Racism without Racists

THIRD EDITION

Racism without Racists

Color-Blind Racism and the Persistence of Racial Inequality in the United States

THIRD EDITION

Eduardo Bonilla-Silva

ROWMAN & LITTLEFIELD PUBLISHERS, INC.
Lanham • Boulder • New York • Toronto • Plymouth, UK

Published by Rowman & Littlefield Publishers, Inc.
A wholly owned subsidiary of The Rowman & Littlefield Publishing Group, Inc.
4501 Forbes Boulevard, Suite 200, Lanham, Maryland 20706
http://www.rowmanlittlefield.com

Estover Road, Plymouth PL6 7PY, United Kingdom

British Library Cataloguing in Publication Information Available

Library of Congress Cataloging-in-Publication Data Available

978-1-4422-0217-7 (cloth : alk. paper)
978-1-4422-0218-4 (pbk. : alk. paper)

♾ ™ The paper used in this publication meets the minimum requirements of American National Standard for Information Sciences—Permanence of Paper for Printed Library Materials, ANSI/NISO Z39.48-1992.

Printed in the United States of America

The good and the bad are part of reality and I take both as part of the dialectics of life. Hence, I dedicate this third edition of *Racism without Racists* to those mainstream sociologists who have tried to hurt my career over the years as well as to the few sociologists of color who have joined them hoping to advance their own careers. Without all of you, I would have not worked as hard as I have; without you, I would not have proof my work is doing what is supposed to do: irritating the powerful who hate to see their *real* reflection in the sociological mirror. Accordingly, your poison has been useful to me much like the venom of the snakes which, when given in small dosages, is a wonderful medicine.

I also dedicate this edition to the "usual suspects" who have loved and supported me over the years: my graduate students; my son Omar, who just got his BA in sociology at Wisconsin; my parents and family in Puerto Rico who still treat me as the young skinny kid who left in 1984; and my Mary—"the good Mary," as folks at Texas A&M call my sweet yet strong wife (she is the only person who can keep me in check). The support you have all given me has been the necessary balm to balance the hate I get from the enemies of humanity. Thanks to all of you and know that I have your back, too.

Contents

Acknowledgments   ix

Preface to the Third Edition of *Racism without Racists*   xiii

1   The Strange Enigma of Race in Contemporary America   1

2   The Central Frames of Color-Blind Racism   25

3   The Style of Color Blindness: How to Talk Nasty about Minorities without Sounding Racist   53

4   "I Didn't Get That Job Because of a Black Man": Color-Blind Racism's Racial Stories   75

5   Peeking Inside the (White) House of Color Blindness: The Significance of Whites' Segregation   103

6   Are All Whites Refined Archie Bunkers? An Examination of White Racial Progressives   131

7   Are Blacks Color Blind, Too?   151

8   *E Pluribus Unum* or the Same Old Perfume in a New Bottle? On the Future of Racial Stratification in the United States   177

9   Will Racism Disappear in *Obamerica*? The Sweet (but Deadly) Enchantment of Color Blindness in Black Face   207

10   Conclusion: "The (Color-Blind) Emperor Has No Clothes": Exposing the Whiteness of Color Blindness   261

Bibliography   277

Index   289

About the Author   301

Note: The following material from the previous edition can be found on the Rowman & Littlefield website at www.rowmanlittlefield.com :

- Queries: Answers to Questions from Concerned Readers
- Postscript: What Is to be Done (For Real)?
- Appendix: In-Depth Interview Schedule DAS 98-Form B

Acknowledgments

The last words my mother told me before I left Puerto Rico in 1984 were: "Son, in the United States you need to walk and behave like a king." She also told me something to the effect that no matter what the "gringos" said about me, I always had to remember that "I was as good if not better than them." At the time, I did not understand her advice. Over twenty years later, I fully understand her enormous wisdom. In this country, racial "others" of dark complexion are always viewed as incapable of doing much; we are regarded and treated as secondary actors only good for doing beds in hotels or working in fast-food restaurants. Therefore, my mother's advice ("walk and behave like a king") helped me develop the much needed emotional *coraza* (shield) to repel all the racial nonsense of "gringolandia" (Frida Kahlo was so right about this country!). Thanks *Mami!*

This *coraza* has come in handy in my sociological career, because at every step of the way, I have encountered people who have tried to block my path one way or another. Fortunately, I have also encountered along the way many people who have helped me in this, my second country. And, in truth, my experience with good and generous people has outweighed that with the bad ones. Many of the former have seen me without my *coraza* and know the real me. At my alma mater (UW-Madison), professors such as Pamela Oliver, Russell Middleton, and Erik Wright were exceedingly generous with me. So were Professors Sam Cohn (now my colleague at Texas A&M), Gay Seidman, and Denis O'Hearn, all of whom I served with as a teaching assistant. Wright and Oliver were even kind enough to read and send me feedback on a working paper I wrote two years after leaving Wisconsin. The paper appeared in 1997 in *ASR* with the title "Rethinking Racism: Toward a Structural Interpretation." But the most important sociological force that affected me at Wisconsin was my adviser, Professor Charles Camic. He was the perfect adviser for me. Camic was knowledgeable, kind, savvy, and had an uncanny under-

ix

standing of the business side of sociology. Then and now, whenever I have a "big (sociological) issue" at hand, he is one of the first people I consult. Thanks, Chas, for being there for me. I hope I am able to repay you in some way.

At Michigan there were a number of colleagues who were very nice to me: Mark Chesler, Julia Adams, Howard Kimeldorf, Muge Gocek, Silvia Pedraza, Jim House, David Williams, and a few others. However, the people who helped me navigate that "peculiar institution" were Professors Donald Deskins Jr., Alford Young II, and Carla O'Connor. These three colleagues were more than my colleagues: they were my friends and allies. Thanks Don, Al, and Carla! I hope the sociological gods allow us to work together one more time before our time expires.

At my sociological house, Texas A&M University, almost everyone has helped me. In my first year there, I received more feedback and love than I did at Michigan in five! Thus, I thank the entire sociology department at A&M for providing me almost unconditional support. I hope I have not disappointed "y'all." Also deserving special mention are two former sociological Aggies, Professors Benigno Aguirre (University of Delaware) and John Boies of the U.S. Census Bureau. They both enriched my sociological and nonsociological life. I miss having lunch with John and coffee with Benigno! Last but not least at A&M, my three outstanding graduate students, David G. Embrick (whom I owe many, many, many thanks for his steadfast loyalty and hard work), Paul Ketchum, and Karen Glover, helped me with some of the data and analysis and have supported me beyond the call of duty. Thanks for all your help and support and I hope to read your own books soon!

Other people who have loved me *de gratis* in sociological Amerikkka are Joe R. Feagin, Hernán Vera, Judith Blau, Tukufu Zuberi, Hayward Horton, Ashley Doane, Gianpaolo Baiocchi, Joane Nagel, Margaret Andersen, Cedric Herring, Abel Valenzuela, Rogelio Saenz, Tyrone A. Forman, Amanda E. Lewis, Walter Allen, Eddie Telles, Michael O. Emerson, Paul Wong, Jose Padin, Veronica Dujon, Carla Goar, William Darity, Geoffrey Ward, Nadia Kim, Ramiro Martinez, Tom Guglielmo, Moon-Kie Jung, and Larry Bobo, among others. I also wish to thank the folks of the Association of Black Sociologists and the ASA Section on Racial and Ethnic Minorities for supporting me over the past five years.

The data for this book were gathered while I was a professor at Michigan. I thank all the people involved with the 1997 Survey of Social Attitudes of College Students (Amanda, Tyrone, and all the undergraduate students who helped me out!) and the 1998 Detroit Area Study (DAS). The 1997 survey was done partly with funding from the ASA-NSF (National Science Foundation) Fund for the Advancement of the Discipline. The 1998 DAS was done with Michigan funds. However, I want to thank Jim House and Earl Lewis for funding the interview component for the 1998 DAS. Without those interviews, the 1998 DAS would have been just another run-of-the-mill survey on racial attitudes.

A significant amount of the drafting of this book was done while I was a visiting research fellow at the University of Houston Law Center in the fall of 2000, under the auspices of Professor Michael A. Olivas, director of the Institute for Higher Education Law and Governance. Michael generously hosted me when I was still an unproven commodity. Thanks Michael, I owe you a lot! While I was in Houston, Professor Russell L. Curtis Jr. from the University of Houston sociology department provided me shelter and friendship. I will never forget our long discussions on almost every possible subject. Thanks Russ!

The final drafting of this book was done at Stanford University, where I was invited to spend a year (2002–2003) as a Hewlett research fellow at the Research Institute for Comparative Studies of Race and Ethnicity, headed by Hazel R. Markus and George Fredrickson. I also wish to thank Leanne Issak, Awino Kuerth, and Dorothy Steele for helping me with all my silly problems during my time there.

This book benefited enormously from the incisive review of Professor Margaret Andersen from the University of Delaware. Maggie read this manuscript from beginning to end and made valuable suggestions that helped me make it a better—although still controversial—book. Thanks Margaret for doing such a terrific job!

Finally, I want to dedicate this book to five very special people in my life. First, to my bother Pedro Juan Bonilla-Silva, who passed away in 2002. Pedro, I wish I had been able to tell you how much I love you, but a bit of machismo and a lot of family history prevented me from doing so. I will always regret that. Second, to my father Jacinto Bonilla. I know I do not say it often, but I respect, admire, and love you. Third, to my sister Karen Bonilla-Silva, the youngest, wisest, and nicest-looking in the Bonilla-Silva clan. Fourth, to my son Omar Francisco Bonilla, who transcribed one of the DAS interviews quoted in this book. Omi, know that I love you and am very proud of your scholarly and artistic accomplishments. Finally, I dedicate this book to the love of my life, Mary Hovsepian. We have marinated our partnership for fifteen years and it is still as sweet and strong as the first day we formalized it. Thanks, Mary, I am eagerly waiting to see what the next fifteen years bring us.

Preface to the Third Edition of
Racism without Racists

This book, like Freddy Krueger, refuses to die. After I finished a second edition in 2003 in which I added a substantive chapter outlining my work on the future of racial stratification in America (the Latin Americanization of racial stratification), another chapter answering questions from readers, and a postscript where I made specific suggestions about how to fight post–Civil Rights racism, I thought I was done. I truly believed I would revisit *Racism without Racists* when my hair was totally white and Rowman and Littlefield asked me to do a silver anniversary edition.

But the gods of history tricked me (perhaps even forced me) by posing a seemingly frontal challenge to many of my claims. How can this nation have a new racial regime in place (what I call the "new racism") and a new color-blind ideology when Americans have just elected a black man as their 44th president? Some readers may even use this event to discount my arguments altogether by claiming Obama's election is a confirmation of the veracity of whites' claims to be color blind (thus challenging a central thesis in this book) and the beginning of a post-racial America. Therefore, this seemingly monumental event forced my hand and pushed me to add an analysis of the meaning of Obama's election as president for race relations in America. Before I outline what I did in this edition, however, I must explain how my own ideas about and analysis of the Obama phenomenon developed.

Like many Americans, I watched the Obama play since before Iowa; since he said he was not running for president even though most commentators believed he was going to get into the field. At the time, I knew very little about Barack Obama (I had seen his speech in the 2004 Democratic Party Convention—and I was not impressed by it—and heard some things about him from friends in Chicago). However, from the outset I felt very uncomfortable with the Messianic element in his campaign and in his political style (charisma is important in politics, but Messiah-like practices are problematic and do not help advance democracy). I also was not too impressed with his policy stands on race matters and on several other fronts. Then one day, I received an e-mail from a colleague from the Association of Black Sociologists, an association I belong to, asking me to co-chair a group called Black and Progressive Sociologists for Obama (the group still exists and maintains a very useful website). I told this person I needed to check a few more things on Obama before making a decision on the matter, but that I had some serious doubts about his campaign and his politics. After a few days, I decided not to co-chair this group, but hoping to stimulate debate (at the time, few members of the Association were engaging publicly the Obama phenomenon), I posted a statement in a listserver titled "*We Are Still The (Dis)United States of America: Will an Obama Presidency Help or Hurt the Cause of Racial Justice in America?*" (The original statement as well as a lecture I delivered before the Association of Humanist Sociologists' Meeting in Boston, November 7th, 2008, titled "The 2008 Elections and the Future of Anti-Racism in 21st Century Amerika or How We Got Drunk with Obama's Hope Liquor and Failed to See Reality" can be found at sociologistsforobama.blogspot.com/search?q = bonilla%27.)

Since I posted that statement in early February of 2008, friends, colleagues, and comrades have expressed their disbelief about my analysis of the Obama phenomenon. Several have told me things such as, "Of all people, how can *you* not be excited about Obama? How can *you* express reservations in public about having a black president? *You* should be ecstatic about Obama as his election to the highest post in the nation represents a monumental leap forward in our history!" A very dear colleague even suggested in an e-mail exchange that Obama's election has ushered in an alternative form of "Americanism" by which he meant that the traditional white-led nationalism (Walters 2003) was challenged in this election by a racially inclusive nationalism that blends the interests of white progressives and liberals and the black and minority masses.

After the cat was out of the bag (that is, after people knew I had many concerns about Obama), I was invited to many places to serve as the counterpoint in "debates" that were mostly Obama love festivals. In some of these events, there was very little space for dissent and I almost had to run for cover. For example, at a debate at Hoftsra University with Rutgers Law Professor David Dante Troutt, the mostly pro-Obama audience accused me of supporting John McCain, being a covert Republican, and of not wanting to admit racial progress in America to "maintain my race business." Even after I told them I did not support *either* of the parties, classified McCain as a stooge for corporate America and a warmonger (I called him other choice names, too), and made clear that as a person of color who suffered *en carne propia* (in my own skin) from America's racial order, I would love to see *real* racial progress in the nation, the audience still continued their relentless attack. Nevertheless, in a situation that became all too familiar for me, not a *single* member of the audience, or the esteemed colleague I debated, challenged the facts I brought to the table.

More troubling, since Obama's election, disgruntled readers of this book and a few "friends" as well as some foes have e-mailed me to tell me in a mocking tone things such as, "So *Professor* Bonilla-Silva, what will you do *now* that we have a black president and are *obviously* a color-blind nation? Will you admit you were *wrong*? Will you finally acknowledge that color blindness has nothing to do with racism? And, by the way, are you looking for a job now that your book has been shown for what it is: a sham?" I dutifully answered all the e-mails I received on this matter and participated on all the debates I could. Now with the chapter on the matter in this book, I take my comments and analysis to a wider audience. The essence of my argument is that Obama is the product of the "new racism" regime and that he and his policies embody to a large extent the color-blind ideology I examine in this book. Furthermore, I suggest that in many ways Obama's policies, politics, and how people are framing his administration may bring us faster than I expected to a Latin America–like racial stratification order (the subject I discuss in chapter 8).

Although what I have said about Obama in public—and what I have written in this book and in several articles in various journals—may be seen by some as "sacrilege," I stand by my analysis and the politics it entails. Unlike so many Obama commentators, I believe I have engaged the matter seriously and done the scholarly work of checking the available facts and data as best as I could. For example, in the chapter on Obama in this edition, I include more than 140 endnotes and offer citations for almost every assertion I make. And though many may fault me for offering commentary on events that are highly fluid and in transition (Obama's stand on Iraq and Afghanistan, the debate on health care reform, the stimulus package, etc.), I believe the moment dictates not waiting until *after the fact* to emit judgment. When nations experience political developments of the magnitude of this one, social analysts must join the debate in the public square or else they become irrelevant. (I have suggested elsewhere that sociologists have been too timid and slow in their interventions on social debates and that this diminishes our discipline.)

Now on to the business of what I did in this third edition. The bulk of what I did in this edition was to add a relatively long, and I believe important, chapter on Obama. Because of the length of the chapter, and to keep the book relatively affordable, I removed chapter 10 ("Queries: Answers to Questions from Concerned Readers"), the appendix with the interview schedule for the 1998 DAS, and the postscript from the text. However, Rowman & Littlefield has placed all of them on their website and they are now accessible to the public. I also edited slightly the original conclusion to include some comments on the Obama matter.

I end this preface by saying I wish historical circumstances had not forced me to write a third edition of this book. But once forced into a fight, one has to deliver. History and readers of this book will decide if my analysis of *Obamerica* (see endnote 1 of the new chapter) is accurate and a healthy contribution to democracy in America. But no matter what y'all say, I know I have done the best I can to win this fight and will continue smiling like the Cheshire cat (this allegory will only make sense to those who read the Obama chapter).

Eduardo Bonilla-Silva
Durham, North Carolina
August 2009

1

~

The Strange Enigma of Race in Contemporary America

There is a strange kind of enigma associated with the problem of racism. No one, or almost no one, wishes to see themselves as racist; still, racism persists, real and tenacious.

—Albert Memmi, *Racism*

RACISM WITHOUT "RACISTS"

Nowadays, except for members of white supremacist organizations,[1] few whites in the United States claim to be "racist." Most whites assert they "don't see any color, just people"; that although the ugly face of discrimination is still with us, it is no longer the central factor determining minorities' life chances; and, finally, that like Dr. Martin Luther King Jr.,[2] they aspire to live in a society where "people are judged by the content of their character, not by the color of their skin." More poignantly, most whites insist that minorities (especially blacks) are the ones responsible for whatever "race problem" we have in this country. They publicly denounce blacks for "playing the race card," for demanding the maintenance of unnecessary and divisive race-based programs, such as affirmative action, and for crying "racism" whenever they are criticized by whites.[3] Most whites believe that if blacks and other minorities would just stop thinking about the past, work hard, and complain less (particularly about racial discrimination), then Americans of all hues could "all get along."[4]

But regardless of whites' "sincere fictions,"[5] racial considerations shade almost everything in America. Blacks and dark-skinned racial minorities

1

lag well behind whites in virtually every area of social life; they are about three times more likely to be poor than whites, earn about 40 percent less than whites, and have about an eighth of the net worth that whites have.[6] They also receive an inferior education compared to whites, even when they attend integrated institutions.[7] In terms of housing, black-owned units comparable to white-owned ones are valued at 35 percent less.[8] Blacks and Latinos also have less access to the entire housing market because whites, through a variety of exclusionary practices by white realtors and homeowners, have been successful in effectively limiting their entrance into many neighborhoods.[9] Blacks receive impolite treatment in stores, in restaurants, and in a host of other commercial transactions.[10] Researchers have also documented that blacks pay more for goods such as cars and houses than do whites.[11] Finally, blacks and dark-skinned Latinos are the targets of racial profiling by the police that, combined with the highly racialized criminal court system, guarantees their overrepresentation among those arrested, prosecuted, incarcerated, and if charged for a capital crime, executed.[12] Racial profiling on the highways has become such a prevalent phenomenon that a term has emerged to describe it: driving while black.[13] In short, blacks and most minorities are, "at the bottom of the well."[14]

How is it possible to have this tremendous degree of racial inequality in a country where most whites claim that race is no longer relevant? More important, how do whites explain the apparent contradiction between their professed color blindness and the United States' color-coded inequality? In this book I attempt to answer both of these questions. I contend that whites have developed powerful explanations—which have ultimately become justifications—for contemporary racial inequality that exculpate them from any responsibility for the status of people of color. These explanations emanate from a new racial ideology that I label *color-blind racism*. This ideology, which acquired cohesiveness and dominance in the late 1960s,[15] explains contemporary racial inequality as the outcome of nonracial dynamics. Whereas Jim Crow racism explained blacks' social standing as the result of their biological and moral inferiority, color-blind racism avoids such facile arguments. Instead, whites rationalize minorities' contemporary status as the product of market dynamics, naturally occurring phenomena, and blacks' imputed cultural limitations.[16] For instance, whites can attribute Latinos' high poverty rate to a relaxed work ethic ("the Hispanics are mañana, mañana, mañana—tomorrow, tomorrow, tomorrow")[17] or residential segregation as the result of natural tendencies among groups ("Does a cat and a dog mix? I can't see it. You can't drink milk and scotch. Certain mixes don't mix").[18]

Color-blind racism became the dominant racial ideology as the mechanisms and practices for keeping blacks and other racial minorities "at the bottom of the well" changed. I have argued elsewhere that contemporary racial inequality is reproduced through "New Racism" practices that are subtle, institutional, and apparently nonracial.[19] In contrast to the Jim Crow era, where racial inequality was enforced through overt means (e.g., signs saying "No Niggers Welcomed Here" or shotgun diplomacy at the voting booth), today racial practices operate in "now you see it, now you don't" fashion. For example, residential segregation, which is almost as high today as it was in the past, is no longer accomplished through overtly discriminatory practices. Instead, covert behaviors such as not showing all the available units, steering minorities and whites into certain neighborhoods, quoting higher rents or prices to minority applicants, or not advertising units at all are the weapons of choice to maintain separate communities.[20] In the economic field, "smiling face" discrimination ("We don't have jobs now, but please check later"), advertising job openings in mostly white networks and ethnic newspapers, and steering highly educated people of color into poorly remunerated jobs or jobs with limited opportunities for mobility are the new ways of keeping minorities in a secondary position.[21] Politically, although the Civil Rights struggles have helped remove many of the obstacles for the electoral participation of people of color, "racial gerrymandering, multimember legislative districts, election runoffs, annexation of predominantly white areas, at-large district elections, and anti–single-shot devices (disallowing concentrating votes in one or two candidates in cities using at-large elections) have become standard practices to disenfranchise" people of color.[22] Whether in banks, restaurants, school admissions, or housing transactions, the maintenance of white privilege is done in a way that defies facile racial readings. Hence, the contours of color-blind racism fit America's new racism quite well.

Compared to Jim Crow racism, the ideology of color blindness seems like "racism lite." Instead of relying on name calling (niggers, Spics, Chinks), color-blind racism otherizes softly ("these people are human, too"); instead of proclaiming God placed minorities in the world in a servile position, it suggests they are behind because they do not work hard enough; instead of viewing interracial marriage as wrong on a straight racial basis, it regards it as "problematic" because of concerns over the children, location, or the extra burden it places on couples. Yet this new ideology has become a formidable political tool for the maintenance of the racial order. Much as Jim Crow racism served as the glue for defending a brutal and overt system of racial oppression in the pre–Civil Rights era, color-blind racism serves today as the ideological armor for a covert and institutionalized system in the post–Civil Rights era. And the beauty of this new ideology is that it aids in the maintenance of white privilege without fanfare, without naming those who it subjects and those who it rewards. It allows a president to state things such as, "I strongly support diversity of all kinds, including racial diversity in higher education," yet, at the same time, to characterize the University of Michigan's affirmation action program as "flawed" and "discriminatory" against whites.[23] Thus whites enunciate positions that safeguard their racial interests without sounding "racist." Shielded by color blindness, whites can express resentment toward minorities; criticize their morality, values, and work ethic; and even claim to be the victims of "reverse racism." This is the thesis I will defend in this book to explain the curious enigma of "racism without racists."[24]

WHITES' RACIAL ATTITUDES IN THE POST–CIVIL RIGHTS ERA

Since the late 1950s surveys on racial attitudes have consistently found that fewer whites subscribe to the views associated with Jim Crow. For example, whereas the majority of whites supported segregated neighborhoods, schools, transportation, jobs, and public accommodations in the 1940s, less than a quarter indicated they did in the 1970s.[25] Similarly, fewer whites than ever now seem to subscribe to stereotypical views of blacks. Although the number is still high (ranging from 20 percent to 50 percent, depending on the stereotype), the proportion of whites who state in surveys that blacks are lazy, stupid, irresponsible, and violent has declined since the 1940s.[26]

These changes in whites' racial attitudes have been explained by the survey community and commentators in four ways. First, are they *racial optimists*. This group of analysts agrees with whites' common sense on racial matters and believes the changes symbolize a profound transition in the United States. Early representatives of this view were Herbert Hyman and Paul B. Sheatsley, who wrote widely influential articles on the subject in *Scientific American*. In a reprint of their earlier work in the influential collection edited by Talcott Parsons and Kenneth Clark, *The Negro American*, Sheatsley rated the changes in white attitudes as "revolutionary" and concluded,

> The mass of white Americans have shown in many ways that they will not follow a racist government and that they will not follow racist leaders. Rather, they are engaged in the painful task of adjusting to an integrated society. It will not be easy for most, but one cannot at this late date doubt the basic commitment. In their hearts they know that the American Negro is right.[27]

In recent times, Glenn Firebaugh and Kenneth Davis, Seymour Lipset, and Paul Sniderman and his coauthors, in particular, have carried the torch for racial optimists.[28] Firebaugh and Davis, for example, based on their analysis of survey results from 1972 to 1984, concluded that the trend toward less antiblack prejudice was across the board. Sniderman and his coauthors, as well as Lipset, go a step further than Firebaugh and Davis because they have openly advocated color-blind politics as *the* way to settle the United States' racial dilemmas. For instance, Sniderman and Edward Carmines made this explicit appeal in their recent book, *Reaching beyond Race,*

> To say that a commitment to a color-blind politics is worth undertaking is to call for a politics centered on the needs of those most in need. It is not to argue for a politics in which race is irrelevant, but in favor of one in which race is relevant so far as it is a gauge of need. Above all, it is a call for a politics which, because it is organized around moral principles that apply regardless of race, can be brought to bear with special force on the issue of race.[29]

The problems with this optimistic interpretation are twofold. First, as I have argued elsewhere,[30] relying on questions that were framed in the Jim Crow era to assess whites' racial views today produces an artificial image of progress. Since the central racial debates and the language used to debate those matters have changed, our analytical focus ought to be dedicated to the analysis of the new racial issues. Insisting on the need to rely on old questions to keep longitudinal (trend) data as the basis for analysis will, by default, produce a rosy picture of race relations that misses what is going on on the ground. Second, and more important, because of the change in the normative climate in the post–Civil Rights era, analysts must exert extreme caution when interpreting attitudinal data, particularly when it comes from single-method research designs. The research strategy that seems more appropriate for our times is mixed research designs (surveys used in combination with interviews, ethnosurveys,[31] etc.), because it allows researchers to cross-examine their results.

A second, more numerous group of analysts exhibit what I have labeled elsewhere as the *racial pesoptimist* position.[32] Racial pesoptimists attempt to strike a "balanced" view and suggest that whites' racial attitudes reflect progress and resistance. The classical example of this stance is Howard Schuman.[33] Schuman has argued for more than thirty years that whites' racial attitudes involve a mixture of tolerance and intolerance, of acceptance of the principles of racial liberalism (equal opportunity for all, end of segregation, etc.) and a rejection of the policies that would make those principles a reality (from affirmative action to busing).[34]

Despite the obvious appeal of this view in the research community (the appearance of neutrality, the pondering of "two sides," and this view's "balanced" component), racial pesoptimists are just closet optimists. Schuman, for example, has pointed out that, although "White responses to questions of principle are . . . more complex than is often portrayed . . . they nevertheless do show in almost every instance a positive movement over time."[35] Furthermore, it is his belief that the normative change in the United States is real and that the issue is that whites are having a hard time translating those norms into personal preferences.

A third group of analysts argues that the changes in whites' attitudes represent the emergence of a *symbolic racism*.[36] This tradition is associated with the work of David Sears and his associate, Donald Kinder.[37] They have defined symbolic racism as "a blend of anti-black affect and the kind of traditional American moral values embodied in the Protestant Ethic."[38] According to these authors, symbolic racism has replaced biological racism as the primary way whites express their racial resentment toward minorities. In Kinder and Sanders's words:

> A new form of prejudice has come to prominence, one that is preoccupied with matters of moral character, informed by the virtues associated with the traditions of individualism. At its center are the contentions that blacks do not try hard enough to overcome the difficulties they face and that they take what they have not earned. Today, we say, prejudice is expressed in the language of American individualism.[39]

Authors in this tradition have been criticized for the slipperiness of the concept "symbolic racism," for claiming that the blend of antiblack affect and individualism is new, and for not explaining why symbolic racism came about. The first critique, developed by Howard Schuman, is that the concept has been "defined and operationalized in complex and varying ways."[40] Despite this conceptual slipperiness, indexes of symbolic racism have been found to be in fact different from those of old-fashioned racism and to be strong predictors of whites' opposition to affirmative action.[41] The two other critiques, made forcefully by Lawrence Bobo, have been partially addressed by Kinder and Sanders in their recent book, *Divided by Color*. First, Kinder and Sanders, as well as Sears, have made clear that their contention is not that this is the first time in history that antiblack affect and elements of the American Creed have combined. Instead, their claim is that this combination has become *central* to the new face of racism. Regarding the third critique, Kinder and Sanders go at length to explain the transition from old-fashioned to symbolic racism. Nevertheless, their explanation hinges on arguing that changes in blacks' tactics (from civil disobedience to urban violence) led to an onslaught of a new form of racial resentment that later found more fuel in controversies over welfare, crime, drugs, family, and affirmative action. What is missing in this explanation is a materially based explanation for why these changes occurred. Instead, their theory of prejudice is rooted in the "process of socialization and the operation of routine cognitive and emotional psychological processes."[42]

Yet, despite its limitations, the symbolic racism tradition has brought attention to key elements of how whites explain racial inequality today. Whether this is "symbolic" of antiblack affect or not is beside the point and hard to assess, since as a former student of mine queried, "How does one test for the unconscious?"[43]

The fourth explanation of whites' contemporary racial attitudes is associated with those who claim that whites' racial views represent a *sense of group position*. This position, forcefully advocated by Lawrence Bobo and James Kluegel, is similar to Jim Sidanius's "social dominance" and Mary Jackman's "group interests" arguments.[44] In essence, the claim of all these authors is that white prejudice is an ideology to defend white privilege. Bobo and his associates have specifically suggested that because of socioeconomic changes that transpired in the 1950s and 1960s, a *laissez-faire racism* emerged that was fitting of the United States' "modern, nationwide, postindustrial free labor economy and polity."[45] Laissez-faire racism "encompasses an ideology that blames blacks themselves for their poorer relative economic standing, seeing it as the function of perceived cultural inferiority."[46]

Some of the basic arguments of authors in the symbolic and modern racism[47] traditions and, particularly, of the laissez-faire racism view are fully compatible with my color-blind racism interpretation. As these authors, I argue that color-blind racism has rearticulated elements of traditional liberalism (work ethic, rewards by merit, equal opportunity, individualism, etc.) for racially illiberal goals. I also argue like them that whites today rely more on cultural rather than biological tropes to explain blacks' position in this country. Finally, I concur with most analysts of post–Civil Rights' matters in arguing that whites do not perceive discrimination to be a central factor shaping blacks' life chances.

Although most of my differences with authors in the symbolic racism and laissez-faire traditions are methodological (see below), I have one central theoretical disagreement with them. Theoretically, most of these authors are still snarled in the prejudice problematic and thus interpret actors' racial views as *individual psychological* dispositions. Although Bobo and his associates have a conceptualization that is closer to mine, they still retain the notion of prejudice and its psychological baggage rooted in interracial hostility.[48] In contrast, my model is not anchored in actors' affective dispositions (although affective dispositions may be manifest or latent in the way many express their racial views). Instead, it is based on a materialist interpretation of racial matters and thus sees the views of actors as corresponding to their systemic location. Those at the bottom of the racial barrel tend to hold oppositional views and those who receive the manifold wages of whiteness tend to hold views in support of the racial status quo. Whether actors express "resentment" or "hostility" toward minorities is largely irrelevant for the maintenance of white privilege. As David Wellman points out in his *Portraits of White Racism*, "[p]rejudiced people are not the only racists in America."[49]

KEY TERMS: RACE, RACIAL STRUCTURE, AND RACIAL IDEOLOGY

One reason why, in general terms, whites and people of color cannot agree on racial matters is because they conceive terms such as "racism" very differently. Whereas for most whites racism is prejudice, for most people of color racism is systemic or institutionalized. Although this is not a theory book, my examination of color-blind racism has etched in it the indelible ink of a "regime of truth"[50] about how the world is organized. Thus, rather than hiding my theoretical assumptions, I state them openly for the benefit of readers and potential critics.

The first key term is the notion of *race*. There is very little formal disagreement among social scientists in accepting the idea that race is a socially constructed category.[51] This means that notions of racial difference are human creations rather than eternal, essential categories. As such, racial categories have a history and are subject to change. And here ends the agreement among social scientists on this matter. There are at least three distinct variations on how social scientists approach this constructionist perspective on race. The first approach, which is gaining popularity among white social scientists, is the idea that because race is socially constructed, it is not a fundamental category of analysis and praxis. Some analysts go as far as to suggest that because race is a constructed category, then it is not real and social scientists who use the category are the ones who make it real.[52]

The second approach, typical of most sociological writing on race, gives lip service to the social constructionist view—usually a line in the beginning of the article or book. Writers in this group then proceed to discuss "racial" differences in academic achievement, crime, and SAT scores as if they were truly racial.[53] This is the central way in which contemporary scholars contribute to the propagation of racist interpretations of racial inequality. By failing to highlight the social dynamics that produce these racial differences, these scholars help reinforce the racial order.[54]

The third approach, and the one I use in this book, acknowledges that race, as other social categories such as class and gender, is constructed but insists that it has a *social* reality. This means that after race—or class or gender—is created, it produces real effects on the actors racialized as "black" or "white." Although race, as other social constructions, is unstable, it has a "changing same"[55] quality at its core.

In order to explain how a socially constructed category produces real race effects, I need to introduce a second key term: the notion of *racial structure*. When race emerged in human history, it formed a social structure (a racialized social system) that awarded systemic privileges to Europeans (the peoples who became "white") over non-Europeans (the peoples who became "nonwhite").[56] Racialized social systems, or white supremacy[57] for short, became global and affected all societies where Europeans extended their reach. I therefore conceive a society's racial structure as *the totality of the social relations and practices that reinforce white privilege*. Accordingly, the task of analysts interested in studying racial structures is to uncover the particular social, economic, political, social control, and ideological mechanisms responsible for the reproduction of racial privilege in a society.

But why are racial structures reproduced in the first place? Would not humans, after discovering the folly of racial thinking, work to abolish race as a category as well as a practice? Racial structures remain in place for the same reasons that other structures do. Since actors racialized as "white"—or as members of the dominant race—receive material benefits from the racial order, they struggle (or passively receive the manifold wages of whiteness) to maintain their privileges. In contrast, those defined as belonging to the subordinate race or races struggle to change the status quo (or become resigned to their position). Therein lies the secret of racial structures and racial inequality the world over.[58] They exist because they benefit members of the dominant race.

If the ultimate goal of the dominant race is to defend its collective interests (i.e., the perpetuation of systemic white privilege), it should surprise no one that this group develops rationalizations to account for the status of the various races. And here I introduce my third key term, the notion of *racial ideology*. By this I mean *the racially based frameworks used by actors to explain and justify* (dominant race) or *challenge* (subordinate race or races) *the racial status quo*. Although all the races in a racialized social system have the *capacity* of developing these frameworks, the frameworks of the dominant race tend to become the master frameworks upon which *all* racial actors ground (for or against) their ideological positions. Why? Because as Marx pointed out in *The German Ideology*, "the ruling *material* force of society, is at the same time its ruling *intellectual* force."[59] This does not mean that ideology is almighty. In fact, as I will show in chapter 6, ideological rule is always partial. Even in periods of hegemonic rule,[60] such as the current one, subordinate racial groups develop oppositional views. However, it would be foolish to believe that those who rule a society do not have the power to at least color (pun intended) the views of the ruled.

Racial ideology can be conceived for analytical purposes as comprising the following elements: common frames, style, and racial stories (details on each can be found in chapters 2, 3, and 4). The frames that bond together a particular racial ideology are rooted in the group-based conditions and experiences of the races and are, at the symbolic level, the representations developed by these groups to explain how the world is or ought to be. And because the group life of the various racially defined groups is based on hierarchy and domination, the ruling ideology expresses as "common sense" the interests of the dominant race, while oppositional ideologies attempt to challenge that common sense by providing alternative frames, ideas, and stories based on the experiences of subordinated races.

Individual actors employ these elements as "building blocks . . . for manufacturing versions on actions, self, and social structures" in communicative situations.[61] The looseness of the elements allows users to maneuver within various contexts (e.g., responding to a race-related survey, discussing racial issues with family, or arguing about affirmative action in a college classroom) and produce various accounts and presentations of self (e.g., appearing ambivalent, tolerant, or strong minded). This loose character enhances the legitimating role of racial ideology because it allows for accommodation of contradictions, exceptions, and new information. As Jackman points out about ideology in general: "Indeed, the strength of an ideology lies in its loose-jointed, flexible application. *An ideology is a political instrument, not an exercise in personal logic:* consistency is rigidity, the only pragmatic effect of which is to box oneself in."[62]

Before I can proceed, two important caveats should be offered. First, although whites, because of their privileged position in the racial order, form a social group (the dominant race), they are fractured along class, gender, sexual orientation, and other forms of "social cleavage." Hence, they have multiple and often contradictory interests that are not easy to disentangle and that predict a priori their mobilizing capacity (Do white workers have more in common with white capitalists than with black workers?). However, because all actors awarded the dominant racial position, regardless of their multiple structural locations (men or women, gay or straight, working class or bourgeois) benefit from what Mills calls the "racial contract,"[63] *most* have historically endorsed the ideas that justify the racial status quo.

Second, although not every single member of the dominant race defends the racial status quo or spouts color-blind racism, *most* do. To explain this point by analogy, although not every capitalist defends capitalism (e.g., Frederick Engels, the coauthor of *The Communist Manifesto*, was a capitalist) and not every man defends patriarchy (e.g., *Achilles Heel* is an English magazine published by feminist men), *most* do in some fashion. In the same vein, although some whites fight white supremacy and do not endorse white common sense, *most* subscribe to substantial portions of it in a casual, uncritical fashion that helps sustain the prevailing racial order.

HOW TO STUDY COLOR-BLIND RACISM

I will rely mostly on interview data to make my case. This choice is based on important conceptual and methodological considerations. Conceptually, my focus is examining whites' racial ideology, and ideology, racial or not, is produced and reproduced in communicative interaction.[64] Hence, although surveys are useful instruments for gathering general information on actors' views, they are severely limited tools for examining how people explain, justify, rationalize, and articulate racial viewpoints. People are less likely to express their positions and emotions about racial issues by answering "yes" and "no" or "strongly agree" and "strongly disagree" to questions. Despite the gallant effort of some survey researchers to produce methodologically correct questionnaires, survey questions still restrict the free flow of ideas and unnecessarily constrain the range of possible answers for respondents.[65]

Methodologically, I argue that because the normative climate in the post–Civil Rights era has made illegitimate the public expression of racially based feelings and viewpoints,[66] surveys on racial attitudes have become like multiple-choice exams in which respondents work hard to choose the "right" answers (i.e., those that fit public norms). For instance, although a variety of data suggest racial considerations are central to whites' residential choices, more than 90 percent of whites state in surveys that they have no problem with the idea of blacks moving into their neighborhoods.[67] Similarly, even though about 80 percent of whites claim they would not have a problem if a member of their family brought a black person home for dinner, research shows that (1) very few whites (fewer than 10 percent) can legitimately claim the proverbial "some of my best friends are blacks" and (2) whites rarely fraternize with blacks.[68]

Of more import yet is the insistence by mainstream survey researchers' on using questions developed in the 1950s and 1960s to assess changes in racial tolerance. This strategy is predicated on the assumption that "racism" (what I label here racial ideology) does not change over time. If instead one regards racial ideology as in fact changing, the reliance on questions developed to tackle issues from the Jim Crow era will produce an artificial image of progress and miss most of whites' contemporary racial nightmares.

Despite my conceptual and methodological concerns with survey research, I believe well-designed surveys are still useful instruments to glance at America's racial reality. Therefore, I report survey results from my own research projects as well as from research conducted by other scholars whenever appropriate. My point, then, is not to deny attitudinal change or to condemn to oblivion survey research on racial attitudes, but to understand whites' new racial beliefs and their implications as well as possible.

DATA SOURCES

The data for this book come primarily from two similarly structured projects. The first is the 1997 Survey of Social Attitudes of College Students, based on a convenient sample of 627 college students (including 451 white students) surveyed at a large midwestern university (MU henceforth), a large southern university (SU), and a medium-sized West Coast university (WU). A 10 percent random sample of the white students who provided information in the survey on how to contact them (about 90 percent) were interviewed (41 students altogether, of which 17 were men and 24 women and of which 31 were from middle- and upper-middle-class backgrounds and 10 were from the working class).

Although the data from this study are very suggestive and, I believe, essentially right, the study has some limitations. First, it is based on a convenient, rather than a representative, sample, limiting the capacity for generalizing the findings to the white population at large. Nevertheless, it is worth pointing out that the bias in that sample is in the direction of *more* racial tolerance, since researchers have consistently found that young, college-educated whites are more likely to be racially tolerant than any other segment of the white population.[69] Another limitation of the study is that interviews were conducted only with white respondents. Thus, this data set does not allow us to examine whether or not their views are different from blacks'. Finally, due to budget constraints, the sample was small, albeit large when compared to most interview-based work.[70]

The second data source for this book is the 1998 Detroit Area Study (DAS). This data set overcomes many of the limitations of the college students' data set, since the former is based on a representative sample and includes a significant number of interviews with both white and black respondents. The 1998 DAS is a probabilistic survey of 400 black and white Detroit metropolitan area residents (323 whites and 67 blacks). The response rate was an acceptable 67.5 percent. As part of this study, 84 respondents (a 21 percent subsample) were randomly selected for in-depth interviews (66 were whites and 17 were blacks). The interviews were race matched, followed a structured interview protocol, were conducted in the respondents' homes, and lasted about one hour.

The major limitation of the 1998 DAS data set is that the respondents are black and white only. As the United States has become a multiracial society, one has to be concerned about the generalizability of an analysis based on findings on blacks and whites. Although I posit color-blind racism is the general ideology of the post–Civil Rights era, I realize that a fuller analysis should include the views of other people of color. Thus, I will bring to bear data from other sources in my conclusion to show how other people of color fit into the notion of color-blind racism. On a final note regarding the 1997 Survey of Social Attitudes of College Students and the 1998 DAS, I am well aware that some readers may question their continued validity. However, both survey research as well as interview-based research (e.g., Bush 2004; Gallagher 2002; etc.) done since have produced similar results, thus adding strength to my arguments in this book.

POLITICS, INTERPRETATION, AND OBJECTIVITY

Social scientific research is always a political enterprise. Despite the Enlightenment's dream[71] of pure objectivity, the problems we pose, the theories we use, the methods we employ, and the analyses we perform are social products themselves and to an extent reflect societal contradictions and power dynamics. This view has become more acceptable in the social sciences today than it was ten or twenty years ago.[72] Accordingly, it is harder for social scientists today to defend sociologist Max Weber's call for a separation between researcher, method, and data.[73]

My scholarly goals in this book are to describe the main components of color-blind racism and explain their functions and to use these components to theorize how future U.S. race relations might look. I hope this effort helps social analysts to get over the present impasse on the nature and meaning of whites' racial views. Yet, by accomplishing my scholarly goals, I also hope to attain a much larger and important political goal: uncovering the basic profile of the main ideology reinforcing contemporary racial inequality. By definition, then, my work is a challenge to post–Civil Rights white common sense; to the view that race no longer matters; and to anyone who believes that the problems afflicting people of color

are fundamentally rooted in their pathological cultures.[74] More specifically, I want to advance an argument (the sophisticated nature of color-
blind racism), an approach (analyzing racial ideology rather than "prejudice"), and a politics (fighting racial domination based on a group
rights'[75] agenda) that assist scholars and activists alike in their research
and struggle against color-blind nonsense. I also hope that this book will
serve as a wake-up call to color-blind liberal and progressive whites and
confused members of minority communities who may favor equal opportunity but not affirmative action, who believe discrimination is not an
important factor shaping the life chances of people of color, or who still
wonder if racial minorities do in fact have an inferior culture that accounts
for their status in America. Nevertheless, recognizing the political nature
of research is not a green light for sloppiness and one-sidedness or for
relying on unsystematically gathered data to make broad generalizations.
Hence, I support my arguments with systematic interview data and reference where my data or analysis differs from that of mainstream analysts
so that readers can find alternative interpretations to mine.

Let me now say a word on the matter of interpretation. It is true that
"the spoken word has always the residue of ambiguity, no matter how
carefully we word the questions and how carefully we report or code the
answers."[76] Hence, it is possible for others to read the data differently. To
satisfy the intellectual concerns of those who doubt my interpretation,
whenever possible I present cases that do not nicely fit my interpretation
(particularly in chapter 7). Nevertheless, I do not eschew the dangerous
but necessary role of the analyst. I will make a strong case for the view
that most whites endorse the ideology of color blindness and that this
ideology is central to the maintenance of white privilege. The alternatives
to this interpretive role of analysts, which I see as more problematic, are
timid descriptions usually accompanied by a forest of caveats in which
actors' self-reports of events becomes the ultimate goal of the research
itself. Although I do not deny that "people's accounts count,"[77] my goals
are interpretive (what do people's accounts mean?) and political (what
do people's accounts help accomplish in society). Description and data
presentation without interpretation, without analysis, is like going to a
beach without a swimsuit.

Does this mean that my interpretation is infallible because I have some
degree of authority, which somehow confers me a special gaze? In truth,
given the situational and partial character of all knowledge,[78] neither I,
nor my potential critics hold the monopoly over the right way of interpreting data. All of us try our best to construct robust explanations of
events and hope that in the tilted market of ideas (tilted toward the interpretations of the powerful) the most plausible ones achieve legitimacy.

But if research is political by nature and my interpretation of the data is guided by my theoretical and political orientation, how can readers ascertain if my interpretation is better than those of other analysts? That is, how can we avoid the trap of relativism,[79] of the idea that "all thinking is merely the expression of interest or power or group membership?" My answer to these questions is that my explanations—as well as those of other analysts—ought to be judged like maps. Judge my cartographic effort of drawing the boundaries of contemporary white racial ideology in terms of its usefulness (Does it help to better understand whites' views?), accuracy (Does it accurately depict whites' arguments about racial matters?), details (Does it highlight elements of whites' collective representations not discussed by others?), and clarity (Does it ultimately help you move from here to there?).[80]

ONE IMPORTANT CAVEAT

The purpose of this book is not to demonize whites or label them "racist." Hunting for "racists" is the sport of choice of those who practice the "clinical approach" to race relations—the careful separation of good and bad, tolerant and intolerant Americans. Because this book is anchored in a structural understanding of race relations,[81] my goal is to uncover the collective practices (in this book, the ideological ones) that help reinforce the contemporary racial order. Historically, many good people supported slavery and Jim Crow. Similarly, most color-blind whites who oppose (or have serious reservations about) affirmative action, believe that blacks' problems are mostly their own doing, and do not see anything wrong with their own white lifestyle are good people, too. The analytical issue, then, is examining how many whites subscribe to an ideology that ultimately helps preserve racial inequality rather than assessing how many hate or love blacks and other minorities.

Even with this caveat, some readers may still feel discomfort while reading this book. Since color-blind racism is the dominant racial ideology, its tentacles have touched us all and thus most readers will subscribe to some—if not most—of its tenets, use its style, and believe many of its racial stories. Unfortunately, there is little I can do to ease the pain of these readers, since when one writes and exposes an ideology that is at play, its supporters "get burned," so to speak. For readers in this situation (good people who may subscribe to many of the frames of color blindness), I urge a personal and political movement away from claiming to be "nonracist" to becoming "antiracist."[82] Being an antiracist begins with understanding the institutional nature of racial matters and accepting that all actors in a racialized society are affected *materially* (receive benefits or disadvantages) and *ideologically* by the racial structure. This stand implies taking responsibility for your unwilling participation in these practices and beginning a new life committed to the goal of achieving real racial equality. The ride will be rough, but after your eyes have been opened, there is no point in standing still.

THE PLAN OF THE BOOK

Color-blind racism emerged as a new racial ideology in the late 1960s, concomitantly with the crystallization of the "new racism" as America's new racial structure. Because the social practices and mechanisms to reproduce racial privilege acquired a new, subtle, and apparently nonracial character, new rationalizations emerged to justify the new racial order. I explore in detail the dominant frameworks of color-blind racism in chapter 2.

All ideologies develop a set of stylistic parameters; a certain way of conveying its ideas to audiences. Color-blind racism is no exception. In chapter 3, I document the main stylistic components of this ideology. In chapter 4, I delve into the story lines ("The past is the past" or "I didn't get a job or promotion—or was not admitted to a certain college—because a black man got it") and personal stories that have emerged in the post–Civil Rights era to provide color blind-racism's gut-level emotionality.

If we take seriously whites' self-profession to color blindness, one would expect significantly high levels of racial interaction with minorities in general and blacks in particular. Using the data from these two projects, in chapter 5 I examine whites' patterns of interracial interactions and conclude that they tend to navigate in what I label as a "white habitus" or a set of primary networks and associations with other whites that reinforces the racial order by fostering racial solidarity among whites and negative affect toward racial "others."

In chapter 6 I address "race traitors,"[83] or whites who do not endorse the ideology of color blindness. After profiling college students and DAS respondents who fit the racial progressive mold, I suggest white women from working-class origins are the most likely candidates to commit racial treason in the United States. Nevertheless, I also show that color-blind racism has affected even these progressive whites. If color-blind racism has affected racial progressives, has it affected blacks, too? Attempting to answer this question is the focus of chapter 7. Using DAS data, I contend that although blacks have developed an oppositional ideology, color-blind racism has affected blacks in a mostly indirect fashion. Rather than totally controlling blacks' field of ideas and cognitions, color-blind racism has confused some issues, restricted the possibility of discussing others, and, overall, blunted the utopian character of blacks' oppositional views. In chapter 8 I challenge the assertions that the United States is still organized along a biracial divide and posit that the United States is slowly moving toward a triracial or "plural" order similar to that found in many Latin American and Caribbean countries. In chapter 9 I examine the Obama phenomenon and suggest it is not emblematic of post-racialism but part of the color-blind drama I examine in this book. In chapter 10 I conclude by assessing the implications of color-blind racism, of the Latin Americanization of racial stratification, and of *Obamerica* for the struggle for racial and social justice in this country.

NOTES

1. Even members of these organizations now claim that they are not racist, simply pro-white. For David Duke's discussion on this matter, see his website, www.duke.org/.

2. Some, such as former president George H. W. Bush, use Dr. King's dictum to oppose affirmative action. Interestingly, when Bush was in Congress, he opposed most of the civil rights legislation advocated by King. Furthermore, few whites have ever read the speech in which King used this phrase. If they had, they would realize that his dream referred to the future, that he emphasized that the "Negro [was] still not free." King also emphasized that there could not be peace without justice. In his words, "There will be neither rest nor tranquility in America until the Negro is granted his citizenship rights. The whirlwinds of revolt will continue to shake the foundations of our nation until the bright day of justice emerges." See Martin Luther King Jr., *A Call to Conscience: The Landmark Speeches of Dr. Martin Luther King, Jr.,* edited by Clayborne Carson and Kris Shephard (New York: Intellectual Properties Management, in association with Warner Books, 2001).

3. These views have been corroborated in survey after survey. For instance, a recent nationwide survey found that 66 percent of whites thought the disadvantaged status of blacks in America was due to blacks' welfare dependency and 63 percent thought blacks lacked the motivation to improve their socioeconomic status. Tom W. Smith, "Intergroup Relations in Contemporary America," in *Intergroup Relations in the United States: Research Perspectives,* edited by Wayne Winborne and Renae Cohen, 69–106 (New York: National Conference for Community and Justice, 2000).

4. This phrase was made popular by Rodney King immediately after his first trial. Curiously, the phrase was provided to King by his white lawyer and a movie producer. See Houston A. Baker, "Scene . . . Not Heard," in *Reading Rodney King, Reading Urban Uprising,* edited by Robert Gooding-Williams, 38–50 (New York: Routledge, 1993), 45.

5. This term was coined in Joe R. Feagin and Hernán Vera, *White Racism: The Basics* (New York: Routledge, 1995), to refer to whites' myths about race in contemporary America, particularly their self-delusions.

6. See Melvin Oliver and Thomas Shapiro, *Black Wealth/White Wealth* (New York: Routledge, 1995). See also Juliane Malveaux, "Black Dollar Power: Economics in the Black Community," *Essence* 10 (October 1999), 88–92; John Goering (ed.), *Fragile Rights in Cities* (Lanham, Md.: Rowman & Littlefield, Forthcoming), and Thomas M. Shapiro, *The Hidden Cost of Being African American: How Wealth Perpetuates Inequality* (London: Oxford University Press, 2004).

7. For a vivid description of the educational inequalities between blacks and whites, see Jonathan Kozol, *Savage Inequalities* (New York: Crown, 1992). For a discussion of resegregation and its consequences, see Gary Orfield, Susan Eaton, and the Harvard Project on School Desegregation, *Dismantling Desegregation: The Quiet Reversal of* Brown v. Board of Education (New York: New York Press, 1996). For a discussion of racial matters in "integrated" campuses, see Joe R. Feagin, Hernán Vera, and Nikitah Imani, *The Agony of Education: Black Students at White Colleges and Universities* (New York: Routledge, 1996); and chapter 2 in Roy Brooks, *Integration or Separation? A Strategy for Racial Equality* (Cambridge, Mass.: Harvard University Press, 1996).

8. William J. Collins and Robert A. Margo, "Race and the Value of Owner-Occupied Housing, 1940–1990," Working Papers Series (Annandale-on-Hudson, N.Y.: Bard College, Levy Economics Institute, August 2000).

9. Douglas Massey and Nancy E. Denton, *American Apartheid* (Cambridge, Mass.: Harvard University Press, 1993); John Yinger, *Closed Doors, Opportunities Lost: The Continuing Costs of Housing Discrimination* (New York: Russell Sage Foundation, 1995); Judith N. Desena, "Local Gatekeeping Practices and Residential Segregation," *Sociological Inquiry* 64, no. 3 (1994): 307–21.

10. Joe R. Feagin and Melvin Sikes, *Living with Racism: The Black Middle Class Experience* (Boston: Beacon, 1994); Peter Siegelman, "Racial Discrimination in 'Everyday' Commercial Transactions: What Do We Know . . . ," in *A National Report Card on Discrimination in America: The Role of Testing*, edited by Michael Fix and Margery Austin Turner, chapter 4 (Washington, D.C.: Urban Institute, March 1999).

11. Oliver and Shapiro, *Black Wealth/White Wealth*; Siegelman, "Racial Discrimination."

12. Katheryn K. Russell, *The Color of Crime* (New York: New York University Press, 1998).

13. David A. Harris, *Driving While Black: Racial Profiling on Our Nation's Highways*, Special Report (New York: American Civil Liberties Union, June 1999).

14. Derrick Bell, *Race, Racism and American Law* (Boston: Little, Brown, 1992).

15. The work of William A. Ryan and Joel Kovel represent early efforts to understand the parameters of post–Civil Rights racial ideology. See William A. Ryan, *Blaming the Victim* (New York: Random House, 1976); Joel Kovel, *White Racism: A Psychohistory* (New York: Columbia University Press, 1985).

16. Melvin Thomas has found that this perspective deeply affects social science research on racial matters. Melvin Thomas, "Anything but Race: The Social Sci-

ence Retreat from Racism," *African American Research Perspectives* (Winter 2000): 79–96.

17. This statement is from the top officer of a cart transport company in Chicago. William Julius Wilson, *When Work Disappears* (New York: Norton, 1996), 112.

18. These comments are from a resident of Canarsie, New York. Jonathan Rieder, *Canarsie: The Jews and Italians of Brooklyn against Liberalism* (Cambridge, Mass.: Harvard University Press, 1985), 58.

19. See my chapter with Amanda E. Lewis, "The 'New Racism': Toward an Analysis of the U.S. Racial Structure, 1960–1990s," in *Race, Nation, and Citizenship*, edited by Paul Wong, 100–150 (Boulder, Colo.: Westview, 1999). For a more recent, updated version, see chapter 3 in my *White Supremacy and Racism in the Post Civil Rights Era* (Boulder, Colo.: Rienner, 2001).

20. For general findings on housing matters, see John Yinger, *Closed Doors*. For gatekeeping practices, see Judith A. Desena, "Local Gatekeeping Practices and Residential Segregation," *Sociological Inquiry* 64, no. 3 (1994): 307–21.

21. Bonilla-Silva, *White Supremacy*, 11–117.

22. Bonilla-Silva, *White Supremacy*, 100–101.

23. CBS, "Bush Enters Affirmative Action Fray," CBS.com, January 16, 2003. For a discussion of the contradiction between President Bush opposing affirmative action and his own affirmative action–like admission to Phillips Academy and Yale, see Ellis Henican, "When It Comes to Hypocrisy, He's Brilliant!" *Newsday.com*, January 17, 2003. In *Grutter v. Bollinger* et al., the Supreme Court decided that Michigan could use race as one factor among many in its admissions policy. Although President Obama has appointed Judge Sonia Sotomayor to the court, the court is still center-right and may further restrict affirmative action.

24. I must caution, however, that at no point in history have dominant groups, whether capitalists, men, or whites, proclaimed that their domination is rooted in unfairness and oppression or characterized their behavior as abominable. Hence, whether in the slavery, Jim Crow, or post–Civil Rights eras, whites have never acknowledged any wrongdoing. From a social-psychological standpoint, this makes perfect sense since, as William Ryan stated in his famous book, *Blaming the Victim*, "no one [wants to think] of himself as a son of a bitch" (20).

25. Howard Schuman et al., *Racial Attitudes in America* (Cambridge, Mass.: Harvard University Press, 1997).

26. For data on stereotypes, see Mark Peffley and Jon Hurwitz, "Whites' Stereotypes of Blacks: Sources and Political Consequences," in *Perception and Prejudice: Race and Politics in the United States*, edited by Jon Hurwitz and Mark Peffley, 58–99 (New Haven, Conn.: Yale University Press); John F. Dovidio and Samuel L. Gaertner, "Changes in the Expression and Assessment of Racial Prejudice," in *Opening Doors*, edited by Harry J. Knopke et al., 119–50 (Tuscaloosa: University of Alabama Press, 1991); Paul M. Sniderman and Edward G. Carmines, *Reaching Beyond Race* (Cambridge, Mass.: Harvard University Press, 1997). See also Anti-Defamation League, *Highlights from the Anti-Defamation League Survey on Racial Attitudes in America* (New York: Anti-Defamation League, 1993).

27. Paul B. Sheatsley, "White Attitudes toward the Negro," in *The Negro Ameri-*

can, edited by Talcott Parsons and Kenneth B. Clark, 303–24 (Boston: Beacon, 1966), 323.

28. Glenn Firebaugh and Kenneth E. Davis, "Trends in Antiblack Prejudice, 1972–1984: Region and Cohort Effects," *American Journal of Sociology* 94 (1988): 251–72; Paul M. Sniderman and Thomas Piazza, *The Scar of Race* (Cambridge, Mass.: Harvard University Press, 1993); Seymour Lipset, *American Exceptionalism* (New York: Norton, 1996); Sniderman and Carmines, *Reaching beyond Race.*

29. Sniderman and Carmines, *Reaching beyond Race,* 138.

30. Eduardo Bonilla-Silva and Tyrone Forman, " 'I Am Not a Racist But . . .': Mapping White College Students' Racial Ideology in the USA," *Discourse and Society* 11, no. 1 (2000): 50–85.

31. For a discussion on this methodology, see Douglas S. Massey, R. Alarcon, J. Durand, and H. Gonzalez, *Return to Aztlan: The Social Process of International Migration from Western Mexico* (Berkeley: University of California Press, 1997).

32. See the introduction to Bonilla-Silva, *White Supremacy.*

33. See Tom W. Smith, "Measuring Inter-Racial Friendships: Experimental Comparisons" (paper presented at the 1999 American Sociological Association meeting in San Francisco).

34. The earliest statement of Schuman's paradoxical views can be found in Angus Campbell and Howard Schuman, *Racial Attitudes in Fifteen American Cities* (Ann Arbor, Mich.: Survey Research Center, June 1968).

35. Schuman et al., *Racial Attitudes in America.*

36. In truth, there are at least four versions of this tradition (symbolic, aversive, modern, and subtle racism). Yet, despite small differences, all of them make the claim that antiblack prejudice has gone underground and is now expressed symbolically through apparently nonracist means.

37. The foundational paper here was David O. Sears and Donald R. Kinder, "Racial Tensions and Voting in Los Angeles," in *Los Angeles: Viability and Prospects for Metropolitan Leadership,* edited by Werner Z. Hirsch (New York: Praeger, 1971).

38. Donald R. Kinder and David O. Sears, "Prejudice and Politics: Symbolic Racism versus Racial Threats to the Good Life," *Journal of Personality and Social Psychology* 40, no. 1 (1981): 414–31, 416.

39. David R. Kinder and Lynn M. Sanders, *Divided by Color: Racial Politics and Democratic Ideals* (Chicago: University of Chicago Press, 1996), 106.

40. Schuman et al., *Racial Attitudes in America,* 293.

41. Michael Hughes, "Symbolic Racism, Old-Fashioned Racism, and Whites' Opposition to Affirmative Action," in *Racial Attitudes in the 1990s,* edited by Steven A. Tuch and Jack K. Martin, 45–75 (Westport, Conn.: Praeger 1997).

42. Lawrence Bobo, James A. Kluegel, and Ryan A. Smith, "Laissez-Faire Racism: The Crystallization of a Kinder, Gentler, Antiblack Ideology," in *Racial Attitudes in the 1990s,* 15–44 (Westport, Conn.: Praeger, 1997), 21. For a similar critique, see chapter 1 in Mary R. Jackman, *The Velvet Glove: Paternalism and Conflict in Gender, Class, and Race Relations* (Berkeley: University of California Press, 1994).

43. This comment was made by Susanna Dolance, a graduate student at Michigan.

44. Jim Sidanius et al., "It's Not Affirmative Action, It's the Blacks," in *Racial-*

ized Politics, edited by David O. Sears, Jim Sidanius, and Lawrence Bobo, 191–235 (Chicago: University of Chicago Press, 2000); Jackman, *The Velvet Glove.*

45. Bobo, Kluegel, and Smith, "Laissez-Faire Racism," 21. Philomena Essed has developed a similar argument and claims that in the modern world the dominant racial ideology is that of "competitive racism." See Philomena Essed, *Diversity: Gender, Color, and Culture* (Amherst: University of Massachusetts Press, 1996). See also my " 'This Is a White Country': Racial Ideological Convergence among the Western Nations of the World-System," *Sociological Inquiry* 70, no. 2 (2000):188–214.

46. Lawrence Bobo and James R. Kluegel, "Status, Ideology, and Dimensions of Whites' Racial Beliefs and Attitudes: Progress and Stagnation," in *Racial Attitudes in the 1990s,* 93–120 (Westport, Conn.: Praeger, 1997), 95.

47. John B. McConahay and J. C. Hough, "Symbolic Racism," *Journal of Social Issues* 32, no. 2 (1976): 23–46; John B. McConahay, "Modern Racism, Ambivalence, and the Modern Racism Scale," in *Prejudice, Discrimination, and Racism,* edited by John F. Dovidio and Samuel L. Gaertner (New York: Academic, 1986).

48. This critique of the prejudice problematic (and of Bobo's work) was issued first by Jackman, *The Velvet Glove,* 55–58.

49. David T. Wellman, *Portraits of White Racism,* 2d ed. (Cambridge: Cambridge University Press, 1993).

50. See Michel Foucault, *The Order of Things: An Archeology of the Human Sciences* (New York: Random House, 1973).

51. A few highly visible social scientists such as Charles Murray, Arthur Jensen, Pierre van den Berghe, and Edward O. Wilson still conceive of race as a biological or primordial category. However, they are in a minority and are severely criticized by most people in academia.

52. For an example of this view, see Yehudi O. Webster, *The Racialization of America* (New York: St. Martin's, 1992). However, this view is much more extensive and has been publicly stated by radical scholars such as Todd Gitlin. I have seen the growing influence of this stance among many "radical" scholars who now proclaim to be disillusioned with what they label as "identity politics" (in truth, they never got onboard with the radical gender and racial agendas of their minority and women's colleagues) and thus argue that gender and race are divisive categories preventing the unity of the working class.

53. For a biting critique of statistical racial reasoning, see Tukufu Zuberi, "Deracializing Social Statistics: Problems in the Quantification of Race," *Annals of the American Academy of Political and Social Science* 568 (2000): 172–85.

54. It is largely irrelevant whether these authors are "racist" (that is, hold negative views about racial minorities) or not. "That knowledge [that produced by race scholars unwilling to accept the centrality of racial stratification as the basic force behind the data they uncover], sometimes wittingly, sometimes unwittingly, operates to reinforce the fear and hatred of others by providing rationales for hierarchizing differences." Thomas L. Dunn, "The New Enclosures: Racism in the Normalized Community," in *Reading Rodney King, Reading Urban Uprising,* edited by Robert Gooding-Williams, 178–95 (New York: Routledge, 1993), 180.

55. I borrow this phrase from Michael G. Hanchard, *Orpheus and Power*

(Princeton, N.J.: Princeton University Press, 1994). Too many postmodern-inspired readings on race insist on the malleability and instability of all social constructions. This, they believe, is the best antidote to essentialism. In my view, however, by focusing on the instability of race as a category, they miss its continuity and social role in shaping everyday dynamics. Even worse, in some cases, the views of some of these authors come close to those of right-wing scholars who advocate the elimination race as a category of analysis and discourse. From the perspective advanced in this book, the elimination of race from above without changing the material conditions that makes race a *socially* real category would just add another layer of defense to white supremacy.

56. I have argued in my work that race emerged as a category of human division in the 15th and 16th centuries as Europeans expanded their nascent world system. However, other analysts believe that the category has existed since antiquity and cite evidence of "racism" from the Roman and Greek civilizations. Although I believe that they confuse xenophobia and ethnocentrism with what I call a racialized social system, our disagreement is not central to the point at hand.

57. Although many analysts resent this concept and think that is inappropriate, I am persuaded by the arguments advanced by philosopher Charles W. Mills. This notion forces the reader to understand the systemic and power elements in a racialized social system, as well as the historical reality that such systems were organized and are still ordained by Western logics. For a discussion on this matter, see my book, *White Supremacy*, or consult Charles W. Mills, *Blackness Visible* (Ithaca, N.Y.: Cornell University Press, 1998).

58. I have been criticized for holding this position (see my debate with Mara Loveman in the pages of the *American Sociological Review*, December 1999), yet the view that race relations have a material foundation has a long history in American sociology. This notion formed part of the classic work of W. Lloyd Warner, in *Social Class in America* (New York: Harper & Row, 1960), and John Dollard, in *Caste and Class in a Southern Town* (New York: Doubleday, 1957); later, it could be found in the work of Herbert Blumer, Hubert Blalock, Stokely Carmichael and Charles Hamilton, and Robert Blauner.

59. My emphasis. Karl Marx, *The German Ideology*, edited and with an introduction by C. J. Arthur (New York: International, 1985), 64.

60. Hegemonic rule means that dominant groups actively attempt to achieve the consent of the subordinated groups through a variety of means.

61. Margaret Wetherell and Jonathan Potter, *Mapping the Language of Racism* (New York: Columbia University Press, 1992), 91.

62. My emphasis. Jackman, *The Velvet Glove*, 69.

63. Black philosopher Charles W. Mills argues that with the advent of modern imperialism (the 15th and 16th centuries onward), whites developed a political, moral, and epistemological "racial contract" to maintain white supremacy over nonwhites. See *The Racial Contract* (Ithaca, N.Y.: Cornell University Press, 1997).

64. Volosinov, the great Russian psychologist, stated a long time ago that ideology, and even self-awareness and consciousness, are "always verbal [communicative], always a matter of finding some specifically suitable verbal complex." Vladimir N. Volosinov, *Freudianism: A Marxist Critique* (New York: Academic,

1976), 86. For treatises on how language is embedded in ideology, see Norman Fairclough, *Language and Power* (London: Longman, 1989) and *Critical Discourse Analysis: The Critical Study of Language* (London: Longman, 1995).

65. For an example of the efforts of survey researchers to craft better survey instruments, see Judith Tanur, ed., *Questions about Questions* (New York: Russell Sage Foundation, 1994).

66. Teun A. van Dijk, *Prejudice in Discourse* (Philadelphia: Benjamins, 1984). See also Howard Schuman et al., *Racial Attitudes in America*.

67. The specific wording of this survey question is: "If a black family with about the same income as you moves into your neighborhood, would you mind it a little, a lot, or not at all?" See Schuman et al., *Racial Attitudes in America*.

68. For data on traditional social distance questions, see chapter 3 in Schuman et al., *Racial Attitudes in America*. For data on the limited level of white-black friendship, see Mary R. Jackman and Marie Crane, " 'Some of My Best Friends are Black . . .': Interracial Friendship and Whites' Racial Attitudes," *Public Opinion Quarterly* 50 (Winter 1986): 459–86. For more recent data on Whites' racial attitudes see Kristen Myers', *Racetalk: Racism Hiding in Plain Sight* (Lanham, Md.: Rowman & Littlefield, 2005) and Melanie Bush's, *Breaking the Code of Good Intentions: Everyday Forms of Whiteness* (Lanham, Md.: Rowman & Littlefield, 2004). Data on limited fraternization between white and black college students will be provided in chapter 5.

69. Lawrence Bobo and Fred Licari, "Education and Political Tolerance: Testing the Effects of Cognitive Sophistication and Target Group Affect," *Public Opinion Quarterly* 53, no. 5 (Fall 1989): 285–308; Schuman et al., *Racial Attitudes in America*.

70. According to Steinar Kvale, *Interviews: An Introduction to Qualitative Research Interviewing* (London: Sage, 1996), most interview-based projects use between ten and fifteen subjects.

71. For a critique of the Enlightenment project as a racialized project, see Zygmut Bauman, *Modernity and Ambivalence* (Ithaca, N.Y.: Cornell University Press, 1991); David T. Goldberg, *Racist Culture: Philosophy and the Politics of Meaning* (Cambridge, Mass.: Blackwell, 1993).

72. See, for example, Norman K. Denzin and Yvonna S. Lincoln, eds., *Handbook of Qualitative Research* (Thousand Oaks, Calif.: Sage, 2000). Yet, this critical approach can be found in Dollard, *Caste and Class*, and more definitely, in Myrdal. For example, Myrdal wrote more than sixty years ago, in addressing the idea that "hard facts" debunk biases: It must be maintained, however, that *biases in social science cannot be erased simply by "keeping to the facts" and by refined methods of statistical treatment of the data*. Facts, and the handling of data, sometimes show themselves even more previous to tendencies toward bias than does "pure thought." . . . When, in an attempt to be factual, the statements of theory are reduced to a minimum, biases are left a freer leeway than if they were more explicitly set forth and discussed. (My emphasis) Gunnar Myrdal, *An American Dilemma: The Negro Problem and Modern Democracy* (New York: Harper & Brothers, 1944), 1041.

73. See Max Weber, "Objectivity in Social Science and Social Policy," edited and translated by Edward A. Shils and H. A. Finch (New York: Free Press, 1949).

74. I am aware that a few blacks and minority scholars and politicians—some

working in very important jobs—endorse these views. However, as I argue in chapter 6, this segment of the black community is very small and does not represent the views of the community at large.

75. This controversial agenda will be developed in chapter 8. My argument is not new. For similar arguments, see Harold Cruse, *Plural but Equal: A Critical Study of Blacks and Minorities and America's Plural Society* (New York: Morrow, 1987); David Ingram, *Group Rights: Reconciling Equality and Difference* (Lawrence: University Press of Kansas, 2000); and, particularly, chapter 8, "Antiracist Strategies and Solutions," in Joe R. Feagin, *Racist America: Roots, Realities, and Future Reparations* (New York: Routledge, 2000).

76. Andrea Fontana and James H. Frey, "The Interview: From Structured Questions to Negotiated Text," in *Handbook of Qualitative Research*, edited by Norman K. Denzin and Yvonna S. Lincoln, 645–72 (Thousand Oaks, Calif.: Sage, 2000).

77. Terri L. Orbuch, "People's Accounts Count: The Sociology of Accounts," *Annual Review of Sociology* 23 (1997): 455–78. The position I am elaborating here has been marvelously captured by philosopher of science Brian Fay. "So must we comprehend others in their own terms? *Yes*, in the sense that we cannot grasp intentional phenomena and their products as intentional without ascertaining what they mean for those engaged in them. But *No*, in the sense that explaining these phenomena often will require outstripping the conceptual resources of those being studied." Brian Fay, *Contemporary Philosophy of Social Science* (Oxford, England: Blackwell, 1996), 134.

78. Situational because those in the business of interpreting the world, "whether they admit it or not, always have points of view, disciplinary orientations, social or political groups with which they identify." (Joel L. Kinchelor and Peter McLaren, "Rethinking Critical Theory and Qualitative Research," in *Handbook of Qualitative Research*, edited by Norman K. Denzin and Yvonna S. Lincoln, 279–314 [Thousand Oaks, Calif.: Sage, 2000], 288.) Partial because we can never capture either the totality of events affecting a process or the process itself.

79. Fay, *Contemporary Philosophy of Social Science*, 220.

80. This idea is also from Fay, *Contemporary Philosophy of Social Science*.

81. For a full elaboration, see my "Rethinking Racism."

82. I owe this idea to Eileen O'Brien, a sociology professor at the State University of New York-New Paltz.

83. I borrow this phrase from the journal *Race Traitors*.

2

The Central Frames of
Color-Blind Racism

The master defense against accurate social perception and change is
always and in every society the tremendous conviction of rightness
about any behavior form which exists.

—John Dollard, *Class and Caste in a Southern Town*

If Jim Crow's racial structure has been replaced by a "new racism,"
what happened to Jim Crow racism? What happened to beliefs about
blacks' mental, moral, and intellectual inferiority, to the idea that "it is
the [black man's] own fault that he is a lower-caste . . . a lower-class man"
or the assertion that blacks "lack initiative, are shiftless, have no sense of
time, or do not wish to better themselves";[1] in short, what happened to
the basic claim that blacks are subhuman?[2] Social analysts of all stripes
agree that most whites no longer subscribe to these tenets. However, this
does not mean the "end of racism,"[3] as a few conservative commentators
have suggested. Instead, a new powerful ideology has emerged to defend
the contemporary racial order: the ideology of color-blind racism. Yet,
color-blind racism is a curious racial ideology. Although it engages, as all
ideologies do, in "blaming the victim," it does so in a very indirect, "now
you see it, now you don't" style that matches the character of the new
racism. Because of the slipperiness of color-blind racism, in this chapter I
examine its central frames and explain how whites use them in ways that
justify racial inequality.

THE FRAMES OF COLOR-BLIND RACISM

Ideologies are about "meaning in the service of power."[4] They are expressions at the symbolic level of the fact of dominance. As such, the ideolo-

gies of the powerful are central in the production and reinforcement of the status quo. They comfort rulers and charm the ruled much like an Indian snake handler. Whereas rulers receive solace by believing they are not involved in the terrible ordeal of creating and maintaining inequality, the ruled are charmed by the almost magic qualities of a hegemonic ideology.[5]

The central component of any dominant racial ideology is its frames or *set paths for interpreting information.* These set paths operate as cul-de-sacs because after people filter issues through them, they explain racial phenomena following a predictable route. Although by definition dominant frames must *mis*represent the world (hide the fact of dominance), this does not mean that they are totally without foundation. (For instance, it is true that people of color in the United States are much better off today than at any other time in history. However, it is also true—facts hidden by color-blind racism—that because people of color still experience *systematic* discrimination and remain appreciably behind whites in many important areas of life, their chances of catching up with whites are very slim.) Dominant racial frames, therefore, provide the intellectual road map used by rulers to navigate the always rocky road of domination and, as I will show in chapter 6, derail the ruled from their track to freedom and equality.

Analysis of the interviews with college students and DAS respondents revealed that color-blind racism has four central frames and that these frames are used by an overwhelming majority of the white respondents. The four frames are *abstract liberalism, naturalization, cultural racism,* and *minimization of racism.* Of the four frames, abstract liberalism is the most important, as it constitutes the foundation of the new racial ideology. It is also the hardest to understand (What is *racial* about opposing busing or affirmative action, policies that clearly interfere with our American individualism?). Thus, I dedicate more space in this chapter to its discussion and to how it plays out in the color-blind drama.

In order to adequately understand the *abstract liberalism* frame, first we need to know what is liberalism. According to John Gray, liberalism, or "liberal humanism," is at the core of modernity; of the philosophical, economic, cultural, and political challenge to the feudal order. Although he acknowledges that liberalism has no "essence," he points out that it has a "set of distinctive features," namely, individualism, universalism, egalitarianism, and meliorism (the idea that people and institutions can be improved).[6] All these components were endorsed and placed at the core of the constitutions of emerging nation-states by a new set of actors: the bourgeoisies of early modern capitalism. When the bourgeoisie lauded freedom, they meant "free trade, free selling and buying"; when they applauded "individualism," they had in mind "the bourgeois . . . the middle-class owner of property"; "The ideas of religious liberty and free-dom of conscience merely gave expression to the sway of free competition within the domain of knowledge."[7]

Hence, classical liberalism was the philosophy of a nascent class that as an aspiring ruling class expressed its needs (political as well as economic) as general societal goals. But the bourgeois goals were not extended to the populace in their own midst until the twentieth century.[8] Moreover, the liberal project was never inclusive of the countries that Spain, Portugal, France, Britain, the Netherlands, Italy, and later on, Germany used as outposts for raw materials and racialized workers (e.g., slaves). Although contemporary commentators debate the merits of liberal humanism as it pertains to current debates about race-based policies, muticulturalism, and "equality of results,"[9] many seem oblivious to the fact that *"European humanism* (and liberalism) *usually meant that only Europeans were human."*[10] Philosophers such as Kant stated that the differences between blacks and whites were "to be as great in regard to mental capacities as in colour." Voltaire, the great French philosopher, said on the same subject that "only a blind man is permitted to doubt that Whites, Blacks, and Albinoes . . . are totally different races." Lastly, even the father of modern liberalism, John Stuart Mill, author of *On Liberty*, justified 19th-century colonialism and supported slavery in antiquity and in certain 19th-century colonial situations.[11] To be clear, my intent here is not to vilify the founders of liberalism, but to point out that modernity, liberalism, and racial exclusion were all part of the same historical movement.

The liberal tradition informed the American Revolution, the U.S. Constitution, and "the leading American liberal thinker of this period, Thomas Jefferson."[12] And in the United States as in Europe, the exclusion of the majority of white men and all white women from the rights of citizenship and the classification of Native Americans and African Americans as subpersons accompanied the development of the new liberal nation-state.[13] Specifically, racially based policies such as slavery, the removal of Native Americans from their lands and their banishment to reservations, the superexploitation and degrading utilization of Mexicans and various Asian groups as contract laborers, Jim Crow, and many other policies were part of the United States' "liberal" history from 1776 until the 1960s.

Nevertheless, I would be remiss if I failed to acknowledge that, in both Europe and the United States, disenfranchised groups and progressive politicians used the liberal rhetoric to advance social and legal reforms (e.g., the Civil Rights Movement, the National Organization of Women, Liberal parties in Europe).[14] Thus liberalism, when extended to its seemingly logical conclusions ("Life, liberty, and the pursuit of happiness for *all*") and connected to social movements, can be progressive. My point, however, is less about social-reform liberalism (although I contend many reform organizations and many white reform-minded individuals[15] have adopted color-blind racism) than about how central elements of liberalism have been *rearticulated* in post–Civil Rights America to rationalize racially unfair situations.

The frame of *abstract liberalism* involves using ideas associated with political liberalism (e.g., "equal opportunity," the idea that force should not be used to achieve social policy) and economic liberalism (e.g., choice, individualism) in an *abstract* manner to explain racial matters. By framing race-related issues in the language of liberalism, whites can appear "reasonable" and even "moral," while opposing almost all practical approaches to deal with de facto racial inequality. For instance, the principle of equal opportunity, central to the agenda of the Civil Rights Movement and whose extension to people of color was vehemently opposed by most whites, is invoked by whites today to oppose affirmative-action policies because they supposedly represent the "preferential treatment" of certain groups. This claim necessitates ignoring the fact that people of color are *severely* underrepresented in most good jobs, schools, and universities and, hence, it is an abstract utilization of the idea of "equal opportunity." Another example is regarding each person as an "individual" with "choices" and using this liberal principle as a justification for whites having the right of choosing to live in segregated neighborhoods or sending their children to segregated schools. This claim requires ignoring the multiple institutional and state-sponsored practices behind segregation and being unconcerned about these practices' negative consequences for minorities.

Naturalization **is a frame that allows whites to explain away racial phenomena by suggesting they are natural occurrences.** For example, whites can claim "segregation" is natural because people from all backgrounds "gravitate toward likeness." Or that their taste for whiteness in friends and partners is just "the way things are." Although the above statements can be interpreted as "racist" and as contradicting the color-blind logic, they are actually used to reinforce the myth of nonracialism. How? By suggesting these preferences are almost biologically driven and typical of all groups in society, preferences for primary associations with members of one's race are rationalized as nonracial because "*they* (racial minorities) do it too."

Cultural racism **is a frame that relies on culturally based arguments such as "Mexicans do not put much emphasis on education" or "blacks have too many babies" to explain the standing of minorities in society.** This frame has been adequately discussed by many commentators and does not require much discussion.[16] During slavery and Jim Crow a central rationale for excluding racial minorities was their presumed biological inferiority. Even as late as 1940, a white newspaper editor in Durham, North Carolina, could confidently state that:

> A Negro is different from other people in that he's an unfortunate branch of the human family who hasn't been able to make out of himself all he is capable of. He is not capable of being rushed because of the background of the jungle. Part of his human nature can't be rushed; it gets him off his balance. . . . You can't wipe away inbred character in one year or a hundred years. It must be nursed along. We look upon him for his lack of culture, as being less reliable, in business and unsafe socially. His passions are aroused easily.[17]

Today only white supremacist organizations spout things such as this in open forums. Yet, these biological views have been replaced by cultural ones that, as I will show, are as effective in defending the racial status quo.[18] For example, George McDermott, one of the white middle-class residents interviewed by Katherine Newman in her *Declining Fortunes*, stated:

> I believe in morality: I believe in ethics: I believe in hard work: I believe in all the old values. I don't believe in handouts. . . . So that the whole welfare system falls into that [category]. . . . The idea of fourteen-year-old kids getting pregnant and then having five children by the time they're twenty is absurd! It's ridiculous! And that's what's causing this country to go downhill.

And as Newman poignantly comments, "George does not see himself as racist. Publicly he would subscribe to the principle everyone in this society deserves a fair shake."[19] Color-blind racism is racism without racists!

Minimization of racism **is a frame that suggests discrimination is no longer a central factor affecting minorities' life chances ("It's better now than in the past" or "There is discrimination, but there are plenty of jobs out there").** This frame allows whites to accept facts such as the racially motivated murder of James Byrd Jr. in Jasper, Texas,[20] the brutal police attack on Rodney King, the Texaco case,[21] the 2005 lawsuit by black workers alleging that Tyson Foods maintained a "Whites Only" bathroom in one of their Alabama plants, the neglect and slow response by government officials toward a mostly black population during Hurricane Katrina, and many other cases and still accuse minorities of being "hypersensitive," of using race as an "excuse," or of "playing the infamous race card." More significantly, this frame also involves regarding discrimination exclusively as all-out racist behavior, which, given the way "new racism" practices operate in post–Civil Rights America (chapter 1), eliminates the bulk of racially motivated actions by individual whites and institutions by fiat.

Before proceeding to illustrate how whites use these frames, I need to clarify a few points about the data and how I present them. First, whites used these frames in combination rather than in pure form. This is understandable, since informal expressions of ideology are a constructive effort, a process of building arguments in situ. Therefore, the examples of how whites use a particular frame may be mixed with other frames. Second, the frames were verbalized by participants in various emotional tones, ranging from sympathy to absolute disgust and outrage toward minorities. This suggests whites with differing levels of sympathy toward minorities resort to the *same* frames when constructing their accounts of racial matters. I attempt to represent this range of emotion in the quotes. Third, because the college student and DAS samples represent two different populations, I present quotes from the two studies separately in the text. I do so to better identify differences in style or content among the two populations. Fourth, the quotes in the chapter were selected to embrace the variety of ways in which the frames are used by respondents. This implies that many outrageously racist quotes were left out for the sake of representing the variance in the samples. Fifth, the interviews were transcribed to be as close to what the respondents uttered as possible. Thus the transcripts include nonlexical expressions (umm, ahh, umhmm), pauses (indicated by ellipses when they are short and by a number in seconds in parentheses representing the duration of the pause, when they are longer than five seconds), emphases (indicated by *italics* or, for notations of the respondent tone, by italic letters in brackets), self-corrections (denoted by a short line, —), and other important discursive matters (laughs and changes in tone are indicated with italic letters in brackets). Whenever I have added words they appear in brackets; the interviewers' interventions appear in brackets and in italic letters. However, to improve its readability, I edited the material lightly.

ABSTRACT LIBERALISM: UNMASKING
REASONABLE RACISM[22]

Because of the curious way in which liberalism's principles are used in the post–Civil Rights era, other analysts label modern racial ideology "laissez-fare racism" or "competitive racism" or argue that modern racism is essentially a combination of the "American Creed" with antiblack resentment.[23] The importance of this frame is evident in that whites use it on issues ranging from affirmative action and interracial friendship and marriage to neighborhood and residential segregation. Because of the pivotal role played by this frame in organizing whites' racial views, I provide numerous examples below.

Rationalizing Racial Unfairness in the Name of Equal Opportunity

An archetype of how white students use the notion of equal opportunity in an abstract manner to oppose racial fairness is Sue, a student at SU.

When asked if minority students should be provided unique opportunities to be admitted into universities, Sue stated:

> I don't think that they should be provided with unique opportunities. I think that they should have the same opportunities as everyone else. You know, it's up to them to meet the standards and whatever that's required for entrance into universities or whatever. I don't think that just because they're a minority that they should, you know, not meet the requirements, you know.

Sue, like most whites, ignored the effects of past and contemporary discrimination on the social, economic, and educational status of minorities. Therefore, by supporting equal opportunity for everyone without a concern for the savage inequalities between whites and blacks, Sue's stance safeguards white privilege. Sue even used the notion of equal opportunity to avoid explaining why blacks tend to perform worse than whites academically: "I don't know . . . um, like I said, I don't see it as a group thing. I see it more as an individual [thing] and I don't know why as a whole they don't do better. I mean, as I see it, they have the same opportunity and everything. They *should* be doing equal."

College students are not the only ones who use this abstract notion of equal opportunity to justify their racial views. For example, Eric, a corporate auditor in his forties, and a very affable man who seemed more tolerant than most members of his generation (e.g., he had dated a black woman for three years, recognized that discrimination happens "a lot" and identified multiple examples, and even said that "the system is . . . is white"), erupted in anger when asked if reparations were due to blacks for the injuries caused by slavery and Jim Crow: "Oh tell them to shut up, OK! I had nothing to do with the whole situation. The opportunity is there, there is no reparation involved and let's not dwell on it. I'm very opinionated about that!" After suggesting that Jews and Japanese are the ones who really deserve reparation, Eric added, "But something that happened three God-damned generations ago, what do you want us to do about it now? Give them opportunity, give them scholarships, but reparations?"

Was Eric just a white with a "principled opposition" to government intervention (see chapter 1 for analysts who make this claim)? This does not seem to be the case since Eric, like most whites, made a distinction between government spending on behalf of victims of child abuse, the homeless, and battered women (whom whites deem as legitimate candidates for assistance) and government spending on blacks (whom whites deem as unworthy candidates for assistance). This finding was consistent with DAS survey results. For instance, whereas 64.3 percent of whites agreed that "we should expand the services that benefit the poor," only 39.6 percent (as opposed to 84 percent of blacks) agreed with the proposition "The government should make every effort to improve the social and economic position of blacks living in the United States." Furthermore, whereas 75.2 percent of white respondents approved of increasing federal spending for the environment and 59.7 percent for social security, only 31.7 percent approved such increases for programs to assist blacks. And when the question dealt with government programs that were not perceived as "racial" in any way,[24] the proportion of whites supporting the program increased even more.

"The Most Qualified . . .": A Meritocratic Way of Defending White Privilege

Another tenet of liberalism whites use to explain racial matters is the Jeffersonian idea of "the cream rises to the top," or meritocracy (reward by merit). And whites seem unconcerned that the color of the "cream" that usually "rises" is white. For example, Diane, a student at SU, expressed her dissatisfaction about providing blacks unique opportunities to be admitted into universities: "I don't think you should admit anyone. It's gotta be, you've gotta be on the level to do it. If they were prepared beforehand to handle the college level to succeed in it, then there you go, anyone can." Diane then added, "They've gotta have the motivation to do well before you get there, I mean, I can't imagine being unprepared to go [to college] like just barely getting by in high school and then coming here to take the classes, you just can't go, 'OK, we want to put minorities in here so put anyone in, you know.'" Diane also used the notion of meritocracy to explain her opposition to affirmative action.

> That's so hard. I still believe in merit, you know, I still believe in equality, you know. If you did have two people with the same qualifications, one's minority and one's not, you know, I'd want to interview them and just maybe a personality stands out that works with the job, I don't know. Just find something other than race to base it on, you know? Let that not be a factor if they qualify.

How could Diane maintain these views and remain "reasonable"? Diane could say these things and seem reasonable because she believes discrimination is not the reason why blacks are worse off than whites. Instead, she relied on the cultural racism frame to explain blacks' status. This view can be seen too in her response to a question on why blacks fare worse academically than whites: "I don't know why. Mine was a personal motivation so, you know, I don't know. I don't want to say they weren't personally motivated to get good grades, but that's what it was for me." Diane expanded on this matter and said, "maybe some of them don't have parents to push them or . . . maybe the schools are not equal." She also speculated, "maybe, you know, they've got in their mind that they can't succeed because they're a minority and they don't try, you know, no one there to tell them 'You can do it, it doesn't matter who you are.'"

Whites from the Detroit metro area used the meritocratic frame as extensively as college students. For instance Jim, a thirty-year-old computer software salesperson from a privileged background, explained in the following way his opposition to affirmative action:

> I think it's unfair top to bottom on everybody and the whole process. It often, you know, discrimination itself is a bad word, right? But you discriminate everyday. You wanna buy a beer at the store and there are six kinda beers you can get, from Natural Light to Sam Adams, right? And you look at the price and you look at the kind of beer, and you . . . *it's a choice.* And a lot of that you have laid out in front of you, which one you get? Now, should the government sponsor Sam Adams and make it cheaper than Natural Light because it's brewed by someone in Boston? That doesn't make much sense, right? Why would we want that or make Sam Adams eight times as expensive because we want people to buy Natural Light? And it's the same thing about getting into school or getting into some place. And universities it's easy, and universities is a hot topic now, and I could bug you, you know, Midwestern University I don't think has a lot of racism in the admissions process. And I think Midwestern University would, would agree with that pretty strongly. So why not just pick people that are going to do well at Midwestern University, pick people by their merit? I think we should stop the whole idea of choosing people based on their color. It's bad to choose someone based on their color; why do we, why do we enforce it in an institutional process?

Since Jim posited hiring decisions are like market choices (choosing between competing brands of beer), he embraced a laissez-faire position on hiring. The problem with Jim's view is that discrimination in the labor market is alive and well (e.g., it affects black and Latino job applicants 30 to 50 percent of the time) and that most jobs (as many as 80 percent) are obtained through informal networks.[25] Jim himself acknowledged that being white is an advantage in America because "there's more people in the world who are white and are racist against people that are black than vice versa." However, Jim also believes that although blacks "perceive or feel" like there is a lot of discrimination, he does not believe there is much discrimination out there. Hence, by upholding a strict laissez-faire view on hiring and, at the same time, ignoring the significant impact of past and contemporary discrimination in the labor market, Jim can safely voice his opposition to affirmative action in an apparently race-neutral way.

"Nothing Should Be Forced upon People": Keeping Things the Way They Are

A central tenet of liberal democracies is that governments should intervene in economic and social matters as little as possible because the "invisible hand of the market" eventually balances states of disequilibrium. A corollary of this tenet, and part of the American mythology, is the idea that social change should be the outcome of a rational and democratic process and not of the government's coercive capacity.[26] During the Jim Crow era, the belief that racial change should happen through a slow, evolutionary process in "peoples' hearts" rather than through governmental actions was expressed in the phrase "you cannot legislate morality."[27] This old standpoint has been curiously reformulated in the modern era to justify keeping racial affairs the way they are. These ideas appeared occasionally in discussions on affirmative action, but most often in discussions about school and residential integration in America.

Sonny, a student at MU, explained in typical fashion her position on whether school segregation is the fault of government, whites, or blacks. As almost all the students, Sonny first stated her belief that school integration is in principle a good thing to have: "In principle, yeah, I think that's a good idea because like with, like with people interacting, they will understand each other better in future generations." But Sonny also, as most students, was not too fond of government attempts to remedy school segregation or, in her words, "I, I don't—I mean, it should be done if people want to do it. If people volunteer for it, and they want that part of their lives, then they should do it, but the government should not force people to bus if they don't want that." When asked to clarify her stance on this matter, she added, "I don't think the government should impose any legislation thinking that it will change people's hearts because people have to change them on their own. You can't force them to say 'Well, OK, now that I have to bus my kid there, I like it.'"

DAS respondents were as adamant as students in arguing that it is not the government's business to remedy racial problems. For example, Lynn, a human resources manager in her early fifties, explained why there has been so little school integration since the 1954 *Brown v. Board of Education* decision:

> I don't and that's another one. *I do not believe in busing.* The reason I don't believe in busing, you know, I said I don't. I didn't encourage my children to play with the neighborhood kids. I still felt that going to school in your community was the key to developing a child's sense of community and I still believe that. One of the reasons, another reason I moved from where I was [was] that I didn't want my children to be bused. I didn't want to have them got on a bus, especially me working. So I don't think that is an answer. I think the answer is education and helping people learn to make a life for themselves and, you know, any type of social program that interacts, that provides interaction between races I think is excellent. But I'm just not a busing person.

Lynn wants equal opportunity in education as well as community schools, a position that sounds perfectly reasonable. However, one would expect Lynn to support doing something to make sure that communities throughout America are diverse, a policy that other things being equal would guarantee school integration. Yet, Lynn took a very strong laissez-faire, antigovernment intervention stance on this matter. Lynn answered as follows the question, "America has lots of all-white and all-black neighborhoods. What do you think of this situation?"

> I don't have a problem with all-white and all-black neighborhoods if that's the choice of the people, the *individuals*. But, if it's *forced* either way, if I'm a black person and I've come into the neighborhood and I want to live here and selectively denied that option, that's wrong. But, again, there still has to be some type of social interaction for growth and if the social interaction takes place then, the cross-integration will take place, I think.

When pressed about what she thought could be done specifically to increase the mixing of the races in neighborhoods, Lynn restated that this could only be achieved "through educating (people) and encouraging businesses." Lynn was not alone in having this abstract view on school and neighborhood integration. Only one of the white respondents who opposed busing in the interviews (69.7 percent of whites opposed busing in the survey) provided a specific proposal that if implemented would increase residential as well as school integration.[28]

Individual Choice or an Excuse for Racial Unfairness and Racially Based Choices?

Individualism[29] today has been recast as a justification for opposing policies to ameliorate racial inequality because they are "group based" rather than "case by case." In addition, the idea of individual choice is used to defend whites' right to live and associate primarily with whites (segregation) and for choosing whites exclusively as their mates. The problem with how whites apply the notion of individualism to our present racial conundrum is that a relation of domination-subordination still ordains race relations in the United States (see chapters 1 and 4 in my *White Supremacy and Racism in the Post–Civil Rights Era*). Thus, if minority groups face group-based discrimination and whites have group-based advantages, demanding individual treatment for all can only benefit the advantaged group.[30] And behind the idea of people having the right of making their own "choices" lays the fallacy of racial pluralism—the false assumption that all racial groups have the same power in the American polity. Because whites have more power, their unfettered, so-called individual choices help reproduce a form of white supremacy in neighborhoods, schools, and society in general.

Lynn, a human resources manager, used the notion of individualism in a very curious way. Although Lynn expressed her support for affirmative action because "there's still a lot of discrimination," she thinks that "there isn't as much discrimination as there used to be." Lynn also acknowledged white males have advantages in society and said "the white male is pretty much instilled" and "very much represses . . . um, people and other minorities." Nevertheless, when it came to the possibility of affirmative action affecting her, Lynn said:

> Um, because affirmative action is based on a group as a whole, but when it comes down to the individual, like if affirmative action were against me one time, like it would anger me. I mean, because, you know, *I* as an individual got ripped off and, you know, getting a job.

DAS respondents also used individualism to justify their racial views and race-based preferences. For example, Mandi, a registered nurse in her thirties, said she had no problems with neighborhood segregation. She justified her potentially problematic position by saying that people have the right to choose where and with whom they live.

> Umm, I think that people select a neighborhood to live in that they are similar to and people, you know, whatever similarities they *find* [*louder voice*], you know, it's race, economical level, religion, or, you know, whatever. When you are looking at somebody you don't know what, what denomination they are or what political preference they have, but you can tell right off in race. I think that they choose to live in a neighborhood that is their race.

NATURALIZATION: DECODING THE MEANING OF "THAT'S THE WAY IT IS"

A frame that has not yet been brought to the fore by social scientists is whites' naturalization of race-related matters. Although the naturalization frame was the least used frame of color-blind racism by respondents in these two projects, about 50 percent of DAS respondents and college students used it, particularly when discussing school or neighborhood matters, to explain the limited contact between whites and minorities, or to rationalize whites' preferences for whites as significant others. The word "natural" or the phrase "that's the way it is" is often interjected to normalize events or actions that could otherwise be interpreted as racially motivated (residential segregation) or racist (preference for whites as friends and partners). But, as social scientists know quite well, few things that happen in the social world are "natural," particularly things pertaining to racial matters. Segregation as well as racial preferences are produced through social processes and that is the delusion/illusion component of this frame.

The importance and usefulness of this frame can be illustrated with Sara, a student at MU who used the frame on three separate occasions. Sara, for example, used the frame to answer the question on black self-segregation.

> Hmm, I don't really think it's a segregation. I mean, I think people, you know, spend time with people that they are like, not necessarily in color, but you know, their ideas and values and, you know, maybe their class has something to do with what they're used to. But I don't really think it's a segregation. I don't think I would have trouble, you know, approaching someone of a different race or color. I don't think it's a problem. It's just that the people that I do hang out with are just the people that I'm with all the time. They're in my organizations and stuff like that.

Sara also used the naturalization frame to explain the paltry level of school integregation in the United States.

> Well, I also think that, you know, where you are in school has to do with the neighborhood that you grow up in and, like, I grew up in mainly all-white communities so that community was who I was going to school with. And if that community had been more black, then that would be, I guess, more integrated and that would be just fine. I don't know if there's any way you can change the places in which people live because I think there *are* gonna be white communities and there are gonna be black communities and, you know, I don't know how you can get two communities like in the same school system.

The interviewer followed up Sara's answer with the question, "Why do you think there are white communities and black communities?" Sara's answer was: "Maybe like I said before, if people like to be with people that they're similar with and it means, you know—well, I don't think it has anything to do with color. I think it has to do with where they. . . ." Sara did not complete her thought as a light seems to have clicked on in her mind. She then proceeded to change her answer and acknowledged that race has a bearing on how people select neighborhoods: "Well, I guess it does [*laughs*]." The interviewer asked Sara if she thought her parents would move into an almost all-black neighborhood. Sara employed all sorts of rhetorical maneuvers (see chapter 3) to defend her parents by conveying the idea that racial considerations would have never been a criterion for selecting a neighborhood.

Finally Liz, a student at SU, suggested that self segregation is a universal process or, in her own words: "I do think they segregate themselves, but I don't necessarily think it's on purpose. I think it's that, you know, *we all try to stay with our own kind* so, therefore, you know, *they get along better with their own people* or whatnot [my emphasis]." By universalizing segregation as a natural phenomenon, Liz was able to justify even her own racial preference for white mates. When asked if she had ever been attracted to minority people, Liz said:

> Um no, just because I wasn't really attracted to them, you know, I'm more attracted to someone that's like kinda more like me. But, you know, and I wouldn't say that, I mean, I like if he's good looking or not, you know, it's not that, it's just I'm more attracted to someone white, I don't know why [*laughs*].

DAS respondents naturalized racial matters too, but in general did it in a more crude fashion. For instance, Bill, a manager in a manufacturing firm, explained the limited level school integration:

> I don't think it's anybody's fault. Because people tend to group with their own people. Whether it's white or black or upper-middle class or lower class or, you now, upper class, you know, Asians. People tend to group with their own. Doesn't mean if a black person moves into your neighborhood, they shouldn't go to your school. They should and you should mix and welcome them and everything else, but you can't force people together. If people want to be together, they should intermix more. [*Interviewer: OK. So the lack of mixing is really just kind of an individual lack of desire?*] Well, individuals, its just the way it is. You know, people group together for lots of different reasons: social, religious. Just as animals in the wild, you know. Elephants group together, cheetahs group together. You bus a cheetah into an elephant herd because they should mix? You can't force that [*laughs*].

Bill's unflattering and unfitting metaphor comparing racial segregation to the separation of species, however, was not the only crude way of using the naturalization frame. For example, Earl, a small-time contractor in his fifties, explained segregation in a matter-of-fact way.

> I think you're never going to change that! I think it's just kind of, you know, it's going to end up that way. . . . Every race sticks together and that's the way it should be, you know. I grew up in a white neighborhood, you know, most of the blacks will live in the black neighborhood. [*Interviewer: So you don't think there's anything wrong?*] No. Well, they can move, they still have the freedom to move anywhere they want anyway.

A significant number of DAS respondents naturalized racial matters in a straightforward manner. For example, Jim, a thirty-year-old computer software salesperson for a large company, naturalized school segregation as follows:

> Eh, you know, it's more of the human nature's fault. It's not the government's fault, right? The government doesn't tell people where to live. So as people decide where to live or where to move into or where they wanna feel comfortable, [they] move to where they feel comfortable. We all kinda hang out with people that are like us. I mean, you look at Detroit, we have a Mexican village, why do we have a Mexican village? Why aren't Mexican people spread out all over on metro Detroit? Well, they like being near other Mexican people; that way they could have a store that suited them close by the, you know, those sort of things probably together. So, it's more human nature that I would blame for it.

Despite whites' belief that residential and school segregation, friendship, and attraction are natural and raceless occurrences, social scientists have documented how racial considerations affect all these issues. For example, residential segregation is created by white buyers searching for white neighborhoods and aided by realtors, bankers, and sellers.[31] As white neighborhoods develop, white schools follow—an outcome that further contributes to the process of racial isolation. Socialized in a "white habitus" (see chapter 5) and influenced by the Eurocentric culture, it is no wonder whites interpret their racialized choices for white significant others as "natural." They are the "natural" consequence of a white socialization process.[32]

"THEY DON'T HAVE IT ALTOGETHER": CULTURAL RACISM

Pierre-André Taguieff has argued that modern European racism does not rely on an essentialist interpretation of minorities' endowments.[33] Instead, it presents their presumed cultural practices as fixed features (hence he labels it as the "biologization of racism") and uses that as the rationale for justifying racial inequality. Thus, Europeans may no longer believe Africans, Arabs, Asian Indians, or blacks from the West Indies are biologically inferior, but they assail them for their presumed lack of hygiene, family disorganization, and lack of morality.[34] This cultural racism frame is very well established in the United States. Originally labeled as the "culture of poverty"[35] in the 1960s, this tradition has resurfaced many times since, resurrected by conservative scholars such as Charles Murray and Lawrence Mead, liberals such as William Julius Wilson, and even radicals such as Cornel West.[36] The essence of the American version of this frame is "blaming the victim," arguing that minorities' standing is a product of their lack of effort, loose family organization, and inappropriate values.

Since there is little disagreement among social scientists about the centrality of this frame in the post–Civil Rights era, I focus my attention on highlighting what this frame allows whites to accomplish. I begin my illustration of this frame with two, clear-cut examples of college students who used it. The students agreed with the premise of the question, "Many whites explain the status of blacks in this country as a result of blacks lacking motivation, not having the proper work ethic, or being lazy. What do you think?" The first student is Kara, an MU student.

> I think, to some extent, that's true. Just from, like, looking at the black people that I've met in my classes and the few that I knew before college, not like they're—I don't want to say waiting for a handout, but to some extent, that's kind of what I'm like hinting at. Like, almost like they feel like they were discriminated against hundreds of years ago, now what are you gonna give me? You know, or maybe even it's just their background, that they've never, like maybe they're the first generation to be in college, so they feel like just that is enough for them.

The second quote is from Kim, a student at SU:

> Yeah, I totally agree with that. I don't think, you know, they're all like that, but, I mean, it's just that if it wasn't that way, why would there be so many blacks living in the projects? You know, why would there be so many poor blacks? If they worked hard, they could make it just as high as anyone else could. You know, I just think that's just, you know, they're raised that way and they see what their parents are like so they assume that's the way it should be. And they just follow the roles their parents had for them and don't go anywhere.

When cultural racism is used in combination with the "minimization of racism" frame, the results are ideologically deadly. If people of color say they experience discrimination, whites, such as Kara and Kim, do not believe them and claim they use discrimination as an "excuse" to hide the central reason why they are behind whites in society: their presumed "laziness."

Although Kara and Kim used the cultural racism frame in a crude form, most students did not. They articulated their culture of poverty views in a gentler, at times even "compassionate," way. For example, Ann, a student at WU, inserted the frame in her answer to a question about why blacks as a group fare worse than whites academically.

> Um, I guess I would have to say primarily family structure. Maybe it's not [being] able to support the child and, you know, in school and really encourage. It might be that it's a single-parent family and it's necessary [for them] to get out and get a job, you know, a full-time job and work a part-time job and still try to go to school. Maybe it's not encouraged as much for, like long term, it's mainly survival. I don't know, something, income; if the family is really skimping by it would be really far fetched, well, it wouldn't be probably necessarily the first thing that a child from [such] a family would think of, you know, expensive college rather than paying the rent, you know what I mean [*laughs*]? So, I mean, you know, the priorities are different.

Although Ann's arguments seem "reasonable" (poor people may have a different set of priorities than other people based on their economic situation), her explanation is wanting because it avoids mentioning the institutional effects of discrimination in the labor, housing, and educational markets and the well-documented[37] impact that discrimination has on middle- and upper-middle-class blacks. More significantly, Ann's failure to recognize how old- and new-fashioned discrimination affects blacks' life chances is not an argumentative slip, but the way in which most whites construe the situation of blacks, as evidenced by how respondents in both samples used similar arguments in answering questions about blacks' status.

This kinder and gentler way of using the cultural frame was the preferred choice of students. For example, Jay, a student at WU, explained as follows why blacks have a worse overall standing than whites:

> Hmm, I think it's due to lack of education. I think because if they didn't grow up in a household that afforded them the time to go to school and they had to go out and get jobs right away, I think it is just a cycle [that] perpetuates things, you know. I mean, I can't say that blacks can't do it because, obviously, there are many, many of them [that] have succeeded in getting good jobs and all that.

Jay, as most whites, admits to the "exceptional black." However, Jay immediately goes back to the gentle cultural argument:

So it's possible that the cycle seems to perpetuate itself because—I mean, let's say they go out and get jobs and they settle down much earlier than they would normally if they had gone to school and then they have kids at a young age and they—these kids—have to go and get jobs and so.

How did DAS respondents use this cultural frame? They relied on this frame as often as students did but were significantly more likely to use it in a straightforward and crude manner. The following two cases exemplify how most DAS respondents used this frame. First is Isaac, an engineer in his fifties. In response to the question comparing blacks' and whites' overall standing, Isaac argued that few blacks have the education to work as engineers. This led to the following exchange between Isaac and the interviewer:

> *Interviewer:* So you feel maybe there's a lack of interest in education that black people have?
> *Isaac:* They want to get a short cut to make money. There's no urgency to get education. They want to make, to get money faster than whites. They don't want to take the time to get educated, they want to get money fast.
> *Interviewer:* So they also don't put the time into developing their educational skills?
> *Isaac:* Yeah the way you learn, the way you grow, is the way you become.
> *Interviewer:* Some people say that minorities are worse off than whites because they lack motivation, are lazy, or do not have the proper values to succeed in our society. What do you think?
> *Isaac:* Right now I think our minorities are lazy. They don't have the patience to keep going.

Ian, the manager of information security at an automotive company, explained why blacks are worse off than whites as follows:

> The majority of 'em just don't strive to do anything, to make themselves better. Again, I've seen that all the way through. "I do this today, I'm fine, I'm happy with it, I don't need anything better." Never, never, never striving or giving extra to, to make themselves better.

Ian's perception of blacks as lazy emerged from his understanding of blacks as culturally deficient. This view was clearly expressed in his response to the question, "Do you think that the races are naturally different?"

> Well I think that genes have something, some play in this, but I think a lot of it is past history of the people and the way they're brought up. You look at Chinese, if you're gonna get ahead in China, you've gotta be very intellectual and you've gotta be willing to, uh, to fight for everything that you're gonna get. Ja-Japan is the same way. For a kid just to get into college, they gonna

take two years of going through entrance exams to get in. Then you kinda look at the blacks' situation. It's like, "Well, because of slavery, I ought to be given this for nothing, so I don't have to work for it, just give it to me." So culture and their upbringing is the big part of this.

Although Ian came close to the old biological view ("Well, I think genes have something, some play in this"), overall he made use of the cultural frame to explain blacks' status (Asians do well because they "gotta be intellectual," whereas blacks believe that because of slavery they do not have to work).

MINIMIZATION OF RACISM: WHITES' DECLINING SIGNIFICANCE OF RACE THESIS

When William Julius Wilson published *The Declining Significance of Race* in 1978, he made many whites in academia feel good about themselves. Wilson's main claim—that class rather than race was the central obstacle for black mobility—was an argument that had been brewing among whites for quite a while. Yet, whites believe that discrimination exists. For example, when white and black respondents in the DAS survey were given the statement, "Discrimination against blacks is no longer a problem in the United States," a high proportion of *both* groups (82.5 percent of whites and 89.5 percent of blacks) "disagreed" or "strongly disagreed" with that statement. Although whites and blacks believe discrimination is still a problem, they dispute its salience as a factor explaining blacks' collective standing. Thus, in response to the more specific statement, "Blacks are in the position that they are today as a group because of present day discrimination," only 32.9 percent of whites "agreed" or "strongly agreed" (compared to 60.5 percent of blacks). This means that in general whites believe discrimination has all but disappeared, whereas blacks believe that discrimination—old and new—is alive and well.

College students were more likely than DAS respondents to give lip service to the existence of discrimination. Because students for this study were taking social science courses at the time of the interviews, they may have become sensitized to the significance of discrimination as well as to the new character of contemporary discrimination. However, despite this sensitization, few believed discrimination and institutionalized racism are the reasons minorities lag behind whites in this society. In general, the students articulated their declining significance of race thesis in three ways. A plurality (18 of 41) used an indirect strategy of denial set by one of the following two phrases, "I am not black" or "I don't see discrimination" (see chapter 3 for an analysis of the functions of these phrases), others (9 of 41) minimized racism directly, and yet others (7 of 41) argued minorities make things look racial when they are not.

The following example illustrates how students used the indirect strategy of denial. The response of Mary, a student at SU, to the statement, "Many blacks and other minorities claim that they do not get access to good jobs because of discrimination and that when they get the jobs they are not promoted at the same speed as their white peers," was:

> I think before you really start talking about hiring practices and promotion practices, you have to look at credentials. I mean, you know, I've only really had one job. I worked for a general contractor so it was basically me in the office all day with him, my boss. But I, in fact, you have to look at credentials. I mean, I don't know if, you know, a white person gets a job over a minority, I can't sit here and say "Well, that's discrimination" because I don't know what the factors were. This person got a master's degree versus a bachelor's degree, or more in-depth training than this person, you know? I mean, I definitely do not doubt that [discrimination] happens, that minorities get passed over for promotions and that they are not hired based on their race. I have absolutely no doubt that it happens. I think that before you can sit there and start calling a lot of things discrimination, you need to look into the background, the credentials behind it.

Rather than stating "I don't believe minorities experience discrimination," Mary suggested they may not get jobs or promotions because they lack the credentials. And although Mary, as most whites, recognizes discrimination exists ("I definitely do not doubt that [discrimination] happens"), she clearly believes most claims are bogus ("I think that before you can sit there and start calling a lot of things discrimination, you need to look into the background, the credentials behind it").

The next example is of students who minimized the significance of racism directly. Andy, a student at WU, answered a question on whether discrimination is the central reason why blacks are behind whites today by saying, "I think they do." Yet his answer was wanting, since he could not provide a meaningful explanation of how discrimination affects minorities' life chances. More importantly, Andy's answers to the other questions minimized the salience of racism. For instance, his answer to the question of whether or not discrimination affects the chances of minorities getting jobs and promotions was, "I think that there's probably less than it used to be, but that it still happens. It's just in isolated places or, you know, it happens in different places, but in most jobs, I think it probably does not happen." When asked to elaborate, Andy stated he believes the reason why blacks do not get good jobs is, "if anything, it's probably education" because "you can't apply for certain jobs without a lot of education."

The last example is of students who argued blacks make situations racial that are not. Janet, an SU student, answered all the questions on discrimination by denying that discrimination is a salient factor in minorities' life chances and suggesting alternative interpretations. For instance, Janet's answer to the same question, on whether or not discrimination is the central reason why blacks lag behind whites was: "I would say it depends on the individual. I'm sure there are some . . . that do and others [that] don't, so. . . ." When asked to clarify, she said, "Right. But I would say for the most part, most of them don't unless they make it out to be the case." When the interviewer asked Janet if she thought most claims of discrimination by minorities were a perception issue, she replied: "If they looked at it as a different way or something, they might see—might not see it as racism, you see what I'm saying? [*Interviewer: You are saying that they are seeing more than is actually out there?*] Right." When asked about discrimination in jobs, Janet answered in a blunt fashion.

> I would say that's a bunch of crap [*laughs*]. I mean, if they're qualified, they'll hire you and if you are not qualified, then you don't get the job. It's the same way with, once you get the job, if you are qualified for a promotion, you'll get the promotion. It's the same way with white, blacks, Asians, whatever. If you do the job, you'll get the job.

DAS respondents used similar argumentative strategies to deny the significance of discrimination. The strategy they used the most was direct minimization (18 of 66), followed by outright denial (13 of 66), stating that minorities make things racial (11 of 66), and indirect minimization (3 of 66). The remaining respondents (20 of 66) include a few who sincerely believe discrimination is important (see chapter 7) and others who denied the centrality of discrimination in their own peculiar way.

The first case exemplifies DAS respondents who minimized the significance of discrimination directly. Joann, a poor white woman in her fifties who works in a large chain store, answered the direct discrimination question by stating, "I don't see any in the store." When asked about discrimination against minorities in general, Joann said:

> I don't think it's as bad as it was. It probably needs improvement. What [society] needs is a knowledgeable crew and I think that is the truth there. I think that the work will have to be done up continually until we're all one big happy family. [*Interviewer: Do you foresee that happening?*] It wouldn't surprise me. My great granddaughter might marry a black, I don't know. *I have no idea!*

The next case is an example of respondents who denied discrimination outright. It is worth pointing out that all the DAS respondents who used this strategy were from working- or lower-class backgrounds. Scott, a twenty-three-year-old drafter for a mechanical engineering company, answered the direct question on discrimination as follows:

> I don't—nowadays I don't, I don't really feel that way, I really don't at all. Maybe like when I was younger I would notice it, but right now I don't really feel that there's too much segregation anymore. If it is because of the person, you know, from their past experience. And, I mean, if you got a record, you're not gonna go too far, you know. So then they might feel like "Just being held back just because, you know, just 'cause I'm black."

The interviewer followed up Scott's answer with the question, "So you don't think that discrimination is a factor in most blacks lives nowadays?" His answer was: "It might be just because of their past and their attitudes toward life. But if you just took it as everyday life and just went with it, no, I don't feel it at all, I don't see it. I don't practice it and my friends, all my friends [don't] practice it."

Next are examples of respondents who argued blacks make things racial that are not. Sandra, a retail salesperson in her early forties, explained her view on discrimination as follows:

> I think if you are looking for discrimination, I think it's there to be *found*. But if you make the best of any situation, and if *you don't use it as an excuse*. I think sometimes it's an excuse because people felt they deserved a job, whatever! I think if things didn't go their way I know a lot of people have tendency to use prejudice or racism as whatever as an *excuse*. I think in some ways, *yes* there is people who are prejudiced. It's not only blacks, it's about Spanish, or women. In a lot of ways there [is] a lot of *reverse* discrimination. It's just what you wanna make of it.

Finally, I provide an example of respondents who used the indirect minimization strategy. Dave, an engineer in his forties who owns a small-time employment agency, answered the direct question on discrimination by saying: "[*laughs*] I don't know any blacks so I don't know. But, in general, I probably have to say it's true." When asked for clarification, Dave stated:

> Oh that's a hard one to just, well, I guess it comes down to stereotypes though like I said earlier. It just—some people may try to say that some blacks don't work as hard as whites. So, in looking for a job they may feel like they didn't get the job because they have been discriminated against because they were black, that's very possible. That may not really be, but as a person, they make the assumption.

Dave explained blacks' inferior status as compared to whites by suggesting that it "really comes down to individuals" and that he has "especially noted that if you want a job, there's jobs out there." In this reply Dave intimates his belief that racial discrimination is not a factor in the labor market since "there's jobs out there."

The last case is of DAS respondents who did not fit the overall strategies and used sui generis arguments to deny the significance of racial discrimination. Henrietta, a transsexual school teacher in his fifties, said the following in response to the question on discrimination:

> [*9-second pause*] Trying to be an unbiased observer because as a transsexual I am discriminated against. I think if people act responsible they will not be discriminated against. People who are acting irresponsible, in other words, demanding things, ah, "I need this" or "You did this because of my skin color" yeah, then they will be discriminated against. People who are intelligent present themselves in a manner that is appropriate for the situation and will not be discriminated against.

Thus, Henrietta suggests that blacks who experience discrimination deserve so because they act irresponsibly or complain too much.

CONCLUSION

In this chapter I illustrated how whites use the four central frames of color-blind racism, namely, abstract liberalism, naturalization, cultural racism, and minimization of racism. These frames are central to the views of whites, young (college-student sample) and old (DAS respondents), and serve them as an interpretive matrix from where to extract arguments to explain a host of racial issues. More significantly, together these frames form an impregnable yet elastic wall that barricades whites from the United States' racial reality. The trick is in the way the frames bundle with each other, that is, in the wall they form. Whites, for example, would have a tough time using the abstract liberalism frame if they could not resort to the minimization of racism frame as well. Precisely because they use these frames the way children use building blocks, whites can say things such as "I am all for equal opportunity, that's why I oppose affirmative action" and also say "Everyone has almost the same opportunities to succeed in this country because discrimination and racism are all but gone." And if anyone dares to point out that in this land of milk and honey there is a tremdendous level of racial inequality—a fact that could deflate the balloon of color blindness—they can argue this is due to minorities' schools, lack of education, family disorganization, or lack of proper values and work ethic. In short, whites can blame minorities (blacks in particular) for their own status.

But what if someone pokes holes in whites' color-blind story by pointing out that whites live mostly in white neighborhoods, marry and befriend mostly whites, interact mostly with whites in their jobs, and send their children to white schools or, if they attend mixed schools, make sure they take most of their classes with white children. Whites have two discursive options to avoid the potentially devastating effects of these arguments. They can resort to the abstract liberalism frame and say something like "I support integration, but I do not believe in forcing people to do anything that they do not want to do" or "People have the right to make their own individual choices and no one can interfere." Alternatively, they can naturalize the whiteness in which they live ("Blacks like living with blacks, and whites like living with whites . . . it's a natural thing"). As I documented in this chapter, whites mix and match arguments as they see fit. Therefore, someone can say, "Segregation is a natural thing" but also say that "I believe that no one has the right of preventing people from moving into a neighborhood." These frames then form a formidable wall because they provide whites a seemingly nonracial way of stating their racial views without appearing irrational or rabidly racist.

But if the ideological wall of color-blind racism were not pliable, a few hard blows would suffice to bring it down. That is why the flexibility of the frames is so useful. Color-blind racism's frames are pliable because they do not rely on absolutes ("All blacks are . . ." or "Discrimination ended in 1965"). Instead, color-blind racism gives some room for exceptions ("Not all blacks are lazy, but most are") and allows for a variety of ways of holding on to the frames—from crude and straightforward to gentle and indirect. Regarding the former, almost every white respondent in these studies mentioned the exceptional black ("Well, Robert, my black friend, is not like that"), agreed in principle with racially progressive notions ("I believe that school integration is great because we can learn so much from each other" or "Gee, I wish I could see the day when we have the first black president"), or even joined Martin Luther King Jr. in the dream of color blindness ("In two or three generations race will disappear and we will all just be Americans"). Regarding the latter, whites used the color-blind frames in crude ways displaying resentment and anger toward minorities ("Blacks are God-damned lazy") or in compassionate ways ("It is terrible the way they live in those neighborhoods, with those schools, without fathers, with crime just around the corner . . . it saddens me whenever I see all that on TV").

The pliability of the color-blind wall is further enhanced by the style of color blindness. For instance, if whites find themselves in a rhetorical bind, such as having disclosed a personal taste for whiteness or a dislike for blackness, they can always utter a disclaimer such as, "I am not prejudiced," or "If I ever fall in love with a black person, the race thing will never be an obstacle for us getting together." They can tiptoe around the most dangerous racial minefields because the stylistic elements of color blindness provide them the necessary tools to get in and out of almost any discussion. I examine these tools in detail in the next chapter.

NOTES

1. John Dollard, *Caste and Class in a Southern Town*, 2d ed. (New York: Doubleday, 1949).

2. For discussions on the "defensive beliefs" that supported Jim Crow, see Dollard, *Caste and Class*; Gunnar Myrdal, *An American Dilemma: The Negro Problem and Modern Democracy* (New York: Harper Brothers, 1944); Allison Davis et al., *Deep South* (Chicago: University of Chicago Press, 1941); and Charles S. Johnson, *Patterns of Negro Segregation* (New York: Harper Brothers, 1943).

3. This is taken from the title of conservative commentator Dinesh D'Souza's book, *The End of Racism: Principles for a Multiracial Society* (New York: Free Press, 1995). This book is, among other things, a crude example of color-blind racism.

4. J. B. Thompson, *Studies in the Theory of Ideology* (Cambridge, UK: Polity, 1984).

5. All ideologies aspire to be hegemonic, to rule the hearts of rulers and ruled. However, only those that incorporate elements of the "common sense" of the oppressed (albeit in partial and refracted manner) can truly become hegemonic.

6. See John Gray, *Liberalism* (Minneapolis: University of Minnesota Press, 1986).

7. All these quotes are from *The Communist Manifesto*. See David McLellan, ed., *Karl Marx: Selected Writings* (London: Oxford University Press, 1982). For a detailed intellectual assault at the farce of liberalism, see Karl Marx and Frederick Engels, *The German Ideology* (New York: International, 1985).

8. For a marvelous discussion of this point and of "racial capitalism," see Cedric J. Robinson, *Black Marxism: The Making of the Black Radical Tradition* (Chapel Hill: University of North Carolina Press, 2000).

9. Good examples of this trend are Andrea T. Baumeister, *Liberalism and the "Politics of Difference"* (Edinburgh: Edinburgh University Press, 2000), and Patrick Neal, *Liberalism and Its Discontents* (New York: New York University Press, 1997). Although Baumeister skillfully shows the tensions in traditional liberal discourse that foreshadow some of today's debates and provides a reasonable philosophical resolution based on "value pluralism," she fails to point out the exclusionary character of liberalism and the Enlightenment. Neal's account produces two interesting modifications of liberalism: the idea that liberal states cannot be neutral and the notion of "modus vivendi liberalism," which entails an open liberal approach to social issues. Yet, like Baumeister, Neal is silent about the racism of

the founding fathers of liberalism and the meaning of their racial exclusions for today's liberal project.

10. Charles W. Mills, *The Racial Contract* (Ithaca, N.Y.: Cornell University Press, 1997), 27.

11. The quotes by Kant and Voltaire as well as the views of Mill on slavery and colonialism can be found in chapter 2 of David Theo Goldberg, *Racist Culture* (Cambridge, UK: Blackwell, 1993). See also Zygmunt Bauman, *Modernity and Ambivalence* (Ithaca, N.Y.: Cornell University Press, 1991).

12. Richard Bellamy, "Liberalism," in *Contemporary Political Ideologies*, edited by Roger Eatwall and Anthony Wright (Boulder, Colo.: Westview, 1993), 23–49.

13. See Dana D. Nelson, *National Citizenship: Capitalist Citizenship and the Imagined Fraternity of White Men* (Durham, N.C.: Duke University Press, 1998), and chapter 5 in Howard Zinn, *A People's History of the United States* (New York: HarperCollins, 1980).

14. From a social movements perspective, "liberal groups are those that attempt to reform social systems for the purpose of giving all groups equal opportunities." Margaret L. Andersen, *Thinking about Women: Sociological Perspectives on Sex and Gender* (New York: Macmillan, 1988), 299.

15. For a scathing critique of color-blind "radicals" such as Todd Gitlin, Michael Tomasky, Richard Rorty, Jim Sleeper, Barbara Epstein, and Eric Hobsbawm, see chapter 4 in Robin D. G. Kelley, *Yo' Mama's Disfunktional: Fighting the Culture Wars in Urban America* (Boston: Beacon, 1997).

16. The classic statement on the subject still is William Ryan, *Blaming the Victim* (New York: Vintage, 1976).

17. Charles S. Johnson, *Racial Attitudes: Interviews Revealing Attitudes of Northern and Southern White Persons, of a Wide Range of Occupational and Educational Levels, toward Negroes* (Nashville, Tenn.: Social Science Institute, Fisk University, 1946), 153.

18. It is important to note that cultural racism was part and parcel of European and American racisms. My point is that this theme has supplanted biological racism in importance and effectiveness.

19. Katherine S. Newman, *Declining Fortunes: The Withering of the American Dream* (New York: Basic, 1993), 168.

20. James Byrd was a black man murdered by three white supremacist ex-convicts in 1998 in Jasper, Texas.

21. High-level Texaco executives were caught on tape saying some racially insensitive things about blacks and other minorities a few years back, which led them to settle a lawsuit brought by minority employees accusing the company of racial discrimination in pay and promotion.

22. I borrow the phrase "reasonable racism" from Jody David Armour, *Negrophobia and Reasonable Racism* (New York: New York University Press, 1997).

23. The former label is used in the works of Lawrence Bobo and his coauthors (see introduction) and the latter by Philomena Essed, in *Diversity: Gender, Color, and Culture* (Amherst: University of Massachusetts Press, 1996).

24. When the question at hand could be perceived as racial, white support declined significantly. Thus, for example, only 21 percent of whites agreed with the proposition to increase welfare spending.

25. The specific citations for these facts can be found in the introduction, or the reader can consult my chapter, coauthored with Amanda E. Lewis, "The 'New Racism': Toward an Analysis of the U.S. Racial Structure, 1960–1990s," in *Race, Nationality, and Citizenship,* edited by Paul Wong (Boulder, Colo.: Westview, 1999).

26. Bringing about social change in this country has never been a rational, civilized feat, particularly when racial considerations have been involved. Force and resistance have accompanied the most significant changes in America's political and racial order. We used force to achieve our independence from Britain, to keep the Union together, and to end state-sanctioned Jim Crow. An excellent little book on this subject is Irving J. Sloan, *Our Violent Past: An American Chronicle* (New York: Random House, 1970).

27. Southern sociologist Howard W. Odum took William Graham Sumner's idea of "mores" and suggested that racial conflicts must be solved through an evolutionary approach that he labeled "racial adjustments." In a similar vein, northern sociologist Robert E. Park argued that race contacts went through "race cycles" that ended in racial assimilation. See Howard W. Odum, *American Social Problems* (New York: Holt, 1939), and Robert E. Park, *Race and Culture* (Glencoe, Ill.: Free Press, 1950).

28. One respondent suggested a tax incentive policy to stimulate residential integration.

29. Despite its elitist origins in American history (see chapter 5 in Zinn, *A People's History of the United States*), the notion of individualism has been used by social reform movements such as the Jacksonian democracy movement of the nineteenth century, the Civil Rights Movement of the 1950s and 1960s ("one man, one vote"), and the Woman's Suffrage Movement of the early 20th century ("one person, one vote") to advance truly inclusive democratic agendas.

30. David Ingram, *Group Rights: Reconciling Equality and Difference* (Lawrence: University Press of Kansas, 2000).

31. For a review, see chapter 4 in my *White Supremacy and Racism in the Post–Civil Rights Era* (Boulder, Colo.: Rienner, 2001).

32. On all these matters, see Beverly Daniel Tatum, *"Why Are All the Black Kids Sitting Together in the Cafeteria?: And Other Conversations about Race"* (New York: Basic, 1997).

33. Most of the work of this important French scholar has not been published in English. A few of his pieces have appeared in *Telos* and, fortunately, the University of Minnesota Press translated his *La Force du préjugé: Essai sur le racisme et ses doubles.* Pierre-André Taguieff, *The Force of Prejudice: Racism and Its Doubles* (Minneapolis: University of Minnesota Press, 2001). See also Pierre-André Taguieff, ed., *Face au racisme, Tome II: Analyse, hypothèses, perspectives* (Paris: La Découverte, 1991).

34. See my " 'This Is a White Country': The Racial Ideology of the Western Nations of the World-System," *Research in Politics and Society* 6, no. 1 (1999): 85–102.

35. The culture of poverty argument was formally developed by anthropologist Oscar Lewis. His claim was that the poor develop a culture based on adaptations to their poverty status, which is then transmitted from generation to generation

and becomes an obstacle for moving out of poverty. Although Lewis formulated his thesis as a class-based one, because the characters in his famous books, *The Children of Sánchez* (1961) and *La Vida* (1965), were Mexican and Puerto Rican, respectively, it was almost impossible not to interpret his argument as especially pertinent for understanding minorities' well-being in America. Lewis's argument was roundly condemned by many of his contemporaries, but it stuck in scholarly policy circles as well as among conservative politicians and a few "liberals" such as Senator Patrick Moynihan.

36. Charles A. Murray, *Losing Ground: American Social Policy, 1950–1980* (New York: Basic, 1984); Lawrence M. Mead, *Beyond Entitlement: The Social Obligations of Citizenship* (New York: Free Press, 1986); William Julius Wilson, *The Truly Disadvantaged: The Inner City, the Underclass, and Public Policy* (Chicago: University of Chicago Press, 1987); Cornel West, *Race Matters* (Boston: Beacon, 1993).

37. See Sharon Collins, *Black Corporate Executives: The Making and Breaking of a Black Middle Class* (Philadelphia: Temple University Press, 1997); Ellis Cose, *The Rage of a Privileged Class* (New York: HarperCollins, 1995); and Joe R. Feagin and Melvin Sikes, *Living with Racism: The Black Middle Class Experience* (Boston: Beacon, 1994).

3

⤳

The Style of Color Blindness

How to Talk Nasty about Minorities without Sounding Racist

Subscribing to an ideology is like wearing a piece of clothing. When you wear it, you also wear a certain style, a certain fashion, a certain way of presenting yourself to the world. The style of an ideology refers to its peculiar *linguistic manners and rhetorical strategies* (or *race talk*),[1] to the technical tools that allow users to articulate its frames and story lines. As such, the style of an ideology is the thread used to join pieces of fabric into garments. The neatness of the garments, however, depends on the context in which they are being stitched. If the garment is being assembled in an open forum (with minorities present or in public venues), dominant actors will weave its fibers carefully ("I am not a racist, but . . .") and not too tight ("I am not black, so I don't know"). If, in contrast, the needlework is being done among friends, the cuts will be rough and the seams loose ("Darned lazy niggers").

I examine in this chapter the basic style of color blindness. At the core of my analysis is the idea that because the normative climate changed dramatically from the Jim Crow to the post–Civil Rights era, the language of color blindness is slippery, apparently contradictory, and often subtle.[2] Thus, analysts must excavate the rhetorical maze of confusing, ambivalent answers to straight questions; of answers speckled with disclaimers such as "I don't know, but . . ." or "Yes and no"; of answers almost unintelligible because of their higher than usual level of incoherence. This is not an easy task and the analyst can end up mistaking honest "I don't knows" for rhetorical moves to save face or nervousness for thematically induced incoherence. Cognizant of this possibility, I offer as much data as possible on each cited case.

Since a full discursive analysis of the stylistic components of color blindness is beyond the scope of this chapter,[3] I focus instead on showcasing five things. First, I document whites' avoidance of direct racial language to expressing their racial views. Second, I analyze the central "semantic moves" (see below) whites use as verbal parachutes to avoid dangerous discussions or to save face. Third, I examine the role of projection in whites' racial discourse. Fourth, I show the role of diminutives in colorblind race talk. Finally, I show how incursions into forbidden issues produce almost total incoherence in many whites. This last element is not part of the stylistic tools of color blindness but the result of talking about racially sensitive matters in a period in which certain things cannot be uttered in public. Nevertheless, because rhetorical incoherence appears often in whites' remarks, it must be regarded as part of the overall language of color blindness.

One concern for readers of this chapter may be whether I am attributing intentionality to whites as they piece together their accounts. That is, am I suggesting white respondents are "racists" trying to cover up their *real* views through these stylistic devices? First, readers need to be reminded that I see the problem of racism as a problem of power (see chapter 1). Therefore, the intentions of individual actors are largely irrelevant to the explanation of social outcomes. Second, based on my structural definition of "racism," it should also be clear that I conceive racial analysis as "beyond good and evil." The analysis of people's racial accounts is not akin to an analysis of people's character or morality. Lastly, ideologies, like grammar, are learned socially and, therefore, the rules of how to speak properly come "naturally" to people socialized in particular societies. Thus, whites construct their accounts with the frames, style, and stories available in color-blind America in a mostly unconscious fashion. As Stuart Hall has pointed out, "we all constantly make use of a whole set of frameworks of interpretation and understanding, often in a very practical unconscious way, and [those] things alone enable us to make sense of what is going on around us, what our position is, and what we are likely to do."[4]

CALLING BLACKS "NIGGER" SOFTLY: RACISM WITHOUT RACIAL EPITHETS

The literature about life in plantations, accounts from frontiersmen, or narratives from cattle ranchers show that whites used to talk about minorities in a straightforward matter. When people of color were property or regarded as secondary human beings, there was no reason to be concerned in talking about them. But the Civil Rights era shattered, among many things, the United States' norms about public discussions on race. Hence using words such as "nigger" and "Spic" and even saying things that sound or can be perceived as racist is deemed immoral. And because the dominant racial ideology purports to be color blind, there is little space for socially sanctioned speech about race-related matters. Does this mean that whites do not talk about minorities in public? As I showed in the previous chapter, whites talk about minorities in public, even in the somewhat formal venue of an interview sponsored by a major research university. But I also showed they talk in a very careful, indirect, hesitant manner and, occasionally, even through coded language.[5]

Almost all whites we interviewed avoided using traditional Jim Crow terminology to refer to blacks. Only one college student and six DAS respondents used terms such as "colored" or "Negroes" to refer to blacks and not a single one used the term "nigger" as a legitimate term. The student who used the term "colored" was Rachel, an MU student who had very conservative racial views. However, it was not clear whether or not she used the term as part of her normal repertoire. She used the term in her answer to a question about who were her friends in college.

> I wouldn't say mostly white. I'd say, it's probably a mix. 'Cause I have like a lot of Asian friends. I have a lot of colored friends,[6] you know, but it wasn't maybe not even the same, like, background either, I don't know. It's hard to tell, you know? From looking at somebody, so. . . .

From this statement, it is unclear whether she used the term in the old sense or wanted to say "people of color" and got confused.

All DAS respondents who used the term "colored" were 60 years of age or older. For example, Pauline, a retired woman in her late seventies, described the racial makeup of the schools she attended while growing up: "They were mixed, you know. [*Interviewer: Mixed of what?*] Well [*raises voice*] we had mostly colored and the white."

Although none of these older respondents were racial progressives, it would be a mistake to regard them as "Archie Bunkers," just because they used the racial language of the past. In truth, all these respondents were whites who have not fully absorbed the racial ideology and style of the post–Civil Rights era. Yet, based on what they said, some of these respondents seemed more open-minded than many younger respondents. For instance, when Pauline was asked if she had black friends while growing up, she said "I always had black friends, even when I worked I had black friends. In fact, I had a couple of my best friends." Although many whites' self-reports on friendship with blacks are suspect (see chapter 5), based on Pauline's own narrative, she seems to have had real associations with blacks. For example, she played with black kids while growing up and remembered fondly her black coworker. More significantly, Pauline, who has a niece who is dating a black "gentleman," seemed less concerned than one would expect:

> I feel like it's none of my business. She's had trouble with ah, she's divorced. She's had a lot of trouble with her ex, and he's very, very abusive. This fellow she's going with is very kind. The kids like him so there you go. So maybe it's gonna be good for her and the kids. And for him too, who knows!

The fact that white youth do not use racial slurs as legitimate terms in *public* does not mean that they do not use these terms or denigrate blacks in *private*. For example, most college students acknowledged listening to or telling racist jokes with friends; six even told the jokes in the interviews. For example, Lynn, an MU student, told the following joke she heard back home.

> *Lynn*: Okay [*laughing*]. It was, it's terrible but, what do you call a car full of niggers driving off a cliff?
> *Interviewer*: What?
> *Lynn*: A good beginning.

Eric, another MU student, told the following joke: "It was, what do you call a black man, a black man in a, in a coat and a tie? And it was, the defendant or something. Yeah, it was the defendant. And that was probably a couple of weeks ago or something that I heard that."

In addition, racist terminology is current in the life of students and DAS respondents, as illustrated by the fact that more than half of them acknowledged that they have friends or close relatives who are "racist." For example, Lee, a WU student, acknowledged that, "My father is pretty racist, so I heard everything, just about every racial slur you could possibly think of I heard it from him and I think that had an effect on me early." He also said that while his family was watching black TV shows such as *Sanford and Son* or *The Jeffersons*, his father would say things such as "Are we gonna watch the nigger shows?" Lee and his brothers would say "Yeah," because it was "just kind of second nature." Although Lee believes he has been able to successfully repel his father's racist influence, he admitted that he had some Nazi leanings while growing up and that although "I wasn't a skinhead or anything, but, you know, every now and again, I would draw a swastika on my notebook or something. . . ."

READING THROUGH THE RHETORICAL MAZE
OF COLOR BLINDNESS

Because post–Civil Rights racial norms disallow the open expression of racial views, whites have developed a concealed way of voicing them. Analysis of post–Civil Rights racial speech suggests whites rely on "semantic moves," or "strategically managed . . . propositions" whose meanings can be determined by the "content of speech act sequences,"[7] to safely state their views. For instance, most whites use apparent denials ("I don't believe that, but . . ."), claims of ignorance ("I don't know"), or other moves in the process of stating their racial views. The moves act as rhetorical shields to save face because whites can always go back to the safety of the disclaimers ("I didn't mean that because, as I told you, *I am not a racist*"). The data in this chapter will show whites often sandwich their racial statements between slices of nonracial utterances. In what follows I showcase the most common verbal strategies of post–Civil Rights' racial speech.

"I am not prejudiced, but . . ." and "Some of my best friends are . . ."

Phrases such as "I am not a racist" or "Some of my best friends are black" have become standard fare of post–Civil Rights racial discourse. They act as discursive buffers before or after someone states something that is or could be interpreted as racist. Therefore, it was not surprising to find that four students and ten DAS respondents used phrases such as "I'm not prejudiced, but" in their answers. One example of how the respondents inserted this semantic move was, Rhonda, a part-time employee in a jewelry store in her sixties. She used the move to safely express her highly racial views on why she thinks blacks are worse off than whites.

> Well, I'm gonna be, you understand I'm, I'm [not] prejudice or racial or whatever. They're always given the smut jobs because they would do it. Then they stopped, they stopped doing [them]. The welfare system got to be very, very easy. And I'm not saying all, there's many, many white people on welfare that shouldn't be. But if you take the percentage in the Tri-city country area, you will find that the majority are white, but all you see is the black people on welfare. But it's a graduation up. Thirty years ago they started it and they continued it, and they continued it, and they continued it. And it was easier to collect welfare from the state rather than go out and get a job. Why work if, if they gonna, if the government's gonna take care of you?

After Rhonda stated that, "I'm, I'm [not] prejudice or racial or whatever," she then gave her account on how she believes the welfare state has spoiled blacks. The ideological value of the "I am not a racist, but . . ." move is clear here.

The phrase "Some of my best friends are . . ." or its equivalent was used by eight students and twelve DAS respondents. Surprisingly, many respondents used it to refer to their Asian friends. For example, Eric, a student at MU, used this phrase after revealing that most of his friends while growing up were white. Specifically, when asked "Okay, and you say mostly whites, were there nonwhite friends along the way?" Eric answered: "Yeah I had a few. I, one of my best friends when I lived in New Jersey was Korean."

Jill, a salesperson in her thirties, used the "Some of my best friends are black" move in a rather odd way. In response to the question, "Have you ever dated racial minorities?" Jill said: "No, but I think one of my best friends is black." The interviewer then asked Jill, "OK, can you talk a little bit about that relationship?" Jill answered:

> Yeah we worked together at Automotive Company and what happened is this man was very bright. He graduated first in his class in economics from Indiana University and he got a fellowship through Automotive Company, which probably helped because he was black. And I also know he got into Harvard because he had terrible GMAT scores, but he did get in. He didn't have terrible, he had in the high fives. He did get in and graduated from Harvard and now he's an investment banker. But you know what? He is a nice guy. What he lacks in intellect he makes up for in . . . he works so hard and he's always trying to improve himself. He should be there because he works harder than anybody I know.

One of Jill's "best friends," according to her own narrative, was "very bright" but had "terrible GMAT scores." Yet, she continued, he "did get in" Harvard, which he deserved because "He is a nice guy" who makes up for "what he lacks in intellect" with hard work (was her "best friend" "very bright" or lacking "in intellect"?). She also sprinkled the story with her veiled concerns about affirmative action (her commentary about Automotive Company helping him "because he was black"). Please also notice this "best friend" is never identified by name.

"I am not black, so I don't know"

Since the aforementioned moves have become cliche (and thus less effective), color-blind racism has produced other semantic moves. These moves, as all the parts of any ideology, have developed collectively through a trial-and-error process and become resources available for the production of people's racial accounts.[8] One such move that appeared frequently among white college students but not among DAS respondents was the phrase "I am not black, so I don't know." After respondents interjected this phrase, they proceeded with statements that indicated they have strong views on the racial issue in question. For example, Brian, a student at SU, inserted the statement in response to the direct question on discrimination.

> I don't know. I believe them. I don't know, I'm not a black person living so I don't hang out with a lot of black people, so I don't see it happen. But I do watch TV and we were watching the stupid talk shows—there's nothing else on—and there's people out there. And just that and just hearing the news and stuff. I'm sure it's less than it used to be, at least that's what everybody keeps saying so . . . I think it's less but I can't say. But I can't speak for like a black person who says they're being harassed or being prejudice or discriminated against.

Brian's statement can be broken down as follows. First, he stated "I'm not a black person," so he did not see discrimination happening. Second, he recognized that discrimination still happens. Third, he carefully stated his own view: "it's less than it used to be."

The second example is Liz, a student at MU. She also used the phrase in her answer to the direct question on discrimination:

> Um, just because I'm not black, I'm not Hispanic, I don't really, don't understand. I don't go through it I guess. But then again, I've seen like racism on, you know, towards whites, scholarships and as far as school goes, which, I mean, which bothers me too. So I guess I can kind of understand.

Liz began her answer with the move and pondered whether or not she could understand minorities' complaints about discrimination because "I don't go through it I guess." But then she changed the topic to the issue of so-called reverse discrimination toward whites in "scholarships and as far as school goes," which "bothers me too." Thus Liz equalized the complaints about discrimination by all groups and concluded that, after all, "I guess I can kind of understand" minorities' claims about discrimination. In a specific question on whether or not blacks experience discrimination in jobs and promotions, Liz answered by avoiding the issue altogether: "Um, I just think that the best qualified should probably get the job and that, you know, like I wouldn't see why someone black wouldn't get a job over someone white who was more qualified or better suited for the job." Since Liz hinted that blacks lie when they make claims of discrimination, the interviewer asked her, "So when they say that [discrimination] happens to them, do you think they're lying or . . . ?" Liz proceeded to make a quick reversal to restore her image of neutrality.

I mean, I don't think they're lying, but I wouldn't, I mean, I guess in my little world, that everything is perfect, I wouldn't see why that would happen. But I guess that there are people who are, you know, racist who do, you know, would not promote someone black just because they're black, which I don't really understand, you know.

Liz's rhetorical back and forth (not understanding minorities' claims of discrimination and then claiming she does) and reversals (hinting that minorities lie when they claim to have experienced discrimination to saying that discrimination happens) typify how dangerous are the waters of color blindness. Negotiating the seemingly contradictory views that "race does not matter" but, at the same time, that "race matters" a little bit for minorities and a lot for whites in the form of reverse discrimination is not an easy task.

"Yes and No, But . . ."

Another semantic move typical of color-blind racism is the "yes and no" strategy. After respondents insert this phrase and, apparently taking or examining all sides, they proceed to take a stand on the issue at hand. Students were more likely than DAS respondents to use this move, a finding that resonates with the fact, discussed in the previous chapter, that DAS respondents were more straightforward in the enunciation of the frames of color-blind racism. An example of how respondents used this move is Emily, a student at SU who answered a question about providing minorities special opportunities to be admitted into universities as follows:

Unique opportunities, I don't know? There might be, I guess, some minorities do get schools [that] aren't as well funded as others. So, I would have to say yes and no. I think they should get an opportunity to come, but I also don't think they should allow other people to come. 'Cause that's sort of like a double-edged sword, maybe because you are discriminating against one group any way you do it and I don't believe in that, and I don't think you should discriminate against one group to give another a better chance. And I don't believe that's fair at all. But I also don't believe that it's fair they have to [attend a] school that can't teach as well or don't have the facilities to teach them like they should. I don't know. I'm kinda wishy-washy on that.

This "yes and no" answer can be interpreted as an expression of whites' ambivalence on a very "controversial" social policy.[9] However, Emily's answer to the direct question on discrimination clearly shows that she is decisively against affirmative action:

I just have a problem with the discrimination, you're gonna discriminate against a group and what happened in the past is horrible and it should never happen again, but I also think that to move forward you have to let go of the past and let go of what happened. You know, and it should really start equaling out, um, 'cause I feel that some of it will go too far and it will swing the other way. One group is going to be discriminated against—I don't believe in that. I don't think one group should have an advantage over another, regardless of what happened in the past.

Thus, Emily opposes affirmative action as it is practiced because she interprets it as reverse discrimination. In turn, she favors programs that are not in place (expanding educational opportunities for minorities before college) or that would not change minorities' status in a significant way (equal opportunity).

Mark, an MU student, used the "yes and no" strategy to express his view on affirmative action:

Yes and no. This is probably the toughest thing I have deciding. I really, 'cause I've thought about this a lot, but I can make a pro-con list and I still wouldn't like. I've heard most of the issues on this subject and I honestly couldn't give a definite answer.

Mark, who was taking a sociology course at the time of the interview, recognized minorities "don't have the same starting points and, if you are starting from so much lower, they should definitely be granted *some* additional opportunities to at least have an equal playing ground." But he immediately added, "I'm gonna be going out for a job next year, and I'll be honest, I'd be upset if I'm just as qualified as someone else, and individually, I'd be upset if a company takes, you know, like an African American over me just because he is an African American." Mark repeats this point when discussing three affirmative action–based hiring scenarios. When asked if he would support the hypothetical company's hiring decisions, Mark said: "If I'm that person, I'm not gonna support it. If I'm that majority getting rejected just because I'm a different race." Hence Mark's philosophical "yes and no" on affirmative action seems to disappear when the policy is discussed in practical terms.

It is important to point out that other respondents did not use the particular phrase "yes and no" but inserted similar buffer statements to safely express their reservations, objections, and at times, opposition to certain policies. For example, Brian, a student at SU, explained his stance on affirmative action: "Man, that's another one where [*laughs*] I kind of support and oppose it [*laughs*], you know? Uh pretty much the same thing I said before was that, I don't know, if I come, I don't know—somebody underqualified shouldn't get chosen, you know?" Brian opposed providing minorities unique opportunities to be admitted into universities and the hiring decisions in the three affirmative action hiring scenarios. This suggests Brian leans more toward the "against" than the "for" stance on affirmative action, regardless of his odd "I kind of support and oppose" stance.

One example of DAS respondents who used this strategy is Sandra. A retail person in her forties, Sandra used the move to voice her opposition to affirmative action. Sandra's answer to the question, "Are you for or against affirmative action?" was:

> **Yes and no.** I feel someone should be able to have *something*, education, job, whatever, because they've earned it, they deserve it, they have the ability to do it. You don't want to put a six year old as a *rocket scientist*. They don't have the ability. It doesn't matter if the kid's black or white. As far as letting one have the job over another one just because of their race or their gender, I don't believe in that.

Sandra's "yes and no" answer on affirmative action seems like truly a strong "no," since she did not find any reason whatsoever for affirmative action programs to be in place. Her "yes and no" at the beginning was followed by a long statement on why affirmative action is wrong and thus she concluded by saying "As far as letting one have the job over another because of their race or their gender [which is the way she interprets affirmative-action policies], I don't believe in that."

Anything but Race

Another rhetorical move akin to the "I am not a racist, but" and "Some of my best friends are" is "Anything but race." This strategy involves interjecting comments such as "is not a prejudice thing" to dismiss the fact that race affects an aspect of the respondent's life. Hence, this tool allows whites to explain away racial fractures in their color-blind story. For example, Ray, a student at MU, dismissed the notion that race had any bearing on the fact that he had no minority friends in high school:

> Yeah, I think, I think that as things got later on, **I don't think there was any type of prejudice involved.** I just think that we really didn't know these kids. You know what I mean? They lived in different neighborhoods, they went to different schools. Um, and there was never any effort made to exclude, and if anything, there was an effort made to cultivate these kids.

Sonny, a student at MU, also used this tool to explain why she did not have minority friends while growing up. Sonny revealed in the interview that she had Italian friends,[10] but suggested that "race never came into play" and that "most of my friends were just normal kids." After revealing that "one of my best friends is Indian" (Asian Indian), she pondered why she and her friends did not have blacks in their crowd:

> I mean, there was so many kids. I don't think we had any black friends. I don't know why. It kind of stuck together and I don't know, it wasn't that we, it wasn't that we wouldn't be like . . . allowing to black people. It's just that there was never, like, an opportunity. There's no population like that around where we lived.

Both Ray and Sonny seemed to realize their almost all-white networks violate their color-blind view of themselves. Thus, in their descriptions, they pointed out that this was a nonracial fact in their lives. My point here is not to accuse whites who do not have minority friends of being "racist" (see my definition of racism in chapter 1). Instead, I want to show that whites explain the product of racialized life (segregated neighborhoods, schools, and friendship networks) as nonracial outcomes and rely on the available stylistic elements of color blindness to produce such accounts.

As college students, DAS respondents used phrases in line with the "anything but race" strategy. For instance, Marge, an unemployed woman in her early fifties, used this rhetorical strategy in her response to the interracial marriage question:

> Very different than what I used to think, I think it doesn't have anything to do with racism. It has to do with how you will all be treated. Now, if it's just a matter of you and the other person and there's no families involved, no kids involved and if you are living in an area [where people have] open minds, I think it's fine. But when you start dragging kids in, no matter how much you love or whether you are a racist or not, that's not the question, it's how those kids are going to be treated. And so my answer is if there are kids, you know, families in and all that involved, and you're living in a racially, you know, racist kind of area, no, I don't believe in marrying somebody of a different race. But if it's you two together and there's nobody else involved, then I say it's fine. But, you know, when you are dragging other people in, you have to think of them too.

Obviously, the phrase "I think it doesn't have anything to do with racism," and the carefully but long-winded statement afterwards, allowed Marge to oppose almost all kinds of interracial unions on a variety of apparently nonracial grounds (but see chapter 5).

"THEY ARE THE RACIST ONES . . .": PROJECTION AS A RHETORICAL TOOL

Psychologists since Freud have argued that projection is part of our normal equipment to defend ourselves.[11] It is also an essential tool in the creation of a corporate identity (Us versus Them).[12] More pertinent to this section, projection helps all of us "escape from guilt and responsibility and affix blame elsewhere."[13] College students and DAS respondents projected racism or racial motivations onto blacks and other minorities as a way of avoiding responsibility and feeling good about themselves. The projections of college students appeared on a variety of issues (e.g., affirmative action, school and residential segregation, interracial friendship and marriage, and the work ethic of blacks), but most often on the hot issue of so-called black self-segregation. For example, Janet, a student at SU, answered a question on whether or not blacks self-segregate, as follows:

> **I think they segregate themselves.** Or, I mean, I don't know how everybody else is, but I would have no problem with talking with or being friends with a black person or any other type of minority. I think they've just got into their heads that they are different and, as a result, they're pulling themselves away.

The interviewer followed up Janet's answer with a question trying to ascertain whether or not Janet had tried to mingle with blacks, but Janet cut her off quickly with the following statement: "They're off to their own kind of little, own world."[14]

Janet projected once more in her answer to the interracial marriage question, but this time not onto blacks, but onto people who marry across the color line.

> I would feel that in most situations they're not really thinking of the, the child. I mean, they might not really think anything of it, *but* in reality I think most of the time when the child is growing up, he's going to be picked on because he has parents from different races and it's gonna ultimately affect the child and, and the end result is they're only thinking of them—of their own happiness, not the happiness of, of the kid.

By projecting selfishness onto people who intermarry ("they're not really thinking of the, the child"), Janet was able to voice safely her otherwise racially problematic opposition to intermarriage. Nevertheless, she admitted that if she or a member of her family ever became involved with someone from a different race, her family "would *not* like it *at all*![*laughs*]."

Other examples of projection among students occurred when they discussed affirmative action. Although most students expressed open resentment on this subject, a few projected the idea that blacks feel "terrible" if they are hired because of their race. For instance, Rachel, the conservative MU student cited above, explained her position on affirmative action as follows:

Affirmative action programs? Like I was saying, I think, I don't know if I do because, I mean, I think the only reason they, you know, established it was to make up for the 200 and some years of slavery. And it's just trying to, like, for us it's just trying to like make up for the past. And on the blacks, on that end, I think they're kind of . . . I would feel bad, you know, because I'm getting in because of the color of my skin, not because of my merits. And I'd feel kind of inferior, you know, like I'd feel that the whole affirmative action system would inferiorize me. Just because maybe I'll get like, you know, a better placement, you know, in a school just because of the color of my skin. I don't know.

This argument appears quite often in whites' objections to affirmative action.[15] The rhetorical beauty of this projection is that it is couched as a "concern" on how blacks feel about affirmative action. Of course, because the market is heavily tilted toward whites, if someone ought to feel "inferior" about market decisions it should be whites, since they are the ones who receive preferential treatment "just because of the color of [their] skin."

DAS respondents projected racism and racial motivations onto blacks and minorities but at a slightly higher rate. Twenty-two of the sixty-six white respondents projected racism or racial motivations onto blacks on a variety of issues. For example Ann, an unemployed woman in her twenties, answered the question on whether blacks are hard to approach or are not welcomed by whites as follows: "I think that, I don't know—they live too much on the past, if you ask me. Some of 'em do. You know, I think blacks are more prejudiced against whites than whites are against blacks."

Francine, a homemaker in her late twenties, answered a question on why blacks and whites see the police and the criminal court system very differently in the following way: "Black people are just prejudiced. They just think that they're out to get them or something."

Pat, an orderly in a psychiatric hospital in her early thirties, balked at the idea of the government establishing programs on blacks' behalf to deal with the effects of discrimination.

On behalf of blacks? No, I think it's equaling out, I mean, if you want to go to school you can. I don't think there should be—Years back [the government] came out with a Negro College Fund. We don't have any United Caucasian Fund, I mean, I don't know why they separate themselves because they are allowed to go to the same schools and colleges and everything as white people. It should be all together. I don't think there should be *specials*, you know what I am saying? [*giggles and snorts*] No, I don't—it should all be the same for everybody. Everybody wants equal rights, equal this and equal this and that will equal everything out.

Beverly, a small-business owner and homemaker in her forties, projected the idea that blacks who are hired through affirmative action feel terrible. She stated that affirmative action is "unfair to black and white." When the interviewer asked her to explain what she meant, Beverly said: "Because a lot of companies they know that they're hired [because they are black]. I mean, it's got to be in their mind, it would be in [my] mind, that's why I'm saying this. 'Was I hired because I was good or because I was black?'"

Racial projections bring to mind the famous statement by DuBois in *The Souls of Black Folk*, "How does it feel to be a problem?"[16] Whites freely lash out at minorities ("*They* self-segregate," "*They* take advantage of the welfare system," "*They* must feel terrible about affirmative action") and seldom exhibit self-reflexivity; minorities are the problem, whites are not.

"IT MAKES ME A LITTLE ANGRY . . .": The Role of Diminutives in Color-Blind Race Talk

Because maintaining a nonracial, color-blind stance is key in the post–Civil Rights era, whites rely on diminutives to soften their racial blows. Hence, when they oppose affirmative action, few say, "I am against affirmative action." Instead, they say something such as, "I am just a little bit against affirmative action." Similarly, few whites who oppose interracial marriage state flatly, "I am against interracial marriage." Instead, they say something such as, "I am just a bit concerned about the welfare of the children."

About half of the college students and a quarter of DAS respondents used diminutives to cushion their views on issues such as interracial marriage and affirmative action. For instance, Andy, a student at WU, used diminutives twice to state his concerns on interracial marriage.[17]

I would say I have a little bit of the same concern about the children just because it's more, I mean, would be more difficult on them. But, I mean, I definitely [*nervous laugh*] have no problem with any form of interracial marriage. That's just, just an extra hurdle that they would have to over, overcome with the children, but, but I—(it) wouldn't be a detriment to the kids, I don't think. That just makes it a little more difficult for them.

Mickey, a student at MU, used diminutives to make the potentially problematic claim that people at MU were oversensitive about matters regarding race or sexual orientation. Andy made his comments in response to a question about whether or not he participated in political activities on campus. After Andy stated in no uncertain terms that he did not participate in any political activity, the interviewer, curious about the tone of the answer, commented "You sounded pretty staunch in your no." To this Andy replied,

> Yeah, I just, I don't know. I think everybody, everybody here just seems like really uptight about that kind of stuff and, I mean, maybe it's just because I never had to deal with that kind of stuff at home, but, you know, it seems like you have to watch everything you say because **if you slip a little bit**, and you never know, there's a protest the next day.

When asked to explain what kind of "little slips" he was referring to, Andy said:

> Like, I mean, if you hear a professor say something, like a racial slur, or **something just like a little bit, you know, a little bit outta hand**, you know. I mean. I would just see it as like, you know, he was just, you took it out of context or something, but, you know, **it's just little things like that**. It's just, it's so touchy. Everything is so touchy it seems like around here. And I don't, like I don't like to get into debates about stuff and, you know, about cultures and stuff like that. 'Cause I've seen it, I've seen it around here, you know, plenty, you know, about like, with religious stuff and gay stuff and minority stuff. And it's just nothin' of that, I just don't like to get into that stuff.

Thus, Mickey uses the diminutives to state that people at MU are hypersensitive because they protest when a professor does "little things" like making "a racial slur" in class or making some insensitive religious or homophobic remarks.

DAS respondents also used diminutives, but consistent with what I have documented for other rhetorical tools and the frames of color blindness, they were less likely to use them. The following two examples illustrate how they used diminutives. First is Rita, an underemployed woman in her twenties. Rita stated her controversial belief that blacks are naturally different from whites as follows: "Well, I can't say that generally they all are, but a lot of the ones I've encountered are **a little more aggressive, a little bit more high tempered**, or whatever."

Obviously, the diminutives and her qualification that her view applies to most but not all blacks muted somewhat her otherwise traditional Jim Crow position.

Judy, a college professor in her forties who throughout the interview signified her "racial progressiveness," softened her opposition to affirmative action by using a diminutive. "**I'm for it a little bit**, not real dramatically. I think it's ah, I think is a temporary solution. I think it's bad when, if you have like, it's used for quotas."

"I, I, I, I DON'T MEAN, YOU KNOW, BUT . . .":
Rhetorical Incoherence and Color Blindness

Rhetorical incoherence (e.g., grammatical mistakes, lengthy pauses, or repetition) is part of all natural speech. Nevertheless, the level of incoherence increases noticeably when people discuss sensitive subjects. Because the new racial climate in America forbids the open expression of racially based feelings, views, and positions, when whites discuss issues that make them feel uncomfortable, they become almost incomprehensible.[18]

Almost all the college students were incoherent when discussing certain racial issues, particularly their personal relationships with blacks. For example, Ray, the MU student cited above and a respondent who was very articulate throughout the interview, became almost incomprehensible when answering the question about whether he had been involved with minorities while in college:

> Um, so to answer that question, no. But I would not, I mean, I would not ever preclude a black woman from being my girlfriend on the basis that she was black. You know, I mean, you know what I mean? If you're looking about it from, you know, the standpoint of just attraction, I mean, I think that, you know, I think, you know, I think, you know, all women are, I mean, all women have a sort of different type of beauty, if you will. And I think that, you know, for black women, it's somewhat different than white women. But I don't think it's, you know, I mean, it's, it's, it's nothing that would ever stop me from like, I mean, I don't know, I mean, I don't if that's, I mean, that's just sort of been my impression. I mean, it's not like I would ever say, "No, I'll never have a black girlfriend," but it just seems to me like I'm not as attracted to black women as I am to white women, for whatever reason. It's not about prejudice, it's just sort of like, you know, whatever. Just sort of the way, way like I see white women as compared to black women, you know?

The interviewer followed up Ray's answer with the question, "Do you have any idea why that would be?" Ray replied: "I, I, I [*sighs*] don't really know. It's just sort of hard to describe. It's just like, you know, who you're more drawn to, you know, for whatever reason, you know?"

Mark, an MU student cited above, answered a direct question on interracial marriage in the following manner:

> I mean, personally, I don't see myself, you know, marrying someone else. I mean, I don't have anything against it. I just I guess I'm just more attracted to, I mean, others. Nothing like, I could not and I would never, and I don't know how my parents would—just on another side, I don't, like, if my parents would feel about anything like that.

Mark was one of three students who openly opposed interracial marriage. Acknowledging this seems to have rattled him emotionally, as his speech pattern became incongruous.

Another issue that made students feel seemingly uncomfortable was discussing their views on the matter of self-segregation. Ann, for example, a WU student, became very hesitant in her answer to the question of whether or not blacks self-segregate (remember, short lines [—] stand for self-corrections).

> Um, no, I don't think they segregate themselves, they just probably just, I guess probably they're, I don't know. Let's see, let's try to—Like we were trying—Like mutual friends, I suppose, maybe and probably maybe it's just your peers that you know, or maybe that they, they have more, more like activities, or classes and clubs, I don't really know, but I don't think it's necessarily conscious, I don't—I wouldn't say that I would feel uncomfortable going and talking to a whole group.

One potential reason why some whites get out of rhythm when discussing self-segregation is the realization that whatever they say about minorities can be said about them. Thus, as they explain their opinions on this issue, respondents make sure they provide nonracial explanations of why minorities may seemingly self-segregate (Ann suggesting friendship networks are based on people sharing similar interests).

DAS respondents were significantly less likely than students to become incoherent, but when they did, it was around the same issues. Dorothy, for instance, a retired automobile company worker in her seventies, who spoke clearly throughout the interview, seemed confused when addressing the topic of interracial marriage.

> Eh, well, I donno, but I, I, I feel that uh, I donno, I just feel like, that uh, you should [*low voice*] stick to your own race for marriage [*Interviewer: And why is that?*] Uh because I feel that there's uh proble—There would be problems on both sides. A girl would feel hurt if, if his parents, you know were. . . . [*End of Tape 1. Interviewer asked her to continue her answer*] Yeah, I really do. Well, I donno—they have a different culture than we do, really and I think that his family would be, would probably be just as upset. I watch this on TV everyday and see how, you know, how they, they have a different, I donno—I hear the men, I know I hear that the black men on TV say that the black women are so, you know, so wild and mad, you know, tempers, you know what I mean. And I just feel that's the limit. I donno, if my dau—If one of my daughters woulda, ah, married one, I would have accepted it because it's my daughter and I would, I wo—And I would have never be, I would never be nasty to them. Because I feel they're just as human as we are. If they treat me decent, I'm gonna treat them decent. That's my feelings!

Dorothy's incoherence "makes sense" in light of her opposition to inter-racial marriage. Because openly opposing interracial marriage is contro-versial and violates the notion of color blindness, Dorothy seemed compelled to qualify her answer and insert the profoundly awkward statement about the equality of the races ("they're just as human as we are").

Lynn, a human resource manager in her early fifties, became incoherent while stating her reservations about dating black men:

> I don't know. Just, well [*high pitched voice*] I think I would have been very uncomfortable, okay, I really do. I mean, it would just be, I [*raises voice*] wouldn't want to go out with a really dark Middle Eastern man, or Indian, or Oriental. I mean, I, I just would be uncomfortable. If they're closer to me in looks, okay. That's just always the way I felt. Not that I didn't like men of ethnic diversity, but I just—You have a certain taste, you know. I think I do.

As with college students, DAS respondents became nervous when dis-cussing some matters other than interracial marriage. For example, Eric, an auditor for an automotive company, became anxious when discussing whether or not he associates with his black coworkers.

> Sure, sure, you can, it's—if you work in that environment the, the race is there obviously. I don't think it will ever go away, but I don't practice it and I see a lot of people who don't practice it. The, they, you know, but it's existing and I know that and I don't. Yeah, I, I, I, I go out with the black guys. I don't even care. It don't matter to me.

CONCLUSION

If the tales of color-blind racism are going to stick, whites need to be able to repair mistakes (or the appearance of mistakes) rhetorically. In this chapter I have documented the variety of tools available to whites to mend racial fissures, to restore a color-blind image when whiteness seeps through discursive cracks. Color-blind racism's race talk avoids racist ter-minology and preserves its mythological nonracialism through semantic moves such as "I am not a racist, but," "Some of my best friends are . . . ," "I am not black, but," "Yes and no," or "Anything but race." Thus, if a school or neighborhood is completely white, they can say "It's not a racial thing" or "It's economics, not race." They can also project the matter onto blacks by saying things such as "They don't want to live with us" or "Blacks are the really prejudiced ones."

But how can whites protect themselves against the charge of racism when they state positions that may be interpreted as racist? They can use diminutives as racial shock absorbers and utter statements such as "I am a little bit against affirmative action because it is terribly unfair to whites" or "I am a bit concerned about interracial marriage because the children suffer so much." And, as in the case of the frames of color-blind racism, whites mix and match the stylistic tools of color-blind racism. Hence, respondents could use a diminutive ("I am a little bit upset with blacks . . ."), followed by a projection (". . . because they cry racism for everything, even though they are the ones who are racist"), and balance out the statement with a semantic move at the end (". . . and I am not being racial about this, it's just that, I don't know").

The interviews also revealed that talking about race in America is a highly emotional matter. Almost all the respondents exhibited a degree of incoherence at some point or other in the interviews. Digressions, long pauses, repetition, and self-corrections were the order of the day. This incoherent talk is the result of talking about race in a world that insists race does not matter, rather than being a tool of color blindness. However, since it is so preeminent in whites' race talk, it must be included as part of the linguistic modalities of color-blind racism.

One final important point to make is that college students were more likely than DAS respondents to use semantic moves such as "I am not a racist, but," "Some of my best friends are . . . ," "Yes and no," and "I am not black, but." The students were also more likely to use diminutives to soften their racial views and to become incoherent when discussing sensitive racial matters. DAS respondents, however, were more likely to project than students. These findings match my findings in the previous chapter. Why is this the case? Preliminary analysis of survey and interview data from these two projects suggest that younger, educated, middle-class people are more likely than older, less-educated, working-class people to make full use of the resources of color-blind racism.

This means white youths are more adept at surfing the dangerous waters of America's contemporary racial landscape. This should not be surprising, since they are the cohort that has been ingrained from day one with the ideology of color blindness. However, it is worth noting that young, educated, middle-class DAS respondents are not too far off from their older, less-educated, working-class counterparts in their crudeness and lack of rhetorical sophistication. This may well mean that, as whites enter the labor market, they feel entitled to vent their resentment in a relatively straightforward manner. No need to sweeten the pill when you feel morally entitled to a job or promotion over all blacks, since you believe they are "not qualified," when you believe the taxes you pay are being largely wasted on "welfare-dependent blacks," when you are convinced that blacks use discrimination as an excuse to cover up for their own inadequacies.

In my substantiation of the frames and style of color blindness, many respondents inserted stories to make their points: stories about the mysterious "black man" who took "their job" or their "spot at Harvard." These stories provide the emotional glue and the seal of authenticity needed to validate strong racial claims. Without these stories, venting racial animosity would be untenable. I examine these stories and their functions in the next chapter.

NOTES

1. For a full discussion of the various stylistic components of a racial ideology, see chapter 3 in my *White Supremacy and Racism in the Post–Civil Rights Era* (Boulder, Colo.: Rienner, 2001).

2. There is no systematic research on whites' *private* racial discourse. I suspect the structured and formal nature of our interview process made it a public matter and thus signified to respondents to be cautious. However, community-based studies on whites and undercover observational studies suggest whites are more likely to use racialized language in private, white spaces. For examples of the former, see Jonathan Rieder, *Carnarsie: The Jews and Italians of Brooklyn against Liberalism* (Cambridge, Mass.: Harvard University Press, 1985), and John Hartigan Jr., *Racial Situations: Class Predicaments of Whiteness in Detroit* (Princeton, N.J.: Princeton University Press, 1999). For an example of the latter, see Lawrence Otis Graham, *Member of the Club* (New York: HarperCollins, 1995). Other notable studies on this subject include Kristen Myers', *Racetalk: Racism Hiding in Plain Sight* (Lanham, Md.: Rowman & Littlefield, 2005) and Melanie Bush's, *Breaking the Code of Good Intentions: Everyday Forms of Whiteness* (Lanham, Md.: Rowman & Littlefield, 2004). See also Joe R. Feagin's forthcoming book *Backstage Racism* (Lanham, Md.: Rowman and Littlefield) where he documents, using students' journals, the extensive level of racist interactions in college campuses.

3. For an example, see Eduardo Bonilla-Silva and Tyrone A. Forman, " 'I Am Not a Racist but . . .': Mapping White College Students' Racial Ideology in the USA," *Discourse and Society* 11, no. 1 (2000): 50–85.

4. Stuart Hall, "The Narrative Construction of Reality," *Southern Review* 17, no. 2 (1984): 7.

5. For a discussion of coded racial discussions on government spending and taxes, see Tomas Edsall and Mary D. Edsall, *Chain Reaction: The Impact of Race, Rights, and Taxes on American Politics* (New York: Norton, 1992).

6. To help readers, all the rhetorical maneuvers used by respondents in this chapter are set in **sans-serif type**. It does not indicate any type of emphasis in tone of voice.

7. Teun van Dijk, *Communicating Racism: Ethnic Prejudice in Cognition and Conversation* (Amsterdam: Benjamins, 1987), 86.

8. On ideology, see Teun van Dijk, *Ideology: A Multidisciplinary Approach* (London: Sage, 1998).

9. Paul Sniderman and Thomas Piazza, *The Scar of Race* (Cambridge, Mass.:

Harvard University Press, 1993); Seymour M. Lipset, *American Exceptionalism* (New York: Norton, 1996); Paul Sniderman and Edward G. Carmines, *Reaching Beyond Race* (Cambridge, Mass.: Harvard University Press, 1997).

10. Italians seem to have a tenuous claim to whiteness, since many "whites" mentioned them as examples of "minority friends" in the interviews.

11. For an excellent analysis of racial projection, see the classic book by Gordon W. Allport, *The Nature of Prejudice* (Garden City, N.Y.: Doubleday/Anchor, 1958).

12. For an excellent analysis of the creation of the antithetical figures of "barbarian" or "wild men" and "civilized men" in Europe and its central role in the creation of the notion of "the other," see Roger Bartra, *Wild Men in the Looking Glass: The Mythic Origins of European Otherness* (Ann Arbor: University of Michigan Press, 1994).

13. Sam Keen, *Faces of the Enemy: Reflections of the Hostile Imagination* (New York: Harper & Row, 1986), 21.

14. On this matter and white college students' lack of self-reflexivity, see Joe R. Feagin and Nikitah Imani, *The Agony of Education* (New York: Routledge, 1996). On the so-called issue of self-segregation, see Beverly Daniel Tatum, *"Why Are All the Black Kids Sitting Together in the Cafeteria?": And Other Conversations about Race* (New York: Basic, 1997).

15. For a critique, see Bryan K. Fair, *Racial Caste Baby: Color Blindness and the End of Affirmative Action* (New York: New York University Press, 1997).

16. W. E. B. DuBois, *The Souls of Black Folk* (New York: Penguin, 1995), 44.

17. The question was: "Twenty-five to thirty-five percent of whites oppose interracial marriage. Many claim they do not have any problem with minorities, but that they are concerned about what would happen to the children. What is your view on this delicate matter?" It is important to point out that we obtained similar "concerns about the children" from the DAS sample, even though we did not include the second part of the question. At any rate, my focus here is on whether or not respondents used diminutives while stating concerns over racially sensitive issues.

18. For a similar finding, see van Dijk, *Communicating Racism*.

4

⌒

"I Didn't Get That Job
Because of a Black Man"

Color-Blind Racism's Racial Stories

S torytelling is central to communication. To a large degree, all communication is about telling stories.[1] We tell stories to our spouses, children, friends, and coworkers. Through stories we present and represent
ourselves and others.[2] Stories have been defined as "social events that
instruct us about social processes, social structures, and social situations."[3] We literally narrate status ("When we were at the Gold Golf
Club . . ."), biases ("This guy, who was not even a member of the GG
Club . . ."), and beliefs about the social order (". . . had the audacity of
asking me out, even though he just drives a Cavalier"). Stories are also
important because they help us reinforce our arguments; they assist us in
our attempt of persuading listeners that we are "right."

Thus, the stories we tell are not random, as they evince the social position of the narrators and belong to what Moscovici labels as "social representations."[4] Storytelling often represents the most ideological moments;
when we tell stories we tell them as if there was *only one way* of telling
them, as the "of course" way of understanding what is happening in the
world. These are moments when we are "least aware that [we] are using
a particular framework, and that if [we] used another framework the
things we are talking about would have different meaning."[5] This is also
the power of storytelling—that the stories seem to lie in the realm of the
given, in the matter-of-fact world. Hence stories help us make sense of the
world but in ways that reinforce the status quo, serving particular interests without appearing to do so.

Not surprisingly, then, since stories are a normal part of social life, they are a central component of color-blind racism. In this chapter I examine the stories people tell as they try to make sense of racial matters in contemporary America. While a number of authors have examined the racial stories people tell,[6] few have specifically focused on the storytelling itself or on the ideological functions of stories. In the pages that follow I delve into modern racial stories as told by college students and DAS respondents. These stories were not research-driven, since I did not probe for them in these projects. Instead, they emerged spontaneously in respondents' answers to questions, in their efforts to punctuate certain points or to underscore the salience of an issue, or as digressions in the middle of racially sensitive discussions.

I examine two kinds of stories in this chapter: *story lines* and *testimonies.* I define *story lines* as the *socially shared tales that are fable-like and incorporate a common scheme and wording.* Racial story lines are fable-like because, unlike testimonies (see below), they are often based on impersonal, generic arguments with little narrative content—they are the ideological "of course" racial narratives. In story lines characters are likely to be underdeveloped and are usually social types (e.g., the " black man" in statements such as "My best friend lost a job to a black man" or the "welfare queen" in "Poor black women are welfare queens"). Furthermore, story lines are social products, a fact revealed by the similar schemata employed by different storytellers in the execution of the story lines—for example, in the use of similar phrases and words (such as "the past is the past") in the accounts. What makes these story lines "ideological" is that storytellers and their audiences share a representational world that makes these stories seem factual. Hence, by telling and retelling these story lines, members of a social group (in this case, the dominant race) strengthen their collective understanding about how and why the world is the way it is; indeed these stories tell and retell a moral story agreed upon by participants. These racial narratives, therefore, do more than assist dominant (and subordinate) groups to make sense of the world in particular ways; they also justify and defend (or challenge, in the case of oppositional stories)[7] current racial arrangements.

Testimonies, by contrast, are *accounts in which the narrator is a central participant in the story or is close to the characters in the story.*[8] Testimonies provide the aura of authenticity and emotionality that only "firsthand" narratives can furnish ("I know this for a fact since I have worked all my life with blacks"). Therefore, these stories help narrators in gaining sympathy from listeners or in persuading them about points they want to convey. Though *seemingly* involving more detail and personal investment than story lines (but see my analysis below), many of the testimonies whites tell still serve rhetorical functions with regard to racial issues, such as saving face, signifying nonracialism, or bolstering their arguments on controversial racial matters. Moreover, they are often tightly linked to the story lines above as personal experiences are understood and interpreted through the lens of more general racial narratives and understandings about the world.

THE MAJOR STORY LINES OF COLOR-BLIND RACISM

During the Jim Crow era the myth of the black rapist became a powerful story line that could be invoked to keep blacks "in their place."[9] In the era of the new racism (see chapter 1), new story lines have emerged that help keep blacks and other minorities in their (new, but still secondary) "place." The major racial story lines of the post–Civil Rights era are "The past is the past," "I did not own slaves," "If (other ethnic groups) have made it, how come blacks have not?," and "I did not get a (job or promotion) because of a black man." Although some of these story lines (e.g., "The past is the past" and "I didn't own any slaves") were often interjected together by respondents, I present my discussion of each separately.

"The Past Is the Past"

"The past is the past" story line is central to color-blind racism since it fits well with the minimization of discrimination frame. Thus more than 50 percent (21 of 41) of the college students and most DAS respondents used the story line most often when discussing affirmative action or government programs targeted for blacks. The core of this story line is that we must put the past behind us and that programs such as affirmative action do exactly the opposite by keeping the racial flame alive. A perfect example of how students inserted this story line was provided by Andy, a student at WU. Andy's answer to the question, "Do you believe that the history of oppression endured by minorities merits the intervention of the government on their behalf?" was:

> I almost—I think that the past is kind of the past and so, history of oppression?[10] I don't know if anyone [is] owed anything because of the, like, past [is] really past history, but to look at things, the way things are right at this moment and to try to move forward from there. Then I support some things, maybe affirmative action, so long as it wasn't a run away sort of. . . .

Emily, a student at SU, used the story line in an exchange with the interviewer on the meaning of affirmative action:

I have, I just have a problem with the discrimination, you're gonna discriminate against a group and what happened in the past is horrible and it should
never happen again, but I also think that to move forward you have to let go
of the past and let go of what happened, you know? And it should really start
equaling out 'cause I feel that some of, some of it will go too far and it'll
swing the other way. One group is going to be discriminated against, I don't,
I don't believe in that. I don't think one group should have an advantage over
another regardless of what happened in the past.

Very few DAS respondents who expressed their displeasure with programs they believe benefit blacks solely because of their racial background did not use a version of this story line. For instance, Jennifer, a
school-district personnel director in her forties, expressed her opposition
to affirmative action in a straightforward manner: "In general I am
against it. I think it had its place. It was necessary." She later reaffirmed
her position using a version of the story line in response to a hypothetical
case dealing with a company that decides to hire a black over a white
applicant because of past discrimination:

Again, I don't think that we can make retribution for things that happened in
the past. I don't think it serves any purpose today to try to fix something that
happened a long time ago that doesn't affect anyone today. All it does is
bring up to the surface that there was a problem.

Jennifer's last statement ("All it does is bring up to the surface that there
was a problem") is the central ideological component of this story line.
For whites, remedial policies are inherently divisive and hence whites'
insistence in forgetting the past.

Kate, a salesperson and part-time college student in her twenties, used
the story line to explain her opposition to government programs for
blacks. Kate first stated: "To make up for what we did in the past, I'd say
no. I mean, we can't still punish the Germans for what happened to the
Jews so if that is to make up for what they did, then I'd say no." Since her
answer left open the possibility there may be cases in which compensatory assistance was reasonable, the interviewer asked for clarification.
After the interviewer read the question to Kate again, she answered:

Am I not elaborating enough? [*Interviewer: Oh, no, no, no, no, we're just* . . .]
No, I don't think that the government should because I think that's saying
"OK, we made a mistake a hundred of years ago so now we're gonna try to
make up for it." But yet, you know, I think that is the past and you have to
move along; I mean, should they admit that they made a mistake? Yes! But
should there be programs for blacks that aren't for whites if they're in the
same position, you know? If they're hurting or they're battered or they're
starving should it be any different because they're not black? No!

Some respondents used the story line while venting lots of anger at the idea of affirmative action or reparations. John II, for instance, a retired architect and homebuilder in his late sixties, vented anger in his response to the question on reparations.

> Not a nickel, not a nickel! I think that's ridiculous. I think that's a great way to go for the black vote. But I think that's a ridiculous assumption because those that say we should pay them because they were slaves back in the past and yet, how often do you hear about the people who were whites that were slaves and ah, the whites that were ah? Boy, we should get reparations, the Irish should get reparations from the English. . . .

But what is ideological about this story? Is it not true that "the past is the past"? First, whites interpreted the past as slavery, even when in some questions we left it open (e.g., questions regarding the "history of oppression") or specified we were referring to "slavery *and* Jim Crow." Since Jim Crow died slowly in the country (1960s to 1970s), their constant reference to a remote past distorts the fact about how recent overt forms of racial oppression impeded black progress. This also means that most whites are still connected to parents and grandparents who participated in Jim Crow in some fashion. Second, the effects of historic discrimination have limited blacks' capacity to accumulate wealth at the same rate as whites. According to Melvin L. Oliver and Thomas M. Shapiro, the "cumulation of disadvantages" has "sedimented" blacks economically so that, even if all forms of economic discrimination blacks face ended today, they would not catch up with whites for several hundred years![11] Third, believing discrimination is a thing of the past helps whites reinforce their staunch opposition to all race-based compensatory programs. This story line, then, is used to deny the enduring effects of historic discrimination as well as to deny the significance of contemporary discrimination. Thus, when one considers the combined effects of historic and contemporary discrimination, the anchor holding minorities in place weighs a ton and cannot be easily dismissed.

"I Didn't Own Any Slaves"

The essence of the "I didn't own any slaves" story line is that present generations are not responsible for the ills of slavery. This story line was used frequently in conjunction with the story line of "The past is the past," but it was inserted less often (nine students and a third of DAS respondents). As with the previous story line, this one was usually invoked in discussions about affirmative action. For instance, Carol, a student at SU, said in response to the question on government intervention:

"I mean, I almost kind of have the 'what happened, happened' attitude. You know, I mean, my generation certainly didn't inflict any of this onto your generation, I mean, if anyone should pay it's the generation that did the inflicting." Because the generation who "did the inflicting" is long gone, her suggestion would not have any impact on blacks today.

Lynn, an MU student, used the story line to explain her opposition to a hypothetical company hiring a black candidate over a white candidate because of past discrimination:

> I think I would, I would, I'd disagree, I think. I mean, yeah, I think I'd dis-agree because, I mean, even though it's kinda what affirmative action—well, it's not really because I don't think like my generation should have to—I mean, in a way, we should, but we shouldn't be punished real harshly for the things that our ancestors did, on the one hand, but on the other hand, I think that now we should try and change the way we do things so that we aren't doing the same things that our ancestors did.

Using the story line here gave credence to Lynn's stance on this case because she had stated before she supported affirmative action and she realized that this case was "kinda what affirmative action" is. It also helped Lynn to regain her composure after a serious bout of rhetorical incoherence ("I think I would, I would, I'd disagree, I think. I mean, yeah, I think I'd disagree because, I mean").

Finally, Sara, a student at SU, used the story line to state her view on government intervention on blacks' behalf.

> Hmm [*long exhalation*], maybe just—Well, I don't know 'cause it seems like people are always wondering if, you know, do we, like do we as white peo-ple owe people as black something their ancestors were, you know, treated so badly. But then, I mean, it wasn't really us that did that, so I don't know. I mean, I think that the race or that culture should, you know, be paid back for something in some way. But I don't think that. . . . I don't know [*laughs*].

DAS respondents used this story line in ways similar to students. For example, Dina, an employment manager for an advertising agency in her early thirties, used the story line to answer the question on government compensation to blacks for past discrimination.

> No, and I, you know, I have to say that I'm pretty supportive of anything to help people, but I don't know why that slavery thing has a—I've got a chip on my shoulder about that. It's like it happened so long ago and you've got these sixteen-year-old kids saying, "Well, I deserve because great, great granddaddy was a slave." Well, you know what, it doesn't affect you. Me, as white person, I had nothing to do with slavery. You, as a black person, you never experienced it. It was so long ago I just don't see how that pertains to

what's happening to the race today so, you know, that's one thing that I'm just like "God, shut up!"

Roland, an electrical engineer in his forties, also used the story line to oppose the idea of reparations.

> I think they've gotten enough. I don't think we need to pay them anything or I think as long as they are afforded opportunities and avail themselves to the opportunities like everybody else, I, I don't know why we should give them any reparation for something that happened, you know. . . . I can't, I *can't* help what happened in the 1400s, the 1500s, or the 1600s, when the blacks were brought over here and put into slavery. I mean, I had no control over that, neither did you, so I don't think we should do anything as far as reparations are concerned.

Although most Detroit-area whites used this story line as part of their argumentative repertoire to explain their opposition to or doubts about affirmative action, occasionally they used them in odd places. For instance, Monica, a medical transcriber in her fifties with a strong commitment to the Jehovah's Witnesses religious viewpoint, used the story line while discussing discrimination. After a long statement arguing that because of past discrimination, blacks developed a cultural outlook based on the idea that they can't succeed because of discrimination, Monica then proceeded to argue: "It's, it's become such a mess and it's perpetuated again by media and by these special interest groups. You and I aren't responsible for what our ancestors did in slavery, that we didn't initiate that slavery."

As can be seen, these two story lines served whites as instruments to object to blacks' demands for compensatory policies. Furthermore, they helped whites stand on a high moral ground while objecting to these policies. But, again, what is ideological about this particular story line? It is a fact that most whites did not participate directly[12] in slavery or came to the country years after slavery had ended.[13] However, this story line ignores the fact that pro-white policies ("preferential treatment") in jobs, housing, elections, and access to social space ("No blacks and Mexicans allowed here!") have had (and continue to have) a positive multiplier effect for all those deemed "white." Thus, not surprisingly, "suspect" racial groups such as the Irish, Italians, and Jews,[14] among others, struggled to become "white" because by doing so, they could receive the manifold "wages of whiteness" (see chapter 1). Hence, the "It wasn't me"[15] approach of this story line does not fit the reality of how racial privilege operated and still operates in America. Although specific whites may not have participated directly in the overt discriminatory practices that injured blacks and other minorities in the past, they all have received unearned privileges[16] by virtue of being regarded as "white" and have benefited from the various incarnations of white supremacy in the United States.

"If Jews, Italians, and Irish Have Made It, How Come Blacks Have Not"?

Another story line that has become quite popular is "If (ethnic groups such as Japanese, Chinese, Jews, and Irish) have made it, how come blacks have not?" This story line is used by whites to suggest blacks' status in America is their own doing, because other groups who experienced discrimination in the past are doing quite well today. Few college students, but ten DAS respondents, used this story line. However, it is important to point out that 35 percent of the students agreed with the premise of this story line when it was asked in the survey.

One example of a student who used this story line is Kim, a student at SU. She inserted a version of the story line in combination with the "The past is the past" story line to explain why she does not favor government intervention on behalf of minorities.

> Um no. I think that, you know, a lot of bad things happened to a lot of people, but you can't sit there and dwell on that. I mean, like the Jewish people, look what happened to them. You know, do you hear them sitting around complaining about it, you know, and attributing, you know, anything bad that happens to them? I've never heard anyone say, "Oh, it's because I'm Jewish." You know, and I know it's a little different because, you know, a black, I mean, you can't really, a lot of, you can't really tell on the outside a lot of times, but, I mean, they don't wallow in what happened to them a long time ago. I mean, it was a horrible thing, I admit, but I think that you need to move on and try to put that behind, you know, put that behind you.

Although DAS respondents were more likely than students to use this story line, they did not use it as frequently as they did the previous two. An example of how they used this story line was provided by Henrietta, a transvestite school teacher in his fifties. Henrietta used the story line in his answer to the question on government spending on blacks' behalf:

> [5-second pause] As a person who was once reversed discriminated against, I would have to say no. Because the government does not need programs if they, if people would be motivated to bring themselves out of the poverty level. When we talk about certain programs, when the Irish came over, when the Italians, the Polish, and the East European Jews, they all were immigrants who lived in terrible conditions, who worked in terrible conditions, too. But they had one thing in common: they all knew that education was the way

out of that poverty. And they did it. I'm not saying the blacks were brought over here maybe not willingly, but if they realize education's the key, that's it. And that's based on individuality.

Mandy, a registered nurse in her forties, used the story line to address the issue of whether or not blacks' standing in this country is due to of their values and laziness:

> *Mandy*: Generally, I think that's probably true. Now are you talking about *all minorities*? [*Interviewer*: *Umhumm*.] 'Cause I don't—when you look at the people coming from Asia, Japan, and China . . . they're making the honor roll. When you look at the honor [roll] here in Rochester, they're all foreign names. You know, some of those kids from minority families figured out that they had to work and strive and work harder if they were going to make it all the way to the top.
> *Interviewer*: Okay. So you're saying that you would classify minorities by race and go from there?
> *Mandy*: Not all minorities are lazy and lay on the couch all the time.

This story line equates the experiences of immigrant groups with that of involuntary "immigrants" (such as enslaved Africans). But as Stephen Steinberg has perceptively pointed out in his *The Ethnic Myth*, most immigrant groups were able to get a foothold on certain economic niches or used resources such as an education or small amounts of capital to achieve social mobility. "In contrast, racial minorities were for the most part relegated to the preindustrial sectors of the national economy and, until the flow of immigration was cut off by the First World War, were denied access to the industrial jobs that lured tens of millions of immigrants. All groups started at the bottom, but as Blauner points out, 'the bottom' has by no means been the same for all groups."[17] Thus, comparing these groups, as this story line does, is comparing apples and pears as a way to "blame the victims" (many minority groups).

"I Did Not Get a Job (or a Promotion), or Was Not Admitted to a College, Because of a Minority"

This story line is extremely useful to whites rhetorically and psychologically. When whites do not get a job or promotion, it must be because of a minority. If they are not admitted into a college, it must be because of a minority. This story line allows whites to never consider the possibility that they are not qualified for a job, promotion, or college. Curiously, the number of actual cases filed on reverse discrimination before the Equal Employment Opportunity Commission is quite small and the immense majority of them are dismissed as lacking any foundation.[18] Furthermore, as I will show, most versions of this story line lack substance, are based on limited data, and rely on less than credible information.[19] This lack of specificity, however, does not detract from the usefulness of this story line, since its sense of veracity is not based on facts, but on commonly held beliefs by whites. Hence, when whites use this story line, precise information need not be included. And because this story line is built upon a personal moral tale, many whites vent personal frustrations or resentment toward minorities while using it.

Almost a quarter of the students (10 of 41) and more than a third of the DAS respondents used this story line. For instance, Bob, the SU student cited above, opposed providing unique opportunities to minorities to be admitted into universities. After anchoring his view in the abstract liberalism frame ("you should be judged on your qualifications, your experience, your education, your background, not of your race"), Bob added:

> I had a friend, he wasn't—I don't like him that much, I think it's my brother's friend, a good friend of my brother's, who didn't get into law school here and he knows for a fact that other students less qualified than him *did*. And that really, and he was considering a lawsuit against the school. But for some reason, he didn't. He had better grades, better LSAT, better everything, and he—other people got in up above him, I don't care who it is, if it's Eskimo, or Australian, or what it is, you should have the best person there.

This is a classic example of this story line. Bob "had a friend" (who was not his friend, but his brother's friend and whom he did not "like that much") who claimed to know "for a fact" (facts he never documents) that minority students who were less qualified than his brother[20] were admitted into SU Law School. Bob uses the story line here to reinforce his view that admission to colleges ought to be strictly based on merits.

Kara, a student from MU, inserted the story line when she was asked if she had been a victim of "reverse discrimination."

> I think applying to schools. I know a couple of people, like, schools like Notre Dame that are, you know, very, like, competitive to get into. Like, I was put on the wait list where this kid in my school who was black was admitted and, like, for me, you know, like, I almost had a four point, you know, I did well on my SATs, and he was kind of a slacker, grade-point wise, and I always thought it *could* have been something else, but it didn't make sense to me and that was the only thing I could put it to.

When asked if she knew of other cases of "reverse discrimination," Kara added, "Yeah, especially my friends that applied to the Ivy League schools." They really felt that they were discriminated against.

Kara claims that while she was not admitted to Notre Dame, a black "kid" in her school who was "kind of a slacker" was. She believes the only logical explanation for this is "reverse discrimination" and that many of her friends experienced it, too. But we do not get any data on how she did on her SAT (she reports doing "well," but does not indicate her score) and, more significantly, we get absolutely no information on how well the black student did on the SAT. Regarding her friends' claims, Kara provides even less information.

This story line was also important for white DAS respondents, since more than a third of them used it. One example is Ann, a young unemployed women. She used the story line in her answer to the question, "Do you think that being white is an advantage or a disadvantage in contemporary America?"

> No. It's, I don't know. [*Interviewer: Why do you think that?*] I don't know, it's [*laughs*], it's weird because my friend that is there, she went for a job interview with two of her white girlfriends. It was her and those three white females and the rest were black. Well, when they were done with the testing they took their scores and they all had the same scores, the three white girls. and they come out and they hire, they said that the two white girls didn't pass their math test, but they said that she passed hers and then they hired her. . . .

Ann claims that a black friend of hers experienced preferential treatment in a job search. As usual in the iterations of this story line, the story is very fuzzy and refers to third parties. In Ann's narrative it is very difficult to assess any of the particularities of the case. How many people went for the job? How many tests did they take? What scores did all the applicants get? Were the applicants interviewed after they were tested? What kind of job were they applying for? The answers to all these questions are uncertain.

Marie, a homemaker in her late thirties, used the story line to explain her position on affirmative action.

> Ah, I'm puzzled a little bit by that. I'm for making sure everybody gets equal opportunity. I think that there are points, though, where it is inappropriate. Just as an example, my sister has a good student that applied for a teaching position at a university and was told that she was one of three final candidates for the position, but the other two candidates, one was a Mexican American and the other was a black female. Unless she could prove she had some active minority in her background, she could not be considered for the position because they had to hire a minority.

Although Marie's story seems more robust than usual, the details do not square with what we know of the academic job market. First, based on the peculiar list of final candidates (peculiar because it is very unusual to have two minority scholars as finalists in a job search), it seems this job required expertise on racial matters. This does not disqualify the white applicant, but it adds some complexity to the story. Second, the argument that she had to prove some minority background to qualify for this position (after she made the final cut) is not credible. Had that been the case, this applicant could have successfully sued this university for discrimination. An alternative reading of the events is that this white applicant lost out to a minority candidate and explained this to herself, her professor, and her peers as many whites do, as a case of reverse discrimination.

Many of the workers in the sample vented lots of anger against what they regarded as "preferential treatment" for minorities, although few knew what affirmative action was. Not surprisingly, many used the story line in its most generic sense. The following two cases illustrate my point. First is Darren, a bus driver in his late forties. He opposed affirmative action by stating that "two wrongs don't make a right" and used the story line to supply evidence on which to base his opinion.

> Ah no, other than I have applied at jobs and been turned down because I was white. *Now, I have nothing* against the black person [if he] was qualified better than I was. But when the guy comes into the interview and I'm off on the side and I can hear them talking and he can't even speak good English, he doesn't know how to read a map, and they're gonna make him a bus driver and hire him over me. I've been doing bus driving off and on since 1973 and I know the guy well enough that [I know] he's a lousy driver. I know why he got the job, and I don't think that's fair.

Darren believed he was turned down for a job as a bus driver because he was white. Furthermore, he claimed that he overheard the interview and that his black competitor could not "even speak good English." But his story is as loose as the others. Both applicants now work in the same company, which suggests Darren got the job there at some point in time. And Darren failed to mention two other factors that may account—besides driving skills, which we cannot ascertain based on the information he provided—for why this other driver may have gotten the job before Darren did. First, this company is located in Detroit and it makes business sense to hire black bus drivers. Second, and more important, Darren has moved a lot in his life and has had more than twelve jobs. Hence, any rational manager must look at his record with some trepidation and wonder why this person has moved so much and whether he would be a reliable worker.

Tony, a carpet installer in his twenties used a very unusual version of the story line to explain why he believes being white is no longer an advantage in America: "Oh yeah. Like when my girlfriend went to get on aid, the lady told her if she was black, she could have got help, but she wasn't black and she wasn't getting no help." Tony's account can be translated as "I did not get welfare because of blacks."

TESTIMONIES AND COLOR BLINDNESS

The role of testimonies in the color-blind drama cannot be underestimated. Almost every respondent in the two studies interpolated them for rhetorical purposes such as saving face, signify nonracialism, or bolstering an argument. Notwithstanding that testimonies were more random than story lines, I classified them into three categories: stories of interactions with blacks (negative and positive), stories of disclosure of knowledge of someone close who is racist, and a residual category of *sui generis* testimonies. The purpose of this discussion is examining the similarities in the narrative form of these stories as well as assessing their rhetorical function. I discuss each story category separately below.

Stories of Interactions with Blacks

Most of the stories of interactions with blacks whites told in these interviews were of two kinds. One type of story portrayed a negative incident with blacks usually used to justify a position taken on some issue (e.g., "Blacks are aggressive. A year ago I was called a racist by . . ."). The other type of story involved a positive incident or relationship with a black person as a way to signify the narrator's good relationships with or views toward blacks. About a third of the students and DAS respondents narrated one of these testimonies at some point in the interview.

Negative Interactions with Blacks

Mickey, a student at MU, acknowledged that his family talks about racial matters often and blamed it on the area they lived in. He said his family lived near Benton Harbor—a formerly white area that has become predominantly black, a neighborhood that has "one of the highest crime rates in, like, the country" and that "now [is] a really dirtiest place." The interviewer asked him whether or not people in his community worried about violence and crime spreading to their community. Mickey acknowledged that he thought "about that a lot" and added:

> But, I mean, nothing really happened horribly. Actually, a neighbor of mine [*laughs*]—kind of a grim story—I have a younger brother who's friends with one of my neighbors just down the street who hangs out with him some-

times. And he was drivin' downtown in Benton Harbor about a couple of months ago, and I think he was trying to get some marijuana or somethin' stupid like that, and he got beat over the head with a baseball bat. Got some black eyes and he had brain damage. He's okay now, but he was in a coma for a little bit. And he's like, I think he's got minor brain damage, irreversible. But nothing that's affecting him, like, too bad but, I mean, that was just one incident that happened a couple of months [ago] that made me think about stuff like this. . . .

This testimony helped Mickey to safely state later in the interview his belief that blacks are "more aggressive" than whites and to suggest the problems of Benton Harbor are moral ones.

Leslie, a student at WU, supported "proposing liberal values" and "having people value the cultural diversity in our country" as a government strategy to increase school integration in America. Nevertheless, she had reservations about busing and narrated the following story to bolster her viewpoint.

There was a time when one of the black kids actually punched out the principal. And there was a time when I was in the P. E. locker room and I set my bag down just to go to the bathroom and then come back out and everything in my locker. I was gone maybe, you know, a minute and I come back and I see a really big woman [with other students] stealing money out of my bag. And I confronted them and they were like "No, we're not doing anything," and so I went to the principal because they stole $60 [*laughs*]. And the only reason I had that much money on me was that I was going shopping after school and I con—confronted like the principal and he confronted them. And they threatened to beat me up, and they were like, "You almost got us suspended." And they like, surrounded me during lunch [*laughs*].

It is hard to determine if Leslie was picked on because she looked different (she was dressing hippie style) in this mixed school, a school that nonetheless was majority white. The important matter, however, is that she believes this is what happened and that her interpretation of this experience informs her stand on busing. Leslie opposes busing and this testimony gives her a convenient rationale for opposing it.

The last example of these stories from college students comes from Rick, a Mormon student at WU. When asked about blacks' claims of experiencing discrimination, Rick suggested, "some people read too much into what other people say." He mentioned that he himself was accused of being racist by a black man in a discussion about affirmative action.

I, I can't remember. It was—I think it was talking about affirmative action or something, and he called me that I was being a racist or something and I said, "I am sorry. I did not mean that in that way, if it was taken that way."

I totally apologized because I, my belief system doesn't incorporate racism, according to me. But maybe I wasn't being as sensitive or maybe he was being oversensitive—I don't know which way it went—but from my experience I kind of developed the attitude that I think too many—Too often we are too easily offended and it goes both ways, not just blacks but whites, you know.

Although Rick stated that his hypersensitivity thesis works both ways, his story was narrated in response to a question about blacks and discrimination. When he was asked again if he believed blacks experienced lots of discrimination, he pointed out, "it depends on the part of country." This answer was used by many respondents to suggest that racism happens "elsewhere." Thus his testimony served him to bolster his belief that blacks falsely accuse whites of discrimination and, therefore, to minimize the significance of racism.

DAS respondents told negative stories of interaction with blacks, too. Bill, a retired school teacher in his eighties, narrated a story to explain why he thinks blacks and whites are different. After pointing out that blacks "seem to be very *religious*" and mentioning that they bought a church in his neighborhood, Bill claimed they forced a restaurant out of business.

They did have a Sweden House on the corner and all the neighbors were happy about it because they could [go] to the Sweden House and have dinner. Well, before long the blacks took over. They are only one mile away and on Sunday afternoon, they come in droves, *in buses* from the churches, *bus loads of 'em*, and they all fill the restaurant and the white people come and see that and turn around and *go*. They burnt it down, the Sweden House. We don't have a Sweden House anymore.

The interviewer asked Bill why they closed the restaurant. Bill said that it closed because "they were not making any money on 'em." He explained this as follows:

They like to eat. They *pile their* dishes just loaded with that stuff and I actually didn't see it, but I saw one lady come in with a full plate of chicken. I didn't pay much attention, but the next thing I know, they are leaving. Now I know she didn't eat all that chicken. She probably put it in her purse and walked out with it. I didn't see that. Lot of them are doing that, how can they make any money? And seeing that they are all *heavy people*, it seems like they do a lot of eating. So I don't know what to say about something like that.

Although most of this story is based on Bill's racist interpretation of events, the fact remains that he uses it to validate his belief that blacks "like to eat," are cheap, and steal.

The second example is Joan, a video store employee in her late thirties. She told a story about a black woman who unfairly accused her of being racist.

> Like black people, they use their excuse that they're black and that's the rea-
> son why white people won't be accepting me. I've seen it, too. I had this
> black person, for instance, who chewed me out at Videobuster. Yelled at me
> a year ago. Started calling me a white honky and every racist slur that you
> could think of happened. My uncle showed up, you know, he works for the
> government and I get to see him often. He came in and I was in tears 'cause
> I was not brought up that way. This woman was totally flabbergasted
> because my uncle asked her if she had a problem and told her I was his niece.
> I just gave him a hug. This woman was calling me names that were totally
> uncalled for. She did not have a receipt. I wouldn't—I do it with everybody.
> You do not have a receipt, you don't get an exchange. She tried to return our
> products, our store rentals without store code on it as a gift from someone
> else. She said I was accusing her of stealing it from the store. I could not
> refund the money. She called me racial names.

Joan's story and case is very interesting, because she considered herself white, even though she claimed to have black, Native American, and Jewish in her background. She was coded as white (and apparently looked the part) because in the original survey she had stated that she was white. The "uncle" she referred to in this story was a black man, but in truth he was just her godfather. The rhetorical goal of this particular story was to punctuate her belief that blacks use race as an excuse, a belief that she repeated often in the interview.

Positive Interactions with Blacks

The number of whites narrating positive testimonies of interactions with blacks was similar to the number of those narrating negative testimonies. These stories had a positive self-presentation rhetorical goal. For instance, Mary, a student at SU, said, in response to the question on whether blacks' self-segregate or are not made to feel welcome by whites, that her family is racist. In this context, Mary narrated her testimony of positive interactions with her black roommate.

> My floor actually, the year I had a black roommate, happened to be predomi-
> nantly African American and so those became some of my best friends, the
> people I was around. And we would actually sit around and talk about ste-
> reotypes and prejudices and I learned so much just about the hair texture,
> you know? What it means for a black person to get a perm versus me, you
> know. I learned *a lot*. And it really, I think, for me, broke down a lot of barri-
> ers and ended a lot of stereotypes I may still [have] had. Because like I said,

I mean, those really became some of my best friends. And even still we don't really keep in touch, but if I see any of 'em on campus, still, you know, we always talk with each other and everything.

Mary's story rings of self-presentation from start to finish. Yet, because Mary was not too refined in her delivery, the story hurt her more than it helped her. For instance, she used the term "those" people twice and pointed out twice that they became "some of my best friends." Furthermore, her claim that she learned a lot from this interaction seems superficial, since she only talked about hair texture and perms. Finally, these nameless "best friends" later became only casual acquaintances after a year of sharing a floor with Mary.

Another example of how students used these positive stories was provided by John, a 40-year-old WU student. In response to the question, "Do you talk about race or racial issues now?" John inserted a story about his cousin marrying a black man.

> Yes I do, there was a cousin of mine—she married a black man. They came to visit me and I had to really look at this really close and consider the fact that he's actually a pretty neat person that she married and I considered it unfair that she should be made to feel saddened and I don't. . . .

John' story helped him project an image of maturity and racial sensitivity. However, based on his answers throughout the entire interview, it is clear that John had some racist views about minorities. For example, John claimed that people from South India smelled differently because "they eat a lot of spices." He also pointed out that blacks exuded a strong body odor that has an "effect on people's psyche, how they react to the racial issue, a subliminal type of thing."

DAS respondents used these positive stories of interaction with blacks for the same purposes. However, because these respondents were older, their stories included a wider range of matters. John II, a semiretired house designer in his sixties, inserted a World War II story of positive interaction with blacks in response to the question on whether blacks are hard to approach or are not made to feel welcome by whites. After stating that he had no experiences upon which to base an opinion on this matter, John II narrated the following story:

> Three Filipino scouts and I were waiting, trying to catch a load south. We had one, probably a 200–300 watt bulb hanging over the intersection to put some light there, and there was an alley that went off on one of the roads that we could hear some shouting. We could see in the dark of that alley, see the light from a door and some three fellows ran out and saw us, the Filipino scouts and I, and thought we [were] the ones that had apparently done

something outrageous and he opened up on us with an automatic carbine. So the Filipino scouts stood farther away from me and they got the cover and I got behind the curb. It wasn't quite enough curb to hide me and the fellow was shooting a full automatic. A jeep came in out of one of the roads and slid to a stop and about the time he said, "Get in!" They said "Let's go!" because I was in laying across the back seat and he took off. When we got down the road, I climbed out of the back seat into the front seat and it was a colored captain. He wouldn't give me his name or anything. He said, "That's all right," but I've always remembered that. He put himself at risk under fire to pick up a man and take him out of a line of fire.

John's testimony served him as a vehicle to state his view that blacks and whites can act civilized toward each other. His story resembles those that so many veterans tell of interracial solidarity during war. However, for John, as for many white veterans, these stories became just stories without much effect on their behavior or attitudes toward blacks after they returned to America.[21] For example, John II, who used the term "colored" to refer to the black man who saved his life, opposed interracial marriage and acknowledged that he is "more comfortable around whites because I've grown up with them" and, thus, had no qualms about neighborhoods or schools being almost completely white. Hence, John II's stand amounts to a modern version of the separate but equal policy of the past; blacks and whites can be civil toward each other, but they should not live near each other or marry each other.

Stories of Disclosure of Knowledge of Someone Close Who Is Racist

Twelve students and eight DAS respondents disclosed information about someone close being racist (usually a parent or grandparent). The narrative form used to disclose this information resembles confession in church, because respondents insert these testimonies as if they were expecting absolution from listeners from the possibility of being regarded as racist. These stories are structured around a trinity formula: confession, example, and self-absolution. The religious motif in these stories is further enhanced by the fact that it is usually through the influence of a woman (mother Mary) that the storyteller hopes to receive absolution. For example, Bob, the SU student previously cited, acknowledged that his father was racist in response to a question on whether his family talked about race while he was growing up.

> Um [*clears throat*], you can tell my parents' background by the way they talk about things. They're both born in New York, a small town in New York. My mom is very open to things, but like my dad, he, he still uses terms like

"them" and "those people" and stuff like that which I don't like at all, which I just don't even talk about and stuff like that with him. We get along, but only there's some things we don't agree with and that's something you can't change. That is, I've tried for twelve years. I remember one time, I think it was my dad asked me something like how come I didn't have any more white friends? And I said, "Well, why don't you go live in a white neighborhood and put me in a white school?" [*laughs*] So that was the end of that conversation.

Bob's story fits perfectly the trinity formula. First, he confesses that his father "uses terms like 'them'" and "those people." He then provides an exculpatory example of how he challenged his father's racist leanings. And throughout the narration, Bob inserts elements ("my mother is very open to things") or comments ("stuff like that which I don't like at all") to indicate he is not like his father, probably because of his mother, who "is very open to things."

Emily, the SU student cited above, in response to the same question Bob answered, admitted that her father was racist.

Um, I don't know if it necessarily was a conversation, but my mom, I mean, she never was racist against people, you know. She always looked at them as people and stuff and I think my sister and I get a lot of that from her. And my dad is racist, but I didn't live with him growing up. My parents were divorced, but she would talk about, you know, that it's not good. And I remember one time, actually, I was a little girl, and I had my best friend was black, and I once said something that was—I don't know if it was racist, it just wasn't a very nice remark, I don't think. And my mom sat me down and said, "How do you think she would feel if she heard you say that?" you know. So she really she would call attention to things so we would pay attention to what was going on.

Emily uses all the elements of the trinity formula: confession ("my dad is racist"), self-absolution ("my sister and I get of lot of that from her"), and example (how her mother corrected her racist comment about her friend). Emily's rhetorical use of the story is clearer than Bob's, given that she focuses on proving that she takes from her mother's rather than from her father's side.

The last example of how college students used this story is from Mike, an MU student. In response to the question, "Do you ever talk about racial issues at home?," Mike said:

Yeah we do. I mean, my dad came from a pretty racist background, I mean, not, you know, like—well, actually, his grandfather, I think, was in the Ku Klux Klan, um, until he got married. And my great grandmother, who I knew—she died, but I knew her—was completely the opposite. And basically when they got married, she said "no way." So *that* ended, but I mean, there was still a certain, you know, racism that pervaded. In his family they were pretty racist, so you'll still hear, you know, racial slurs slip out every once in a while, but I think he makes a conscious effort not to, I mean, he certainly didn't ever try to teach me things like that, you know. For one thing, my dad was in the navy for a long time, so I grew up with my mom for the first five years or so, and then he worked and my mom stayed at home with me. So my dad's influence was not nearly as much as my mom's to begin with, and even when it was, I wouldn't say that influenced me a lot, but there were definitely, I mean, racist ideas in his family. And I see that with my grandparents, you know, his parents.

Mike confesses that his dad comes from a "pretty racist background." Then he mentions that his father's grandfather was in the KKK. Finally, he concludes the story by suggesting he was immune to this background, because his father "didn't try to teach me things like that" and because he was raised mainly by his mother.

Since we did not pose the question on whether respondents talked about race while growing up to DAS respondents, few (8 of 66) used this personal story; and when they did, their delivery of the story was somewhat more disorganized than that of students. Yet, when DAS respondents inserted the story, it was also organized around the trinity formula. Scott, a 23-year-old drafter, while explaining his view on whether blacks self-segregate or are not made to feel welcome by whites, revealed that his father was racist. In response to the specific question, "Do you think that (white workers) are apprehensive about approaching their black colleagues or the same?" Scott stated:

> The same way just reversed, you know, just 'cause you know. I mean, my dad grew up in Detroit in a real bad neighborhood and he was brought on that way, I mean, he is real prejudice. I brought one of my buddies home one time and he was like, "No, I don't want you hanging out with him," you know, he don't trust them.

Scott immediately added, "That's my dad though, but that's not me. I take, you know, I take people for what they are and I don't judge people by word of mouth, you know, just treat you the way you treat me." The interviewer then asked Scott how come he did not develop the same attitudes toward blacks as his dad. Scott stated that it was due to his mom because "she went to Catholic school all the way up until high school. So, she's got a lot of Catholic values so, can't really be prejudice if you're, you're religious. So my mom always shunned on being prejudice." Scott's story is clearly framed by the trinity formula. First, he confesses his father is "real prejudice." Then, he uses the example of his father's racist views about his friend. Finally, Scott suggests he is not like his dad because of his mother's Catholic influence. However, among young DAS respondents, Scott had some of the most highly racialized views on a number of issues (see his views on interracial marriage in chapter 6).

The last example of a DAS respondent using this story is Jenny, a public-school administrator in her fifties. In response to the question on how she felt about the neighborhood where she grew up, Jenny stated that many of her neighbors were closed-minded and she labeled them as "Archie Bunkers." After narrating an incident in which one black kid was refused as a dance partner by a girl in her school, Jenny said:

> My grand, my grandmother, who was—she was Scandinavian. But she used to make fun of blacks. And when we would drive through a black neighborhood she would say things like, "Look at all the little chocolate drops." And I can remember being a young child—maybe five, six, or seven years old—and being offended by her remarks. My parents never, ever said anything like that. My parents were very open-minded and broad-minded.

Again, Jenny uses the same formula. First, she provides the confession about her grandmother harboring racist views. Then, she supplies the example of her grandmother making denigrating remarks about black children. Finally, Jenny distances herself from this relative by pointing out that she was "offended by her (grandmothers') remarks" as well as by saying that her parents were "very open-minded."

Am I making these stories seem racial? Is it not possible for whites to tell stories of family members who are racist without these stories being connected to color-blind racism? Is it not true that sometimes a story is just a story? If these testimonies were just random stories that people tell without any ideological content, one would not be able to find a similar structure in them and would have difficulty assigning any rhetorical function. Furthermore, the fact they were told at similar points in the interviews suggests they are part of what John Dollard labeled almost seventy years ago as "defensive beliefs."[22] In contrast, when white racial progressives mentioned having racist family members or growing up in racist neighborhoods, they did not use the trinity formula typical of this testimony (see chapter 6). From an analytical perspective, then, these testimonies cannot be seen as expressions of "facts" or just plain stories.

Other Personal Stories

The final group of personal testimonies is a residual category of race-related stories. These stories were even more sui generis and even less prevalent among respondents. Furthermore, they seemed to be of the last resort variety and were not helpful all the time to respondents' attempts to save face. The two that appeared most often were stories about someone close being involved with a minority person and stories about having had good black friends in the distant past.

Someone Close to Me Married or Dated a Minority

These stories are kindred to the rhetorical move of "Some of my best friends are . . . ," discussed in chapter 3. Their purpose is mostly positive self-presentation. Because I do not think generalizations can be extrapolated from these stories, I just present one example of each. The example of the first testimony came from Trudy, a salesperson in her late twenties. When asked if she had ever dated a black man, she said: "No, no. No nev—There was this one guy I kind of liked. He was Oriental." When asked her view on interracial marriage, Trudy replied:

> I don't really know how I feel about that. I don't think there's anything wrong with it. I don't know if I had a child and they wanted to marry a black person, I don't know how I would feel. I think it might be kind of odd for the children. And in fact, my husband has this real good friend at work, her name is Laverne. She's black and her husband's white and, you know, they'll have us for dinner. I mean, real *nice couple*! I mean, I don't see anything wrong, you know, if that's what they want to do, I don't have a problem. Me, personally, I don't know if I would feel comfortable, you know.

The purpose of the story about her husband's "real good friend" seems obvious. By including this story, Trudy is able to express her personal concerns about interracial marriage as if they are nonracial because, after all, her husband has a black friend who is married to a white guy and they seem like a "real *nice couple*" and invite them for dinner. However, the oddity of the story and the fact she referred to her Asian date as "Oriental" does not make this an ideologically useful testimony.

I Used to Have Very Good Black Friends

White respondents who did not have any associations with blacks could not use the "Some of my best friends are blacks" move to signify color blindness. Thus, some of the respondents in this predicament claimed they *had* very good black friends in the past. As with the testimony above, I provide just one example. Lucy, a part-time cook for a vending company in her late sixties, had very few interactions with blacks throughout her life. However, when asked to describe the racial composition of her workplace, she said, "we used to have three colored girls, but since then, they have quit." Later on, in response to a question on her interaction with her coworkers, Lucy said the "commissary kitchen (people) were good friends," that she would "go out to dinner with people that used to work there and (the) ones that still do," and that they even "have a barbecue once a year and a picnic in the summer." Nevertheless, when asked if blacks participated in these activities, she said "Uh, no, no." Because this answer did not fit very well the color-blind outlook that Lucy wanted to portray, she tried to amend it in her answer to the next question, dealing with the subject of so-called black self-segregation.

> Well, like I told you, we had some of 'em and Kathleen, she'd go out to dinner with us. You know and so, the individuals I think—her other girlfriend, she, she moved out of town and she came in, she came in to see us. And you know, we're real happy for her and in fact another one was just in not too long ago. She has—we told her, you know, well, she has made some mistakes, a couple of children and didn't get married. And we says, you know, "Deanna, go back to school." Well, she came back to tell us she listened to us and she's doing real well and a good job, you know. I suppose, you know, they're still friends of ours, you know. We don't see 'em that much anymore, but they did come back and say that they were happy they listened to us.

By resuscitating black acquaintances from the past and making them her friends (see chapter 5), Lucy attempted to rebuild her investment in color blindness. However, this rhetorical attempt was not very successful because Lucy is still trapped in the language of the past ("colored" and "some of 'em") and narrated a story pregnant with Jim Crow paternalism.

CONCLUSION

At the outset of this chapter I stated that we make stories and that these stories, in turn, make us. I described two types of racial stories, story lines and testimonies. These racial stories "make" whites, but also help them navigate the turbulent waters of contemporary public discussions on race. The four story lines I analyzed, "The past is the past," "I did not own slaves," "If (other ethnic groups such as Italians or Jews) have made it, how come blacks have not?" and "I did not get a (job or promotion) because of a black man," help whites discursively since they provide "evidence" to solidify their viewpoints. For example, if whites object to the idea of affirmative action or reparations, they can insert "The past is the past" or "I did not own any slaves" story lines to strengthen the apparent reasonableness of their argument. If the issue at hand is explaining blacks' status in America, the story line of "If (other ethnic groups such as Italians or Jews) have made it, how come blacks have not?" is very appropriate. Finally, because the story line of "I did not get a (job or promotion) because of a black man" seems personal (in truth, the facts included in this story line tend to be secondhand or based on racialized impressions of social outcomes), it has become a powerful rhetorical weapon to win arguments ("I know for a *fact* that . . .").

In addition to the rhetorical role filled by story lines, they also serve whites as vehicles to vent deep-seated emotions[23] about racial matters. In case after case, whether students or whites from the Detroit area, respondents vented anger about what they interpreted as blacks' whining ("I didn't own any slaves and I do not understand why they keep asking for things when slavery ended 200 *God-damned* years ago!") or about not getting into certain jobs or universities because of minorities ("A friend of mine was not admitted into SU Law School, but many *unqualified* black students were and that's *wrong*"). The story lines then serve whites as legitimate conduits for expressing anger, animosity, and resentment toward racial minorities.

Although testimonies are more loose and unstructured than story lines, they are as important in whites' rhetorical arsenal. Almost every respondent used them at some point or another in the interviews. Even though these stories were more random, compared to story lines, I organized them into three categories, namely, stories of interactions with blacks (negative and positive), stories of disclosure of someone close who is racist, and other stories. The testimonies of disclosure of someone close who is racist serve clear self-presentational purposes ("I am not a racist like my dad, uncle, or friend"). Stories of positive interactions with blacks were also used for self-presentational purposes. For example, if a respondent had a "good experience" in the past with a black person, that experience could be used to cover up for a present that blacks are not part of, that is, for a totally white life—an apparent blemish in the color-blind fable. Testimonies of "bad experiences" with blacks were mostly used to give credence to respondents' negative views about blacks. For example, if respondents believe blacks are aggressive, narrating a story of a black person behaving in an aggressive manner helps them make the point.

Although the last category of personal stories is a residual one, I highlighted two that appeared more often in the interviews and seemed more structured, namely, "Someone close to me married or dated a minority" and "I used to have very good black friends." Respondents who used these stories usually had a positive self-presentational concern, even though these stories were largely ineffectual and extremely odd ("I am not a racist because my sister dated a black guy some time ago"). However, these stories were probably the *only* vehicles for signaling nonracialism for respondents who lived totally submerged in whiteness. Likewise, respondents who used the personal stories of "I used to have very good black friends" navigated completely white environments and hence depended on these recollections to validate their claim to color blindness.

A final point on story lines and testimonies: because these story lines are *social* products, the media play an important role in reinforcing them.[24] News reports on affirmative action seldom address the whiteness of academia or the workplace and its implications;[25] sensational reports on welfare cheats never address the reality of welfare, that people on welfare live below the poverty line;[26] stories of "bad" behavior by black and Latino youths are presented as "normal," whereas stories depicting "bad" behavior by white youths are not.[27] News reports on minorities thus tend to be presented as morality tales that support the various racial stories of the color-blind era. These reports are then recycled by the white audience as absolute truths ("Didn't you hear about that black guy who couldn't read and was admitted into Harvard? It was in the news"). Therefore, the media uses the racial stories we create and makes them as if they were independent creations that validate our racial angst.[28]

One of the things I have shown indirectly in this and previous chapters is that whites tend to interact mostly with whites. This fact, and its implications, has not been adequately examined by social scientists. Few have asked questions such as, What are the sociological and social-psychological consequences of whites living in primarily white environments? How can whites develop empathy and gain an understanding of blacks if so few of them develop meaningful interactions with them? I turn my attention to these and related matters in the next chapter.

NOTES

1. For an interesting discussion of stories and a superb story on how affirmative action is being undercut from within in academia, see Adalberto Aguirre Jr., "Academic Storytelling: A Critical Race Theory Story of Affirmative Action," *Sociological Perspectives*, 43, no. 2 (2000): 319–39.

2. On this issue, see Margaret Somers, "The Narrative Constitution of Identity: A Relational and Network Approach," *Theory and Society* 23, no. 3 (1994): 605–49.

3. Aguirre, "Academic Storytelling," 320.

4. Stuart Hall, "The Narrative Construction of Reality," *Southern Review* 17, no. 2 (1984): 8.

5. Hall, "Narrative Construction," 8.

6. See most notably Ruth Frankenberg, *White Women, Race Matters* (Minneapolis: University of Minnesota Press, 1993). For an attempt at examining the ideological role of modern racial storytelling in America, see James Fraser and Edward Kick, "The Interpretive Repertoires of Whites on Race-Targeted Policies: Claims Making of Reverse Discrimination," *Sociological Perspectives* 43, no. 1 (2000): 13–28.

See also Nina Eliasoph, " 'Everyday Racism' in a Culture of Political Avoidance: Civil Society, Speech, and Taboo," *Social Problems* 46, no. 4 (1997): 479–502.

7. In this chapter, I focus on the *dominant* racial stories. The questions included in these projects did not elicit oppositional racial stories from blacks.

8. See Norman K. Denzin, *The Research Act* (Englewood Cliffs, N.J.: Prentice Hall, 1989).

9. Patricia Hill-Collins, *Black Feminist Thought* (New York: Routledge, 1990); Catherine Clinton, *The Plantation Mistress* (New York: Pantheon, 1982).

10. As in the previous chapter, I set off the pertinent phrase with a different font not to signify emphasis from the respondents, but to help readers identify the racial story.

11. Melvin L. Oliver and Thomas Shapiro, *Black Wealth/White Wealth* (New York: Routledge, 1995); Thomas M. Shapiro, *The Hidden Cost of Being African American: How Wealth Perpetuates Inequality* (London: Oxford University Press, 2004). For an estimate of how much America owes blacks, see Richard F. America, *Paying the Social Debt: What White America Owes Black America* (Westport, Conn.: Praeger, 1993). See also William A. Darity, Jr., "Stratification Economics: The Role of Intergroup Inequality," *Journal of Economics and Finance"* 29, no. 2 (2005): 144–53.

12. Most of the white population in the South participated in slavery as a social institution in, for example by participating in the patrol system, which sought to catch runaway slaves. See George P. Rawick, *From Sundown to Sunup: The Making of the Black Community* (Westport, Conn.: Greenwood, 1972).

13. Jim Goad, in his *The Redneck Manifesto* (New York: Touchstone, 1998), states that at the peak of slavery (1860), only one out of every fifteen whites was a slaveholder. However, Goad, whose manifesto includes a number of interesting ideas, fails to analyze how slavery formed a social system in which all whites participated (in patrols, in the war effort, in catching fugitives).

14. See David Roediger, *The Wages of Whiteness* (London: Verso, 1994); Noel Ignatiev, *How the Irish Became White* (New York: Routledge, 1995); and Karen Brodkin, *How Jews Became White Folks and What That Says about Race in America* (New Brunswick, N.J.: Rutgers University Press, 1998).

15. Eduardo Bonilla-Silva, Tyrone A. Forman, Amanda E. Lewis, and David G. Embrick, " 'It Wasn't Me': Race and Racism in 21st Century America," *Research in Political Sociology* (2003).

16. On this point, see Joe R. Feagin, *Racist America: Roots, Realities, and Future Reparations* (New York: Routledge, 2000).

17. Stephen Steinberg, *The Ethnic Myth* (Boston: Beacon, 1989).

18. See Tom Wicker, *Tragic Failure* (New York: Morrow, 1996).

19. For a similar finding based on data from the Los Angeles Study of Urban Inequality (part of the Multi City Study of Urban Inequality), see chapter 14, by Lawrence Bobo and Susan Suh, "Surveying Racial Discrimination: Analyses from a Multiethnic Labor Market," in *Prismatic Metropolis: Inequality in Los Angeles,* edited by Laurence Bobo et al., 523–60 (New York: Russell Sage Foundation, 2000).

20. As Beverly Daniel Tatum points out, "When these stories are told, I wonder how the speaker knows so much about the person of color's resume." Tatum,

"Why Are All the Black Kids Sitting Together in the Cafeteria?": *And Other Conversations about Race* (New York: Basic, 1997), 115.

21. S. A. Stouffer, *The American Soldier*, vols. I and II (Princeton, N.J.: Princeton University Press, 1949). See also Gordon W. Allport, *The Nature of Prejudice* (New York: Doubleday, 1954).

22. John Dollard, *Caste and Class in a Southern Town* (New York: Doubleday/Anchor, 1957).

23. In his recent *Racist America*, Feagin has forcefully argued that emotions are a central part of "systemic racism."

24. The classic study on racism and the media is Paul Hartmann, *Racism and the Mass Media: A Study of the Role of the Mass Media in the Formation of White Beliefs and Attitudes in Britain* (Totowa, N.J.: Rowman & Littlefield, 1974). See also the important contributions of Teun van Dijk, in *News as Discourse* (Hillsdale, N.J.: Erlbaum, 1988) and *Racism and the Press* (London: Routledge, 1991), and by Darnell Hunt, in *Screening the Los Angeles "Riots": Race, Seeing, and Resistance* (New York: Cambridge University Press, 1996) and *O. J. Simpson Facts and Fictions: News Rituals in the Construction of Reality* (Cambridge: Cambridge University Press, 1999).

25. On this point, see Joe R. Feagin, Hernán Vera, and Nikitah Imani, *The Agony of Education: Black Students at White Colleges and Universities* (New York: Routledge, 1996).

26. On the realities of how women survive on welfare, see Kathryn Edin, *Making Ends Meet: How Single Mothers Survive Welfare and Long-Wage Work* (New York: Russell Sage Foundation, 1997). For a discussion on the limited supply of good jobs and its implications, see Gordon Lafer, *The Job Training Charade* (Ithaca, N.Y.: Cornell University Press, 2002).

27. For example, whereas gang-related activity in urban areas is naturalized, gang-like activity in the suburbs (such as drug selling and drug use, the many recent mass murders in schools, prostitution) is presented as exceptional behavior that we need to think long and hard about to prevent. For an example of the latter, see "Born to Be Bad," *Dateline NBC*, April 27, 1999.

28. Here I am borrowing Marx's idea of "commodity fetishism" to explain how these media stories operate.

5

~

Peeking Inside the (White) House of Color Blindness

The Significance of Whites' Segregation

In every racial ghetto there are particular "racial problems" unique to the lives and conditions of the people in that ghetto. [In] our white society, although we are not accustomed to thinking of ourselves as ghettoized people, we have a "white life style" and "white racial problems" which have emerged as a result of our confinement in a prison built by racism. . . . The language we speak, the food we eat, the people we marry, the songs we sing, and the organizations we belong to are unique because of our separate residential and cultural life.

—Joseph Barndt, *Liberating Our White Ghetto*

S ocial scientists in various fields have amply shown the serious repercussions of social and spatial isolation for blacks. For example, in the 1960s, observers of black ghetto life argued vigorously that the segregation experienced by blacks had led them to live in a "culture of poverty."[1] In the late 1970s and 1980s, this idea resurfaced in the work of conservative commentators such as Charles Murray and Lawrence Mead, liberal commentators such as William Julius Wilson and Ken Auletta, and even radical commentators such as Cornel West.[2] All these authors have argued that blacks segregated in ghettos have developed a cultural outlook that does not foster a sense of personal responsibility (Murray and Mead), produces pathological behavior (Wilson and Auletta), or that creates a profound sense of despair and nihilism (West). Other commentators have argued that segregation and isolation have led blacks in ghettos to develop a unique style ("cool pose"), an anti-intellectual strategy embodied in an "oppositional identity" to deal with educational barriers and to protect their self-esteem (Ogbu), and even a "code of the street" to conduct public interactions (Anderson).[3] Scholars have made analogous arguments about Latinos in similar circumstances[4] (For critiques of these arguments that tend to "blame the victims," see Amanda E. Lewis, *Race in the Schoolyard: Negotiating the Colorline in Classrooms and Communities* (New Jersey: Rutgers University Press, 2003) and Judith Blau, *'Race in the Schools:' Perpetuating White Dominance* (Boulder, Colo.: Lynne Rienner Publishers, 2003).

One of the most lucid examples of this type of analysis is Massey and Denton's *American Apartheid*. In this book the authors clearly show the incredibly high levels of residential segregation and isolation experienced by blacks and speculate, based on the work of others, that these realities foment in blacks what they label "the culture of segregation" or "a set of behaviors, attitudes, and values that are increasingly at variance with those held in the wider society."[5] According to these authors, some of the major characteristics of this culture are little concern with marriage, a drug-related lifestyle, and even a "language of segregation."

Despite the serious limitations of this subcultural approach to the lifestyle of poor blacks,[6] no one should doubt that, in general, the social and spatial isolation of one group from others leads to differentiation of those groups as well as the development of group cohesion and identity in the segregated group. If this idea applies to racial minorities, it must apply to whites, too, and because whites experience even *higher* levels of social and spatial isolation than blacks, the "racial problems" related to their "confinement in the prison built by racism" must be as consequential as those produced by black and Latino ghettoization. Therefore, in this chapter I explore how whites' high levels of social and spatial segregation and isolation from minorities creates what I label as a "white *habitus*,"[7] a racialized, uninterrupted socialization process that *conditions* and *creates* whites' racial taste, perceptions, feelings, and emotions and their views on racial matters.

One of the central consequences of the white habitus is that it promotes a sense of group belonging (a white culture of solidarity) and negative views about nonwhites.[8] The analysis focuses on blacks in particular because of the data I have (see chapter 1), but also because blacks are still the racial antithesis of whites in the racial spectrum. I first examine whites' levels of residential segregation and personal association with blacks. Second, I explore how they interpret their racial segregation and isolation from blacks. Third, I present data that suggest some of the potential consequences of whites' limited level of interaction with blacks.

WHITES' RACIAL SEGREGATION
AND ISOLATION

In surveys, whites express openness to and, in many cases, even preference for an interracial lifestyle.[9] The answers of both college students and
DAS respondents to questions about residential and school integration as
well as others indicating support for the principle of integration bear this
out (see table 5.1).[10] Similarly, on traditional "social distance"[11] questions,
such as whether respondents object to a family member inviting a black
friend for dinner or whether they approve of marriage between blacks
and whites, a large number of whites agreed with the racially tolerant
response. Thus, 92 percent of the students (and 87.2 percent of the DAS
respondents) indicated they had "no objection" to the former; 80.4 percent of students (and 57.7 percent of DAS respondents) approved of the
latter.

However, based on their answers to questions dealing with their own
behavior, whites seemed less committed to an interracial life. For example, when students were asked about the five people with whom they
interacted most on a daily basis, 67.7 percent stated that none of these five
people were black. Similarly, to the social-distance question, "Have you
invited a black person for lunch or dinner recently?" 68.5 percent said
"no" (see nontraditional items in table 5.1 below). In line with these findings, 87 percent of white DAS respondents admitted that none of their
three closest friends were black, 89 percent that they had never had a
romantic relationship with a black person, and 94.5 percent[12] had a white
spouse at the time of the interview. Of the 323 white respondents in the
DAS survey, only one was married to a black person at the time of the
interview! In this section I begin to deconstruct the apparent "paradox"[13]
between whites' commitment to the principle of interracialism and their
mostly white pattern of association based on their answers to a series of
questions about their past and present lives.

"It Was a White Neighborhood": Facts of Whites'
Segregation and Isolation

If the survey results suggest that few whites live an integrated life, the
interview data confirm it. For example, only 4 of the 41 white students
interviewed for this project reported having resided in neighborhoods
with a significant black or other minority presence (i.e., where minorities
made up at least 20 percent of their neighbors). Similarly, only 8 of the 66
whites interviewed for DAS grew up in racially mixed neighborhoods.
These findings are consistent with research on residential segregation.[14]

As perplexing as these numbers are, the facts of "whiteness" (levels of

Table 5.1 White's Views on Social Distance Items

Social Distance Questions	Survey Sample (N = 451)	Interview Sample (N = 41)	DAS Sample (N = 323)
Traditional Items			
B2. If a black family with about the same income and education as you moved next door, would you mind it a lot, a little, or not at all?			
1. Not at all[a]	92.4%	95.1%	90.9%
B12. Do you approve or disapprove of marriage between whites and blacks?			
1. Approve	80.4	90.2	57.5
2. Not Sure[b]	12.9	4.9	—
3. Disapprove	6.7	4.9	42.5
B7. How strongly would you object if a member of your family had a friendship with a black person?			
1. No objection[a]	92.4	92.7	87.2
Nontraditional Items			
A13. Think of the five people with whom you interact the most on an almost daily basis. Of these five, how many of them are black?			
1. None	67.7	68.3	NA
2. One	20.0	24.4	
3. Two or more	12.2	7.3	
A15. Have you invited a black person for lunch or dinner recently?			
1. No	68.5	75.0	NA
2. Yes	31.5	25.0	
A6. Think of your three closest friends, other than relatives. How often do you engage in social activities with them:			
1. More than once a week			21.7
2. Once a week			29.5
3. Once a month	NA	NA	28.9
4. Less than once a month			17.1
5. Never			2.8
A7. How many of these (three) friends are (white/black)?			
0. None			87.0
1. One			11.2
2. Two	NA	NA	1.2
3. Three			0.6

H10. Does your spouse consider (himself/herself),
primarily white or Caucasian, black or African
American, American Indian or Alaskan Native,
Asian or Pacific Islander, or something else?

1. White			94.5
2. Black			0.5
3. Native	NA	NA	0.5
4. Asian			1.5
7. Other			3.0

Have you ever had a romantic relationship with a
(black/white) person?

1. Yes	NA	NA	10.3
2. No			89.7

Sources: 1997 Survey of Social Attitudes of College Students and 1998 Detroit Area Study.
Notes: The option of "not sure" was not included in the survey.
ᵃ Percentages in other categories were insignificant and thus are not reported here.
ᵇ The option of "not sure" was not included in the survey.

racial isolation and segregation from blacks) get more disturbing yet. For instance, two of the four college students who grew up in racially mixed neighborhoods did not associate with minorities and another one related to minorities in a racialized way.[15] Of the eight DAS respondents who grew up in mixed neighborhoods, two had no meaningful interactions with blacks and four had very limited interactions.

Not surprisingly, given whites' racial isolation, few reported having close minority or black friends. Although "friendship" is a hard concept to operationalize given its historically and culturally contingent nature and unclear boundaries, most researchers agree that close friends exhibit a high degree of *interaction, interdependence,* and *closeness.*[16] In fact, when researchers ask people about good friends, they have found that the most common metaphor for describing closeness is kinship. Thus, good friends are like family members.[17]

Based on these criteria and on respondents' self-reports on interracial "friendship," 34 of the 41 college students did not have black friends while growing up (schools and neighborhoods). After cross-validating[18] the answers of those who reported friendship with blacks, *only* 3 of the remaining 7 students had black friends while growing up. Among DAS respondents, 60 of the 66 reported not having close black friends in their neighborhoods. And, as with college students, after carefully examining the answers of the 6 respondents who claimed to have had black friends, only 3 could be regarded as having had a close black friend.

Since my claim that many whites inflate their reports on friendship with blacks is controversial, I provide two examples to illustrate how this process works. The first case is Sally, a student at MU. She grew up in Novi, Michigan, a neighborhood she described as "a hundred percent white and upper middle class." Consequently, all her neighborhood friends were white. Yet, Sally attended mostly "integrated" schools while growing up. When asked, "who did you hang out with in school?," she responded:

> It wasn't bad. Everyone hung with everyone. In particularly, I'd have to say my three best friends were white girls, but I definitely had an excellent girl-friend that was African American and I had several acquaintances that were Asian. That's about it, never really any. . . .

Sally's "excellent African American friend" did not participate in any of the activities she enjoyed with her "three best friends" on the weekends, such as playing tennis, going shopping, or just hanging out. Neither did Sally point to anything that indicated closeness nor interdependence between her and her black friend.

The second case is Pauline, a retired woman in her seventies. She grew up in Hamtramic, Michigan, a neighborhood where "there were a few (black families), but not many." When asked who her close friends were while growing up, Pauline said: "the majority were white." The interviewer followed up this answer with the question, "Do you remember having any black friends growing up?" Pauline's reply was: "I always had black friends, even when I worked[19] I had black friends. In fact, I had a couple of my best friends." Pauline also claimed having had black friends in schools because "I had *lots* of friends" and "I was popular at school." In both cases, Pauline seems to be referring to being "friendly" toward blacks rather than developing a meaningful personal interaction with blacks. This follows from her claim that she was trained to "respect everybody."

These findings are consistent with research on interracial friendship, which usually finds that fewer than 10 percent of whites have black friends.[20] Furthermore, the promotion of black associates into friends is consistent with recent research by survey expert Tom W. Smith. He shows that when whites are asked directly whether or not they have black friends, a large proportion (about 20 percent) says they do. When the question is filtered by asking first whether or not the respondent has friends, the proportion of respondents then claiming to have black friends declines significantly. Finally, when the respondents are asked first whether or not they have friends, then what their names are, and, finally, whether or not any of these friends are black, the proportion of whites claiming to have black friends declines precipitously.[21]

Can the low proportion of whites who befriend blacks be attributed to *hypersegregation,* as some researchers suggest?[22] Alternatively, if whites had the demographic chance of interacting with blacks of similar status, would they do so? Based on the data from my two studies, neither students nor Detroiters who had the demographic chance of interacting with blacks did so. For example, of the 21 students who attended "integrated" schools, only 2 developed meaningful associations with blacks. A higher proportion of DAS respondents (50 of 66) attended predominantly white schools, but of the 16 who attended integrated schools, 5 had black acquaintances, 5 had no black associates, and only 6 had black friends.

Why is it that integrated schools have not provided a meaningful platform for interracial contacts? First, the structure of "desegregated" schools is such that interracial interactions do not lead to significant cross-racial relationships.[23] For instance, even when whites are bused to predominantly minority schools, tracking guarantees they have a mostly white experience in their schools.[24] Case in point: almost all of our respondents described their classes (academic track) as "mostly white," even in cases where the schools were described as 40 percent or more minority! Our respondents also rarely remembered being in classes or clubs in which students of color were the majority. Second, school integration typically occurs late in the lives of whites (usually in high school). By that time, they have already developed emotional attachments to whites as their primary social group, learned a number of stereotypes about minorities, and bypassed the development of the skills necessary to navigate multicultural situations. Ray, a student at MU, explained aptly this last point.

> *Interviewer:* Uh, so what about middle school or high school? Did it change much (compared to his previously all-white educational experiences)?[25]
> *Ray:* Yeah, middle school, things began to change a little bit. Because there were more areas being included. And things did become a little bit more diversified, but mostly, it was pretty much the same, the same song and dance, you know what I mean? Because, I don't know if this was the way they had it set up, but it was almost like they didn't want the sort of lower areas to assimilate with the upper areas until high school. And so that meant that it wasn't a whole new ball game in high school; the people that were friends before were pretty much stayed friends through there. And that's not a hundred percent true, but it seemed to me that things were pretty segmented in high school.

Another possible place for meaningful cross-racial interaction is college; because of "the emphasis on individual achievement and universalism in higher education, the college educated may be less likely to identify themselves with their social and cultural roots."[26] Yet, based on both survey and interview results of the two studies, the precollege pattern of limited and superficial interaction with blacks is maintained in college. As I stated earlier, nearly 70 percent of college students reported they neither have a black person among "the five people with whom they interact the most on an almost daily basis" nor have "invited a Black person for lunch or dinner recently."[27] This finding was confirmed in the interviews. Of the 38 students who did not have black friends before college, only 2 developed friendships with blacks in college. Among the 3 subjects who had black friends before going to college, only 1 befriended a black in college (her boyfriend, who was also from her hometown). Altogether, only 3 of the 41 college students had a black friend at the time of the interview. This finding is also consistent with previous research about the limited extent of white-black interaction in college settings.[28]

In the case of DAS respondents, since all of them were 18 years or older, the question that led us to assess their current level of interaction or association with blacks was, "Are you currently in college, employed, searching for a job, or something else?" By far most white DAS respondents (44) were working at the time of the interview, followed by retirees (10), homemakers (6), people working part time (3), and unemployed (3). Of the whites in these various situations, 41 found themselves in virtually all-white environments, but 25 were not. Of these 25 whites, 8 did not associate with blacks at all, 10 had superficial relationships with blacks, and only 7 had black friends.

Once again, I found that a high proportion of the respondents promoted black acquaintances to "good friends" or even "best friends." Among college students, nearly 50 percent (19 of 41) stated they had black "friends" or that they "hung out" with blacks. After their claims were analyzed, however, it was clear that only 3 truly had black friends by the criteria discussed above. And among DAS respondents, a little more than a third (24 of 66) made such claims, even though only 10 interacted with blacks in a serious fashion.[29] The following two cases exemplify respondents who promoted black acquaintances to friends in the college or work setting. The first case is Emily, a student at MU, who in response to a question about her college friends said, "almost, well, mostly white." Yet, almost immediately she added, "I have a few black friends." Since I instructed my interviewers to follow up whites' claims of friendship with blacks (I also asked them to do the same when blacks claimed friendship with whites, see chapter 7) to assess the degree of closeness of these relationships, the interviewer inquired about Emily's friends.

Interviewer: Okay, and so, other than Jessica (her best white friend), who else? Are there other people that you really spend a lot of time with? Or . . .
Emily: No. Just here and there, but I am really busy . . .
Interviewer: So who, if you can give me a rundown of some of these other

people that you mentioned, like a bigger crowd of people that you might hang out with? Maybe your roommate[30] is one of them. Um, who are those people? So, it sounds like Jessica is the person that you spend the most time with.

Emily: Well, my roommate is—I'm friends with some girls in my hall. And they are all black and they are really nice. And I hang out with them and my roommate, sometimes we do stuff together like go to the mall or—it's not like I'm really good friends with them, but we do stuff together.

At the end, Emily recognized that "it's not like I'm really good friends with them," but the claim of friendship with blacks helped her maintain a pluralistic, color-blind outlook.

Jannis, a manager of human resources for a manufacturing firm she described as "55 percent black," when asked if she had friends in her job said, she had with "a certain amount of them." The interviewer then asked the racial background of her job friends and Jannis responded "It really makes no difference" and that "staff members who are both black and white, we have shared meals with." But Jannis did not associate with any of these black friends outside her job or demonstrate having ever confided in them. Furthermore, Jannis believes self-segregation is natural because "no matter what racial group you are, you do, um, sort of *gather with* those people that are alike." This may explain why she described interracial marriage as "salmons swimming upstream."

Three things are noteworthy about these self-reports of friendship with blacks. First, blacks tend to be "otherized" ("these people," "them," and so forth) denoting the respondents' social distance from blacks. For example, black "friends" are hardly ever identified by their first names. Second, superficial contacts (for college students, sports, music,[31] and the occasional friendly talk with a black student and, for Detroit residents, the occasional lunch or talk at work with blacks) are used as self-evident facts of friendship. Missing from these reports of friendship with blacks is evidence of trust, of the capacity of confiding, and of interactions with these friends beyond the place or situation of formal contact (classroom, assigned roommates, or job). Finally, these "friendships" with blacks always disappear after the reason for the formal interaction ends—taking a class, rooming, playing in a band or in a sports team, or working in the same company.

"IT'S JUST THE WAY THINGS WERE": WHITES' INTERPRETATION OF THEIR OWN RACIAL SEGREGATION

Thus far I have shown that whites have very little contact with blacks in neighborhoods, schools, colleges, and jobs. But how do whites interpret their segregation and isolation from blacks? How do they feel about this racial reality that seems to contradict their endorsement of color blindness? The most significant finding in this section is that whites do not interpret their hypersegregation from blacks as a problem, because they do not interpret this as a *racial* phenomenon. Instead, they normalize this crucial aspect of their lives by either not regarding it as an issue or interpreting is as "normal," as "just the way things are." For instance, most respondents who lived in segregated neighborhoods described them as "all white," "predominantly white," or "primarily white," but when asked how they felt about this fact, few stopped to think this was problematic at all. Among college students, only five thought that the racial composition of their neighborhood was a problem and, among DAS respondents, only eight made such comments. Among the eight DAS respondents who commented negatively on the whiteness of the racial composition of their neighborhoods, one was a Jewish woman who complained about anti-Semitism, another was a Dutch person who complained about feeling isolated as a foreigner, and two others were whites who lived in minority neighborhoods while growing up. Therefore, only four DAS respondents recognized their racial isolation from minorities as a problem.

The typical college students described their feelings about their neighborhoods' racial makeups with statements such as, "I liked it, it was fine to me" (Kim, SU); "When I was growing up, I didn't think about it much. I mean, it was fine for me, it doesn't really bother me that much" (Brian, SU); "I really didn't think about it" (Mary, MU); "Yeah, really comfortable" (Kara, MU); "I didn't care, which is pretty standard, I think, for the kids. It's taken for granted" (Bill, WU). The interpretation of hypersegregation as a normal, matter-of-fact affair was expressed by students with statements such as, "it's like the perfect American neighborhood" and "the sort of white upper-middle-class, *Leave It to Beaver*'s what I think of" (Ray, MU) and "It was a middle-class normal neighborhood" (Rick, WU). DAS respondents' answers to a similar question produced responses such as "I loved it! Everybody was one big happy family" (Jill), "Well, its a very comfortable town because if anybody had a problem, then the rest of the town was there to help you" (Monica), "Oh, it was great. They were all basically the same kind of people" (Don), and "They were good people. *It was a good neighborhood*" (Pat).

This lack of reflexivity is not surprising since, as psychologist Beverly Tatum argues, dominant identities tend to remain inarticulate precisely because they are seen as the "norm" and, therefore, "Whites can easily reach adulthood without thinking much about their racial group."[32] Thus, whereas whiteness is not perceived as a racial category, other categories are; whereas a white neighborhood is a "normal" neighborhood, a black neighborhood is "racially segregated." Nevertheless, besides white racial

progressives (see chapter 6) who recognized racial segregation and isolation as a problem, a few other respondents realized in the interview that
the racial composition of their neighborhoods or networks of friends *could*
be regarded as problematic. For these respondents, however, the issue
was explaining these matters as not involving prejudice on their part. For
instance, Carol, an SU student, said about the racial mix of her neighborhood, "Never, never entered my mind, it was just my neighborhood,"
and she stressed that her community was thoroughly mixed. However,
when asked who her friends were, she pointed out that they were almost
all white (she had one "Hispanic" friend). At this point Carol seemed to
realize the contradiction between claiming that she lived in a mixed
neighborhood and having virtually all-white friends. Hence, Carol
remarked in a rather indignant tone: "I mean, I don't think it, like me
being friends with them had anything to do with them being I guess
white, it's just they lived like next door and across the street from me."
Carol added that her friends' race was just the result of "location."

Sonny, an MU student, explained the limited interaction among blacks
and whites in her school as a product of demography:

> I don't think we had any black friends. I don't know why. It kind of stuck
> together and, I don't know, it wasn't that we, it wasn't that we wouldn't be,
> like allowing to black people, it's just that there was never, like, an opportu-
> nity. There's no population like around where I lived.

Ray, the MU student cited above, addressed the same issue in a rather
defensive way:

> I don't think there was any type of prejudice involved, I just think that we
> really didn't know these kids. You know what I mean? They lived in differ-
> ent neighborhoods, they went to different schools. And there was never any
> effort made to exclude, and if anything, there was effort made to cultivate
> these kids. Any type of discrimination in terms of anything was really just
> taboo at East Lansing. It wasn't like people were trying to exclude them, it's
> just that they didn't know them. It's just the way things were.

Naturalizing whites' racial isolation ("It's just the way things were";
see chapter 2) was a strategy adopted by most college students to rationalize their limited contact with blacks. For example, Daniel, a WU student and a recent immigrant to this country, stated about segregation
that, "I guess in American society it seems sort of, it sort of comes natural,
it appears to be the way of things." Andy, another WU student, said
about segregation that, "I would agree that we don't, or Caucasian people, or the majority does not make things necessarily comfortable for
them, but not like intentionally, so I think it just sort of comes up that way
[*laughs*]." Sue, a student at SU, commented about the whiteness of her

neighborhood that, "I lived there since I was two, I don't really have much of an opinion on it. I just sort of, that's how it was."

The few DAS respondents who realized their limited interaction with blacks could be interpreted as "racist" were also keen in pointing out that race had no bearing in their lives. As college students, many used the demographic excuse to explain why they did not interact with minorities. For example, Kim, a housewife in her late twenties, had a racial life typical of DAS respondents. Kim grew up in various cities in Michigan with few blacks around and had no interactions with them. At the time of the interview she lived in a neighborhood she described as "mostly white." When asked if she had black friends in school, Kim said, "I never had close black friends." Kim then inserted a personal story about her father being racist (for a discussion on these stories, see chapter 4). Later on, when discussing with whom she interacted as a homemaker, Kim said:

> Yep, yep, my husband has some black friends in, you know. You just don't see 'em [*respondent is referring to blacks here*]. They move or whatever, we don't see 'em. It's just—I wished I did so I could just say, you know, "I do" [have black friends]. They are just not around, they don't live in our area.

Trudy, a salesperson at a large retail store in her late twenties, also had the typical white life. She grew up in Warren, Michigan, an area she described as "pretty much white." She attended both private and public schools that she also described as "mostly white." In neither her neighborhoods nor the schools she attended did Trudy develop friendships with blacks. However, 20 percent of her coworkers are black. Yet, when asked about friends in her job, she reported they are "mostly white." When asked if she had any black friends in her job, Trudy said, "Yeah, mostly like acquaintances, not like real good friends." Asked about this situation, Trudy said she "didn't do a whole lot" with her black acquaintances because "I mean, I don't get a lot of opportunity because there are not a whole lot of black people that I work with."

Lastly, Rita, an underemployed worker at a cookie company in her twenties, explained her lack of black friends while attending racially mixed schools in Detroit: "No, but it wasn't because I didn't want to. It's not, it's not because—I didn't have a problem with them. It just, I never socialized with them. Yeah more like they actually never socialized with me."

Like Rita, whites' lack of reflexivity about how race fractures their own lives is evident in their racial projections on a variety of issues (for a discussion on the role of projection, see chapter 3). For example, Kara, an MU student, commented on so-called black self-segregation that, "they just kind of clique with those people and at first I was like, I guess you are always kind of taken aback by it when you see, like, a whole table of minorities, it's harder to go up to people and talk to them when there's a whole group of them." Mickey, another MU student, said on the same issue: "I've definitely seen that. I think the one thing that sticks out the most, the one example, is just like, like dining facilities. Like it's never, it's never integrated. It's always, they always they have their own place to eat." The interviewer asked Mickey if he thought this practice was exclusive to blacks and he answered, "That's mainly just African American people, yeah." Finally, Dan, another student from WU, noted that the fact that blacks have "their own dorms, activities, clubs, and such might be a contributing factor because it kind of encourages them to spend more time with each other and not worry [about] interact[ing] with other people." Kara does not see white cliquing, Mickey does not see white tables, and Dan does not see white anything!

Many DAS respondents also projected racial motivations onto blacks. For example, Ian, a manager of information security for an automotive company in his fifties, addressed this issue as follows:

> I think they're hard to approach at times. At least the ones I have dealt with and deal with on a day-to-day basis. If you question 'em, they take it personally, very defensive. And I try not to, not to make race an issue because I do have to deal with, you know, Indians and Chinese and everything and, as long as, you know, they can do the job, I have no problem with it. But when you constantly go to somebody and say—just follow up with 'em, "Did you do this? Did you do that? Did you make sure of this?" and they take it personally, I have a problem with that. You know, 'cause it's not, you know, we're not bothering to check anybody's integrity. It's just, "Did you get the job done?" and, at times they don't like to be questioned.

When asked if he thought this was "more a problem of self-segregating or a problem of not feeling welcomed" by whites, Ian answered without any hesitation: "Self-segregating."

Matt, a city worker in his twenties, provided a similar one-sided explanation:

> Yeah right. I don't know about hard to approach but from ah, where I've worked in the past and presently, it seems they're not open to any information or ideas from white folks. That they're, you know, set in their own way or maybe their way is a better way, which may or may not be true. But they're, they're not hard to approach. I have no problem approaching them, but when I do, it's like it goes in one ear and out of the other. They don't really, you know, take what you have to say as either encouragement or support or help. And, you know, just view a white guy talking for no reason.

Finally, various respondents made direct statements that signify they regard whiteness as "normal" and, therefore, nonracial. For example,

Rick, a WU student, said that blacks are into the "me syndrome," which he thinks is "so stupid," and added that in his dealings with people from other ethnic groups the question of segregation "wasn't even approached, we were just friends and because I grew up in a white neighborhood, I really didn't see race." What allows Rick to say that because he "grew up in a white neighborhood" he "didn't see race" is that he interprets "race" as something that only racial minorities have.

Lee, another WU student, complained about the monotony of his neighborhood because it was "all white people, but we lived pretty close to Washington, D.C., and there was a lot of culture there, I mean." Therefore for Lee,[33] culture, which he defines narrowly as music, food, and arts, was the prerogative of D.C., an area that is more than two-thirds black. For Lee, then, blacks and Latinos have "culture," but whites (who are not regarded as a race) do not.

Many DAS respondents also saw blacks and other minorities as the only actors who could be regarded as racial. Although this can be inferred from the way they answered many questions, a few used expressions that showed this directly. For example, Susie, a social worker in her late forties, said about the racial mix in her school, "I don't think there was *any* racial children in my, you know, public schools." Susie repeated the expression (racial children) when describing the racial makeup of her workplace:

> Oh, jeez, I just had an employee with that. Umhum [*raises voice*] I think it's probably 52/48 [percent], 52 being Caucasian, 48 being black, close to 50/50. But she indicated [*referring to a black "friend" at work*] there's a few blacks missing [*lowers voice*], one of my racial friends.

The data presented in this section indicates that whites do not see or interpret their own racial segregation and isolation as a racial issue at all. This blindness is central for understanding their views on a host of racial matters. Recognizing whites' lack of realization that race matters in their lives, combined with their limited interracial socialization, helps decipher the apparent contradiction between their stated preference for a color-blind approach to life (which corresponds to their perception of how they live their own lives) and the white reality of their lives. I examine this apparent contradiction by focusing on their views on the sensitive matter of interracial relations.

"IF TWO PEOPLE ARE IN LOVE . . .": WHITES' VIEWS ON INTERRACIAL MARRIAGE

Despite whites' stake in color blindness, in surveys they are more likely to oppose interracial marriage than any other form of interracial association.[34] For example, only 57.5 percent of white DAS respondents approved of interracial marriage in the survey. Although the approval rate was higher among college students—80 percent for white-black unions and 86 percent for white-Mexican unions—it was still lower among students than was support for other social-distance questions (see table 5.1). This latter finding about college students fits research that suggests educated people are more likely to express approval for the principles of integration.[35]

Nevertheless, most DAS respondents and even the few college students who admitted they had problems with interracial marriage in the interviews brandished a laissez-fare or color-blind view on love. Love was described as a matter of personal choice between two people and, thus, as no one else's business because "love conquers all obstacles" (see my discussion of abstract liberalism in chapter 2).[36] Yet, this endorsement of color blindness in romantic relationships cannot be interpreted in a straightforward manner. Most respondents *qualified* their support in such a way or live such segregated lifestyles that their laissez-faire positions on this subject seem empty. Furthermore, too many whites express an aversion for blackness ("negrophobia") that casts doubt on their professed color blindness.

In table 5.2 I map respondents' answers to the interracial marriage question. The classifications are not mutually exclusive (e.g., some respondents I classified as 2s could have been classified as 4s) and cannot be read as an ordinal scale, that is, as moving from racial progressives to racial reactionaries (e.g., some respondents I classified as 3s or 4s were in fact more racially progressive than some who were 2s). The purpose of this taxonomy is just to organize answers to this question rather than provide the ultimate analysis of which respondents are truly "for" or "against" these unions.

Table 5.2   Respondents' Answers to the Interracial Marriage Question

DAS Students	Respondents	
Respondents' Views on Interracial Marriage	(%)	(%)
1. Support marriage/Interracial life	5 (12.5)	7 (11.0)
2. Support marriage/Primary white networks	8 (20.0)	14 (22.0)
3. Reservations toward intermarriage/Interracial life	4 (10.0)	2 (3.0)
4. Reservations toward intermarriage/Primary white networks	21 (52.5)	21 (32.0)
5. Opposes intermarriage/Interracial life	0 (0.0)	7 (11.0)
6. Opposes intermarriage/Primary white networks	2 (5.0)	14 (22.0)
Total number of respondents	40[a]	65[a]

[a] The question was not as asked to one of the students and one of the DAS respondents.

In the case of college students, the typical response was category 4, respondents who qualified their support with expressions of concern for the children, family reactions, or location, or with rhetorical maneuvers indicative of little personal commitment to these unions ("*They* can have all the fun *they* want, it doesn't bother *me* at all"). Eight students supported interracial marriage but had all-white associations[37] and two admitted directly that they would not do it themselves. Among DAS respondents, the typical response was also category 4 (32 percent), followed closely by respondents who opposed interracial marriage (22 percent). A similar proportion of DAS respondents and college students stated their support for interracial marriage in the interviews (32.5 percent to 33 percent).

Since the responses to this sensitive question are complex, I present various examples from each category. First I provide examples of respondents' answers in category 1—those who approved of interracial marriage and had an interracial lifestyle.[38] Kay, a student at MU, answered the interracial question in the following manner: "I don't see anything wrong with it [*laughs*]." Kay laughed because before this question was posed to her she had said that her boyfriend was black (she was the only white dating or married to a black among the 107 whites interviewed in these two projects). Franci, a homemaker in her twenties, answered the question similarly: "As long as they're happy, go for it!" Although many other whites used expressions such as this one, they immediately added long-winded statements qualifying their support. In contrast, respondents in this category answered without hesitation and had an interracial lifestyle that included in some cases having dated across the color line. Franci, for example, had dated *four* minority men, one of whom was black.

But even in this category, which was the most internally consistent, there was some variance. For instance, Scott, a mechanical drafter in his twenties, answered the interracial question as follows: "If you are comfortable with it, do it. You know, I mean, I'm looking for a Vietnamese—half-Vietnamese, half-Chinese right now. That's my dream woman right there. I love Asian women." Scott, who had dated Asian (half-Vietnamese), Latino, and Arab women in the past, seems like a clear example of respondents in category 1. Yet, Scott's fascination for Asian women was highly racialized (he stated he liked them because their food "is awesome," they are "just so attractive to me," and he "just love[s] the Asian race, it's mystical to me in a way") and in tune with the way that many white men think of Asian women today.[39] Even more problematic was Scott's response in a follow-up to the interracial marriage question. After Scott stated he would have "no problem" marrying someone of a different race, the interviewer asked him, "So what do you think about people who are absolutely against it, you know, who want to keep the races pure or whatever?" His answer was:

> I mean, I kind of, I feel that way also because I kind of, I don't know, I kinda wanna stay with my nationality in a way, you know. I think once, once you start breaking away, you start losing your own like deep home family values and in a way, you get mixed emotions, you know. But then again, it's just like the old times are gone, you know it's all modern-day now. So really you[r] nationality really don't, shouldn't count. But then again some people don't want to have so much blood within their family, within their name, you know. I know people that will not marry unless they're a hundred percent Italian. I got a couple of people who will not date anyone unless they're hundred percent Italian, so. . . .

Based on this response and the fact that Scott was classified as having an interracial lifestyle because he had *one* black friend while growing up, he could have been classified as someone who opposes interracial marriage.

Respondents in category 2—those who approved of interracial marriage but associated primarily with whites—had more diverse responses. Some were respondents on the "racial progressive" side (see chapter 7) such as Sam, a warehouse laborer in his twenties. His response to the intermarriage question was: "I have no problems with it. I just did it." Sam was married to a Mexican American woman and stated he had been "attracted [to black women] but I've really never dated anyone like that." Others were supportive of interracial marriage, but had a racial preference for white mates. For example, Ray, an MU student cited above, answered the interracial marriage question as follows:

> I think that there's, I think that interracial marriage is totally legitimate. I think if two people love each other and they want to spend the rest of their lives together, I think they should definitely get married. And race should in no way be an inhibitive factor.

Although Ray seems supportive of interracial marriage (despite using some indirectness), his life before college and in college was centered exclusively around whites. He grew up in a midsize city in the Midwest in an upper-middle-class neighborhood that he characterized as "all white" and described his friends as "what the average suburban kid is like nowadays." More significantly, Ray, who was extremely articulate in the interview, stuttered remarkably over the question (asked before the one on intermarriage) dealing with whether or not he had ever been attracted to blacks (see chapter 3 for Ray's answer). Ray's hesitation was due to the fact he is not attracted to black women, something that clashes with his self-proclaimed color-blind approach to love and his apparent support for interracial marriages.

The third and fourth categories include respondents who had reservations about interracial marriage. I discuss them together because there are no meaningful variations in these two categories and I provide many examples, as a large number of respondents (nearly 50 percent) were in one of these two kindred categories. Most of the respondents in categories 3 and 4 stated they had no problem with interracial marriage but proceeded to cite reasons why these marriages are more difficult. A typical example is Olga, a software salesperson for an insurance company in her forties:

> Well, I guess my only concern is always if there's children and how those children will be accepted or not accepted. And it would be nice to think that the world would be lovely and wonderful but, you know, I think people should be allowed to do whatever they want to do. I don't think you should look at people's skin color or their origin or anything to determine what it is you want to do. However, what are you putting those kids through when they're a mixed that *neither* culture would accept because the cultures are sometimes just as bad about sticking together as they are about claiming that no one will let them in and out of each other's areas. So sometimes that really affects the kids and neither culture will accept the child as being their culture or the other. So that concerns me, but in general, I don't have any problem with any of that.

Joann, a clerk in a department store in her early sixties, stated that, "except for someone that might be extremely young, I think that [if] they want to marry outside their race and put up with what they [will face], that's their problem." But Joann acknowledged that interracial marriage could not have happened in her own family because:

> I, that I never [*very loud*] even though—because my husband was "whites marry whites, blacks marry blacks," he was very prejudice about it. He grew up with that made up [in] his mind and that was it. Any white could marry any whites but blacks marry blacks and that is the way it was.

Ian, the manager of information security cited above, said in typical fashion about interracial marriage, "I don't have a problem with it at all," but added,

> There's gonna be problems. White and Chinese, white and even Italian, there's gonna be problems, white and black. I have no problems with it, but they better face the facts of life, they're gonna have a lot of problems. And they're not gonna be accepted, I don't, at least, I don't think very well by either side.

College students in these categories answered in similar fashion. For instance, Sally, an MU student, stated her view on interracial marriage as follows:

> I certainly don't oppose the marriage, not at all, depending on where I am, if I had to have a concern, yes, it would be for the children. You know, it can be nasty and then other kids wouldn't even notice. I think I could care less what anyone else does with their lives, as long as they are really happy. And if the parents can set a really strong foundation at home, it can be conquered, but I'm sure, in some places, it could cause a problem.

Sally's apprehension matched the nature of her life and her specific views on blacks. Sally's network of relationships was, in terms of interactions, relationships, and residence, an almost entirely white one. When asked about her romantic life, Sally said that she had never dated a person of color and recognized that, "I've never been attracted to a black person" and that, "I never look at what they look like, it just hasn't occurred in my life."

Some respondents in these two categories could have been classified as people who opposed interracial marriage, even though they did not say so. For example, Mandi, a nurse working in a nursing home in her thirties, answered the question on intermarriage by saying, "I wouldn't do it." When asked for her general position, she said: "I don't think I could tell people what to do. I think it's hard on people when they marry outside their race. The children." Thus Mandi relies on abstract liberalism for her general position on interracial marriage, but is clear that interracial marriage is not for her.

Another example is Dina, an employment manager for an advertising agency in her twenties. Her answer to the interracial marriage question was:

> I don't have an issue with it at all. You know, I personally, I don't [date people] of another race so it's very difficult for me to say, but I don't think [*sighs*] I can't see myself ever doing that, marrying someone of another race. But we have friends in interrational—interracial relationships and. . . .

Interestingly, Dina had dated a black man for a week in high school. Yet, she pointed out that "he was kinda like a white person, you know, he acted white, he talked white" and that she did it to "kinda just to tick off my grandpa." In general, Dina said, "the guys I dated were white jocks kinda guys."

Finally, I present respondents answers in categories 5 and 6, those who opposed interracial marriage. The first example is Janet, a married student at SU. Janet, like a number of respondents, accused people in interracial relationships of being selfish:

> I would feel that in most situations they're not really thinking of, of the child. I mean, they might not really think anything of it, *but* in reality I think most of the time the child is growing up, he's going to be picked on because he has parents from different races, and it's gonna, and it's gonna ultimately affect the child and, and the end result is they're only thinking of them—of their own happiness, not the happiness of the kid.

The interviewer followed up by asking, "How do you think your family would deal with it if you or someone else in your family became involved with someone of another race?" Janet's answer was: "They would *not* like it *at all* [*laughs*]!"

Most older respondents expressed their disapproval of interracial marriage without hesitation and relied on Jim Crow tenets to justify their position. For example, Jim, a retired man in his seventies, stated:

> Well, I'm against it. I think scripture says that we should be very careful how we should choose our mates. I may love the girl I want to marry and she's black, but I just can't look at that situation. I have to look at what's going to happen afterwards, what's going to happen to our kids. They're the ones who take a beating. You're not white, you're not black.

However, some older respondents expressed their opposition in a more refined manner. For instance, Rhonda, a part-time salesperson in a golf store and of Jewish background, used the movie *Fiddler in the Roof* to state her view on this matter: "A bird and a fish can fall in love but where do they go to nest?" After saying this, Rhonda narrated a testimony (see chapter 4) to suggest blacks and whites should not marry because it causes many problems for the children. She then commented: "The children are the ones that are—they're the ones that are not going to be, they're the ones that don't [know] where they belong. They don't know if they are white, they don't know if they're black."

As the previous examples illustrate, the argument of the children (or concerns for family) are not much different than those of respondents in categories 3 and 4. More significantly, a few respondents in these categories (those who opposed interracial marriage) used the jargon of color blindness in their responses. For example, Henrietta, a transsexual school teacher in his fifties, answered the question on intermarriage as follows: "[*5-second pause*] If two people [*3-second pause*] are [in love] . . . I see nothing wrong with it. It's their business." Henrietta seems to have a laissez-faire view on interracial marriage. However, after stating his view, Henrietta proceeded to discuss the problems he has seen among biracial children in his school. In this discussion, Henrietta seemed to change his mind and said: "I would say I would have to be against it." The interviewer then asked him, "So then it sounds like you yourself would not consider marrying someone of another race or . . . ?" Henrietta responded: "It depends. It depends on how I feel about the person due to my upbringing, could I, if you're asking me could I marry a black man? No. If you are asking me if I could marry an Asiatic man or an American, Native American man? Yes."

There are three things clear from the answers of the respondents in these studies to the question on interracial marriage. First, although most use the language of color blindness ("I have no problem with it" or "If two people are in love"), their answers reveal a deep level of reservation if not outright opposition toward these unions. Second, a large number of whites express a clear preference for whites as mates that seems to violate their professed color blindness. Third, even though whites do not have much contact with blacks or with people in interracial marriages, they reject these unions because of presumed "problems" that transpire in these marriages.

I suggest whites' answers to the interracial marriage question are prima facie evidence of one of the consequences of the white habitus. Whites' answers signify they have serious difficulties in thinking about these relationships as normal. From a social-psychological perspective, this is not a mystery. How can whites fall in love with people whom they never see, whom they regard as "different," and with whom they hardly associate? Hence, what their answers to the interracial question betray is that whiteness as a lifestyle fosters whiteness as a choice for friends and partners. Their answers also reveal concerns for not sounding "racist," concerns that fit well what I have discussed about color-blind racism so far.

CONCLUSION

At the outset of this chapter I argued that whites live a white habitus that creates and conditions their views, cognitions, and even sense of beauty and, more importantly, fosters a sense of racial solidarity. This postulate fits the arguments and findings of the status construction and social identity theories. Whereas work in the social identity tradition has amply demonstrated how little it takes to create antagonistic groups, work in the status construction tradition has shown that once there are two or more status groups in a social system, those at the top tend to adjudicate the status differences to nominal characteristics such as race and gender.[40] Research in these traditions has also uncovered that when status differences between groups exist, as in the case between whites and blacks, the advantaged group develops its own "groupthink," values, and norms to account for and rationalize these differences.

In this chapter I documented three things related to the white habitus. First, I showed that whites experience tremendous levels of racial segregation and isolation while growing up. That isolation continues in college and in the workplace, even when blacks are present in these environments. Second, I documented how whites, for the most part, do not interpret their racial isolation and segregation from blacks as racial. Instead, they either do not see any need to explain this or explain it as a nonracial matter ("Race has nothing to do with it" or "That's the way things are"). Lastly, I examined their answers to the interracial marriage question and suggested that they are an example of what the white habitus produces, as they signify, despite the color-blind rhetoric, that whites are not very likely to engage in interracial unions with blacks.

The social psychology produced by the white habitus leads to the creation of positive self-views ("We are nice, normal people") and negative other views ("They are lazy").[41] The more distant the group in question is from the white "norm," other things being equal, the more negative whites will view the group. Because blacks are the group farthest from whites residentially and socially in this country[42]—although not necessarily culturally[43]—they are the most likely candidates for debasement.[44] In previous chapters I documented how whites see blacks in a negative light. For example, they regard blacks as lazy, as welfare-dependent, and as receiving preferential treatment. They also believe blacks complain too much about racism and discrimination. This negative view on blacks extends to the most personal realm: close interracial associations as friends and significant others. Although most whites rely on color blindness ("race doesn't matter"), a free-market logic on human relationships ("if two people are in love"), and liberal individualism ("I don't think that anyone should have the right to tell anyone else whether or not they should marry") to articulate their views on interracial marriage, few seem to support these relationships and, more significantly, to be in a position to ever engage in one or even to be neutral in case a close family member enters into one.

Whites' lack of true empathy for or interest in interracial marriage with blacks should not be a shock or a mystery to readers. People cannot like or love people they don't see or interact with. This truism has been corroborated by social psychologists, who for years have maintained that friendship and love emerge when people share activities, proximity, familiarity, and status.[45] Thus, whites' extreme racial isolation from blacks does not provide fertile soil upon which primary interracial associations can flourish, regardless of blacks' level of assimilation. Therefore, whites' theoretical support for interracial associations with blacks is not likely to lead to significant increases in their personal associations with blacks.

The social and political implications of the white habitus are very significant. The universe of whiteness navigated on an everyday basis by most whites fosters a high degree of homogeneity of racial views and even of the manners in which whites express these views. Despite the civil rights revolution, whites, young and old, live a fundamentally segregated life that has attitudinal, emotional, and political implications. Yet it is important to underscore the existence of racial progressives in these samples. Their existence suggests that although the white habitus conditions whites' lives, whites can, as Marx said, "make their own history."[46] I found a number of respondents who lived interracial lifestyles, understood the significance of contemporary discrimination, and did not rely on color blindness to articulate their racial views. I turn my attention to this group of racial progressives in the next chapter.

NOTES

1. The premier author in this tradition was Oscar Lewis, *La Vida: A Puerto Rican Family in the Culture of Poverty* (New York: Random House, 1966). For a radical version of this theory at the time, see Michael Harrington, *The Other America: Poverty in the United States* (New York: Macmillan, 1962).

2. Charles A. Murray, *Losing Ground: American Social Policy, 1950–1980* (New York: Basic, 1984); Lawrence M. Mead, *Beyond Entitlement: The Social Obligations of Citizenship* (New York: Free Press, 1986); William Julius Wilson, *The Truly Disadvantaged: The Inner City, the Underclass, and Public Policy* (Chicago: University of Chicago Press, 1987); Ken Auletta, *The Underclass*, updated and revised (Woodstock, N.Y.: Overlook, 1999); and Cornel West, *Race Matters* (Boston: Beacon, 1993).

3. John Ogbu, *Minority Education and Caste: The American System in Cross-Cultural Perspective* (New York: Academic, 1978), and Elijah Anderson, *Streetwise* (Chicago: University of Chicago Press, 1990).

4. Hints of this stand can be seen in James Diego Vigil, *Barrio Gangs: Street Life and Identity in Southern California* (Austin: University of Texas Press, 1988), but more clearly in Philippe Bourgeois, *In Search of Respect: Selling Crack in El Barrio* (New York: Cambridge University Press, 1995).

5. Douglas Massey and Nancy Denton, *American Apartheid* (Chicago: University of Chicago Press, 1993), 165–66.

6. See the introduction to my *White Supremacy and Racism in the Post–Civil Rights Era* (Boulder, Colo.: Rienner, 2001).

7. Bourdieu defines habitus as "not only a structuring structure, which organizes practices and the perception of practices, but also a structured structure: the principles of division into logical classes which organizes the perception of the social world is itself the product of internalization of the division into social classes." The most important contribution of this concept, however, is that it

shapes an actor's "perception, appreciation and action" through routinization, without express calculation, and with little need for external constraints. I extend his class-inspired notion of habitus to the field of race. Pierre Bourdieu, *Distinction* (Cambridge, Mass.: Harvard University Press, 1984), 170, and *Pascalian Meditations* (Stanford, Calif.: Stanford University Press, 1997), 138.

8. On this point, see Matthhijs Kalmijn, "Intermarriage and Homogamy: Causes, Patterns, Trends," *Annual Review of Sociology* 24 (1998): 395–421.

9. Howard Schuman et al., *Racial Attitudes in America: Trends and Interpretations* (Cambridge, Mass.: Harvard University Press, 1997).

10. Recent surveys, however, have found that whites and blacks are growing increasingly comfortable with the idea of segregation, so long as it is not enforced through violent means, that is, so long as it is by "choice." See Peter Grier and James N. Thurman, "Youth's Shifting Attitudes on Race," *Christian Science Monitor*, August, 18, 1999.

11. Gordon Allport, *The Nature of Prejudice* (New York: Doubleday, 1954).

12. This proportion is in line with the general population, as 93 percent of whites do not intermarry. See Rachel Moran, *Interracial Intimacy: The Regulation of Race and Romance* (London: University of Chicago Press, 2001).

13. Schuman et al., in their *Racial Attitudes in America*, label the gap between the number of whites who approve of the principle of integration and the policies to implement integration a "paradox." I suggest this is just an apparent paradox the mystery behind which becomes clear when it is viewed within an ideological framework. Whites adopt an *abstract* notion of liberalism that has little import to their life, relations, and attitudes about a variety of *real* and *concrete* racial matters.

14. Massey and Denton, *American Apartheid;* Reynolds Farley, *The New American Reality* (New York: Russell Sage Foundation, 1996); and Kalmijn, "Intermarriage and Homogamy."

15. Kara, the respondent in question, referred to her Asian friend as "Oriental" and had very stereotypical views on blacks. In the survey, however, she claimed that she interacted almost daily with a black person. This person was her black maid.

16. Michael Argyle and Monika Henderson, *The Anatomy of Relationships* (London: Routledge, 1985), and Beverly Fehr, *Friendship Process* (Newbury Park, Calif.: Sage, 1996).

17. On this point, see Lillian B. Rubin, *Just Friends: The Role of Friendship in Our Lives* (New York: HarperCollins, 1985).

18. We cross-examined whites about their self-reports of friendship with blacks because (1) previous research suggested that race is among the most salient similarity factors upon which friendships are based (Helen Gouldner and Mary Strong, *Speaking of Friendship: Middle-Class Women and Their Friends* [New York: Greenwood, 1987]); (2) survey research has found that few whites (7 to 10 percent) have black friends (Mary R. Jackman and Marie Crane, " 'Some of My Best Friends Are Black . . .': Interracial Friendship and Whites' Racial Attitudes," *Public Opinion Quarterly* 50 [Winter 1986]: 459–86); and (3) self-reports by whites on friendship with blacks are highly unreliable (Benjamin DeMott, *The Trouble with Friendship: Why Americans Can't Think Straight about Race* [New York: Atlantic

Monthly, 1995]). Thus, we followed up every respondent's self-report of friendship with blacks with questions such as "What kind of things do you do with your black friend?" and "How often?" We did the same with black respondents.

19. I did not find any reference to these black friends at work in any part of the interview.

20. Jackman and Crane, "Some of My Best Friends"; Maureen Hallinan and Richard A. Williams, "The Stability of Students' Interracial Friendships," *American Sociological Review* 52, no. 2 (October 1987): 653–64. See also Bonilla-Silva, Embrick, Ketchum, and Saenz, "Where is the Love?: Why Whites Have Limited Interaction with Blacks," *Journal of Intergroup Relations* 32, no. 1 (2004): 24–38; Bonilla-Silva and Embrick (Forthcoming), "'Every Place Has a Ghetto . . .': The Significance of Whites' Social and Residential Segregation," *Journal of Symbolic Interaction*.

21. Tom W. Smith. "Measuring Inter-Racial Friendships: Experimental Comparisons" (paper presented at the annual meeting of the American Sociological Association, August 6, 1999, in Chicago).

22. Massey and Denton, *American Apartheid*; Farley, *New American Reality*.

23. Clairette P. Armstrong and A. James Gregor, "Integrated Schools and Negro Character," in *White Racism and Black Americans*, edited by David G. Bromley et al. (Cambridge, Mass.: Schenkman, 1972); P. Rosenbaum, "Five Perspectives on Desegregation in Schools: A Summary," in *When Schools Are Desegregated: Problems and Possibilities for Students, Educators, Parents, and the Community*, edited by M. L. Wax (Washington, D.C.: National Institute of Education, 1979). For a recent estimate of the high levels of racial isolation of all racial/ethnic groups in schools, see Kara Joyner and Grace Kao, "School Racial Composition and Racial Homophily," *Social Science Quarterly* 81 (2000): 810–25. For recent studies on how race is reproduced in schools, see Amanda E. Lewis, *Race in the Schoolyard: Negotiating the Colorline in Classrooms and Communities* (New Jersey: Rutgers University Press, 2003); Judith Blau, *'Race in the Schools:' Perpetuating White Dominance* (Boulder, Colo.: Lynne Rienner Publishers, 2003).

24. J. L. Epstein, "After the Bus Arrives: Resegregation in Desegregated Schools," *Journal of Social Issues* 41, no. 3 (1985): 23–43; Gary Orfield and Susan Eaton, *Dismantling Desegregation* (New York: New York Press, 1996).

25. First, the names of all the respondents are fictitious. Second, the responses were transcribed as close as possible to the spoken utterances, because lapses, self-corrections, and pauses were relevant data. Third, all the italics in the quotes were added to emphasize important material.

26. Kalmijn, "Intermarriage and Homogamy," 401; Sean-Shong Hwang, Rogelio Saenz, and Benigno E. Aguirre, "Structural and Individual Determinants of Outmarriage among Chinese-, Filipino-, and Japanese-Americans in California," *Sociological Inquiry* 64, no. 4 (1994): 396–414.

27. The Bogardus social distance scale has seven items, ranging from would "admit to close kinship by marriage" to would "exclude from my country." See Gordon Allport, *The Nature of Prejudice* (New York: Doubleday, 1954). For examples of traditional survey questions on social distance, see Schuman et al., *Racial Attitudes in America*.

28. Joe R. Feagin, Hernán Vera, and Nikitah Imani, *The Agony of Education: Black Students at White Colleges and Universities* (New York: Routledge, 1996).

29. I counted as friends those who interacted with blacks outside their jobs. This was a more flexible criterion for DAS respondents than it was for college students. For example, it included two respondents who just bowled or played basketball with blacks.

30. Emily had said that her roommate was "Korean . . . from Hawaii," that she was "really nice," and that they "got along really well." However, Sally never mentioned her roommate's name and said that she had "her own friends, I have mine."

31. Although sports and music are central to the repertoire of social activities of youth, the fact that most of these reports on friendship with blacks were around these two activities suggests that (1) the associations involve a small degree of emotional commitment and (2) that whites may still think that blacks only care about sports and music. For a historical explanation of the latter, see John Hoberman, *Darwin's Athletes* (Boston: Houghton Mifflin, 1997).

32. Beverly Daniel Tatum, *"Why Are All the Black Kids Sitting Together in the Cafeteria?": And Other Conversations about Race* (New York: Basic, 1997), 93. See also Ashley W. Doane, "White Identity and Race Relations in the 1990s," in *Perspectives on Current Social Problems*, edited by Gregg Lee Carter, 151–59 (Boston: Allyn and Bacon, 1997).

33. Lee had mentioned in the interview he is majoring in music and that he is totally into black music.

34. Schuman et al., *Racial Attitudes in America*; Eduardo Bonilla-Silva, DAS 1998.

35. Schuman et al., *Racial Attitudes in America*.

36. Yanick St. Jean, "Let People Speak for Themselves: Interracial Unions and the General Social Survey," *Journal of Black Studies* 28, no. 3 (1998): 398–414.

37. I am not suggesting that people who have an entirely white network of associations are "racist." Conceptually, I argue that racism ought to be studied in a *structural* manner. In my work, I use the term "racism" exclusively to designate the racial ideology of a *racialized social system* and, thus, labeling someone as "racist" represents a regression to an individualist and subjectivist reading of racial matters. The issue here is assessing the real degree of support for interracial relationships among whites. Thus, it is necessary to have a larger picture in view to clearly demarcate the *meaning* and *implications* of respondents' self-reported approval of interracial relationships. By including elements from the respondents' lives (such as lack of meaningful interracial interaction or fear of blacks), I am able to interpret their positions on interracial marriages in terms of a larger context.

38. We were flexible in the classification of respondents as having an interracial lifestyle. Hence respondents who had one black friend at *any* point in time were regarded as having an interracial lifestyle.

39. Asian women are viewed by many white men as highly "desirable" because they are supposed to be subservient and sensual, as "China Dolls," the label given to this stereotype by the Media Action Network for Asian Americans. See Media Action Network for Asian Americans, *A Memo from MANAA to Hollywood: Asian Stereotypes* (www.janet.org/ manaa/a_stereotypes).

40. This literature has also uncovered that when status differences between groups exist, as in the case between whites and blacks, the advantaged group develops its own "groupthink," values, and norms to account for and rationalize these differences. See Cecilia Ridgeway and James Balkwell, "Group Processes and the Diffusion of Status Beliefs," *Social Psychology Quarterly* 60, no. 1 (1997): 14–31; Cecilia Ridgeway, Elizabeth Heger Boyle, Kathy J. Kuipers, and Dawn T. Robinson, "How Do Status Beliefs Develop? The Role of Resources and Interactional Experience," *American Sociological Review* 63 (June 1998): 331–50.

41. Interestingly, a recent review of the past 30 years of work in the area of social psychology labels the area "color blind" and concludes that "social psychologists . . . have given race and ethnicity less attention than it warrants."Hence, we still lack serious social-psychological analyses of the various ways in which race affects multiple social processes. Matthew O. Hunt, Pamela Braboy Jackson, Brian Powell, and Lala Carr Steelman, "Color Blind: The Treatment of Race and Ethnicity in Social Psychology," *Social Psychology Quarterly* 63, no. 4 (2000): 360–61. See also Carla Goar's article, "Even the Rats are White: White Supremacy in Experimental Methodology" in *White Logic, White Methods: Racism and Methodology*, edited by Eduardo Bonilla-Silva and Tukufu Zuberi (Forthcoming).

42. For data on segregation by groups, see Douglas S. Massey and Nancy A. Denton, "Trends in the Residential Segregation of Blacks, Hispanics, and Asians: 1970–1980," *American Sociological Review* 52, no. 6 (December 1987): 802–25. For data on interracial perceptions of social ranking of the races, see Lawrence D. Bobo and Devon Johnson, "Racial Attitudes in a Prismatic Metropolis: Mapping Identity, Competition, and Views on Affirmative Action," in *Prismatic Metropolis: Inequality in Los Angeles*, edited by Lawrence D. Bobo et al., 81–163 (New York: Russell Sage Foundation, 2000).

43. Greeks, Arabs, and Armenians, for instance, are, culturally speaking, farther from "whites" than blacks, yet they have been incorporated into whiteness.

44. As Joe R. Feagin points out in his *Racist America: Roots, Realities, and Future Reparations* (New York: Routledge, 2000: 132) Because of the racial demography and ecology of everyday life, the majority of blacks spend much more time interacting with whites than the majority of whites spend interacting with blacks. Most blacks work, shop, or travel with large numbers of white Americans, whereas relatively few whites do the same with large numbers of black men and women. White views of blacks are not likely to be grounded in numerous equal-status contacts with blacks. The sense of white superiority is reinforced by the continuing process in which whites live separated from black Americans or other Americans of color. White isolation and lack of contact feeds negative stereotyping, and there is little chance to unlearn inherited antiblack attitudes. For a recent update, see Joe R. Feagin's latest book, *Systemic Racism: A Theory of Oppression* (New York: Routledge, 2006).

45. John Sabini, *Social Psychology* (New York: Norton, 1992).

46. The phrase is "Men make their own history, but they do not make it just as they please"; it appears in *The Eighteenth Brumaire of Louis Bonaparte*. David McLellan, *Karl Marx: Selected Writings* (New York: Oxford University Press, 1982).

6

~

Are All Whites Refined
Archie Bunkers?

An Examination of White
Racial Progressives

M ost whites in the United States rely on the ideology of color-blind
racism to articulate their views (by relying on the frames of the ideology), present their ideas (by using the style of the ideology), and interpret interactions with people of color (by sharing the racial stories of the
ideology). They believe blacks are culturally deficient, welfare-dependent, and lazy. They regard affirmative action and reparations as tanta-
mount to "reverse discrimination." And because whites believe
discrimination is a thing of the past, minorities' protestations about being
racially profiled, experiencing discrimination in the housing and labor
markets, and being discriminated against in restaurants, stores, and other
social settings are interpreted as "excuses." Following the color-blind
script, whites support almost all the goals of the Civil Rights Movement
in principle, but object in practice to almost all the policies that have been
developed to make these goals a reality. Although they abhor what they
regard as blacks' "self-segregation," they do not have any problem with
their own racial segregation because they do not see it as a racial phenomenon. Finally, although they sing loudly the color-blind song, as I showed
in the previous chapter, they live a white color-coded life.

Does this mean that all whites are refined Archie Bunkers? Does every
single white subscribe to the frames, racial stories, and style associated
with color-blind racism? The answer is obviously not. Historically, racial
progress in America has always transpired because of the joint efforts of

131

racial minorities and white progressives. No one can forget the coura-
geous efforts of whites such as John Brown, Thaddeus Stevens, Charles
Sumner, Lydia Maria Child, the Grimke sisters, and the many whites who
joined the Civil Rights Movement; no one should ever ignore white mili-
tants who struggled for racial equality and who risked their lives for this
goal.[1] Therefore today, as yesterday, a portion of the white population is
not singing the tune of color blindness. Who are these modern-day
"white traitors"?[2] Are they middle-class, educated, racially enlightened
whites, as most social scientists contend?[3] Are they more likely to be
socialized outside the white habitus (see chapter 5)? Are racial progressives beyond racial contradictions? These are some of the questions I
examine in this chapter.

THE SURPRISING DEMOGRAPHY
OF RACIAL PROGRESSIVES

Interview data from the 1997 Survey on Social Attitudes of College Students and the 1998 Detroit Area Study suggest young, working-class
women are the most likely candidates to be racial progressives.[4] This
finding contradicts the claims of most of the media and scholars (from
Theodor Adorno's *The Authoritarian Personality* onward), who contend
"racists" are poor or working-class whites.[5] These commentators contend
poor whites project their fears, their sense of losing out, and their concerns with demographic, civil, and political changes in America onto
racial minorities. These opinion-shaping agents also propagate the view
that most whites, whom they classify as "middle class," are racially tolerant. But if racism is systemic,[6] this view of "good" and "bad" whites
distorts reality. Systems of privilege are defended by most of their bene-
ficiaries in a variety of ways. Some actors defend systemic privilege
through violence, but most do so by following the normal customs and
practices that help keep the system in place. Hence, the analytical (and
political) issue regarding "racism" (racial ideology) ought always to be,
What segment of the dominant race does not subscribe to the dominant
racial ideology and why not?

I classified as racial progressives respondents who support affirmative
action and interracial marriage and who recognize the significance of discrimination in the United States. In cases in which respondents exhibited
reservations on one of the issues, I made an effort to search for other elements disclosed in the interview to help me classify the respondents (e.g.,
whether they had meaningful relationships with minorities or the degree
of racial progressiveness on other race-related issues discussed in the
interviews). Based on these criteria, I classified 15 percent of college stu-

dents (6 of 41) and 12 percent of the DAS respondents (8 of 66) as racial progressives.

PROFILES OF RACIAL PROGRESSIVES: COLLEGE STUDENTS

I classified two students at WU and three at MU as racial progressives. Common characteristics of these five respondents were their class background (four belonged to the working or lower-middle class), gender (all were women), and being in college. Other elements that affected their degree of racial progressiveness were having meaningful associations or friendships with people of color (three of these women had dated black or Latino men) and having a very liberal or radical political ideology. I profile three of these students in the following pages.

Beth: "Being a White Male I Guess You Don't Realize Shit Unless It's Shoved in Your Face"

Beth was a student at WU at the time of the interview. She grew up in southeast Portland in a lower-middle-class neighborhood and, although she classified herself as middle class, she acknowledged that while she was a child, her parents were not "making a whole lot." This element, the fact that her father was a supervisor in a factory and had only a high-school diploma, and the neighborhood where she grew up suggest Beth had a strong working-class influence in her formative years.

Beth was exposed early on in her life to people from many backgrounds. Of the four friends she mentioned from her childhood, one was half black, another was an adopted Thai, and another was Chinese. Among the four friends she mentioned having had in middle school, one was a girl from Trinidad and another was from China. Although Beth had only dated white males in her life (one had some Native American ancestry but, as she pointed out, "he doesn't appear as stereotypical minority, he just looks white"), she acknowledged having had a "major crush on a black guy in middle school." When probed on this matter, Beth stated she did not make a move because she was "too shy." In addition, she mentioned that this black boy dated one of her white friends later on, which made her "so mad."

Beth described herself politically as "very liberal" and, based on what she said throughout the interview about a number of social issues, the label fit. For instance, she supported interracial marriage strongly. Beth's answer to the interracial question was different from those of most whites:

I don't think that there is a problem with it at all. Yeah, it's going to be different when the races are not so able to clearly define anymore. I mean, it's going to be a whole new identity for us to label again, but I don't know, I think the labeling just after a while, its going to become obsolete.

Her views on affirmative action were equally strong. For example, Beth said in reference to a white male in one of her classes who opposed affirmative action that, "Being a white male I guess you don't realize shit unless it's shoved in your face." Furthermore, Beth mentioned that she told this student the following in reference to his view on affirmative action:

I said, "Well, if you think it's a quota system, well you're wrong" and that maybe it's hard to see what these people go through all their life and, I mean—me too, being female, what you go through, just the slight discrimination here and there, this like common slur, you don't understand that. You just think it's a harmless joke, but it's not. It builds up [*giggles*]. He was just not getting it.

Beth understood that discrimination affects the life chances of minorities and even supported programs compensating minorities for past discrimination, because "it's hard to start when you have hit rock bottom, it's hard to climb back up." Although three of the other progressive students had difficulty understanding the significance of school and neighborhood integration, Beth argued that "integration can change [people's] hearts" and that "if people learn to get along they can, but if they're kept apart from each other they won't know how to communicate."

Yet, as with all the progressives in the sample, Beth's radicalism had some limitations. For example, although Beth had an impressive level of interaction with minorities before she entered college, she acknowledged, "I don't have a lot of contact with minorities here." Beth also interprets affirmative action exclusively as a program to guarantee equal opportunity for minorities to compete fairly with whites or, in Beth's words, as a program that "just gives them the chance to at least try."[7] Despite this limited interpretation of affirmative action, Beth supported providing unique educational opportunities for minorities because "many won't get a chance otherwise in any way, shape, or form" and supported hiring the minority applicant in two of the hypothetical cases of the ABZ company. Also, when asked if the decisions of this hypothetical company could be regarded as reverse discrimination, she said, "Well, look at the workplace. It's 97 percent white and who is getting the preferential treatment?"

Mandy: "I Think That It Is People Who Oppose Interracial Relationships Based on the Problem They Would Have with Kids [That] Make the Problems for Their Kids"

The second case is Mandy, a half Cherokee[8] student from WU. She was one of the few students who acknowledged in the survey as well as in the interview that she came from a working-class background. Mandy reported that she lived in "a section of town that was considered to be for all the white trash." Mandy, who is married, described her household as "poor" and stated that she and her husband earned less than $20,000 a year.

In the survey Mandy pointed out that she was "extremely liberal" on economic and social issues and said in the interview she had participated in feminist organizations as well as in groups defending the rights of gays and lesbians. Although she grew up in an area she described as "98 percent white," she indicated she had Native American, black, and Asian friends. She dated a black man and mentioned that he "is still a very good friend of mine." In line with this history, Mandy supported interracial unions in a strong fashion.

> I think that it is people who oppose interracial relationships based on the problem they would have with kids [that] make the problems for their kids [*laughs*]. I have a lot of friends who are in interracial marriages and they have children and those children are well loved, they are well socialized, they know who they are, where they come from. And I just think it's people who oppose it who create the most problems.

Mandy was very clear about the impact of discrimination on racial minorities and narrated two incidents she witnessed to illustrate her position. One of these incidents reveals how clearly she understands the new face of discrimination.

> I was in a country store and I had my backpack, which was empty. And I was trying to figure out something to take to a pot luck for school, and I was in there forever, walking around, and the guy at the counter didn't care. And I could've stuck anything in my backpack if I wanted to. So I went up to pay for the item, "Well, how are you doing ma'am?" and "Are you having a good day?" And all of sudden, I saw his face change and he was looking past me, and he just had this weird look on his face. So I turned around and there was a black man standing behind me. He went over to the guns, picking out a gun. And I'm standing there with money in my hand, and this guy goes, "Can I help you?" to the guy. He says, "Do you need something, Sir? Is there anything you need?" And just kept looking at him. And so I said, you know, "Here's my money [*laughs*] if you want to take it." And he's all so sorry and

he's taking my money, but he's still keeping an eye on this guy. And I looked at the guy and he had this look on his face that just broke my heart because you could tell that he has to deal with this and I have never had to deal with that.

Because Mandy understood that discrimination happens today, she was one of the few whites who supported providing some kind of financial compensation to minorities for past discrimination, either through government programs or direct payments.

Although Mandy hesitated in her support of affirmative action in the direct question, her answers to the specific ABZ company decisions were positive. For example, whereas most whites thought hiring a black job candidate who scored slightly less than a white on a test amounted to reverse discrimination, Mandy opined "the country had a history of hiring only white people over black people, then it's about damn time they hired a black person and, if it is discriminatory toward the white person, too bad." She was also one of the few who pointed out that "five percentage points wasn't enough of a difference in terms of score." When asked about the notion of reverse discrimination, Mandy said: "Discrimination in reverse? The minute you were born in this country white male you have so many more privileges than the rest of the people, it's unbelievable."

Of the 41 college students, Mandy was the most consistently racially progressive respondent (see the beginning of this chapter for the discussion of the elements involved in classifying respondents as "progressives"). The only troublesome issues in her answers were a comment about her being "a little hesitant" if she had to sit at an all-black table, her overt concern with merits as the basis for affirmative action programs, and the fact that she described her extended family as "very racist." Although the story was not delivered as an ideological testimony (it did not use the trinity formula; see chapter 4), having family members who are "very racist" bears on anybody's life. My point is not to make her racist by association. Instead, I suggest that having family members who are "very racist" imprints some of her actions and views whether she wants it to or not. For example, she acknowledged her family had "a hard time" when she dated the black man. She also acknowledged that her brother believes he has been a victim of "reverse discrimination," although she disagrees adamantly with him on this issue. However, on the latter issue, she used arguments similar to those of her own brother to support affirmative action. Thus, Mandy's associations with her family will continue to be a part of her social milieu, as few people can dissociate themselves totally from the important people in their lives.[9]

Kay: "I've Been Going Out with the Same Guy Since My Sophomore Year in High School. He's Black"

Kay was a sophomore at MU when she was interviewed. As with most racial progressives, Kay is from a lower-class background. She grew up in Cassopolis, a small but very diverse community in Michigan. Kay stated that the community was "30 to 40 percent black" and "10 to 20 percent" Laotian. She had minority friends while growing up and attended the local public school, which was more than 50 percent minority.

While at MU, she was dating a young black man from Cassopolis with whom she had been since high school. Her association with this black man brought her into contact at MU with other people of color. Therefore, Kay's answer to the interracial marriage question was: "I don't see anything wrong with it." Kay appreciated racial diversity and stated:

> I think it's a very good thing, because I'm glad that I came from a diverse environment. Because the white friends that I do have here, like, came from Catholic schools that were all white and all girls, and it's just—they are *so* different from me, and they are *so* sheltered. And I'm really glad and, like, proud of where I came from.

She also supported affirmative action and connected it to her own admission to MU.

> Because I'm, like, compared to lots of other people, my grade point average isn't high and it's good they look at other, like, your activities and not just your grade point average, because that doesn't reflect, you know, how good of a student you are, just your grade point average. You know, they need to look at lots of other things.

Kay was one of the few respondents in the two studies who understood that affirmative action was not just about race and that many colleges admit a portion of their students based on criteria other than grade point average and SAT scores. Nevertheless, Kay was the most tenuous racial progressive among college students. For example, even though she supported affirmative action and claimed that diversity had been very important in her life, she objected to the hypothetical ABZ company hiring an equally qualified black over a white applicant for diversity concerns.

> Well, I guess if I was, like, put in the situation and, like, I think about if I was in that situation, if *I* was the applicant, *I* would be very upset. If I found out that was the reason, you know, I don't think that's a very good reason. Just because, you know, we have a lack of diversity. I mean, you need, I don't know [*laughs*] I'll just shut up [*laughs*].

All of Kay's answers to the questions about the hypothetical ABZ company were problematic and similar to those of most whites. This was also the only subject in the interview that made her hesitate to the point of becoming rhetorically incoherent (see chapter 3).

Kay also opposed busing and used the frame of abstract liberalism to explain her stance. When asked if the government should intervene to make sure school integration becomes a reality, she said: "I think people should be able to go to school where they want to go to school. I mean, not be forced to have so many, you know, so many black people at this school, so many Asian people at this school, you know, that's difficult." Kay's specific view on busing was: "I don't know if you've heard of Benton Harbor, Michigan. Like, they bus the black people *in* from there *to* their school because their community is, like, all white. I don't know exactly why they did it, but I just think it's kind of ridiculous."

Finally, as with most whites who dated or interacted heavily with blacks, Kay's parents objected to it. For instance, she explained "my parents always told me that I could be friends with black people, but I couldn't date them." As in Mandy's case, this fact of Kay's life does not condemn her to racism for life, however, racialized considerations will affect her decision-making process in the future, so long as she interacts with her family.

PROFILES OF RACIAL PROGRESSIVES: DETROIT AREA RESIDENTS

Although I classified eight DAS respondents as racial progressives, four were distinctly more progressive than the others. As with the college students, these respondents were mostly women (7 of 8), from working-class or lower-middle-class backgrounds (6 of 8), and had an interracial lifestyle. I profile two of the most progressive whites from the 1998 DAS first, followed by two somewhat less progressive ones.

Sara: "Why [Was the Company 97 Percent White]? Because That's, Well, the Fact There Is Racism"

Sara is an unemployed woman in her twenties who was born and raised in Detroit city in a low-income neighborhood. She characterized the diversity in her neighborhood as "just a bunch of different people." This description corresponds to the friends she had: one Arab, one black, one white, and one Mexican. Sara still lives in the neighborhood she grew up in, which she describes as "all low-income" and as very racially diverse. The schools she attended were also diverse and her best friend was a black girl named Bridget. She and Bridget hung out together in school and even skipped classes together.

Sara's interracial lifestyle included having "an affair with a black guy," whom she described as "real sweet." Although later on she clarified that this "affair" was "just a date," Sara seemed to truly have an interracial life. For example, her current boyfriend was "Hispanic" and her own sister was marrying a black man with whom she had had two children. Therefore, her answer to the interracial marriage question was a straight "I think if you love that person, it's your business; no one else has a right to say anything."

Her answers to the discrimination question were consistently progressive. She believes blacks experience daily discrimination and that they are not more lazy than whites, and even supports the idea of government spending on blacks' behalf to compensate for past discrimination. Sara, as many of the poor and uneducated whites in the sample, had very little knowledge about programs such as "busing" or "affirmative action" and could not provide sensible answers to questions about them. Yet, when affirmative action–type hiring situations were posed to her through the hypothetical ABZ company, she opposed the three decisions. Nevertheless, she was one of the few whites who, when asked to explain why this company was 97 percent white, said, "*Why?* Because that's, well, the fact there is racism." Furthermore, she expressed a strong view against whites who are angry about an almost all-white company hiring blacks:

> I couldn't, I couldn't say that they should be angry about it. You know, but, you know, they should try to, they need more black people in there, yes they do. They have to have the fairness to because if they, if they can do that *job*, then let them have that job. Don't—I think that's so stupid about the discrimination bullshit [referring to whites who claim they experience discrimination].

Sara's answer to the last question of the interview, "If you were the president of the USA, what would you do to eliminate racial inequality and ease racial tensions?" was yet another example of her progressiveness:

> [*raises her voice*] I would put down that it should be equal to each and every person that's out there. Equal school, equal jobs, everything should be equal. I don't think one should get more than another. It should be right down the middle, equal. Equal to them both.

When asked if there was anything else she wanted to add, Sara said: "Um, I know a lot of people out there don't believe in whites and blacks mixing in marriages and stuff, but I think that's wrong. I think that if they love each other, then that's their business. I think people should leave them alone."

Sue: "I Suppose If You Keep Running Your Head into the Wall, After a While You Just Say, 'No More'"

Sue's class background is confusing. Although she grew up in an upper-middle-class household, she seems to be in a different class today. Sue is a retired school teacher in her early fifties, but as many older, single adults, has experienced a step back in her class status. She described her current job situation as follows: "I do real estate and estate cleanup on the side [*laughs*] to supplement my income so that's about where I'm at. Or for free rent or whatever, like, I'm here for free rent [indecipherable] paint it up, clean it, no bills. That'd be a good business for you [*addressing the interviewer*]."

Sue seems to have had a mostly white network of associates from childhood until adulthood, but she pointed out that she became (and still is) close to the "cleaning lady" that worked for her father and that "I had friends at college of color and I never had any problem with it." Later on, she referred to her "black acquaintances" and the "hard way to go" they have in the workplace. Although Sue's connections to blacks are tenuous, they are real. For example, she remained in contact with the "cleaning lady" who worked for her father after the employment situation ended.

Sue believes discrimination is an important factor explaining blacks' status and she acknowledged that, "People have not given them the chances." She said she had seen this since early on in her life with the "Kentucky and hillbilly attitude." When asked if laziness had anything to do with blacks' contemporary situation, Sue answered:

> I don't think it's true. I think many of 'em work twice as hard as [*indecipherable*] because it's made so difficult for them. Others, I don't know if I agree with this or whatever, I suppose if you keep running your head into the wall after a while you just say, "No more."

Sue supports affirmative action, believes that being white is an advantage, and thinks that whites' anger about it stems from their fear of losing control.

> I think because they feel they're gonna loose control of what they assume is a weaker entity of society. And I don't think they want them to have the opportunities to become equals, because they don't want them sitting next to them in the country club or sitting next to them in the office place. They just like to keep 'em right where they are at, underneath their feet. You know, I think a lot of it is fear. Because I think anger is repressed fear, it's

repressed. Fear, they are scared and I don't know why, you know, what its cause is; it's obviously their background, too.

But as all white racial progressives, Sue had some contradictions. First, her stance on interracial marriage was not very progressive. Although Sue stated that, "I don't have a problem with it" and pointed out that there are several members of her family in interracial marriages, she also said: "I wonder about the children, if it's fair because society I don't think gives 'em a fair chance and sometimes I feel sorry for the kids. I have some empathy there, I don't know about—reserve my judgment on that."

Furthermore, Sue herself would not get involved in interracial marriages because of "a very bad experience with a [black] man that worked for my father in our home." Although she says that now she feels "very comfortable with men of color," she has not been able to "totally erase that."[10]

Sue also interpreted some of the differences between whites and blacks as biological. For example, although Sue believes the differences between whites and blacks are "cultivated," she said that "the fat, wider noses makes them, it's easier for them to [be] high altitude runners." Later on, she added, to accentuate her position, that "I mean, I have no rhythm, I mean, black friends of mine [have it]." Fortuitously, she ended this problematic discussion by saying "I think they do get a lot of practice."

Lastly, Sue's mostly white network of interaction and the fact that her boyfriend and some of her friends are prejudiced, must affect her cognitions and views. For instance, why would a racial progressive date (and remain with) someone who is "prejudiced"? Do the views of her prejudiced boyfriend and friends affect her own views? Can associating with color-blind or outright Jim Crow–prejudiced whites muffle Sue's racial progressiveness? Susan admitted that "my boyfriend, he's prejudiced" and, as part of her answer to the question on white advantage, said that her boyfriend says "he wishes he was a black woman, you know, 'cause [*laughing*] he'd be up many levels." Sue stated she supports affirmative action, but used the frame of abstract liberalism to oppose *all* the hiring decisions of the hypothetical ABZ company. Once again, I am not suggesting she is guilty of racism by association. However, my point again is to underscore that networks of social interaction matter whether actors are aware of it or not.

Staci: "Probably Because of Racism"

Staci was a school custodian in her fifties. She grew up in Troy, Michigan, in a middle-class community (her parents even owned a small cottage in northern Michigan). The majority of her networks until she began her life as a worker were completely white. However, Staci has worked as a hair stylist and now works as a custodian, which has brought her to a high level of interaction with blacks over the past 25 years of her life. Although Staci has never dated across the color line, she has no objections to interracial marriage. In her answer to the question on this matter Staci included just a minor qualification:

> I think it's just fine. You know, if you find someone that, you know, is your soul mate, I see nothing wrong with it whatsoever. It's a—I think it's probably difficult because of the way other people will, you know, view you but if they're a strong enough person to handle that, then I think it's just fine.

Staci believes discrimination against blacks is daily and pointed out how she thinks it happens.

> Probably in a million different ways: from buying something at, you know, waiting in line just to buy—not waiting in line but at a counter to buy something at a store and maybe you're the first [to] buy [and] you don't get waited on, you know, in proper sequence or. . . . You know, I hadn't experienced it myself, so it's hard to say but I'm sure there's many ways for that to occur.

When asked why blacks are worse off than whites, Staci answered point blank, "Probably because of racism." She also believes being white is an advantage and described white-skin privilege as follows:

> Things are more accessible to you, you know. You don't walk into somewhere and you're not automatically judged by your skin color. You know, you're just more or less accepted until, you know, people find out whether or not they like you and if they're going to give you the benefit of the doubt, you know, second chances like that. That would be an advantage.

Nevertheless, color-blind racism has affected racial progressives too. Thus, Staci believes blacks do not deserve any special government assistance and used the "The past is the past" story line to punctuate her view: "people have to let go of the past." To explain her stance on reparations, she used yet another story line: "You've got the Irish, your Italians, all kinds of people that came over here to this country that weren't treated nicely when they first arrived and, you know, you can't give reparations to everyone that has been mistreated." Staci also opposed busing and believed residential segregation is "more a matter of economics than anything" (this is the "Anything but racism" semantic move). When pressed in a follow-up question on this subject, she used the abstract liberalism frame and said that "the government can't start telling people where to live" and that residential choice was "one of the things you strive for in life to be able to, you know, live in a neighborhood where you want, to go to schools that you feel would be right for your children and I don't think that's any of the government's business where people live." Finally, Staci also opposed affirmative action and two of the three ABZ company hiring decisions.

Judy: "I'm for It [Affirmative Action] a Little Bit, Not Real Dramatically"

Judy is a college professor of nursing in her forties. She grew up between Kalamazoo and Royal Oak, Michigan, areas she described as "mainly Caucasian." Her neighborhood as well as school friends while growing up were all white, but that changed in college as she developed friendships with black women. She meets once a month with one of her black friends to have dinner, share life stories, and "trade poems." In her current job, most of the staff and 30 percent of the professors are black. When asked if she interacts with her black peers, she said: "Oh yeah! I interact pretty heavily with the minority faculty because I chair the cultural relations committee in our college, so I've done that for the last couple of years so I *deliberately* engage them in conversation and interaction."

Judy realizes discrimination is still important and described various examples of old- and new-style discrimination. For example, Judy said that a black man told her that he was not served "at Henry Ford Hospital" because he was black. Judy also said that many blacks are used as guinea pigs because they are black and poor. Finally, she mentioned that a black woman told her that when she shops in the suburbs "she notices that people won't give her change in her hand" because they are "fearful of her and that bugs her to death." As with many racial progressives, Judy's experience as a woman helped her empathize with blacks' plight. For instance, while explaining how the few blacks that move up in society "feel always on display," she connected it to her experiences as a woman:

> It's kind of like women, you know. I have to be that much better just because of various conditions and practices that occur. So in that way I can understand it because it's difficult being a woman in this society. It is planned, it's organized by men. It's set up for them and we've had to struggle to become equal. It's just that way for people of color.

Although I classified Judy as a racial progressive, almost all her answers to crucial racial questions were not completely progressive and, on occasion, they were not different from those of most whites. For example, her answer to the interracial marriage question was typical:

Oh, I have—I think its acceptable. Naturally, its [*lowers voice*]—the [*raises her voice*] problems with it I think only occur as it surrounds the kids and growing up in a culture that does not support, you know, such a—it doesn't really support interracial marriage, our culture. So I think that the couple is—are adults when they take this on and it's a choice and they know what they are doing and [I] think they have more struggles because they don't really have a culture that says, "OK, great, whoever you are is fine!" So that's kind of a problem; that's the biggest problem I see.

When asked if she would have considered interracial marriage herself, she said: "I don't think at the time I married I would [have], which would have been, you know, twenty-five years ago." However, she added immediately that, "Currently I would."

Similarly, on the crucial question of affirmative action, Judy said that, "I'm a little bit for it, not real dramatically." She then proceeded to state that it is a "temporary solution," that "it's bad" when "it's used for quotas," that it should not be used for "*real jobs*," and that it is not "consistent with the rest of the marketplace values." Therefore, when asked if she thought affirmative action was unfair to whites, Judy said that "it can be unfair to whites" when it is used in the workplace. She also had lots of difficulties accepting any of the hiring decisions of the hypothetical ABZ company.

Finally, she could see almost no role for the government in dealing with racial inequality or residential and school segregation. Throughout the interview, when asked to specify a solution to these problems, Judy suggested education and dialogues as the solutions. For example, Judy's solution to residential segregation is "town meetings." The government intervention she favors is "day-care centers and schools and I think maybe more education programs would be best." Judy also stated that she liked Bill Clinton's racial dialogues because "we need to dialogue about this rather than trying to fix it through these, like affirmative action program[s], after the fact." And when asked what she would do to eliminate racial inequality and ease racial tension if she were the president of the United States, Judy said, "Start with educational programs" and "Keep the education coming and spend money on it."

CONCLUSION

In this chapter I profiled white racial progressives. Contrary to those who hold the "commonsense" view on racial matters, racial progressives are more likely to come from working-class backgrounds. Specifically, I found that young, working-class women are more likely than any other segment of the white community to be racially progressive. They were more likely to support affirmative action and interracial marriage, have close personal relations with minorities in general and blacks in particular, and understand that discrimination is a central factor shaping the life chances of minorities in this country. Most also admitted that being white is an advantage in this country.

Although these respondents were substantially different in their views from most whites in these two studies, many of their views denoted the influence of color-blind racism. For example, all these respondents, though to various degrees, have been influenced by the frames of color blindness and, hence, on some issues had *exactly* the same views as most whites. Many had problems with affirmative action programs and policies; a few had serious problems with them. Others pondered the "problems" children of interracial couples would face. Yet others thought residential and school decisions ought to be left to "people's choices" and, thus, saw no reason for governmental intervention on these matters.

Elsewhere I have argued that whiteness is *"embodied racial power"* because "all actors socially regarded as 'white' . . . receive systemic privileges just by virtue of wearing the white outfit whereas those regarded as nonwhite are denied those privileges."[11] However, the wages of whiteness are not equally distributed. Poor and working-class whites receive a better deal than their minority brethren, but their material share of the benefits of whiteness is low, as they remain too close to the economic abyss.[12] Hence, white workers have a powerful reason to exhibit more solidarity toward minorities than whites in other classes.

But if this is so, why have most workers in the United States been historically antiblack, antiminority, and anti-immigrant?[13] I believe the answer has to do with the interaction between race and gender. It has been white *male* workers who have historically supported the racial order. Why? Because whether in periods of economic security or insecurity, white masculinity has provided white men with economic and noneconomic benefits.[14] During good times, working-class men have been "the kings of the castle" (the home) and, during bad times (when "their" women have had to work in the paid labor force), they have been able to maintain a sense of control by demanding a traditional patriarchal organization of the home and by "patrolling neighborhoods" and the family from racial "pollution" (see reference on Fine and Weis in note 14).[15] The white male bond[16] thus has prevented working-class white men from joining progressive racial movements en masse.

In line with this argument, one can also understand why white women are the most likely segment to express solidarity with racial minorities. Since systems of domination are always "articulated,"[17] actors who experience multiple oppressions are more likely to share literally a "social space" as well as a set of experiences that tend to develop a sense of "commonality."[18] Since the 1960s, the percentages of racial minorities and white women in the working class have increased. According to Yates (2005) the majority of minimum wage workers and workers making no more than a dollar above the minimum wage are women (nearly 60 percent in either case). Furthermore, research by Mitra Toossi (2002) illustrate that by 2050 the share of white non-Hispanics in the U.S. labor force will decrease from 73 to 53 percent. In contrast, blacks are expected to increase their numbers in the workforce from 12 percent to 14 percent and Hispanics and Asians are expected to more than double their numbers in the labor force (from 11 to 24 percent for the former and from 5 to 11 percent for the latter).[19] The complex workings of contemporary racialized capitalism have created a situation in which white women and racial minorities increasingly share similar class conditions in the workplace[20] as well as social debasement, a situation that already is producing high levels of joint political action in a variety of areas.[21]

In my two projects, racially progressive women, one after the other, used their own experiences of discrimination as women as a lens through which to comprehend minorities' racial oppression. It was also clear that their shared class vulnerability with minorities (such as bad jobs and low wages) was involved in their racial progressiveness and it may even be the reason why they were the most likely subgroup of all the whites in these samples to have dated across the color line. As Gordon Allport argues, race contacts among *equals* lead to better race relations.[22]

Besides the class/gender background of this group of whites, what other attributes do they share that may explain their high propensity for racial progressiveness? First, most of these respondents grew up in racially mixed neighborhoods. Although growing up in "integrated" neighborhoods does not necessarily lead to racial progressiveness (e.g., Bob, a respondent from SU, grew up in an integrated neighborhood), it increases the likelihood of equal-status contacts between whites and people of color, which may in turn increase the likelihood of whites appreciating minorities as their equals. Second, and maybe related to the first attribute, almost all these respondents had minority friends while growing up. As I pointed out in chapter 6, whites' own racial segregation and isolation leads them to a white habitus that impedes the development of empathy toward people of color and fosters a sense (and the views that accompany this sense) of "us versus them." This "(white) racial solidarity" is less likely to develop among whites who have real friendships with minorities, because race "can be a function of experiences and ties";[23] the more positive experiences and ties whites have with people of color, the more likely they are to see them in their full humanity. Third, many of these respondents were, in general terms, either politically progressive or radical. Hence, they were able to make connections that few whites are able to make (e.g., connecting patriarchal, class, and racial oppression).

Fourth, many of these respondents had dated across the color line. Although dating or marrying someone of a different race does not translate into beliefs of racial equality (e.g., Scott, a 23-year-old mechanic, had dated Asian and Arab women but regarded them as racialized and sexualized objects), the work most people in these relations do *before* and *during* the interaction requires dealing with many of the central racial aspects of American society.[24]

These findings can be used for research and politics. Other researchers must examine systematically whether or not my findings can be replicated. They may lead us away from the idea that racial tolerance is increased through mere education and into more specific formulations on what education does and does not do and for whom. We should also examine whether or not the four additional variables I mention above (growing up in mixed neighborhoods, having black friends, being politically progressive, and dating across the color line) do in fact increase, separately or together (what social scientists call "the interaction effect"), the likelihood of being racially progressive. Politically, my findings point to the need of a new kind of working-class politics in America (see chapter 8). If working-class women are more likely to be racially progressive, organizations seeking progressive social change must rethink their politics. It may be that, after all, class will be the uniting factor in progressive politics, but it will be class solidarity through race and gender prisms.[25]

If racial progressives are influenced by color-blind racism, are blacks influenced too? That is, are blacks as color blind as whites—progressive or not? Do they use the frames of color-blind racism as much as whites? Do they resort to the style of color blindness when expressing their racial views? Do blacks use the racial stories of color blindness to punctuate their racial positions? I examine these matters in the next chapter.

NOTES

1. On antiracist whites from 1619 until the Civil War, see Herbert Aptheker, *Anti-Racism in U.S. History: The First Two Hundred Years* (New York: Greenwood, 1992). On white women in the struggle for racial equality, see Gerda Lerner, *The Grimké Sisters from South Carolina. Rebels: Pioneers for Woman's Rights and Abolition* (New York: Schocken, 1967). On whites in the struggle for equality in the twentieth century, see Manning Marable, *Race, Reform, and Rebellion: The Second Reconstruction in Black America, 1945–1990* (Jackson: University Press of Mississippi, 1991).

2. I borrow the phrase "white traitors" from the journal *Race Traitors*.

3. Lawrence Bobo and Fred Licari Bobo, "Education and Political Tolerance: Testing the Effects of Cognitive Sophistication and Target Group Affect," *Public Opinion Quarterly* 53, no. 5 (1989): 547–59; Lincoln Quillian, "Group Threat and

Regional Change in Attitudes toward African-Americans," *American Journal of Sociology* 102, no. 3 (1996): 816–60.

4. My finding corresponds to the recent findings of two social psychologists who studied high-school seniors from 1976 to 1992. They point out that these young women were "more willing to be friends with people of other races, to live near them and work with them, and to have their future children associate with them." Monica Kirkpatrick Johnson and Margaret Mooney Marini, "Bridging the Racial Divide in the United States: The Effect of Gender," *Social Psychology Quarterly* 61, no. 3 (1998): 247–58. See also Emily W. Kane, "Racial and Ethnic Variations in Gender-Related Attitudes," *Annual Review of Sociology* 26 (2000): 419–39.

5. Jack Levin and Jack McDevitt, in their 1993 *Hate Crimes*, suggest that, "Hate crimes are more often committed under ordinary circumstances by otherwise unremarkable types—neighbors, a coworker at the next desk, or groups of youngsters looking for a thrill" (5). The authors also report an increase in racist attitudes and violence among white students across America. See *Hate Crimes: The Rising Tide of Bigotry and Bloodshed* (New York: Plenum, 1993). For a scathing critique of white middle-class liberals who blame the problem of racism on poor whites, see chapter 10 in Jim Goad, *The Redneck Manifesto* (New York: Touchstone, 1997).

6. See Eduardo Bonilla-Silva, "Rethinking Racism," *American Sociological Review* 62, no. 3 (1997): 465–80. For a more accessible formulation, see Joe R. Feagin, *Racist America: Roots, Realities, and Future Reparations* (New York: Routledge, 2000).

7. If affirmative action programs do not include goals, concerns about how race affects the scores of minorities in examinations, and a true interest for diversity, affirmative action is no more than window dressing and it does not make a significant dent in narrowing the gap between minorities and the majority. See Edward Dorn, *Rules and Racial Equality* (New Haven, Conn.: Yale University Press, 1979).

8. Mandy was in our sample because on the survey question on racial identity she identified herself as "white." She also added that she "looks white."

9. We noted in the interviews that when people said that their family was "racist," "conservative," or "very racist," that this had a bearing on their own racial views. For example, on many occasions the respondents even quoted some of the racist members of their families as sources of authority on an issue.

10. This is a racialized interpretation of the sexual incident. Although most white women experience terrible things with white men, it is when they have such encounters with blacks that they develop "negrophobia." That is, when white men molest them, they do not develop "whitephobia." On this point, see Alexander Thomas and Samuel Sillen, *Racism and Psychiatry* (New York: Brunner/Mazel, 1972).

11. Eduardo Bonilla-Silva and Ashley Doane Jr., eds., "New Racism, Color-Blind Racism, and the Future of Whiteness in America," in *Whiteout: The Continuing Significance of Racism,* (New York: Routledge, 2003).

12. I agree with David Roediger that white workers receive a psychological wage from whiteness, but I insist that they receive other important material incentives too (better jobs and more job security, slightly higher wages, better access to

good schools and neighborhoods). If the "wages of whiteness" were just psycho-logical, one would expect more whites to become "white traitors." See David Roe-diger, *The Wages of Whiteness* (London: Verso, 1994).

13. See David Goldberg, *The Color of Politics: Race and the Mainsprings of Ameri-can Politics* (New York: New York Press, 1997).

14. See Michelle Fine and Lois Weis, *The Unknown City: Lives of Poor and Working-Class Young Adults* (Boston: Beacon, 1998); Lillian B. Rubin, *Families on the Fault Lines: America's Working Class Speaks about the Family, the Economy, Race, and Ethnicity* (New York: HarperCollins, 1994); and Dana D. Nelson, *National Manhood: Capitalist Citizenship and the Imagined Fraternity of White Men* (Durham, N.C.: Duke University Press, 1998).

15. This is not a novel argument. See Catherine Clinton, *The Plantation Mistress* (New York: Pantheon, 1982).

16. I owe this concept to David G. Embrick, who studied the various forms of exclusion of minorities and women in a bread company while he was a graduate student in sociology at Texas A&M University.

17. For a discussion on the notion of articulation, see Jennifer Daryl Slack, "The Theory and Method of Articulation in Cultural Studies," in *Stuart Hall: Critical Dialogues in Cultural Studies,* edited by David Morley and Kuan-Hsing Chen, 112–27 (London: Routledge, 1996).

18. Pierre Bordieau, "Social Space and Symbolic Power," *Sociological Theory* 7 (Spring 1980): 12–25.

19. Data from Mitra Toossi, "A Century of Change: The U.S. Labor Force, 1950–2050." *Monthly Labor Review* (May 2002) and David Roediger, "What If Labor Were Not White and Male?" For similar claim, see pages 179–92 in David R. Roediger, *Colored White: Transcending the Racial Past* (Berkeley: University of California Press, 2000; London: Verso, 2002).

20. See Barbara Reskin and Irene Padavic, *Women and Men at Work* (Thousand Oaks, Calif.: Pine Forge, 2002).

21. David Roediger, *Colored White.* See also Robin R. Kelley, *Yo' Mama's Disfunk-tional: Fighting the Culture Wars in Urban America* (Boston: Beacon, 1997). For a sim-ilar argument, see Joe R. Feagin and Hernán Vera, *White Racism: The Basics* (New York: Routledge, 1995).

22. Gordon Allport, *The Nature of Prejudice* (New York: Doubleday, 1954).

23. Rachel F. Moran, *Interracial Intimacy: The Regulation of Race and Romance* (Chicago: University of Chicago Press, 2001), 81.

24. On this point, see Beverly Daniel Tatum, *"Why Are All the Black Kids Sitting Together in the Cafeteria?": And Other Conversations about Race* (New York: Basic, 1997), 96.

25. "Class is not a unified group, and people similarly situated in this social space will not necessarily form specific groups or organizations. Yet the complex historical workings of capitalism create changing conditions, physical spaces, and opportunities for people to engage in a range of possibilities of resistance in a variety of different kinds of collectivities. Class as serial structure constrains and enables action, but does not determine it." Sonya O. Rose, "Class Formation and the Quintessential Worker," in *Reworking Class,* edited by John R. Hall, 133–66 (Ithaca, N.Y.: Cornell University Press, 1997), 151.

7

◯

Are Blacks Color Blind, Too?

Survey researchers are mostly in agreement about blacks' racial attitudes. Although they all underscore that blacks share basic elements
of "Americanism" or the "American Creed," such as the belief that those
who work hard will be compensated in life, they also point out that blacks
have vastly different positions than whites on central racial issues.[1] For
example, in surveys blacks and whites consistently have polar views on
issues such as the significance of discrimination in America, the merits of
affirmative action, support for certain government programs, and busing.
Surveys even find significant differences in the level of support for interracial social interaction (twenty percentage points on some items).[2]

The survey results of the 1998 DAS are in line with these findings too.
For instance, whereas 53 percent of whites stated their preference for
neighborhoods that are "all" or "mostly" white, only 22 percent of blacks
preferred neighborhoods described as "all" or "mostly" black. In fact, 62
percent of blacks preferred neighborhoods described as "half and half."
Regarding the policy of busing, 69 percent of whites opposed it, compared to 26 percent of blacks. On the hot issue of affirmative action, 50
percent of whites stated they would support a proposal similar to that
passed in California in 1996 to eliminate affirmative action, if such a proposal were put on the ballot in the state of Michigan. In stark contrast,
only 6 percent of blacks said they would support such a proposal. Finally,
whereas 56 percent of whites agreed that this country has experienced a
lot of racial progress, only 29 percent of blacks agreed with this position.

Have these observed attitudinal differences between blacks and whites
been corroborated in qualitative studies? The answer to this question is
not clear, because qualitative studies of blacks' attitudes are sparse,
single-issue driven, and based on segments of the black community, and
they usually do not cover a wide range of racial issues. Most qualitative

data on blacks' views are part of larger studies on the woes of the black upper or middle class, the working class, the working poor, or the black underclass.[3] Other qualitative research on blacks addresses specific aspects of their lives, such as their experiences in historically white colleges or with interracial friendship.[4]

Given the limited number of systematic, qualitative studies of blacks' views, in this chapter, using interview data I gathered as part of the 1998 DAS, I examine black Detroiters' racial views. My specific goal is to assess the extent to which blacks rely on the frames, style, and racial stories of color blindness to articulate their positions. I recognize, however, that the relatively small size of the sample (N 17) limits the possibility of generalizing from this study. Yet, because the cases were randomly selected from a randomly chosen larger sample (see chapter 1), I believe the results are robust and will be corroborated in studies with larger samples of blacks.

I proceed as follows: first, I assess the influence of the frames of color blindness on blacks; second, I examine the extent to which blacks rely on the style of color-blind racism; finally, I explore whether or not blacks have adopted the racial stories of color-blind racism.

SLIGHTLY COLOR BLIND: COLOR-BLIND RACISM'S FRAMES AND BLACKS

Do blacks endorse the frames of color-blind racism? Do they use its frames as the foundation upon which to articulate their views on racial matters? Content analysis of the interviews with black and white DAS respondents suggests blacks are significantly less likely than whites to use the frames of color blindness directly. As table 7.1 shows, whereas all these frames are essential to whites' explanations of racial matters, only three (abstract liberalism, cultural racism, and naturalization of racial matters) have impacted blacks' consciousness.

Because the direct effect of the frames of color-blind racism on blacks is minimal, it is plausible to argue that blacks and whites navigate two totally different ideological worlds and thus that color-blind racism is partially ineffective. However, an ideology is not dominant because it affects all actors in a social system in the *same* way and to the *same* degree. Instead, an ideology is dominant if *most* members (dominant and subordinate) of a social system have to accommodate their views vis-à-vis that ideology.[5] If an ideology dominates the space of what people think is feasible and thinkable, and even provides the parameters to oppose the status quo, then that ideology is dominant. In this section I analyze how the different frames of color-blind racism have affected blacks. My main contention is that color-blind racism has affected blacks *indirectly* and that this has consequences for the likelihood of blacks developing an all-out oppositional ideology to color-blind racism.

Abstract Liberalism and Blacks

Abstract liberalism is the explanatory well from which whites gather ideas to account for residential and school segregation, limited levels of interracial marriage, and a host of other racial issues. Slightly more than a third of the blacks in this study used this frame directly in their answers.[6] I will illustrate in this section how this frame has affected blacks' views on two issues, namely, affirmative action and school and residential segregation.

Affirmative Action

Affirmative action has become emblematic of racial tensions in contemporary America. Not surprisingly, the frames of color blindness had very little direct and indirect influence on blacks on this important subject. Blacks overwhelmingly expressed support for affirmative action and other race-targeted programs and rebuked white opposition to them. A typical response to the question "Are you for or against affirmative action?" was that of Edward, an unemployed man in his fifties:

> I'd say that I would have to be for affirmative action simply because you still have ignorant people. Some of these ignorant people are in control and have a little more power than I'd like to think they should have in regards to what they can do to prevent other people from having opportunities that means that they can't have growth and development. Affirmative action is a means and method. Then it's like a key when you got a locked door. You've got to have it.

When asked, "What would you say to those who say affirmative action is unfair to whites?" Edward responded: "I tell them that 'What do you call fair?' If you got everything, it's kind of like saying you are upset because you got ice cream and you don't have a cone. Then put it in a bowl, you already got everything. Don't worry about it."

Regina, a poor homemaker in her early fifties with little formal education, expressed her support for affirmative action in clear terms. Her answer to the affirmative action question was "I'm for it." In the followup question about whether affirmative action could be regarded as unfair to whites, Regina stated: "Well, I say the colored race have had a *hard time* all they lives and the whites, it's been easy for them. I think they should give them [blacks] a break."

Finally, Joe, an electronic technician in his thirties, echoed the views of

Table 7.1   Deployment of Color-Blind Frames by White and Black Respondents, DAS 1998

Frames	Whites	Blacks
Abstract Liberalism	64/67 (96%)	6/17 (35%)
On Affirmative Action	59/67 (88%)	1/17 (6%)
Cultural Racism	59/67 (88%)	4/17 (24%)
Naturalization	27/67 (43%)	4/17 (24%)
Denial of Discrimination's Systemic Nature	56/67 (84%)	1/17 (6%)

the previous respondents on whites' concerns about the unfairness of affirmative action: *"They need to wake up and smell the roses."*

Only one black respondent, Irma, an accounting clerk in her early thirties, opposed affirmative action. She explained her opposition to affirmative action in a way that resonates with how whites explain their opposition to this program: "Affirmative action [*draws out the words*], I guess I would say I'm against because I believe you should have the equal opportunity not just be given something just because of your race. I think it's just for equal opportunity." However, Irma's stand on affirmative action was more complex than this answer suggests. For instance, Irma believes discrimination is an everyday matter and she provided personal examples. When asked, "Have you yourself experienced that type of discrimination," she said "[*answers immediately*] Oh yeah, umhum." At the interviewer's request, Irma elaborated about her personal encounters with discrimination: "Um, we've experienced discrimination in our neighborhoods growing up as kids walking down the street. Police officers were, you know, call you names, you know, the white race would call you names, throw chocolate milk at you." Consistent with this answer, Irma supported the decision of the hypothetical ABZ company, described as 97 percent white, to hire a black over a white candidate to redress past discrimination. And when she was asked, "What do you say to those who think that this is preferential treatment," Irma replied,

> We say some blacks take so much discrimination that sometimes, I guess, we deserve a break. But I still think that given, put on the same playing field and same rules and same kind of scores and everything like that, whoever gets the highest scores should be able to fill that position.

Irma realizes that "blacks take so much discrimination," but hopes to live in a society where race does not matter in hiring decisions. Yet, since Irma realizes that employers are not color blind; when asked why she thought the hypothetical company in the question was 97 percent white, she suggested, "Probably 'cause they wanted to keep it like that."

School and Residential Segregation

In contrast to the issue of affirmative action, abstract liberalism had a profound influence on how blacks interpreted segregation. Although a large number of blacks blamed the government, whites, or racism for residential segregation (7 of 17) and a majority blamed them for school segregation (12 of 17) and demanded school equality (in funding and otherwise), blacks' views were not monolithic. Four blacks believed school or residential segregation was "natural," three that blacks had something to do with residential segregation or that it was "no ones fault," and two that racial segregation was not a problem. More significantly, six blacks used the abstract liberalism frame directly to account for school or residential segregation. (Note that the numbers do not add up here because some respondents blamed whites for segregation and still used the abstract liberalism frame or claimed that blacks had something to do with it too.)

First, let me provide one example of how *most* blacks answered the questions on residential and school segregation. Latasha, a self-employed nail polisher in her late twenties, blamed government for the lack of school integration. She pointed out that whereas schools in the suburbs "might get $2,500 per child," public schools in Detroit city "only get $1,000 per child." She asserted in her discussion on busing that "the problem you come about education, it's the money, that's what the main thing is, is the money with the kids." Latasha's concern with the limited funding received by inner-city schools was echoed by most blacks.

Latasha aspires to live in a society where race does not affect people's residential choices, or in her words: "you shouldn't have to single yourself to this area or single yourself to that area because you're [of a] different race." However, because Latasha realizes discrimination has not disappeared in America, her color-blind dream is not like that of whites. After stating her hope for a race-neutral housing market, for example, Latasha acknowledged of race that *"sometimes it is"* a factor. More specifically, Latasha commented she has experienced discrimination herself while shopping in downtown Detroit. Therefore, she supported government intervention to guarantee blacks access to all neighborhoods and programs to improve the neighborhoods where most blacks live.

Although most blacks blame whites or the government for the high level of segregation in the United States, their views are more mixed and contradictory. For example, Tyrone, an unemployed man in his early forties, supported school and residential integration. Tyrone stated his support for residential integration, a choice supported by 62 percent of blacks in the survey, as follows: "I think all the neighborhoods should be mixed. Then every—then there wouldn't be no concept of how different people are. They would know how each race would be." However, Tyrone opposed government intervention to guarantee residential integration: "Well, you can't tell people where [to] live. They got to pay for their own house, so people are going to live where they want to live. So you can't do that." Tyrone used the abstract liberalism frame ("you can't tell people where to live" and "They got to pay for their own house") to oppose doing anything about one of the central factors behind blacks' contemporary plight in America.[7] Interestingly, Tyrone, as I will show below, was a strong supporter of government intervention on many other racial matters.

Tyrone's contradictory position on this issue was not unique. For example, Mark, a bus driver in his thirties, recognized the role of white violence in the maintenance of school segregation. Yet he opposed government intervention to increase residential integration.

> No more than if blacks or whites attempt to integrate an area and are faced with, are faced with . . . [*Mark whispers to himself: "I can't think of the word"*] aggression when attempting to do so. And I can't say necessarily the federal government, but on a local level, they should be afforded every protection or opportunity that they deserve and that is their right.

Mark's answer, particularly his insistence on governmental intervention to guarantee individuals' access to housing markets, is almost verbatim the standard answer offered by most whites to this question.

One good example of how abstract liberalism has blurred blacks' views on some issues was provided by Nel, a retired janitor in her early seventies who thought racism was an important force behind neighborhood segregation. However, Nel believed blacks were partly responsible for this situation.

> Well, [the] only thing I can say is, I believe the whites don't want to live around blacks and some of the blacks don't want to live around the whites. It is because they have, well, they have a chip on their shoulder. I think a neighborhood is much better when it's mixed, you know. We got the little thing that's racism. That's what causes a lot of this, too, between black and white.

The consequence of interpreting neighborhood segregation as the outcome of people's choices ("some blacks don't want to live around the whites") is that Nel did not see any role for government to help remedy this situation.[8] Hence Nel stated in a pessimistic manner the following about the prospects of the government redressing residential segregation in America: "They go [*laughs*] ah, if they were right it would be good if they could do something about it, but I don't see much [they can do]."

Finally, one extreme example of blacks' reliance on abstract liberalism to explain segregation is Carla, an executive secretary in her forties. She believed that school segregation was a matter of choice:

> I think it's everybody's fault except for the government. White people and black people choose to put their children in [the] school that they wanted them to be into and a lot of time you go into a school and they say "there's a lot of black people enrolled and I'm going to send you to this one" or "it's more white people here than black so I'm going to send you to this one." So it's more so the parents' fault.

For Carla, neighborhood segregation is the product of people's choices. Therefore, she does not believe anything can be done about it. She says of the prospects of changing the situation: "Nothing, I mean, nothing as far as showing anybody anything or telling anyone anything. They will only do what they want to do so you can tell them and stress it but if they choose not to, they won't."

Cultural Racism and Blacks

Whites' cultural explanation of blacks' standing in America affected directly only a few blacks (3 of 17). The typical black respondent argued this is a ruse used by whites to hide their role in blacks' contemporary situation. For example, Jimmy, a social worker in his forties, explained blacks' lower standing compared to whites as follows:

> Because the whites are in the majority and all and they're in a position of power. They got the wealth, they do the hiring, they [are] the employers opposed to the employees. They—we have the last hired, the first fired, and we get the lowest jobs and those [are] the things that perpetuate those situations and all.

Another example of blacks' typical responses to this question is Trisha, a homemaker in her early forties: "I wouldn't say they lazy. I think they just say you lazy 'cause you black. But I don't think they is. They just don't want to give them a chance to prove themselves that they can achieve more."

Despite the fact that few blacks bought completely this cultural explanation, this *bounded* the way many blacks discuss issues such as discrimination or the specific charge that they are lazy. The direct and indirect influence of this cultural frame in the interviews did not come as a total surprise, since in the survey a significant proportion of blacks agreed with many stereotypes about blacks. For instance, 32 percent of blacks agreed with the proposition that blacks are "violent," 32 percent with the idea that blacks are "lazy," and 30 percent with the notion that blacks are "welfare-dependent" (50 percent, 20 percent, and 53 percent of whites agreed with these stereotypes, respectively).

The two examples below illustrate how this frame has bounded blacks' views. First is Vonda, a homemaker in her late fifties with very little education. She explained blacks' lower standing compared to whites in the following way: "Ah. [*8-second pause*] I don't know, I don't know how to answer that one. Maybe if they get off their butts and get an education like white, I don't know. Maybe that's it."

When asked specifically if she believes blacks are worse off than whites because they are lazy, Vonda stated, *"Yeah, I think they probably more and more lazy than white are."* Although Vonda's answer sounds much like those of whites on this issue, it is important to point out that she agreed with the majority of blacks on most of the other issues.

Next is Regina, a homemaker in her early fifties who shared most positions on race issues with the majority of blacks in the sample. Yet, the cultural theme framed the way she explained why blacks are worse off than whites in this country.

> Well, I don't think they [lack] the proper, you know, things to succeed, but the ones that wants to have, they can have. But it's just some don't want to have anything. They can't blame it on other person, *which I don't.* I don't blame it on anyone 'cause I don't have anything. I blame it on myself 'cause I think I should have did better when I was coming up and got a better education.

Nevertheless, Regina, as most blacks, believes discrimination is important and stated without hesitation and with emphasis that being white is still an *"Advantage!"* When she was asked, "Why?" Regina replied, "Because of they *color.*" In her responses to the questions on discrimination, Regina said blacks experience "a lot of discrimination" and that the reason why blacks have a lower standing than whites is because "they don't have the education that they should have."

There are two significant things to underscore about Vonda's and Regina's answers. First, both accept the cultural premise to explain blacks' status in America (laziness is a central reason why blacks are behind whites in this country) although Regina limits it to some blacks. The second point is that, as most blacks, both of these respondents believe discrimination is a central factor behind blacks' current standing in America. Their puzzling stance (believing that blacks are lazy but that discrimination is central) exemplifies how color-blind racism has affected some blacks on central racial matters.

Naturalization of Racial Matters and Blacks

Although blacks do not have a cohesive view on segregation, their explanations of why segregation exists are different from those of whites. Most blacks point out that whites have something to do with segregation or that whites do not want to live or share resources with blacks. For example, Jimmy, the social worker cited above, said about school segregation:

> Yeah, I think the mixing of the races in the school, to me, is probably the whites' fault, to me. And, if it's a better school, and blacks try to go there and all, I think they are not really welcome and given an opportunity to [develop] and then they don't get the—In the inner city and all, it's not—the schooling the funding or whatever is not the same. If it was equal here in the black and white areas and all, they might not even want to go there. But I think this, if they, [when] they try to go to better schooling, I think they're prohibited from going there more so by whites and the government and all.

Yet, some blacks (3 of 17) relied on the naturalization frame mixed with abstract liberalism to explain segregation. For instance, although Jimmy underscored the role of discrimination in school segregation, he attributed neighborhood segregation to natural tendencies in people.

> Well, I'm sure that people clique by choice and all. I mean whites tend to stay with whites because they're comfortable. But given, you know—I'd say if we tried to mix a little more, we might tend to get together more and all, integrate more and all, but as it stands now and all, we tend to be comfortable [with] our race and that's the way it generally goes.

Natasha, a licensed practical nurse in her early thirties, blamed the government for the low level of school integration in this country "because they make the laws." She also supported busing because it is "a good thing because you get to know about other peoples' cultures and their way of living." However, Natasha believes neighborhood segregation is the product of peoples' natural choices or, in her own words:

> I really don't [think about this situation] 'cause I move basically [*giggles*] where I can afford it. I don't think that any one race shouldn't be allowed anywhere in this world. It's a free country, so. I think they just choose to be with *their* kind. Blacks choose to live around blacks and whites choose to live around whites.

Therefore, when asked if she believes the government can play a role in remedying residential segregation, Natasha said,

No, but I think that [there] shouldn't be any limitations on that one man, one black woman moving into an all-white neighborhood. He shouldn't get treated any different. But I know that [*lowers voice*] [I am] fantasizing [*very loudly and giggles*]. I mean, you never know, it may work out. I really don't think the government should get into it because I don't think they'd say, "OK, this is a white [*raises voice*] neighborhood," you know what I'm saying? Like I said, people tend to segregate together."

The third respondent who used the naturalization frame was Mark, the bus driver cited above. Mark believes school segregation is maintained by whites—often through violent means—to the detriment of "many bright African American students in urban areas [who do] not have the means to get to predominantly white schools to be afforded greater learning experiences." However, Mark explained neighborhood segregation as the outcome of natural tendencies in people.

It's something that's gonna naturally occur. And both because of economic and social grievances, there are gonna be some whites that are economically better off than other whites and other blacks and they are gonna want to be along with other races. And that holds true with both blacks also.

Minimization of Racism and Blacks

Notwithstanding how color-blind racism affects blacks' understandings of various racial issues, the reality of discrimination is such that few blacks believe discrimination is no longer very significant. An overwhelming majority of blacks stated that antiblack discrimination is still central in America. In the survey questions regarding this issue, blacks' answers confirming discrimination were twenty to thirty percentage points higher than those of whites. More significantly, 61 percent of blacks, compared with only 33 percent of whites, agreed with the statement "Blacks are in the position that they are as a group because of present day discrimination."

Blacks' answers to the questions about discrimination in the in-depth interview were as strong, if not stronger, than their answers in the survey. For example, Tyrone, the unemployed man cited above, said about blacks facing discrimination:

I think sometimes you do. 'Cause I used to work in Sterling Heights [a neighborhood in Detroit]. I used to be out their waiting on the bus, somebody would drive by and call me a "black-ass nigger" at least three times out of the week [*laughs*] and I'm just trying to work and come home [*Interviewer: Wow!*].

Likewise, when he was asked why he thinks blacks have a lower standing than whites in America, he cited racial discrimination as a factor:

> Well, 'cause who is the boss? He want to give you the worse job 'cause of the color of your skin. I been through that up in Sterling Heights. Me and Dwayne was the only two blacks in the maintenance department. Me and Dwayne got the nastiest jobs they was. They go, "Go get them they'll do it!" And they'd come get me and Dwayne. Me and Dwayne got the nastiest jobs.

Accordingly, Tyrone was a strong supporter of affirmative action, government programs for blacks, and even of reparations. He stated his support for reparations as follows:

> They should get something [*raises his voice*], they should get something. They was suppose to give the black man forty acres and a mule. Where's my forty acres of land at or my money that you going to pay me for these forty acres I *was supposed to get?* You know, give me a tractor, give me some money, give me something!

Natalie, a data entry clerk in her twenties, said about whether or not blacks experience lots of discrimination, "I think some blacks do experience it." When asked to give examples, Natalie, as most blacks,[9] narrated a personal experience.

> Yes, I agree with that because I have had, store [*stutters slightly*] people that work in stores follow me around [*raises her voice*] "*May I help you?*" you know, they do it in a way that you, if you weren't paying attention, you wouldn't think that they were following you but they are, and they tend to follow black people more than they do other people.

Consistent with her view on discrimination, Natalie believes blacks are worse off than whites because of "racism" and thus supported government intervention on blacks' behalf. Her response to the question on whether government should intervene on blacks' behalf was:

> Yes, because they tend to have, they [*raises her voice*] have *programs* for other people who suffered past discrimination. They help like Japanese people and stuff, so why can't they help us? I mean, basically, the reason that we were discriminated against and people from Japan were discriminated against their own people by their own people, but we helped them out. Why they can't help some black people like they do them?

Other respondents narrated incidents typical of post–Civil Rights discrimination.[10] For example, Jimmy, the social worker cited above, said of discrimination:

Well, I think it's real and it's true and all and if you really—it's just hard to get the evidence and put it on the table and expose it and all. But examples are like when you see a black and a white go out together to apply for an apartment and the white get told one thing and given the better break and the black being told the opposite thing and a worse break. It's just one way to expose it and all. But it is real and it does exist and it's just hard to uncover and all.

Latasha, the self-employed nail polisher cited before, answered the question about the significance of discrimination for blacks in a personal way:

You do, you do, you really do because you have some people that just won't let it go. You know, they put on a lot of front and a lot of air and you have some people that just won't let go and some people just won't hide it. They'll slap it right in your face and do it right in front of you.

When asked if she could provide any examples, she narrated how her own supervisor avoids dealing with her directly and relegates this task to some of her white coworkers.

Thelma, a widow in her late sixties, answered the discrimination question by saying: "By whites? [*Interviewer: Or by whomever, yeah anyone.*] Yeah!" When prompted to say more on this subject, Thelma said: "Because it's like me or you go to a job and apply for a job, right. They turn us down and this white man or white female walks up there and they hire her like this. So that's discrimination right there!"

One of the scariest incidents of overt discrimination was narrated by Edward, the unemployed forty-one-year-old man cited above. As part of his explanation about the interactions he used to have with whites in jobs, he narrated the following incident:

I even had an argument when I was hired at Cross Company, and guess what it was about? They said how violent we were and I was commenting about "Well, look, man, y'all ain't no different." And guess what? I had somebody jump up behind me—and we are in an engineering office—and he called me. And who I thought was a fairly decent person, I thought who I was on good terms with. And they started this conversation about racism, about the difference between black and white people. It wasn't me. I'm the only black person in the office. I'd exchanged my viewpoint with people in the office. He jumps up and he wasn't necessarily being insulted. He jumps us and calls me an African Nigger. He comes around the drafting board and I coaxing him along because I'm thinking that he's not gonna do anything. But the guy swings at me and clips me in the jaw.

So far I have shown that blacks believe discrimination is salient, that it affects them personally, and that it operates in crude and subtle ways. Yet, the minimization of racism frame has affected how *some* blacks think about discrimination. For example, most whites regard discrimination *exclusively* as old-fashioned, one-on-one racist behavior by whites against minorities and, therefore, think discrimination is declining in significance. Some blacks agree with this view and do not think discrimination is important. For instance, Carla, the executive secretary mentioned above, answered the discrimination question by stating: "I don't experience ah, did you say racial discrimination? I don't experience discrimination in daily life, maybe on one or two occasions but not" every day.

Other blacks who regarded discrimination as overtly racist behavior believed that only blacks who work with whites experience lots of discrimination. For example, Alma, a homemaker and part-time worker, answered the discrimination question as follows:

Well, if they are [giggles], I mean, that's kind of hard to say for everybody because on the average most people don't be around another race every day in order to consider discrimination. But probably a person that works on [a] mixed, you know, with whites and blacks, it's well, yeah those I've heard have the discrimination.

Yet other blacks qualified their answers ("some blacks experience discrimination, but . . .") and used the cultural and abstract liberalism frames to explain the status of blacks. For instance, Natasha, the practical nurse cited above, answered the discrimination question as follows: "I'd say [*high-pitched voice*] some probably do, they probably do. It depends on what plan in their life, where they are, besides their job, what type of job, they would get some discrimination." When pressed by the interviewer with the question, "How much do you think it affects, you know, black people, this discrimination, in their daily lives?" Natasha stated:

It don't—it [doesn't stop] anything as far as that goes, you know. You know what I am saying? You might have to deal with it, but you have to keep going. I don't think it really puts an impact on it, on your day, or inhibits anybody from doing what they want to do or being what they want to be. That's up to the individuals.

Vonda, the homemaker cited above, could not even assess whether or not discrimination affects blacks a lot: "[*8-second pause*] I don't know how to, you know, I don't know how to answer that one."

THE STYLE OF COLOR-BLIND RACISM AND BLACKS

I suggested in chapter 3 that the style of color blindness is oblique, indirect, subtle, and full of apparent ambivalence and even flat-out contradictions. My main finding in this section is that blacks have not been affected in any meaningful way by the style of color-blind racism. Because the influence of the style of this ideology on blacks is virtually nonexistent in some areas (racist terminology, racial projections, and diminutives), here I examine only its impact in the areas of semantic moves and rhetorical incoherence.

Semantic Moves and Blacks

Whites use a number of verbal pirouettes to avoid appearing "racist." Specifically, I argue that color blindness has a peculiar *race talk* that includes semantic moves in situations in which whites feel they may sound racist. Although some analysts might expect blacks to be as conscious of not being perceived as antiwhite as whites are of being perceived as antiblack, or that they might be as conscious as whites of being seen as having strong racial views, my findings suggest otherwise—a finding that is consistent with previous work.[11] In general, blacks call it as they see it. If they oppose interracial marriage, they are significantly less likely than whites to beat around the bush. If they do not have white friends or do not associate with whites, they say so without promoting a white acquaintance to the friend status.[12] If blacks agree or disagree with a policy, they usually state their opinion clearly. I suggest this straightforwardness reflects the fact that blacks have very little to hide—or very little to lose—in the contemporary racial order.[13] Whereas in slavery or Jim Crow, blacks had to be "stage Negroes"[14] if they wanted to survive, as a consequence of new norms, whites now have to be "stage whites." Therefore, being at the bottom of the racial order in post–Civil Rights America gives blacks at least the freedom to speak their minds.

An area that potentially could have made blacks defensive and brought out some rhetorical hesitation was the issue of "reverse discrimination." Nevertheless, blacks were clear in their beliefs that this idea is nonsense. Jimmy, the social worker cited above, said that whites who talk about "reverse discrimination" are "just hollerin'." Jimmy's response to a question about whether or not the decision of a hypothetical company hiring a black over a white job candidate was discriminatory against whites[15] was as follows:

> Yeah it's discriminating against whites, but in the sense that you already got all the power of a position and all. And it's like you're a hundred percent and all and if I say go down to 97 percent you'll holla' you're discriminating against me and all. But, you know what I mean, you need some discrimination [*laughs*].

Although Jimmy interprets affirmative action as "discriminatory," he believes it is necessary to improve blacks' status. Malcolm, a construction worker in his forties, expressed views similar to Jimmy's and in a straightforward manner as well. For instance, when asked about his view on affirmative action, he answered "I'm for it." His response to a follow-up question asking if he thought this program was unfair to whites was: "Well, racism affects all blacks but affirmative action affects a certain percentage of whites. So you really can't compare. You know, like this, they call it anti-[*lowers his voice*] discrimination or, you know, you can't compare the two."

Although most blacks answered the questions without filtering them through the rhetorical maze of color blindness, a few answered questions using phrases similar to those of color blindness. However, I suggest these respondents, unlike whites, were not trying to buffer polemical or racist views. Instead, they were usually pointing out contradictions between the way things *ought to be* and the way things *are*. For example, Tyrone, the unemployed worker I cited before, used what could be seen as the "Yes and no" move to explain his view on affirmative action.

> Well one way I'm for it, one way I'm against it. Now, if everybody had equal chance, there's nothing against the color of your skin or nothing, we wouldn't need affirmative action. But by the way not giving people chances, we need it. You gotta have something, you know, to help.

Although his answer seems to include the "yes and no" move ("one way I'm for it, one way I'm against it"), Tyrone does not hesitate at all in stating that because America is not color blind, we need affirmative action ("You gotta have something to help"). By contrast, when whites used the "Yes and no, but" move, they added other phrases to signify ambivalence and insecurity (e.g., "I am not sure" or "I don't know), even when they were making a strong case one way or the other (see chapter 3). Tyrone did not do that. Further evidence that Tyrone was not ambivalent or trying to hide his views on affirmative action discursively comes from his answer to the question about whether or not the decisions of the hypothetical company were discriminatory against whites. His answer was: "How can they discriminate against whites when the employment is 97 percent white? That's no discrimination! You got 97 percent white people and 3 percent of a different race."

In the same vein, when he was asked to explain why so many whites seem to be angry about affirmative action, Tyrone replied in a way that is consistent with his strong support for affirmative action:

> Well some of them figure out that they are not getting a fair chance. Some of them don't like it just because it's helping the blacks. But to me, you know,

like I said, if we all had a fair chance, we wouldn't need affirmative action. They ought to know. See, they not black and how can they say this is what they go through? They ain't never been black. They ain't never been through what we go through.

Another semantic move that has become quite popular among whites is "Some of my best friends are black." I did not find a single black respondent who used the analogous phrase "Some of my best friends are white." Whereas whites used this phrase to inflate their associations with blacks and, occasionally, to be able to say something very negative about blacks, blacks did not resort to similar phrases to state their views about whites. For example, blacks who did not have white friends had no problem stating it. The following examples illustrate how blacks who did not have white friends described this situation. Mark, the bus driver previously cited, when questioned about whether or not he had close white friends in school, responded: "At Renaissance I didn't have any close white friends. I had some that I interacted with that were associates and acquaintances." Later in the interview, when asked if he had white friends on his current job, Mark said "I can't say I have any friends. I have those whites that I associate with basically on the job." Natasha, the young practical nurse cited above, when asked, "Did you have any close white friends in school," replied: "Ah no, I didn't have any." Regina, the homemaker cited above, stated in no uncertain terms that she did not have white friends while growing up: "No, not down [*raises her voice*], not in Louisiana. No."

Rhetorical Incoherence and Blacks

Most whites in these studies were incoherent at some point in the interviews because of the racially sensitive nature of the subject of discussion. In contrast, when blacks were incoherent, it was because either that was their usual speech pattern or they lacked knowledge of the issue at hand. For example, whereas the topic of intermarriage led many whites to virtual muteness, blacks stated their views on this matter without much hesitation. Their behavior on this subject corresponds to the survey results. Fifty-eight percent of whites and 88 percent of blacks in the DAS survey approved of interracial marriage. However, when the question was "Suppose your own child married (a white/a black) person. Would you mind it a lot, a little, or not at all," 58 percent of whites said they would mind it "a lot" while 32 percent said they would mind it "a little," whereas 84 percent of blacks said that they would not mind it at all, a number that almost matches the 88 percent who approved of interracial unions. This suggests blacks have more consistent views on this sensitive matter and, therefore, may be less likely than whites to try to provide socially desirable answers.

Whether blacks approved of interracial marriage and would do it themselves (8 of 17), approved of it but would never do it themselves (7 of 17), approved of it but pointed out problems the couples might face (2 of 17), or were opposed to these relationships (1 of 17), they stated their answers in a clearer manner than white respondents (numbers add up to 18 rather than 17, because the answer of one respondent fit two categories). Before proceeding with my analysis, I need to add two caveats. First, I am interested in highlighting the *form* or *style* of their answers rather than examining the ultimate meaning of their answers. Second, I must point out the asymmetric interpretation of these questions for black and white respondents.[16] Whereas for whites the question of interracial marriage seems to evoke visceral reactions based on racialized readings of black bodies, for blacks—particularly for older blacks—the question evokes a history of rejection, exclusion, and even the not well-studied social and family training among blacks of avoiding these relationships to stay out of trouble. This means that blacks' and whites' disapproval of interracial marriage means different things because the issue evokes different historical and personal circumstances and reactions.

An example of a black respondent who had no problems with interracial marriage but would not do it herself was Nel, the retired janitor cited above.

> *Interviewer:* OK, thank you. Now can you tell me, I guess the, you know, [who] were the people that you dated and married, were they—what race were they?
> *Nel:* Black [*laughs*].
> *Interviewer:* They were all black?
> *Nel:* Yeah.
> *Interviewer:* All right, thank you. Let's see, now, did you ever have any romantic interest in a white person?
> *Nel:* I never even dreamed, you know, thought of it.
> *Interviewer:* Now why is that?
> *Nel:* I don't know. You're talking 'bout like romance, no? [*unintelligible*] I really can't answer that question.

Nel's answers in this series of questions were, for the most part, very straightforward. Only on the last question, dealing with why she did not have any romantic interest in whites, did Nel not provide a satisfactory answer. However, the demeanor, tone, and rhetoric used by Nel and the other respondents to questions in this category suggest they were not trying to hide or distort their feelings and opinions on this sensitive matter.

Nel's straightforward style, for example, surfaced even when she was asked her opinion on interracial marriage. Nel's answer was a simple: "I don't think there's anything wrong with it." When the interviewer asked Nel to explain this answer, she stated "I don't see anything, really, I don't see any difference no more than the skin tone." Although this answer *could* be interpreted as a baseless one similar to that of most whites, Nel did not qualify her support for these marriages, as most whites did. Moreover, Nel added the following piece of information that bolstered the credibility of her answer: "But now I have a brother who's still [alive] and his [white] wife. And they was just so nice, you know. They lived up in Minnesota but they were nice, you know. Maybe that's why I don't think anything about it, you know."

Eight black respondents approved of interracial marriage and said they would do it themselves. Their answers to the interracial questions were similar to that of Irma, the young conservative accounting clerk previously cited:

> *Irma:* I, it doesn't matter to me. If, if the persons [are] in love, then it don't matter.
> *Interviewer:* Would you yourself have considered marrying someone from a different race?
> *Irma:* Yeah if I had, if the opportunity were, yeah I guess.

An extreme example of blacks who subscribed to this view is Carla, the executive secretary previously cited. She is also an example of how straight blacks were in answering the interracial marriage question. Her answer was: "If you like it, I love it." Asked if she would consider marrying outside her race, she said "Yes." These answers were unusual for blacks but fit Carla's answers on this and other subjects. For example, when Carla was asked if she had ever had any romantic interest in people of other races, she said "[I] always wanted to." And when she was asked if she had ever been interested in whites, she said "Yes."

Black respondents who opposed interracial marriage said so without much hesitation. For instance, Joe, an electronic mechanic in his forties, opposed interracial relationships without hesitation:

> *Interviewer:* Did you ever have any white relationships?
> *Joe:* No.
> *Interviewer:* Did you ever have any romantic interest in a white person?
> *Joe:* No.
> *Interviewer:* And why would you think that is so?
> *Joe:* My preference.
> *Interviewer:* Is your spouse the same racial background as you are?
> *Joe:* Yes.

Interviewer: People have mixed feelings about marrying outside their race. What is your view on this delicate matter?

Joe: [*clears throat*] I feel people of the same race should stay together instead of interacting.

Interviewer: So you yourself would not consider marrying someone or would not have considered marrying someone of a different race?

Joe: I would say that. I would say that.

Joe answered all these difficult questions the same way he answered all the questions throughout the interview: in a short and precise manner.

Of all the blacks in this sample, I found only two who hesitated in a notable way on the interracial marriage question. The hesitation of one of these respondents came when the interviewer asked him a question that was not part of the interview protocol. Malcolm, the construction worker cited above, hesitated somewhat in his answer to the question "Did you think you could see yourself having a romantic interest in another black person here?" Malcolm's answer to this question was "I probably would. I, I, if it happened like that, then I'd say either way." The interviewer posed this rather unusual question to Malcolm, a man in his forties, because he described himself as a "solitary person" but said he had dated a few women while he was in the "service" in Germany and *all of them* were white! His hesitation, then, could be attributed to the interviewer addressing a sensitive issue but on a different front: a forty-something man not involved with *any woman* (was he concerned that the interviewer was checking his sexual orientation?) or his exclusive interest in *white* women (was he concerned that the interviewer thought he was a negrophobic black?).

RACIAL STORIES OF
COLOR BLINDNESS AND BLACKS

In chapter 4 I documented the salience of four color-blind story lines, namely, "The past is the past," "I didn't own any slaves," "I did not get a (job/promotion) because of a black man," and "If (ethnic groups such as Jews and Italians) have made it, how come blacks have not?" I also discussed the role that testimonies or personal stories have in the color-blind ideology. I argued that racial stories help whites seal tightly their larger color-blind fable by providing gut-level, emotional arguments to validate some important myths about race relations in America. Notwithstanding that color blindness has tainted the way blacks formulate many issues, based on my analysis of the 17 interviews it seems that blacks are not buying into these stories in any significant way. I could not detect any influence of the latter two story lines, even among conservative black respondents, and I could detect none whatsoever of testimonies. Nevertheless, the story lines "The past is the past" and "I never owned any slaves" affected one black respondent directly and four indirectly.

The first two stories, which tend to appear together, were used directly by Carla, the conservative executive secretary. She answered the question on reparations as most whites did:

> That became [a] topic in school. I don't remember what I said but right now I feel that was so long ago that the people who are here now didn't have anything to do with it. So I don't feel it would, I mean, you can say you're sorry but it's not, it's not going to take back what happened. Therefore, I don't think it's necessary.

Although these stories and their logic affected very few blacks directly, they affected four blacks indirectly. For example, Natasha, the young practical nurse, answered the question on reparations as follows: "Yeah, I think so. But are there any of those people around? Would it go to that, to those surviving family members?"

Although Natasha supports reparations, she seems influenced by the idea that only people who were *directly* affected by slavery can demand compensation. This idea, mentioned by many white respondents, operates under the assumption that discrimination is a matter of a distant past that does not affect blacks' life chances today. If discrimination ended in the 1860s, then blacks who were affected by it are long gone and reparations and other forms of government intervention on blacks' behalf are unnecessary.

Another example of the indirect influence of these stories is Edward, the unemployed 41-year-old man. His answer on reparations was: "Oh bullshit, no, no! I think that America needs to think about its people now and the American people are all kind of folks." Edward exhibits the same emotion as many whites when answering this question ("Oh bullshit, no, no!") and thinks, like most whites, that the issue is helping all Americans now rather than dwelling on the past.

CONCLUSION

In this chapter I examined the extent and ways in which color-blind racism affects blacks. First, I showed that blacks, for the most part, do not subscribe wholeheartedly to the frames of color blindness. Furthermore, I pointed out that blacks have oppositional views on many important issues. For example, they believe discrimination is a central factor shaping their life chances in this country, firmly support affirmative action, and are very clear about whites' advantageous position in this society. However, I also documented that some of the frames and ideas of color blindness have had a significant *indirect* effect on blacks. For example, the frame of abstract liberalism has shaped the way many blacks explain school and residential segregation. Second, I documented that the style of color-blind racism has had a very limited impact on blacks. Whereas whites hesitate and use double-talk to state their views on racial matters, blacks state their views clearly and without much hesitation, even when the topic of discussion is interracial marriage. Finally, I suggested that only two of the four story lines of color blindness have had some impact on blacks. Although most of the impact of these stories was indirect, the fact that 5 of the 17 blacks were directly or indirectly affected by these stories suggests the ideological transmission belt is working well. Thus, I regard the ideology of color blindness as the current *dominant* racial ideology because it binds whites together and blurs, shapes, and provides many of the terms of the debate for blacks.

For students of ideology my findings should not be surprising. Dominant actors (men, capitalists, whites), by virtue of their centrality in the social system and their superior resources, are able to frame the terrain of debates and influence the views of subordinated groups. Therefore, as I argued above, a dominant ideology is effective not by establishing ideological uniformity, but by providing the frames to organize difference.[17] As Nicos Poulantzas wrote about dominant class ideology:

> The dominance of [an ideology] is shown by the fact that the dominated classes live their conditions of political existence through the forms of dominant political discourse: this means that often they live *even their revolt* against domination of the system within the frame of reference of the dominant legitimacy.[18]

Women and workers, for example, may have views that are different from those of men and capitalists, but they share enough of their views and ideas, and more important, the *terrain* of political discourse, so that even their challenges to patriarchy and capitalism fall within the limits of what is "legitimate" for men and capitalists. Women and workers may demand "equal opportunity"—a demand that does not subvert the parameters of gender or class rule—but they are less likely to struggle for proportional representation and rewards in all social networks and institutions or for wealth redistribution.

What is the significance of my findings? On the one hand, my findings reveal in some detail the precise way in which blacks disagree with whites on central racial issues of our time. For example, unlike whites, blacks realize that racism is structural and that lack of power and differential access to rewards is at the heart of America's racial situation. Therefore, they strongly support programs such as affirmative action, despite the relentless ideological campaign against this program. On this, I concur with those[19] who claim that blacks and whites have different views on most racial issues. On the other hand, my findings reveal quite clearly that blacks are influenced *directly* (e.g., the cultural rationale and naturalization of racial matters) and *indirectly* (e.g., the free-market rationale and laissez-faire racism) by the frames of color blindness. For example, although one would expect blacks to have a strong tendency against the "culture of poverty" concept, I found that too many buy into substantial parts of this argument. This ideological infiltration of the frames of color blindness into blacks' political consciousness hinders the development of an all-out oppositional ideology or "utopia"[20] to fight contemporary white supremacy. Thus, because so many blacks are swayed by elements of color blindness, the struggle against color-blind racism will have to be waged not only against color-blind whites, who cannot see the centrality of race in America, but also against the many *slightly* color-blind blacks.

One burning question that many readers may have is whether blacks are as "racist" as whites. To properly answer this question, I need to go back to the theoretical framework that anchors this book: the racialized social-system framework (see chapter 1). My concern has been describing the dominant racial ideology of the post–Civil Rights era in detail and exploring how it affects whites and blacks. In this process, I have avoided moralizing the analysis (attempting to identify "good" and "bad" people). My overall findings are that *most* whites believe this new ideology wholeheartedly and rely on its various elements to articulate their views on racial matters and that a significant number of blacks are indirectly affected by this ideology and use some elements of it, too.

But I do not want to avoid what may be the real question for some readers: are blacks as "racist" (meaning antiwhite) as whites (meaning antiblack)? This question, which was formulated by some white respondents in my studies, has received some legitimacy in liberal and radical circles by the position articulated by Michael Omi and Howard Winant in the 1994 edition of their important book, *Racial Formation in the United States*.[21] In this book, Omi and Winant argue racism amounts to any practice that *"creates or reproduces structures of domination based on essentialist categories of race."*[22] Based on this criterion, they conclude blacks can be "racist," too, and that, in fact, some are. From the racialized social system framework vantage point I have developed, the answer to this question is different. First, the question needs to be rephrased from "are blacks as 'racist' as whites?" to "are blacks as 'prejudiced' as whites." I do so because the concept of "racism," as used by most social scientists and commentators, is grounded on methodological individualism (the separation of "racist" and "nonracist" individuals) and psychologism (assuming "racist" individuals are pathological, whereas those who are not "racist" are normal). In contrast, I have attempted to conceptualize racism as a sociopolitical concept that refers exclusively to racial ideology that glues a particular racial order. Thus, I have suggested that color-blind racism is the ideology of the "new racism" era. My answer, then, to this rephrased question is that any race (or ethnic group) can be "prejudiced" against any other race or races (e.g., blacks can be anti-Jewish and Jews can be antiblack). Regarding the matter of the degree to which blacks are antiwhite, most research suggests they are *less likely* to be antiwhite than whites are to be antiblack. In fact, the most interesting finding on prejudice research is that blacks are almost as likely as whites to believe many of the antiblack stereotypes.[23]

If the question is, "Are blacks *likely* to develop a racialized social system in the United States with blacks as the dominant race?" the answer is absolutely not. Blacks lack the power[24] (organizational capacity and resources) to carry out a nationalist program[25] to create a pro-black racial state. Blacks also lack the demographic capacity (numbers) needed to mount a revolution like blacks did in Haiti in the eighteenth century. In fact, given current changes in the racial demography of the nation (blacks are no longer the largest minority group in the nation), the most likely scenario for the future is that race relations will become Latin America–like, that is, that a new, triracial order will emerge with a pigmentocratic component to it.[26] As a Latin America–like society, any form of race-based contestation will become increasingly more difficult, which, as in Latin America, will allow white supremacy to reign supreme, hidden from public debate.

In the next chapter, I hypothetize what the future of racial stratification in the United States might look like in the future.

NOTES

1. Jennifer Hochschild, *Facing Up to the American Dream* (Princeton, N.J.: Princeton University Press, 1995).

2. Michael Dawson, *Behind the Mule: Race and Class in African American Politics* (Princeton, N.J.: Princeton University Press, 1994); Hochschild, *Facing Up*; Lee Sigelman and Susan Welch, *Black Americans' View of Racial Inequality: The Dream Deferred* (Cambridge: Cambridge University Press, 1991); Howard Schuman et al., *Racial Attitudes in America* (Cambridge, Mass.: Harvard University Press, 1997).

3. On the black upper middle class, see Sharon Collins, *Black Corporate Executives: The Making and Breaking of a Black Middle Class* (Philadelphia: Temple University Press, 1997). On the black middle class, see Joe R. Feagin and Melvin Sikes,

Living with Racism: The Black Middle Class Experience (Boston: Beacon, 1994). An example of work on the black working class is Lillian Rubin, *Families on the Fault Line: America's Working Class Speaks about the Family, the Economy, Race, and Ethnicity* (New York: HarperCollins, 1994). On the black working poor, see Michelle Fine and Lois Weis, *The Unknown City: Lives of Poor and Working-Class Young Adults* (Boston: Beacon, 1998). Finally, on the black underclass, see Elijah Anderson, *Streetwise* (Chicago: University of Chicago Press, 1990).

4. Examples are Joe R. Feagin, Hernán Vera, and Nikitah Imani, *The Agony of Education: Black Students at White Colleges and Universities* (New York: Routledge, 1996) or, on interracial friendship, Mary W. McCullough, *Black and White as Friends: Building Cross-Race Friendships* (Cresskill, N.J.: Hampton, 1998). Two exceptions to this trend are Robert Blauner's *Black Lives, White Lives* and Studs Terkel's *Race: How Blacks and Whites Feel and Think about the American Obsession* (New York: Doubleday, 1993). Although these two books are exceptional examples of interview-based research with blacks, both are based on *unsystematic* samples and lack a rigorous analytical strategy.

5. Mary R. Jackman, *The Velvet Glove: Paternalism and Conflict in Gender, Class, and Race Relations* (Berkeley: University of California Press, 1994).

6. It is worthwhile to point out that blacks subscribed to traditional laissez-faire views (not race related) in the survey at rates similar to those of whites. For example, 94 percent of blacks and 95 percent of whites agreed with the statement, "Any person who is willing to work hard has a good chance of succeeding." Similarly, 59 percent of blacks and 71 percent of whites agreed with the statement, "Most people who don't get ahead should not blame the system; they have only themselves to blame." For similar findings, see Lawrence Bobo and James Kluegel, "Opposition to Race-Targeting: Self-Interest, Stratification Ideology, or Racial Attitudes?" *American Sociological Review* 58, no. 4 (1993): 443–64.

7. Douglas Massey and Nancy Denton, *American Apartheid* (Chicago: University of Chicago Press, 1993).

8. It is important to point out that blacks were significantly more likely than whites to report having friends from the other group (39 percent of blacks reported having one or more white friends, whereas only 13 percent of whites reported having one or more black friends) and to have a preference for living in integrated neighborhoods.

9. Most blacks reported personal examples of old-fashioned discrimination in stores, with coworkers, supervisors, or police, and in encounters with regular white folks.

10. See chapter 3 in Eduardo Bonilla-Silva, *White Supremacy and Racism in the Post–Civil Rights Era* (Boulder, Colo.: Rienner, 2001).

11. Blacks' straight talk on racial matters can be seen in Blauner, *Black Lives, White Lives;* Rubin, *Families on the Fault Line;* and Fine and Wise, *The Unknown City.*

12. See chapter 5. See also Tom W. Smith, "Measuring Inter-Racial Friendships: Experimental Comparisons" (paper presented at the annual meeting of the American Sociological Association, August 6, 1999, in Chicago), in which he documents through survey experiments how whites inflate the number of black friends they have.

13. Based on 1998 research by Public Agenda—a nonpartisan and nonprofit public opinion research organization—with 1,600 white and black parents, the organization concluded that,

> Conventional wisdom in research circles says an African-American moderator is necessary to ensure forthright focus group conversations with African Americans. But one of the earliest observations in this project was that it was far easier for a white moderator to talk with an all-black group about race and schools than for a white moderator to discuss these issues with an all-white group.

In the same report, the organization suggested the following about the implications of whites' silence about their true views:

> But the reticence of white parents to talk explicitly means their fears and anxieties remain beneath the surface. One consequence is that while the views of African-American parents are resolved and focused, the views of whites about race and the schools often seem murky and ambivalent, replete with twists and turns in attitudes that are difficult to unravel because they are sometimes hidden—sometimes not worked-through—and rarely discussed.

See www.publicagenda.org/specials/moveon/moveon8.htm.

14. David R. Goldfield, *Black, White, and Southern: Race Relations and Southern Culture, 1940 to the Present* (Baton Rouge: Louisiana State University Press, 1990).

15. The scenarios were varied (equal qualifications, white slightly more qualified, and decision based on past discrimination by the company) to allow examination of the strength and consistency of respondents' views on this sensitive issue.

16. This is an interpretative problem that plagues survey research. The interpretation of the survey questions and the meaning of the answers often hinge on the respondents' race. Thus, for example, when whites and blacks both agree that discrimination is still important in America, they mean totally different things (see chapter 4).

17. See William H. Sewell Jr., "The Concepts(s) of Culture," in *Beyond the Cultural Turn*, edited by Victoria E. Bonnell and Lynn Hunt, 35–61 (Berkeley: University of California Press, 1999).

18. My emphasis. Nicos Poulantzas, *Political Power and Social Classes* (London: Verso, 1984), 223.

19. Dawson, *Behind the Mule;* Donald Kinder and Lynn Sanders, *Divided by Color* (Chicago: University of Chicago Press, 1996).

20. Teun van Dijk, *Ideology: A Multidisciplinary Approach* (London: Sage, 1998), 182.

21. Michael Omi and Howard Winant, *Racial Formation in the United States* (New York: Routledge, 1994). For disclosure purposes, I argue in my *White Supremacy and Racism in the Post–Civil Rights Era* that "most radical writing on race in the 1990s has been inspired by Omi and Winant" and that "my own theory owes heavily to their work." However, I also point out some of the serious limitations of their "racial formation" perspective. I also wish to acknowledge that Omi and Winant are extraordinarily collegial and generous comrades and that I am

indebted to them in many ways. Yet, I disagree profoundly with them on the matter of "black racism."

22. Omi and Winant, *Racial Formation*, 71.

23. See Lawrence Bobo and Devon Johnson, "Racial Attitudes in a Prismatic Metropolis." For a discussion of the historical roots of why whites are more likely to be antiblack than blacks are to be antiwhite, see Mia Bay, *The White Image in the Black Mind: African-American Ideas about White People, 1830–1925* (New York: Oxford University Press, 2000).

24. I also disagree with Omi and Winant's assertion that blacks have "power." If by power they mean the capacity to enact their racial interest into concrete policies and crystallize it into institutions, blacks have very little power and seem to be losing the little they have by the day. As a matter of fact, given the new racial demography of the nation, blacks are likely to continue losing power in the future. On the concept of power, see Keith Dowding, *Power* (Minneapolis: University of Minnesota Press, 1996), and the always indispensable Nicos Poulantzas, *Political Power and Social Classes*.

25. However, and as one would expect from any oppressed people, blacks have had nationalist tendencies from slavery until today. For a historical analysis of black nationalist forces and programs in the twentieth century, see Roderick Bush, *We Are Not What We Seem: Black Nationalism and Class Struggle in the American Century* (New York: New York University Press, 1999). For a recent analysis of nationalism among blacks, see Michael C. Dawson, *Black Visions: The Roots of Contemporary African-American Political Ideologies* (Chicago: University of Chicago Press, 2001).

26. Eduardo Bonilla-Silva and Karen Glover, "'We are all Americans': The Latin Americanization of Race Relations in the USA," in *The Changing Terrain of Race and Ethnicity: Theory, Methods and Public Policy*, edited by Amanda E. Lewis and Maria Krysan (New York: Russell Sage Foundation, 2004).

8

❧

E Pluribus Unum or the Same Old Perfume in a New Bottle?

On the Future of Racial Stratification in the United States

WHAT DOES ALL THE RACIAL NOISE MEAN? A SKETCH OF THINGS TO COME

L atinos are now officially the largest minority group in the nation. According to the Census Bureau, while blacks comprise 12.3 percent of the U.S. population, Latinos are almost 14 percent.[1] This Latino population explosion, generated by immigration, has already created a number of visible fractures in the United States that seem to be shifting the racial terrain. In academic circles, for instance, conservative scholars have begun attacking the new racial demography as devastating for the future of the country. An example of these scholars is Harvard's political scientist, Samuel Huntington, who in his recent book, *Who Are We? The Challenges to America's National Identity*, argued that Latino immigration threatens Anglo-Saxon American culture as well as the political integrity of the country.[2] And politicians in both parties as well as prominent newscasters such as Lou Dobbs—since 2003 or so, he has addressed every night the topic of illegal immigration in his show *Lou Dobbs Tonight* in his nightly segment "Broken Borders"—[3] and almost all *Fox News* commentators (e.g., Brit Hume, Tony Snow, Sean Hannity, John Gibson, and Fox's most vitriolic newscaster, Bill O'Reilly) articulate and inflame the anti-immigrant fears for the wider public.

In addition to the Latino population explosion, other trends have emerged that challenge our traditional biracial divide (white vs. non-white) and, more specifically, our black-white understanding of racial politics in the United States. For example, another group that has gained visibility in our racial discussions is Asian Americans, partly because of

177

their demographic gains (they are now 5 percent of the population), partly because as a group, they are perceived as doing very well economically and educationally, and, more importantly, partly because they are still viewed by most Americans through the lenses of developments in South East Asia.[4] On this last point, the commercial rise of Japan and, particularly, of China, has generated a fear of the East that can be seen in movies (e.g., *Red Corner* [1997], *Mulan* [1998], etc.), political scandals, and in the way China is discussed almost every night in the news.[5]

Yet another illustration of the changing racial terrain in the United States is our recent national discussion on the status of "multiracial" and "biracial" people.[6] Two events shaped our collective engagement on these matters over the last ten years. First, phenom golfer Tiger Woods, son of a black father and a Tai mother, made a public statement suggesting he was not black but rather "Cablanasian" (a mixture of Caucasian, black, and Asian). This led to a furious public debate on what it means to be "black" or "mixed" and whether or not people could claim a racial identity other than those already inscribed in our racial pentagram (Who had ever heard of such a thing as a Cablanasian)? Second, the struggle by people in the multiracial movement[7] to force changes in the way the Census Bureau gathered racial data—specifically, to include a multiracial category, which coincided with efforts by Republican politicians to end the collection of racial data altogether—ended with the addition of the "More than one race" item in the 2000 Census schedule.

Finally, and related to some of the developments mentioned above, the rate of interracial dating and marriage between Latinos and whites and Asians and whites has skyrocketed.[8] In general, interracial marriage, which accounted for less than 1 percent of all marriages in the country, accounts today for 5.4 percent. Many demographers and a few public intellectuals have heralded this development as signifying the erosion of racial boundaries and maybe pointing the way out of our national racial quagmire.[9]

Thus, as I write this revised edition, we all ponder about what will be the future of race in America. How will the Latino population explosion affect the 300-year-old racial drama of the country? Will Latinos replace blacks as the racial boogeyman[10] or will they become white, as some analysts have suggested?[11] And how will Asians fit in the emerging racial totem pole? Will they be treated as white or vilified as the enemies within, as happened to Japanese Americans during World War II? Or do all these trends signify that I have wasted my time (and your money) writing this book because, as some public commentators have argued, we live in the time of "the end of racism" or, at least, of "the declining significance of race"?[12]

These are the kinds of issues that prompted me to write this chapter.

My basic claim, unlike the romantic predictions of assimilationists[13] or the racialized pessimism of Anglo-Saxonists such as Huntington, is that all this reshuffling denotes that the biracial order typical of the United States, which was the exception in the world racial system,[14] is evolving into a complex and loosely organized triracial stratification system similar to that of many Latin American and Caribbean nations. Specifically, I contend that the emerging triracial system will be comprised of "whites" at the top, an intermediary group of "honorary whites"—similar to the coloreds in South Africa during formal apartheid, and a nonwhite group or the "collective black" at the bottom. I sketch in figure 8.1 what these three groups may look like. I hypothesize that the white group will include "traditional" whites, new "white" immigrants and, in the near future, totally assimilated white Latinos (e.g., former Secretary of Education Lauro Cabazos, the football coach of the University of Wisconsin Barry Alvarez, and actors such as Martin Sheen), lighter-skinned multi-racials, and other subgroups; the intermediate racial group or honorary whites will comprise most light-skinned Latinos (e.g., most Cubans and segments of the Mexican and Puerto Rican communities), Japanese Americans, Korean Americans, Asian Indians, Chinese Americans, and most Middle Eastern Americans Americans; and, finally, that the collective black group will include blacks, dark-skinned Latinos, Vietnamese, Cambodians, Filipinos, and Laotians.

As a triracial system (or Latin- or Caribbean-like racial order), race conflict will be buffered by the intermediate group, much like class conflict is when the class structure includes a large middle class. Furthermore, color gradations, which have always been important matters of within-group differentiation, will become more salient factors of stratification. Lastly, Americans, like people in complex racial stratification orders, will begin making nationalists appeals ("We are all Americans"), decry their racial past, and claim they are "beyond race."

This new order, I argue, will be apparently more pluralistic and exhibit more racial fluidity than the order it is replacing. However, this new system will serve as a formidable fortress for white supremacy. Its "we are beyond race" lyrics and color-blind music will drown the voices of those fighting for racial equality ("Why continue talking about race and racism when we are all Americans?") and may even eclipse the space for talking about race altogether. Hence, in this emerging Latin America-like America, racial inequality will remain—and may even increase—yet there will be a restricted space to fight it.

I must state a few important caveats before I proceed any further. First, figure 8.1 is heuristic rather than definitive and thus is included here just as a guide of how I think the various ethnic groups will line-up in the emerging racial order. I acknowledge, however, that the position of some

Figure 8.1 Preliminary Map of Triracial Order in the USA

"Whites"
> Whites
> New whites (Russians, Albanians, etc.)
> Assimilated white Latinos
> Some multiracials
> Assimilated (urban) Native Americans
> A few Asian-origin people

"Honorary Whites"
> Light-skinned Latinos
> Japanese Americans
> Korean Americans
> Asian Indians
> Chinese Americans
> Middle Eastern Americans
> Most multiracials

"Collective Black"
> Vietnamese Americans
> Filipino Americans
> Hmong Americans
> Laotian Americans
> Dark-skinned Latinos
> Blacks
> New West Indian and African immigrants
> Reservation-bound Native Americans

groups may change (e.g., Chinese Americans, Asian Indians, and, particularly, Arab Americans—on this, please see my comments at the end of the chapter), that the map is not inclusive of all the groups in the United States (for instance, Samoans, Micronesians, and Eskimos, among others, are not in the map), that it is *possible* that more than three racial strata emerge, and that at this early stage of this project and given some serious data limitations, some groups may end up in a different racial strata altogether (for example, Filipinos may become "honorary whites" rather than another group in the "collective black" strata). More significantly, if my Latin Americanization thesis is accurate, there will be categorical porosity as well as "pigmentocracy" making the map useful for group- rather than individual-level predictions. The former refers to individual members of a racial strata moving up (or down) the stratification system (e.g., a light-skin middle-class black person marrying a white woman and moving to the "honorary white" strata) and the latter refers to the rank ordering of groups and members of groups according to phenotype and cultural characteristics (e.g., Filipinos being at the top of the "collective black" given their high level of education and income as well as high rate of interracial marriage with whites). Lastly, since I am predicting the future, I truly hope that we can prevent the crystallization of this racial order altogether or at least derail it partially.

In this chapter I proceed as follows. First, since I am suggesting the United States is becoming Latin America-like, I enumerate succinctly a few of the major features of racial stratification in Latin America. Second, I explain why I contend a triracial system is emerging. Third, I examine a few available objective (e.g., data on income and education), subjective (e.g., racial attitudes and racial self-classification), and social interaction indicators (intermarriage and residential choices) to see if they fit the expectations of my Latin Americanization thesis. Lastly, I discuss the implications of this new order for the racial politics of the future.

HOW RACIAL STRATIFICATION WORKS IN THE AMERICAS

Despite claims of nonracialism ("We don't have racism here. That is an American problem"), racial minorities in Latin American countries tend to be worse off, comparatively speaking, than racial minorities in Western nations. Yet, few revolts in the 20th- and 21st-centuries in Latin America have had a clear racial component (important exceptions such as the Zapatista movement notwithstanding). This apparent contradiction is explained by the fact that race has very limited "discursive space" in Latin America and, in order for people to struggle along an axis of social division, that axis must be visible and real to them. "Prejudice"—Latin Americans do not talk about "racism"—is regarded as a legacy from slavery and colonialism and "racial" inequality (again, Latin Americans and Caribbeans do not believe race is part of their social reality) is regarded as the product of class dynamics.

Since examining the long history that produced this state of affairs is beyond the scope of this chapter, I just sketch[15] six central features of Latin American (and Caribbean) racial stratification.

1) *Miscegenation or "Mestizaje"*

Latin American nation-states, with a few exceptions, are thoroughly racially mixed. Racial mixing, however, in no way challenged white supremacy in colonial or postcolonial Latin America since: (1) the mixing was between white men and Indian or black women, maintaining the race/gender order in place (2) the men were fundamentally poor and/or working class, which helped maintain the race/class order in place; (3)

the mixing followed a racially hierarchical pattern with "whitening" as a goal; and (4) marriages among people in the three main racial groups were (and still are) mostly homogamous (among people from the same racial strata).

2) Plural Racial Stratification Systems

Although Portuguese and Spanish colonial states wanted to create "two societies," the demographic realities of colonial life superseded their wishes. Because most colonial outposts attracted very few Europeans, these societies developed intermediate groups of "browns," "pardos," or "mestizos" that buffered sociopolitical conflicts. Even though these groups did not achieve the status of "white" anywhere, they nonetheless had a better status than the Indian or black masses and, therefore, developed their own distinct interest.

3) Colorism or Pigmentocracy

There is yet another layer of complexity in Latin American racial stratification systems. The plural racial strata are also internally stratified by "color" (in quotation marks because in addition to skin tone, phenotype, hair texture, eye color, culture and education, and class matter in the racial classification of individuals in Latin America), a phenomenon known in the literature as pigmentocracy or colorism.

4) "Blanqueamiento": Whitening as Ideology and Practice

"Blanqueamiento" (whitening) has been treated in the Latin American literature as an ideology. However, blanqueamiento was and is a real economic, political, and personal process. At the personal level, families can be colored or even racially divided and exhibit differential treatment toward dark-skinned members. Thus, rather than showing Latin American racial flexibility, racial mixing oriented by the goal of whitening shows the effectiveness of the logic of white supremacy.

5) National Ideology of "Mestizaje"

National independence in Latin America meant, among other things, silencing any discussion about race and forging the myth of national unity. After years of attempting to unite Latin American nations under the banner of Hispanidad, a more formidable ideology crystallized: the ideology of mestizaje (racial mixing). Although Latin American writers and politicians have praised the virtues of mestizaje, this notion has worked as an ideology to help keep race below the social radar and better safeguard white power.

6) *"We Are All 'Latinoamericanos'":* Race as Nationality/Culture

Most Latin Americans refuse to identify themselves in racial terms. Instead, they prefer to use national (or cultural) descriptors such as "I am Puerto Rican or Brazilian." This behavior is cited as an example of the fluidity of race in Latin America. However, defining the nation and the "people" as the "fusion of cultures" (even though the fusion is viewed in a Eurocentric manner), is the logical outcome of all of the factors mentioned above. Nationalist statements such as "We are all Puerto Ricans" are not evidence of nonracialism, but the direct manifestation of the racial stratification peculiar to Latin America.

WHY LATIN AMERICANIZATION NOW?

What are the reasons behind racial stratification becoming Latin America-like at this point in our history? The reasons, in my estimation, are multiple. First, as I discussed above, the demography of the nation is changing. Racial minorities are now about 30 percent of the population and, as population projections suggest, may become the numeric majority by the year 2050. This rapid darkening of America is creating a situation similar to that of Puerto Rico, Cuba, or Venezuela in the 16th and 17th centuries, or Argentina, Chile, and Uruguay in the late 18th and early 19th centuries. In both historical periods, the elites realized their countries were becoming majority "black" (or "nonwhite") and devised a number of strategies (unsuccessful in the former and successful in the latter) to whiten their population.[16] Although whitening the population through immigration or by classifying many newcomers as white is a possible solution to the new American demography, for reasons discussed below, I do not think this is likely.[17] Hence, a more plausible accommodation to the new racial reality is to (1) create an intermediate racial group to buffer racial conflict,[18] (2) allow some newcomers into the white racial strata, and (3) incorporate most immigrants into the collective black strata.

Second, as part of the tremendous reorganization that transpired in America in the post–Civil Rights era, a new kinder and gentler white supremacy emerged which I labeled elsewhere as the "new racism" (for a quick summary of my argument, see chapter 1 in this book or chapter 4 in my 2001 book *White Supremacy and Racism in the Post–Civil Rights Era*). In post–Civil Rights America the maintenance of systemic white privilege is accomplished socially, economically, and politically through institutional, covert, and apparently nonracial practices. Whether in banks or Universities, in stores or housing markets, smiling discrimination tends to be the order of the day. This "softer" kind of discrimination is in line with the way discrimination operates in Latin America and will ease the transition to a discourse of "racism is declining in significance here."

This new white supremacy has also produced an accompanying ideology that rings Latin America all over: the ideology of color-blind racism. This ideology, as it is the norm all over Latin America, denies the salience of race, scorns those who talk about race, and increasingly proclaims that "We are all Americans." (This is the main subject of this book and thus needs little discussion here.)

Third, race relations have become globalized. The once almost all-white Western nations have now "interiorized the other."[19] The new world systemic need for capital accumulation has led to the incorporation of "dark" foreigners as "guest workers" and even as permanent workers. Thus today European nations have racial minorities in their midst who are progressively becoming an underclass,[20] have developed an internal "racial structure" (see chapter 1) to maintain white power, and have a curious racial ideology that combines ethnonationalism with a race-blind ideology similar to the color-blind racism of the United States today.[21]

This new global racial reality, I believe, will reinforce the Latin Americanization trend in the United States as versions of color-blind racism will become prevalent in most Western nations. Furthermore, as many formerly almost-all-white Western countries (e.g., Germany, France, England, etc.) become more and more diverse, the Latin American model of racial stratification may surface in these societies too.

Fourth, the convergence of the political and ideological actions of the Republican Party, conservative commentators and activists, and the so-called multiracial movement has created the space for the radical transformation of the way we gather racial data in America. One possible outcome of the Census Bureau categorical back-and-forth on racial and ethnic classifications is either the dilution of racial data or the elimination of race as an official category. At this point, Ward Connerly and his cronies lost the first round in their California Racial Privacy, but I believe they may be successful in other states and given the changes in the Supreme Court, their efforts may bear fruit in the near future.

If race disappears as a category of official division, as it has in most of the world, this will facilitate the emergence of a plural racial order where the groups exist in *practice* but are not officially recognized—and any one trying to address racial divisions is likely to be chided for racializing the population. This is, as I have argued elsewhere, the secret of race in Latin America.[22]

Lastly, the attack on affirmative action, which is part of what Stephen Steinberg (1995) has labeled as the "racial retreat,"[23] is the clarion call signaling the end of race-based social policy in the United States. The recent Supreme Court *Grutter v. Bollinger* decision, hailed by some observers as a victory, is at best a weak victory because it allows for a "narrowly tailored" employment of race in college admissions, imposes an artificial 25-year deadline for the program, and encourages a monumental case-by-case analysis for admitting students that is likely to create chaos and push institutions into making admissions decisions based on test scores. Again, this trend reinforces the trend toward Latin Americanization because the elimination of race-based social policy is, among other things, predicated on the notion that race no longer affects the life chances of Americans. Nevertheless, as in Latin America, we may eliminate race by decree and maintain—or even see an increase in—the degree of racial inequality.

A LOOK AT THE DATA

To recapitulate, I contend that because of a number of important demographic, sociopolitical, and international changes, the United States is developing a more complex system of racial stratification that resembles those typical of Latin American societies. I suggest three racial strata will develop, namely, whites, honorary whites, and the collective black and that "phenotype" will be a central factor determining where groups and members of racial and ethnic groups will fit—lighter people at the top, medium in the middle, and dark at the bottom.[24] Although I posit that Latin Americanization will not fully materialize for several more decades, in the following sections I provide a cursory analysis of various objective, subjective, and social interaction indicators to see if the trends support my thesis.

A) Objective Standing of "Whites," "Honorary Whites," and "Blacks"

If Latin Americanization is happening in the United States, gaps in income, poverty rates, education, and occupational standing between whites, honorary whites, and the collective black should be developing. The available data suggests this is the case. In terms of income, as table 8.1 shows, "white" Latinos (Argentines, Chileans, Costa Ricans, and Cubans) are doing much better than dark-skinned Latinos (Mexicans, Puerto Ricans, etc.). The apparent exceptions in table 8.1 (Bolivians and Panamanians) are examples of self-selection among these immigrant groups. For example, four of the largest ten concentrations of Bolivians in the United States are in Virginia, a state with just 7.2 percent Latinos (Census Bureau 2000).[25]

Table 8.1 also shows that Asians exhibit a pattern similar to that of Latinos. Hence, a severe income gap is emerging between groups I label as

Table 8.1   Mean Per Capita Income[1] ($) of Selected Asian and Latino Ethnic Groups, 2000

Latinos	Mean Income	Asian Americans	Mean Income
Mexicans	9,467.30	Chinese	20,728.54
Puerto Ricans	11,314.95	Japanese	23,786.13
Cubans	16,741.89	Koreans	16,976.19
Guatemalans	11,178.60	Asian Indians	25,682.15
Salvadorans	11,371.92	Filipinos	19,051.53
Costa Ricans	14,226.92	Taiwanese	22,998.05
Panamanians	16,181.20	Hmong	5,175.34
Argentines	23,589.99	Vietnamese	14,306.74
Chileans	18,272.04	Cambodians	8,680.48
Bolivians	16,322.53	Laotians	10,375.57
Whites	17,968.87	Whites	17,968.87
Blacks	11,366.74	Blacks	11,366.74

Source: 2000 PUMS 5% Sample.

[1] I use per capita income because family income distorts the status of some groups as some groups have more individuals contributing toward the family income than other groups (e.g., the case of most Asian families).

honorary white Asians (Japanese, Koreans, Filipinos, and Chinese) and those I suggest belong to the collective black (Vietnamese, Cambodian, Hmong, and Laotians).

The analysis of data on education, occupations, and unemployment reveals similar patterns (for tables on these matters, see the chapter referred to in footnote 15). That is, light-skinned Latinos and elite Asians do significantly better than their darker brethren in all these areas.

B) Subjective Standing of Racial Strata

Social psychologists have amply demonstrated that it takes very little for groups to form, develop a common view, and adjudicate status positions to nominal characteristics.[26] Thus, it should not be surprising if gaps in income, occupational status, education, and employment among these various strata are leading to early stages of group formation. For example, members of the groups I label as likely to become honorary white may be classifying themselves as "white" and believing they are different (better) than those I argue likely to comprise the collective black category. If this is happening, members of these groups should also be in the process of developing white-like racial attitudes befitting of their new social position and differentiating (distancing) themselves from the members of the group I believe will comprise the collective black.

In line with my thesis, I expect whites to be making distinctions between honorary whites and the collective black, specifically, exhibiting a more positive outlook toward honorary whites than toward members of the collective black. Finally, if Latin Americanization is happening, I speculate that members of the collective black should exhibit a diffused and contradictory racial consciousness as blacks and Indians do throughout Latin America and the Caribbean.[27] I examine some of these matters in the following subsections.

SOCIAL IDENTITY OF HONORARY WHITES

1) Self-Reports on Race: The Case of Latinos

Historically, most Latinos have classified themselves as "white" but the proportion of Latinos who self-classify as such varies tremendously by group. Hence, as table 8.2 shows, whereas 60 percent or more of the members of the Latino groups I regard as honorary white self-classify as white, 50 percent or fewer of the members of the groups I regard as belonging to the collective black do so. As a case in point, whereas Mexicans, Dominicans, and Central Americans are very likely to report "Other" as their preferred "racial" classification, most Costa Ricans, Cubans, Chileans, and Argentines choose the "white" descriptor.[28] Hence, the data in this table seems to fit my thesis.

2) "Racial" Distinctions among Asians

Although for political matters, Asians tend to vote panethnically,[29] distinctions between native-born and foreign-born (e.g., American-born Chi-

Table 8.2   Racial Self-Classification by Selected Latin America Origin Latino Ethnic Groups, 2000

	White	Black	Other	Native American	Asian
Dominicans	28.21	10.93	59.21	1.07	0.57
Salvadorans	41.01	0.82	56.95	0.81	0.41
Guatemalans	42.95	1.24	53.43	2.09	0.28
Hondurans	48.51	6.56	43.41	1.24	0.29
Mexicans	50.47	0.92	46.73	1.42	0.45
Puerto Ricans	52.42	7.32	38.85	0.64	0.77
Costa Ricans	64.83	5.91	28.18	0.56	0.53
Bolivians	65.52	0.32	32.79	1.32	0.05
Colombians	69.01	1.53	28.54	0.49	0.44
Venezuelans	75.89	2.58	20.56	0.36	0.60
Chileans	77.04	0.68	21.27	0.44	0.56
Cubans	88.26	4.02	7.26	0.17	0.29
Argentines	88.70	0.33	10.54	0.08	0.35

Source: 2000 PUMS 5% Sample.

nese and foreign-born Chinese) and between economically successful and unsuccessful Asians are developing. In fact, according to various analysts, given the tremendous diversity of experiences among Asian Americans "all talk of Asian panethnicity should now be abandoned as useless speculation."[30] Leland Saito (1998), in his *Race and Politics*, points out that many Asians have reacted to the "Asian flack" they are experiencing with the rise in Asian immigration by fleeing the cities of immigration, disidentifying from new Asians, and invoking the image of the "good immigrant." In some communities, this has led to older, assimilated segments of a community to dissociate from recent migrants. For example, a Nisei returning to his community after years of overseas military service, told his dad the following about the city's new demography:

> Goddamn dad, where the hell did all these Chinese came from? Shit, this isn't even our town anymore.[31]

To be clear, my point is not that Asian Americans have not engaged in coalition politics and, in various locations, participated in concerted efforts to elect Asian American candidates. My point instead is that the group labeled "Asian Americans" is profoundly divided along many axes and thus I forecast that many of those already existing divisions will be racialized by whites (e.g., sexploitation of Asian women by lonely white men in the "Oriental bride" market) as well as by Asian American themselves (e.g., intra-Asian preferences seem to follow a racialized hierarchy of desire).[32]

RACIAL ATTITUDES OF VARIOUS RACIAL STRATA

1) Latinos' Racial Attitudes

Although researchers have shown that Latinos tend to hold negative views of blacks and positive views of whites,[33] the picture is more complex. Immigrant Latinos tend to have more negative views about blacks than native-born Latinos. For instance, a study of Latinos in Houston, Texas, found that 38 percent of native-born Latinos compared to 47 percent of foreign-born held negative stereotypes of blacks. This may explain why 63 percent of native-born Latinos versus 34 percent of foreign-born report frequent contact with blacks.[34]

But the incorporation of the majority of Latinos as "colonial subjects" (Puerto Ricans), refugees from wars (Central Americans), or illegal migrant workers (Mexicans) has foreshadowed subsequent patterns of integration into the racial order. In a similar vein, the incorporation of a minority of Latinos as "political refugees" (Cubans, Chileans, and Argentines) or as "neutral" immigrants trying to better their economic situation (Costa Rica, Colombia) has allowed them a more comfortable ride in America's racial boat. Therefore, whereas the incorporation of most Latinos in the United States has meant becoming "nonwhite," for a few it has meant becoming almost white.

Nevertheless, given that most Latinos experience discrimination in labor and housing markets as well as in schools, they quickly realize their "nonwhite" status. This leads them, as Nilda Flores-Gonzales (1999) and Suzanne Oboler (1995) have shown, to adopt a plurality of identities that signify "otherness."[35] Thus, dark-skinned Latinos are even calling themselves "black" or "Afro-Dominicans" or "Afro-Puerto Rican."[36] For example, José Ali, a Latino interviewed by Clara Rodríguez (2000) in her book *Changing Race*, stated,

> By inheritance I am Hispanic. However, I identify more with blacks because to white America, if you are my color, you are a nigger. I can't change my color, and I do not wish to do so.

When asked, "Why do you see yourself as black?" he said,

> Because when I was jumped by whites, I was not called "spic," but I was called a "nigger."[37]

The identification of most Latinos as "racial others" has led them to be more likely to be pro-black than pro-white. For example, data on Latinos' racial affects toward various groups indicates that the proportion of Mexicans and Puerto Ricans who feel very warm toward blacks is much higher (about 12 percentage points for Mexicans and 14 percentage points for Puerto Ricans) than toward Asians (the readings in the "thermometer" range from 0 to 100 and the higher the "temperature" is, the more positive are the feelings toward the group in question). In contrast, the proportion of Cubans who feel very warm toward blacks is 10 to 14 percentage points *lower* than Mexicans and Puerto Ricans. Cubans are also more likely to feel very warm toward Asians than toward blacks (table not shown here). More fitting of my thesis, analysis of the same data in table 8.3 shows that Latinos who identify as "white" express similar empathy toward blacks and Asians, those who identify as "black" express the most positive affect toward blacks—about 20 degrees warmer toward black than toward Asians (data now shown here). Again, this finding is fitting of my thesis.

Table 8.3   Proportion of Latinos Who Express High Affect toward Blacks and Asians

Degrees of Feeling Thermometer	Blacks	Asians
Mexicans		
51–74	11.9	11.8
75–100	34.3	22.2
Puerto Ricans		
51–74	11.8	9.0
75–100	39.5	25.3
Cubans		
51–74	14.5	9.9
75–100	25.1	29.9

Source: Forman, Martinez, and Bonilla-Silva, "Latinos' Perceptions of Blacks and Asians: Testing the Immigrant Hypothesis" (Unpublished manuscript).

2) Asians' Racial Attitudes

Various studies have documented that Asians tend to hold antiblack and anti-Latino attitudes. For instance, a study found that Chinese residents of Los Angeles expressed negative racial attitudes toward blacks.[38] One Chinese resident stated, "Blacks in general seem to be overly lazy" and another asserted, "Blacks have a definite attitude problem."[39] Studies on Korean shopkeepers in various locales have found that over 70 percent of them hold anti-black attitudes.[40]

These general findings are confirmed in table 8.4. This table has data on the degree (in a scale running from 1 to 7) to which various racial groups subscribe to stereotypes about the intelligence and welfare dependency of other groups. The table clearly shows that Asians (in this study, Koreans, Chinese, and Japanese) are more likely than even whites to hold anti-black and anti-Latino views (for example, whereas whites score 3.79 and 3.96 for blacks and Latinos, Asians score 4.39 and 4.46). In line with this finding, they hold, comparatively speaking, more positive views about whites than Latinos and blacks.[41] Thus, as in many Latin American and Caribbean societies, members of the intermediate racial strata buffer racial matters by holding more pro-white attitudes than whites themselves.

3) The Collective Black and Whites' Racial Attitudes

After a protracted conflict over the meaning of whites' racial attitudes (for a discussion, see Bonilla-Silva and Lewis 1999), survey researchers seem to have reached an agreement: "a hierarchical racial order continues to shape all aspects of American life" (Dawson 2000, 344). Whites express/defend their social position on issues such as affirmative action

Table 8.4   Relationship between Race/Ethnicity and Racial Stereotypes on Intelligence and Welfare Dependency of Blacks, Latinos, Asians, and Whites in Los Angeles, 1993–1994

	Group Stereotyped			
	Blacks	*Latinos*	*Asians*	*Whites*
Group Stereotyping				
Unintelligent?				
White	3.79	3.96	2.90	3.09
Asians	4.39	4.46	2.90	3.25
Latinos	3.93	3.57	2.74	2.87
Blacks	3.31	3.96	3.21	3.32
F-ratio	***	***	***	***
Prefer Welfare?				
White	4.22	4.08	2.30	2.48
Asians	5.10	5.08	2.52	2.93
Latinos	5.57	4.49	2.77	2.77
Blacks	4.12	4.29	2.67	2.77
F-ratio	***	***	***	***

Source: Los Angeles Study of Urban Inequality, 1993–1994.

and reparations, school integration and busing, neighborhood integration, welfare reform, and even the death penalty (see Sears, Sidanius, and Bobo 2000; Tuch and Martin 1997; Bonilla-Silva 2001). Regarding how whites think about Latinos and Asians, not many researchers have separated the groups that comprise "Latinos" and "Asians" to assess if whites are making distinctions amongst them. However, the available evidence suggests whites regard Asians highly and are significantly less likely to hold Latinos in high regard.[42] Thus, when judged on a host of racial stereotypes, whites rate themselves and Asians almost identically (favorable stereotype rating) and rate negatively (at an almost equal level) both blacks and Latinos.

Bobo and Johnson also show that Latinos tend to rate blacks negatively and that blacks tend to do the same regarding Latinos. They also find that Latinos, irrespective of national ancestry, self-rate lower than whites and Asians (blacks, however, self-rate at the same level with whites and as better than Asians). This pattern seems to confirm Latin Americanization as those at the bottom in Latin America tend to exhibit a diffused rather than clear racial consciousness. My contention seems to be also bolstered by their findings that "blacks give themselves ratings that tilt in an unfavorable dimension on the traits of welfare dependency and involvement with gangs" and that "for Latinos three of the dimensions tilt in the direction of negative in-group ratings."[43]

SOCIAL INTERACTION AMONG MEMBERS OF
THE THREE RACIAL STRATA

If Latin Americanization is happening, one would expect more social (e.g., friendship, associations as neighbors, etc.) and intimate (e.g., marriage) contact between whites and members of the groups I label honorary white than between whites (and honorary whites) and members of the collective black. A cursory analysis of the available data suggests this is in fact the case.

1) Interracial Marriage

Although most marriages in America are still intraracial, the rates vary substantially by group. Whereas 93 percent of whites and blacks marry within-group, 70 percent of Latinos and Asians do so, and only 33 percent Native Americans marry Native Americans.[44] More significantly, when one disentangles the generic terms "Asians" and "Latinos," the data fits even more closely the Latin Americanization thesis. For example, among Latinos, Cuban, Mexican, Central American, and South Americans have higher rates of outmarriage than Puerto Ricans and Dominicans.[45] Although interpreting the Asian American outmarriage patterns is very complex (groups such as Filipinos and Vietnamese have higher than expected rates in part due to the Vietnam War and the military bases in the Philippines), it is worth pointing out that the highest rate belongs to Japanese Americans and Chinese and the lowest to Southeast Asians, a pattern that seems to fit the contours of my Latin Americanization argument.[46]

Furthermore, racial assimilation through marriage ("whitening") is significantly more likely for the children of Asian-white and Latino-white unions than for those of black-white unions, a fact that bolsters my Latin Americanization thesis. Hence, whereas only 22 percent of the children of black fathers and white mothers are classified as white, the children of similar unions among Asians are twice as likely to be classified as white (Waters 1997). For Latinos, the data fits even closer my thesis as Latinos of Cuban, Mexican, and South American origin have high rates of exogamy compared to Puerto Ricans and Dominicans (Gilbertson, Fitzpatrick, and Yang 1996). We concur with Moran's (2001) speculation that this may reflect the fact that because Puerto Ricans and Dominicans have far more dark-skinned members, they have restricted chances for outmarriage to whites in a highly racialized marriage market.

2) Residential Segregation among Racial Strata

An imperfect measure of interracial interaction is the level of neighborhood "integration."[47] Nevertheless, the various indices devised by demographers to assess the level of residential segregation allow us to gauge in broad strokes the level of interracial contact in various cities. In this section, I focus on the segregation of Latinos and Asians as the high segregation experienced by blacks is very well known.[48]

RESIDENTIAL SEGREGATION AMONG LATINOS

Researchers have shown that Latinos are less segregated from and are more exposed to whites than blacks.[49] Yet, they have also documented that dark-skinned Latinos experience black-like rates of residential segregation from whites. Early research on Latino immigrant settlement patterns in Chicago, for example, showed that Mexicans and Puerto Ricans were relegated to spaces largely occupied by blacks, in part because of skin color discrimination.[50] More recent studies find also this race effect on Latino residential segregation patterns. Latinos who identify as white, primarily Cubans and South Americans, are considerably more likely to reside in areas with non-Latino whites than are Latinos who identity as black, mainly Dominicans and Puerto Ricans.[51]

RESIDENTIAL SEGREGATION AMONG ASIANS

Of all minority groups, Asian Americans are the least segregated from whites. However, they have experienced an increase in residential segregation in recent years.[52] In a recent review Zubrinsky Charles (2003) found that from 1980 to 2000, the index of dissimilarity for Asians had increased 3 points (from 37 to 40) while the index of exposure to whites had declined 16 points (from 88 to 62).[53] Part of the increase in segregation (and the concomitant decrease in exposure) may be the result of the arrival of newer and poorer immigrants from Southeast Asia.[54] For example, the Vietnamese—a group I predict will be part of the collective black—almost doubled its size between 1990 and 2000. While the majority of residential segregation studies are based on black, Latino, and Asian proximity to whites, which limits an examination of intragroup differences among Asians and Latinos, the fact that Asians have much lower dissimilarity indexes and higher exposure indexes vis-à-vis Latinos and blacks, fits my overall claim that the majority of Asians will belong to the honorary white category.

DISCUSSION

I have presented a broad and bold thesis about the future of racial stratification in the United States.[55] However, at this early stage of the analysis and given the serious limitations of the data on "Latinos" and "Asians" (most of the data is not parceled out by subgroups and hardly anything is provided by skin tone), it is hard to make a conclusive case. I acknowledge that factors such as nativity or socioeconomic characteristics may explain some of the patterns I documented.[56] Nevertheless, the fact that almost all the objective, subjective, and social interaction indicators I reviewed were in the direction I predicted, supports my Latin Americanization thesis. For example, the objective data clearly shows substantive gaps between the groups I labeled "white," "honorary whites," and the "collective black." In terms of income and education, whites tend to be slightly better off than honorary whites who tend to be significantly better off than the collective black. Not surprisingly, a variety of subjective indicators signal the emergence of *internal* stratification among racial minorities. For example, whereas some Latinos (e.g., Cubans, Argentines, Chileans, etc.) are very likely to self-classify as whites, others are not (e.g., Dominicans and Puerto Ricans living in the United States). This has led them to develop a racial attitudinal profile, at least in terms of subscription to stereotypical views about groups, similar to that of whites. Finally, the objective and subjective indicators had a correlate at the level of social interaction. Data on interracial marriage and residential segregation shows that whites are significantly more likely to live nearby honorary whites and to intermarry them than members of the collective black.

I also acknowledge that my racial map and arguments can be debated and, since I have already heard some critiques, I wish to take the opportunity to defend my case. The three criticisms of my work I hear most often are the following: (1) Why do I classify Arab Americans as "honorary white" at a time when all Arabs, and folks who look like them, are being labeled terrorists? (2) How can I predict that color blindness will become even more salient when there seems to be a resurgence of old-fashioned racism? (3) Why do I suggest a triracial order will emerge when many Latinos and whites fight to become white?

The first person with whom I debated some of these points was my wife, who happens to be a Palestinian woman. And I will state here exactly what I told her in the privacy of our home. Regarding the first point, I used a semantic move and told her "I love you baby, but . . ." and proceeded to explain to her that this map is heuristic and, thus, that it is not definitive. Groups may move up or down and I am willing to contemplate this possibility *if the data warrants it.* However, because the data in this chapter—and in forthcoming work—does not show that Arab Americans or Asian Indians (a group that is, for many reasons, in a similar location in whites' imaginary to Arab Americans) have changed their racial politics, I am not inclined to move them to the "collective black" category. In fact, I suggest their historical position is analogous to that of Japanese

Americans during World War II. (In their case, the record shows that despite suffering from the horrible ignominy of internment, Japanese Americans returned rather quickly to an in-between status in the racial order and as the favored minorities for whites. Furthermore, they did not shift their political lenses and join in the struggle with other minorities in the sixties and seventies. In contrast to Latinos, Blacks, and Native Americans, Japanese Americans hardly participated in the civil rights movement.) Thus, Arab Americans may be suffering from a sort of collective punishment from whites by being regarded as terrorists, as fundamentalist, as uncivilized or differently civilized, but I do not see systematic evidence suggesting they are developing an oppositional identity such as that exhibited by other minorities. But, as I also told my wife, if I see data suggesting that "Arab Americans"[57] are in fact becoming members of the "collective black" and behaving as such in terms of their patterns of interaction, I am willing to revise my map.

Regarding the second point, I still maintain that color blindness will become the glue that will bind the triracial order. This does not mean that Jim Crow racism is totally dead or that it may not temporarily gain space-making Amerika feel more like Amerikkka. However, we must understand that because color blindness is about maintaining white power, this ideology, as all ideologies, can bend in many ways to help in this task. Even the material I included in the main text of the book showed that it is possible for whites to claim they are color blind and still talk about race in crude ways. Examples of this phenomenon abound. For instance, every night you can watch Lou Dobbs on CNN attack so-called illegal aliens, talk about China and India as if they were the real economic threat for America, trash Arab nations, and make fun of so-called political correctness in a color-blind way. And "in point of fact," to use one of Lou Dobbs's favorite verbal mannerisms, whenever anyone calls him "racist" or claims he is "being racist," he gets indignant and claims to be above the racial fray. Similarly, the way President Bush and his cabinet have attempted to thread the needle in this "War on Terror," fits the logic of color blindness. Their rhetorical plan seems to be, "Say a lot about the 'enemy,' but use disclaimers so that you can never be pinned down as intolerant or racist."

Lastly, on the matter of whether Asians and Latinos will join the ranks of whites, I simply state almost verbatim what I stated in a debate on this matter in a recent edited book with my colleague, George Yancey, author of *Who Is White? Latinos, Asians, and the New Black/Nonblack Divide.*[58] Although Yancey's claim is meritorious—he claims that because most Asians and Latinos self-identify as white in the Census, they should therefore be considered as such—and I have many coincidences with him (I too argue that many Latinos and Asians will become white), I believe his overall claim is unlikely. There are four reasons why I think his general prediction is unlikely. First, Latinos and Asians are not "new immigrants." They have been in the United States since at least the 19th century! Therefore, if they were going to become white, that process should have started in the 1830s (for Mexican Americans) and 1840s for (Chinese Americans). The fact that this has not happened in mass (I acknowledge that some Asians and Latinos, like light-skinned blacks in the past, became white through passing) suggest that the racialization of these groups is different from that of people of European descent.

Second, all racial categories are historico-political constructions and, therefore, always exhibit malleability and porosity. However, the incorporation of groups into the USA white category has shown, so far, to have some epidermic boundaries, that is, groups and individuals added to the category have been European-looking. Hence, *groups* lacking epidermic capital, such as Latinos and Asians, will have more trouble getting admission into whiteness (but I point out that individual members of these groups can use their individual racial capital, such as light skin color, eye color, etc., to move up the racial ladder).

Third, the kind of assimilation process experienced by many of the groups that are presumed to become white (e.g., Mexican-Americans, Dominicans, Puerto Ricans, Filipinos, etc.) seems different from that of European immigrants in the early part of the 20th century. Thus, analysts now talk about "segmented assimilation" to refer to the variety of outcomes of these groups (Rumbaut and Portes 2001).

And fourth, the class and cultural distance between the masses of Mexican, Central American, and some Asian immigrants and whites is such that it is unlikely that most of them will be able to become white. The Mexican, Puerto Rican, Dominican barrios and the Chinese, Korean, Vietnamese towns across the nation are not like the temporary ethnic ghettos of the past. Some of these neighborhoods have more than 100 years of existence, a very long time to be regarded as "transition neighborhoods."

I restate for the record that I acknowledge that many of these new immigrants as well as many of the old minority citizens will either become white or near-white (honorary white). My big difference with Yancey and others is that I believe that most of these people will not become white and will accompany blacks in the large loosely organized racial strata at the bottom of the racial order.

Race Struggle in a Latin America-Like United States

If my predictions are right, what will the consequences of Latin Americans be for race relations in the United States? First, racial politics will change dramatically. The "us" versus "them" racial dynamic will lessen as "honorary whites" grow in size and social importance. They are likely to buffer racial conflict—or derail it altogether—as intermediate groups do in many Latin American and Caribbean countries.

Second, the ideology of color-blind racism that I examined in this book is likely to become even more salient in the United States. Color-blind racism is in fact an ideology similar to that prevailing in Latin American and Caribbean societies and like there, it will help glue the emerging racial order and buffer racial conflict.

Third, if the state decides to stop gathering racial statistics, the struggle to document the impact of race in a variety of social venues will become monumental. More significantly, because state actions always impact civil society, if the state decides to erase race from above, the *social* recognition of "races" in the polity may become harder. We may develop a Latin American-like "disgust" for even mentioning anything that is race-related.

Fourth, the deep history of black-white divisions in the United States has been such that the centrality of the black identity will not dissipate. For instance, research on the "black elite" shows that it exhibits racial attitudes in line with their racial group.[59] That identity, as I suggested in this chapter, may be even taken up by dark-skinned Latinos as it is being rapidly taken up by most West Indians. For example, Al, a 53-year-old Jamaican engineer interviewed by Milton Vickerman (1999), stated:

> I have nothing against Haitians; I have nothing against black Americans. . . . If you're a nigger, you're a nigger, regardless of whether you are from Timbuktu. . . . There isn't the unity that one would like to see. . . . Blacks have to appreciate blacks, no matter where they are from. Just look at it the way I look at it: That you're the same. [60]

However, I expect some important changes to take place even among the black population. Their racial consciousness, I argue, will become more diffused. For example, blacks will be more likely to accept many stereotypes about themselves (e.g., "We are lazier than whites") and exhibit what I label here as a "blunted oppositional consciousness" (see chapter 6). Furthermore, the external pressure of "multiracials" in white contexts[61] and the internal pressure of "ethnic" blacks may change the notion of "blackness" and even the position of some "blacks" in the system. Colorism may become an even more important factor as a way of making social distinctions among "blacks."[62]

Fifth, the new racial stratification system will be more effective in maintaining white supremacy. Whites will still be at the top of the social structure but will face fewer race-based challenges. And, to avoid confusion about my claim regarding "honorary whites," let me clarify that I believe their standing and status will be ultimately dependent upon whites' wishes and practices.[63] "Honorary" means that they will remain secondary, will still face discrimination, and will not receive equal treatment in society. For example, although Arab Americans should be regarded as "honorary whites," their treatment in the post-September 11 era suggests their status as "white" and as "Americans" is tenuous at best. Although some analysts and commentators may welcome Latin Americanization as a positive trend in American race relations,[64] those at the bottom of the racial hierarchy will soon discover that behind the statement "We are all Americans," hides a deeper, hegemonic way of maintaining white supremacy. As a Latin America-*like* society,[65] the United States will become a society with more rather than less racial inequality but with a reduced forum for racial contestation. The apparent blessing of "not seeing race" will become a curse for those struggling for racial justice in years to come. We may become "All Americans," as commercials in recent times suggest, but paraphrasing George Orwell, "some will be more American than others."

In the next chapter of this book, I will tackle the meaning of the election of President Obama. Although many commentators and analysts believe his election signifies "the end of racism" or a monumental change in our long racial history, I will argue that it is in line with color-blind racism.

NOTES

1. Data calculated from table 3, "Annual Estimates of the Population by Sex, Race and Hispanic or Latino Origin for the United States: April 1, 2000 to July 1, 2004," in American Fact Finder, a website sponsored by the U.S. Census Bureau which can be found at the following address: http://factfinder.census.gov/home/saff/main.html?_lang=en.

2. The reference for Huntington's book is, *Who Are We?* (New York: Simon & Schuster, 2004). As a quick refutation, the United States has never had an "Anglo-Saxon" because the culture of the country has always reflected waves of incorporation of peoples as colonial subjects (e.g., Mexicans and Indians), as immigrants (e.g., Italians, Scandinavians, etc.), and slaves (e.g., Africans).

3. For a critique of the way Lou Dobbs frames the immigration debate, skews his list of invitees, and distorts the data on immigration he presents in his show, see Peter Hart's article, "Dobbs' Choice: CNN host picks immigration as his ax to grind," February 2004 in the website of FAIR (Fairness and Accuracy in Reporting).

4. Asian Americans were, from the first time they set foot in this country, a very small group (about 1 percent of the population) very regionally concentrated (mostly on the West Coast). But since the enactment of the 1965 Immigration Act, this group has grown in size exponentially and is now represented in most states. And this group, perceived as a success story, has in fact the highest proportion of college graduates (50 percent) and a high level of income. For recent data on this

group, see the U.S. Census Bureau release, "Asian/Pacific American heritage Month, May 2005," located in www.census.gov/Press-Release/www/releases/archives/facts_for_featur es_special _editions/004522.html. For critiques of the "model minority" myth and explanations of the success story of Asian Americans, see Frank H. Wu, *Yellow: Race in America Beyond Black and White* (New York: Basic Books, 2003).

5. On the political scandals, one just need to remember how easy it was for the Republican Party to accuse the Democratic Party of selling the nation's sovereignty to China in the 2000 election because they allegedly accepted contributions from Chinese citizens. (For a critique, see Wu's book which I cite in the previous footnote.) For examples on the anti-Chinese views expressed in the news, tune in to almost any channel every night and see how they frame trade issues ("They are taking us for a ride!,") energy issues ("They are using too much energy!"), or intellectual property right issues ("They are stealing our intellectual property!"). On the latter point, we must always remember that if we super exploit nations all over the world, we have no moral ground to defend intellectual property rights. It is simply another case of the rooster coming back home to roost.

6. I place these two concepts in quotation marks for two reasons. First, since we are all one species, the notions such as "multiracial" or "bi-racial" reify biological interpretation of race. Second, all humans are "multiracial" (in the sociological sense of the notion of race) since we are the product of two million years or mixing, migrating from place to place, and mixing some more. What has allowed people to signify their multiracialism in the United States nowadays is the transition from the Jim Crow era—when all people were either white or nonwhite—to the post–Civil Rights racial era in which there is seemingly more space and fluidity for individuals to choose their identity, racial or otherwise.

7. I have said elsewhere that there is no multiracial movement per se, if by that one means a social movement. What we have is many organizations, without much coherence, articulating the views and angst of either parents (usually white mothers) of bi-racial children or the organizations of biracial children in colleges and professional circles.

8. For a perceptive examination of interracial marriage and now race still ordains our mate selection, see Rachel Moran, *Interracial Intimacy: The Regulation of Race and Romance* (Chicago and London: University of Chicago Press, 2001).

9. The comments on demographers, and the data on rates of interracial marriage, refer to Sharon Lee and Barry Edmonston, "New Marriages, New Families: U.S. Racial and Hispanic Intermarriage," *Population Bulletin*, June 2005. An example of a public intellectual heralding interracial marriage as the solution to America's racial problems is Randal Kennedy, *Interracial Intimacies* (New York: Pantheon, 2003).

10. Jennifer Wilbank's story of the Georgia woman who disappeared the day before her wedding in the summer of 2005, shows that Latinos may be moving into a position in our culture analogous to that of blacks. Wilbanks claimed she was kidnapped by a Hispanic man and a white woman. Initially, the story was believed but soon after, the police realized the story was fabricated. But of interest in this case is that Wilbanks did not rely on the traditional "black man story" and

used what seems to be the new game in town: "The Hispanic man did it." Also, the fact that we believed her story until we were told it was not true suggests there is a new racial sensitivity or fear emerging in the country.

11. See, for example, George Yancey, *Who is White?: Latinos, Asians, and the New Black/Nonblack Divide* (Boulder, Colo.: Lynne Rienner Publishers, 2003).

12. Denish D'Souza, *The End of Racism* (New York: Free Press, 1995). William J. Wilson, *The Declining Significance of Race* (Chicago: University of Chicago Press, 1978).

13. See, for example, Richard Alba and Victor Nee, *Remaking the American Mainstream: Assimilation and Contemporary Immigration* (Boston and London: Harvard University Press, 2004).

14. The arguments and data for this chapter come from my ongoing project titled " 'We Are All Americans!' The Latin Americanization of Racial Stratification in the United States." For a discussion on the racialization of the world system, see Etienne Balibar and Immanuel Wallerstein, *Race, Nation, and Class: Ambiguous Identities* (London: Verso, 1991).

15. Experts interested in the references on this section should consult my chapter, " 'We Are All Americans!' The Latin Americanization of Racial Stratification in the United States," in *The Changing Terrain of Race and Ethnicity*, edited by Maria Krysan and Amanda E. Lewis, (New York: Russell Sage Foundation, 2004), 149–83.

16. Aline Helg, "Race in Argentina and Cuba, 1880–1930: Theory, Policies, and Popular Reaction," in *The Idea of Race in Latin America, 1870–1940*, edited by Richard Graham (Austin: University of Texas Press, 1990).

17. Two example of this posture are Herbert J. Gans, "The Possibility of a New Racial Hierarchy in the Twenty-first Century United States," in *The Cultural Territories of Race: Black and White Boundaries*, edited by Michele Lamont (Chicago: University of Chicago Press, 1999), and Jonathan W. Warren and France Winddance Twine, "White Americans, the New Minority?: Non-Blacks and the Ever-Expanding Boundaries of Whiteness," *Journal of Black Studies* 28, no. 2 (1997): 200–218. A quick rebuttal of their view is that Latinos and Asians have been here for a long time and have not become white en masse. Thus, I expect that the bulk of the Latino and Asian immigrants coming to America (increasingly poor and many in a tenuous legal status in the country) will not join the ranks of the white group as these analysts predict.

18. Any social stratification order that does not have intermediate strata is more likely to be fraught with conflict of the " 'We' versus 'Them' " kind and require a more heavy investment in coercion as a way of keeping social order. On this point, see Gerhard E. Lenski, *Power and Privilege: A Theory of Social Stratification* (Chapel Hill: University of North Carolina Press, 1984). Hence, my claim here is that the development of this intermediate group will act as a "buffer" for social conflict. The white-nonwhite dynamic typical of the American racial order will be blurred by more complex racial lines of contestation.

19. See Robert Miles, *Racism after Race Relations* (London and New York: Routledge, 1993) and Robin Cohen, *Global Diasporas: An Introduction* (Seattle: University of Washington Press, 1997).

20. See Stephen Castles and Mark Miller, *The Age of Migration: International Population Movements in the Modern World* (Hong Kong: Macmillan, 1993).

21. For more on this argument, see my "This Is a White Country": The Racial Ideology of the Western Nations of the World-System," *Sociological Inquiry* 70, no. 3 (2000): 188–214.

22. See, Eduardo Bonilla-Silva, "The Essential Social Fact of Race: A Reply to Loveman," *American Sociological Review*, 64 (2000): 899–906.

23. Stephen Steinberg, *Turning Back: The Retreat from Racial Justice in American Thought and Policy* (Boston: Beacon Press, 1995).

24. However, phenotype in Latin America can be perceptually and socially "lightened" (or "darkened") by nonphenotypical characteristics such as education, language, culture, class, and occupational background. A black-looking person with a Ph.D. from Harvard who makes lots of money may not be regarded as black in Puerto Rico or Brazil. Similarly, I believe that although most Asian Indians range in color from dark to quite dark, they are likely to be regarded as honorary whites because of their mastery of the English language, high levels of education, and other nonphenotypical factors.

25. Whereas the Bolivian Census of 2001 reports that 71 percent of the Bolivians self-identify as Indian, less than 20 percent have more than a high school diploma, and 58.6 percent live below the poverty line, 66 percent of Bolivians in the United States self-identify as white, 64 percent has 12 or more years of education, and have a per capita income comparable to that of whites. Thus, this seems like a case of self-selection, that is, Bolivians in the United States do not represent Bolivians in Bolivia. The information on Bolivia comes from Censo Nacional de Población y Vivienda, *Bolivia: Caraterísticas de la Población*, Serie Resultados (Vol. 4. La Paz: Ministerio de Hacienda, 2002).

26. On this see the classic work of Henri Tajfel, "Experiments in Intergroup Discrimination," *Scientific American* 223 (1970): 96–102. See also the contributions of Cecilia Ridgeway. For a example, see her "The Social Construction of Status Value: Gender and Other Nominal Characteristics," *Social Forces* 70, no. 2 (1991): 367–86.

27. Michael G. Hanchard, *Orpheus and Power: The Morimiento Negro of Rio de Janeiro and São Paulo, Brazil, 1945–1988* (New Jersey: Princeton University Press, 1994).

28. Survey experiments have shown that if the question on Hispanic origin is asked first, the proportion of Latinos who report to be "white" increases from 25 to 39 percent (Martin, Demaio, and Campanelli 1990). The same research also shows that when Latinos report to belong to the "Other" category, they are not mistaken, that is, they do want to signify they are neither black nor white. Unfortunately, we do not have results by national groups. Are Cubans more likely to claim to be white if the order of the questions is changed? Or is the finding symmetrical for all groups? Regardless we think this finding does not alter the direction of the overall findings on the self-identification of various Latino groups.

29. See, Yen Le Espiritu Espiritu, *Asian American Panethnicity: Bridging Institutions and Identities* (Philadelphia: Temple University Press, 1992).

30. E. San Juan Jr. "The Limits of Ethnicity and the Horizon of Historical Mate-

rialism," in *Asian American Studies: Identity, Images, Issues Past and Present* edited by Esther Mikyung Ghymn (New York: Peter Lang, 2000), 10.

31. Leland T. Saito, *Race and Politics: Asian Americans, Latinos, and Whites in a Los Angeles Suburb* (Urbana: University of Illinois Press, 1998), 59.

32. My comments on Asian Americans, in case some readers have doubts, apply to Latinos, too. Latinos, as I have argued so far, are not a monolithic group and have serious divisions that mimic elements of the divisions seen among Asian Americans. For instance, a study on Latino attitudes toward immigration released in June 2005 reported that, "Although an overwhelming majority of Hispanics expresses positive attitudes toward immigrants . . . a significant minority, concentrated among native-born Latinos, is concerned that unauthorized migrants are hurting the economy." The study estimates the size of this group as 30 percent of the native-born population, but does not go further in attempting to identify the characteristics of this segment. Perhaps they are the light-skinned, well-educated, Hispanics that I label here honorary white. See Robert Suro, "Attitudes Towards Immigrants and Immigration Policies: Surveys among Latinos in the U.S. and Mexico," *Pew Hispanic Center*, August 16, 2005.

33. On the racial attitudes of Latinos, see Wallace Lambert and Donald Taylor, *Coping with Cultural and Racial Diversity in Urban America* (Westport, Conn.: Praeger, 1990) and, particularly, Tatcho Mindiola Jr., Yolanda Flores Niemann, and Nestor Rodriguez, *Black-Brown Relations and Stereotypes* (Austin: University of Texas Press, 2002).

34. Mindiola, Niemann, and Rodriguez 2002.

35. See Nilda Flores-Gonzales, "The Racialization of Latinos: The Meaning of Latino Identity for the Second Generation," *Latino Studies Journal* 10, no. 3 (1999): 3–31 and Suzanne Oboler, *Ethnic Labels, Latino Lives: Identity and the Politics of (Re)Presentation in the United States* (Minneapolis: University of Minnesota Press, 1995).

36. On Dominicans and their racial history, see David Howard, *Coloring the Nation: Race and Ethnicity in the Dominican Republic* (Boulder, Colo.: Lynne Rienner Publishers, 2001).

37. Clara Rodríguez, *Changing Race: Latinos, the Census, and the History of Ethnicity in the United States* (New York: New York University Press, 2000) 56.

38. Lawrence Bobo, Camille Zubrinksy, James Johnson Jr., and Melvin Oliver, "Work Orientation, Job Discrimination, and Ethnicity," *Research in the Sociology of Work* 5 (1995): 45–85.

39. Bobo, Zubrinsky, Johnson, and Oliver, p. 78. See also Lawrence Bobo and Devon Johnson, "Racial Attitudes in Prismatic Metropolis: Mapping Identity, Stereotypes, Competition, and Views on Affirmative Action," in *Prismatic Metropolis*, edited by Lawrence Bobo, Melvin Oliver, James Johnson, and Abel Valenzuela (New York: Russell Sage Foundation, 2000).

40. On the views of Asian Americans, see Ronald Weitzer, "Racial Prejudice among Korean Merchants in African American Neighborhoods," *Sociological Quarterly* 38, no. 4 (1997): 587–606; In-jin Yoon, *On My Own: Korean Businesses and Race Relations in America* (Chicago: University of Chicago Press, 1997); and Pyong Gap Min, *Caught in the Middle: Korean Communities in New York and Los Angeles* (Berkeley: University of California Press, 1996).

41. For a more thorough analysis, see Bobo and Johnson 2000.

42. Bobo and Johnson 2000.

43. Bobo and Johnson 2000, 103.

44. Moran 2001, 103.

45. Greta A. Gilbertson, Joseph P. Fitzpatrick, and Lijun Yang, "Hispanic Out-marriage in New York City—New Evidence from 1991," *International Immigration Review* 30 (1996).

46. See Harry L. Kitano and Roger Daniels, *Asian Americans: Emerging Minorities*, (New Jersey: Prentice Hall, 2000).

47. For some of the limitations of this index, see Eduardo Bonilla-Silva and Gianpaolo Baiocchi, "Anything but Racism: How Sociologists Limit the Significance of Racism," *Race and Society* 4 (2001): 117–31.

48. See, for example, Douglass S. Massey and Nancy A. Denton, *American Apartheid* (Cambridge, Mass.: Harvard University Press, 1993) and Milton Yinger, *Closed Doors, Opportunities Lost: The Continuing Costs of Housing Discrimination* (New York: Russell Sage Foundation, 1995).

49. See Douglass S. Massey and Nancy A. Denton, "Trends in the Residential Segregation of Blacks, Hispanics, and Asians: 1970–1980," *American Sociological Review* 52, no. 6 (1987): 802–25. For a recent review of the overall trends, see Camille Zubrinsky Charles, "The Dynamics of Racial Residential Segregation," *Annual Review of Sociology* 29 (2003): 167–207.

50. See John J. Betancur, "The Settlement Experience of Latinos in Chicago: Segregation, Speculation, and the Ecology Model," *Social Forces* 74 (1996): 1299–1324.

51. See John R. Logan, "How Race Counts for Hispanic Americans." Lewis Mumford Center, University of Albany, 2003. Retrieved from http://mumford1 .dyndns.org/cen2000/BlackLatinoReport/BlackLatino01.htm.

52. On this point, see William H. Frey and Reynolds Farley, "Latino, Asian, and Black Segregation in U.S. Metropolitan Areas: Are Multi-ethnic Metros Different?" *Demography* 33, no. 1 (1996): 35–50 and Michael J. White, Ann E. Biddlecom, and Shenyang Guo, "Immigration, Naturalization, and Residential Assimilation among Asian Americans in 1980," *Social Forces* 72, no. 1 (1993).

53. The dissimilarity index expresses the percentage of a minority population that would have to move to result in a perfectly even distribution of the population across census tracts. This index runs from 0 (no segregation) to 100 (total segregation) and it is symmetrical (not affected by population size). The exposure index measures the degree of potential contact between two populations (majority and minority) and expresses the probability of a member of a minority group meeting a member of the majority group. Like the dissimilarity index, it runs from 0 to 100, but unlike it, it is asymmetrical (it is affected by population size). Zubrinsky Charles (2003).

54. See Frey and Farley, 1996.

55. I am not alone in making this kind of prediction. Scholars such as Arthur K. Spears, Suzanne Oboler, Gary Okihiro, and Mari Matsuda have made similar claims recently. See Arthur K. Spears contribution in his edited book, *Race and Ideology: Language, Symbolism, and Popular Culture* (Detroit: Wayne State University

Press, 1999); Suzanne Oboler, " 'It Must be a Fake!' Racial Ideologies, Identities, and the Question of Rights in Hispanics/Latinos," in *The United States: Ethnicity, Race, and Rights*, edited by Jorge J. E. Garcia and Pablo De Greiff (New York: Routledge, 2000); Gary Okihiro, *Margins and Mainstreams: Asians in American History and Culture* (Seattle: University of Washington Press, 1994); and Mary J. Matsuda, *Where Is Your Body? And Other Essays on Race, Gender and the Law* (Boston: Beacon Press, 1996).

56. An important matter to disentangle empirically is whether it is color or nativity, education, or class what determines where groups fit in our scheme. A powerful alternative explanation to many of my preliminary findings is that the groups I label "honorary whites" come with high levels of human capital *before* they achieve honorary white status in the United States, that is, they fit this intermediate position because of neither their color nor their race, but rather because of their class background. Although this is a plausible alternative explanation that we hope examine in the future, some of the available data suggests that race/ color has something to do with the success of immigrants in the United States. For example, the case of West Indians—who come to the United States with class advantages (e.g., educational and otherwise) and yet "fade to black" in a few generations—suggests that the "racial" status of the group has an independent effect in this process. It is also important to point out that even when some of these groups may do "well" objectively, when one checks their returns to their characteristics is when one realizes how little they get for what they bring to the fore. And, as Waters and Eschbach (1995: 442) stated in a review of the literature on immigration, "the evidence indicates that direct discrimination is still an important factor for all minority subgroups except very highly educated Asians." Mary C. Waters, Mary C. Eschbach, and Karl Eschbach, "Immigration and Ethnic and Racial Inequality in the United States," *Annual Review of Sociology* (1995). However, even highly educated and acculturated Asians, such as Filipinos, report high levels of racial discrimination in the labor market. Not surprisingly, second and third-generation Filipinos self-identity as Filipino-American rather than as white or "American." For references on all these matters and a slightly more elaborate discussion, see Bonilla-Silva (2004).

57. The term Arab Americans may in fact be too wide to hide multiple realities. My wife Mary Hovsepian, a sociologist at Duke, has suggested to me that maybe Christian Arabs will become white-like and Muslim Arabs will become black-like. Although I still have not seen data suggestive of this trend, I remain observant of this possibility.

58. George Yancey, *Who Is White?: Latinos, Asians, and the New Black/Nonblack Divide* (Boulder, Colo.: Lynne Rienner Publishers, 2003).

59. See Michael Dawson, *Behind the Mule: Race and Class in African American Politics* (Princeton, N.J.: Princeton University Press, 1994).

60. Milton Vickerman, *Crosscurrents: West Indian Immigrants and Race* (New York: Oxford University Press, 1999), 199.

61. Kerry Ann Rockquemore, Kerry Ann Brunsma, and David L. Brunsma, *Beyond Black: Biracial Identity in America* (Thousand Oaks, Calif.: Sage, 2002).

62. For a recent discussion and analysis on this matter, see Cedric Herring,

Verna M. Keith, and Hayward D. Horton, *Skin Deep: How Race and Complexion Matter in the "Color-Blind" Era* (Urbana: University of Illinois Press, 2003).

63. The work of Claire Jean Kim on "triangulation" seems appropriate here. She argues that Asian Americans have been triangulated vis-à-vis blacks and whites. On the one hand, although whites value Asian Americans as a model minority worthy of praise, but at the same time, they ostracize them civically as unworthy of assimilation. Albeit my data on marital assimilation and neighborhood segregation suggests that the second pole is more complex than Kim suggests, her point is well-taken. See Claire Jean Kim, "The Racial Triangulation of Asian Americans," *Politics and Society* 27, no. 1 (March 1999): 105–38. For a similar point with tons of examples, please see Frank H. Wu, *Yellow: Race in America Beyond Black and White* (New York: Basic, 2003).

64. In the last few years, Harvard political scientist Jennifer Hochschild has been working on a project dealing with the significance of color for Americans. Although her project is similar to mine and we have shared platforms a few times, she believes that this development may be progressive as it will lessen racial boundaries. I, as a black-looking man who lived for 21 years in a so-called racial democracy, know that colorism is no solution to racialization but is in fact a different version of it.

65. Latin America-like does not mean exactly like Latin America. The 400-year history of the American racial formation has stained the racial stratification order forever. Thus I expect some important differences in this new American racial stratification system compared to that "typical" of Latin American societies. First, phenotype-based discrimination will not work perfectly. Hence, for example, although Asian Indians are dark-skinned, they will still be higher as a group in the stratification system than, for example, Mexican American *mestizos*. Second, Arabs, Asian Indians, and other non-Christian groups are unlikely to be allowed complete upward mobility unless they engage in passing. The events of September 11, 2001, and our intervention in Afghanistan and Iraq—both of which may force the U.S. military to remain in the area for a long time—are reinforcing the traditional view of whiteness as a Christian-only identity. Third, because of the 300 years of dramatic racialization and group formation, most members of the historically nonwhite groups will maintain "ethnic" (Puerto Ricans) or racial claims (e.g., blacks) and demand group-based rights.

9

⌇

Will Racism Disappear in *Obamerica*?

The Sweet (but Deadly) Enchantment of Color Blindness in Black Face

> Madness is rare in individuals—but in groups, parties, nations, and
> ages it is the rule.
>
> Friedrich Nietzsche, *Beyond Good and Evil* (1966): 90

"WE ARE ALL MAD HERE." ON MADNESS IN THE AMERICAN WONDERLAND

Since the 2008 presidential campaign, Americans have behaved much like the characters in the upside down world of *Alice's Adventures in Wonderland*.[1] In many ways the entire nation succumbed to *Obamania*.[2] Thankfully some progressive[3] critics had a shield that protected them from this social current. They were able to navigate the turbulence for two reasons. First, given that this country does not have a traditional left and has extremely weak labor unions (Aronowitz 1991) it has never been easy to be a progressive in America. Second, now that Obama is the president, many feel vindicated as many of the concerns, issues, and predictions they made during the campaign have become a reality. Unfortunately, this vindication is somewhat Pyrrhic as Obama's victory has increased (hopefully temporarily) the madness in the nation and reduced even further the space for criticizing him and his polices from the left.[4]

I was one of those progressives[5] who offered a critique of the Obama phenomenon and, since an early intervention on the matter, I was criticized by many friends and foes alike (see the preface to this edition). Accordingly, my agenda in this chapter is partly personal (I answer my critics), partly political (I explain in a more systematic way the commentary I offered during the 2008 campaign), and partly scholarly (I argue the Obama phenomenon fits quite well my argument about the centrality of color-blind racism and my prediction about the Latin Americanization of racial stratification in the United States). First and foremost, this chapter is my explanation—which I dare call sociological[6]—of the "miracle": the election of a black man as president of the United States. My explanation runs counter to those who believe his victory represents the "end of racism" and the beginning of the era of "no more excuses"[7] for people of color. In contrast, I contend Obama's ascendancy to the presidency is part and parcel of the "new racism" and the *All in the* (Color-Blind) *Family* soap opera that began running on a U.S. TV station in the early 1970s. Second, this chapter is a call to progressives and liberals who believed in Obama's message of hope and change to get serious. The election is over and it is time for them to put their thinking caps back on. Obama is now the president and we must all scrutinize his actions as we have done with all presidents before.

Because I know my views will anger some—perhaps many—readers who may shout like the Queen in the famous story, "Off with *his* head," I state five caveats hoping my would-be executioners forget their decree. First, although I hesitated, I voted for Obama (I thought of voting for Cynthia McKinney). Second, my criticism of Obama is neither of all he stands for nor of all of his actions in office (after all, I label his politics center-right, not right-wing). At the end of the chapter I enumerate some of the good things he has done so far and outline a course of action to make sure he delivers more good things for "we the people." Third, although I will criticize President Obama's image, politics, and policies, I want to be absolutely clear on one important point: in comparison to the president he replaced and the Republican candidate he faced, Obama seems like pure gold. Fourth, since Obama emerged as a viable candidate, the bulk of the American intelligentsia ceased its critical mission. Being critical (or analytical) is part of the job of intellectuals in any society and when they are not, they abdicate their responsibility. Fifth, I include material I used in speeches for two reasons: (1) to give the writing some character and a sense of urgency and (2) to provide readers with the *exact* arguments I articulated from February 2008 onward. This makes the text seem "personal" in some parts, but I hope readers can separate the grain from the straw. With these caveats out of the way, I can now begin the slow ascent out of the rabbit-hole I call *Obamerica*.

"DOWN THE RABBIT HOLE": THE REAL
QUESTION POSED BY OBAMA'S VICTORY

George Orwell stated a long time ago that "To see what is in front of one's nose needs constant struggle" (Orwell 1946). In the 2008 election cycle Americans did not see what was in front of their noses; they saw what they wanted and longed to see. Whereas blacks and other people of color saw in Obama the impossible dream come true, whites saw the confirmation of their belief that America is indeed a color-blind nation. But facts are, as John Adams said,[8] "stubborn things" and astute social analysts knew that since the late 1970s racial progress in the United States had stagnated and, in many areas, regressed. The evidence of such state of affairs was, as the title of a report of the early 1990s put it, "clear and convincing."[9] All socioeconomic indicators revealed severe racial gaps in income, wealth, housing, and educational and occupational standing. Since I have addressed these inequalities in this book and in previous work (particularly, in Chapter 4, Bonilla-Silva 2001), I review here some economic disparities for 2008—the year Obama was elected president. All the statistics I cite, unless otherwise specified, come from the 2009 report "State of the Dream 2009: The Silent Depression,"[10] a very useful compendium of information from sources such as the Census Bureau and the Bureau of Labor Statistics (BLS).

> The Black unemployment rate is currently 11.9%. Among young Black males age 16–19, unemployment is 32.8% (v). [Unemployment for whites in 2008 was 5.8%; see page 13.]

According to data from the BLS, by April 2009 the rate increased to 15.0% for blacks, 11.3% for Latinos, and 8% for whites.[11] (As I put the finishing touches to this chapter, the general unemployment rate is 9.6 and economists are predicting it will reach 10 to 11% in 2010.)

> The median household incomes of Blacks and Latinos are $38,269 and $40,000, respectively, while the median household income of whites is $61,280 (v).

> People of color are disproportionately poor in the United States. Blacks and Latinos have poverty rates of 24% and 21% respectively, compared to a 10% poverty rate for whites (v).

> People of color are more likely to be poor (24.5%), remain poor (54%), and move back into poverty from any income class status than their white counterparts (vi).

> Nearly 30% of Blacks have zero or negative worth, versus 15% of whites (vi).

Citing data from the "State of Black America 2009" report by the Urban League, Earl Graves, Jr., from *Black Enterprise*, said on the wealth disparity the following:

> Nationally, the typical African-American family today possesses less than 10 percent of the net worth of the average white family. Almost 30 percent of black families have zero or negative net worth. And far fewer blacks than whites benefit from inherited wealth or assets.[12]

> Only 18% of people of color have retirement accounts, compared to 43.4% of their white Counterparts (vi).

> On the *median*, for every dollar of white wealth, people of color have 15 cents. On *average*, people of color have 8 cents for every dollar of white wealth (vi).

The racial inequality that existed in 2008 and which remains today is not the product of "impersonal market forces" (Wilson 1978, 1987) or due to the presumed cultural, moral, ethical, intellectual, or family "deficiencies" of people of color, as conservative commentators such as Charles Murray in *Losing Ground* (1984), Murray and Herrnstein in *The Bell Curve: Intelligence and Class Structure in American Life* (1994), Abigail and Stephan Thernstrom in *America in Black and White* (1997), and many others have argued. Racial inequality today is due to the "continuing significance" of racial discrimination.[13] The scholarly community has documented the persistence of discrimination in the labor and housing markets and has uncovered the co-existence of old-fashioned as well as subtle "smiling discrimination" (Brooks 1996).[14]

But racial discrimination is not just about jobs and housing. Discrimination affects almost every aspect of the lives of people of color. It affects them in hospitals (Blanchard and Lurie 2004; Penner et al. 2009), restaurants (Rusche and Brewster 2008), trying to buy cars (Ayres 2002) or hail a cab (Kovaleski and Chan 2003), driving (Meehan and Ponder 2002) or flying (Harris 2001), or doing almost anything in America. Indeed, "living while black [or brown]"[15] is quite hard and affects the health (physical and mental) of people of color tremendously as they seem to always be on a "fight or flight" mode.[16]

Indicators of subjective matters denote trouble in paradise, too (I limit the discussion to racial attitudes, but could include data on perceptions of well-being and the like). Although the first wave of researchers in the 1960s and 1970s assumed tremendous or moderate racial progress in whites' racial attitudes, most[17] contemporary researchers believe that since the 1970s whites developed a new way of justifying the racial status quo distinct from the "in your face" prejudice of the past (see discussion in chapter 1). Analysts have labeled whites' post–Civil Rights racial attitudes as "modern racism," "subtle racism," "aversive racism," "social dominance," "competitive racism," "Jim Crow racism," or the term I prefer, "color-blind racism." But regardless of the name given to whites' new way of framing race matters, their switch from WK–Jim Crow racism to the WK–color-blind racism T.V. station did not change the basics as the new station is as good, if not better, than the old one in safeguarding the racial order. Despite its suave, apparently nonracial character, the new racial ideology is still about justifying the various social arrangements and practices that maintain white privilege (see chapters 2, 3, and 4).

The overall contemporary racial situation I have described is compounded by a mean-spirited white racial animus. The first component of this animus is the anti-affirmative action and "reverse racism" mentality that emerged in the early 1970s and that took a firm hold of whites' racial imagination since the 1980s (Pincus 2003; chapter 2 in Crosby 2004). This mentality—which became so transparent during the confirmation hearings in July 2009 of Judge Sotomayor for the Supreme Court—and its connection to "racial prejudice" is well-documented (Unzueta, Lowery, and Knowles 2007) and I have addressed it in this book. The second component of the racial climate people of color face is the anti-immigration mood that started slowly in the latter part of the 20th century and has become one of the central axes of racial politics in the early part of the 21st century (Esses, Dovidio, and Hodson 2002). When the first edition of this book appeared in 2003, the anti-immigration sentiment did not seem or feel as intense as today.[18] With the economy in shambles and agitators such as Lou Dobbs[19] fueling enmity towards undocumented workers (he calls them "illegal aliens"), a thick nativist mood is palpable and finding expression in draconian anti-immigrant measures enacted in localities across the nation.[20]

The last element of the contemporary racial climate is a derivative of the ill-conceived and ineptly labeled "war on terror."[21] In the late 1990s and during the first few months of President Bush's administration, a brief national discussion about racial profiling ensued. President Bush even classified racial profiling as a serious problem in the second presidential debate in 2000 and promised that if elected, he would enact a federal law against it.[22] However, that inchoate debate collapsed along with the Twin Towers. After 9/11 the discussion about racial profiling ceased and the practice became, in the eyes of many, a legitimate weapon in the fight against terrorism. In 2003 President Bush issued a ban on racial profiling governing the actions of seventy federal agencies, but left wide open the use of race and ethnicity as valid criteria when "national security" or "terrorism" was at stake.[23] Thus 9/11 has muddled the waters for challenging racial profiling as a racist and, ultimately, ineffective[24] policing tactic.

"And then out of nowhere," paraphrasing the much-maligned Father Pfleger, came a relatively unknown black politician who said, "Hey, I am Barack Obama" and almost the entire nation said like Hillary, "Oh damn, where did this black man come from?"[25] Since January of 2008 the nation has been mesmerized by Obama; by his "Yes we can"; by his appeal to our "better angels"; and by his relentless call for national unity. And many Americans have felt inspired, proud, and a few, like MSNBC's Chris Matthews, have even felt a "thrill going up [their] leg."[26] But the question we must ponder now that Obama is the president of the still (Dis)United States of Amerika[27] is: *Were we all wrong?* Were neo-liberal and conservative analysts right when they claimed America had seen D'Souza's "the end of racism" (1995) or, at least, William Julius Wilson's "declining significance of race" (1978)? Were the white masses right in their claim that America had become a color-blind nation and that minority folks were the ones who kept race alive by playing the infamous "race card"?

Analytically and politically, too many liberal and progressive commentators dug a deep hole for themselves in the 2008 election as they either went with the flow and assumed Obama was truly about social and racial change or took the stand that white racism would prevent Obama from getting elected.[28] But there is a more fitting, historically accurate, and sociologically viable explanation—and one I advanced *before* Obama was elected.[29] The "miracle"—the fact that race matters in America tremendously yet we elected a black man as our president—is but an apparent one. Obama, his campaign, and his "success" are the outcome of forty years of racial transition from the Jim Crow racial order to the racial regime I have referred to in my work as the "new racism" (2001). In the new America that presumably began on November 4, 2008, racism will remain firmly in place and, even worse, may become a more daunting obstacle. The apparent blessing of having a black man (and I should truly say *"this* black man") in the White House is likely to become a curse for black and brown folks.

In the remaining of this chapter I do four things. First, I describe the context that made it possible for someone like Obama to be elected president. Second, I discuss what Obama did in order to be elected president. Third, I review some specific predictions I made during the campaign and offer a few more predictions based on Obama's ongoing record as president. Finally, I conclude by discussing a few things we can do if we wish to attain real change at this juncture when so many whites (and many people of color) believe we are finally beyond race even though racial inequality remains entrenched.[30]

"BEGIN AT THE BEGINNING . . .": THE
CONTEXT THAT ALLOWED THE "MIRACLE"

In the midst of the trial against the Knight of Hearts in *Alice's Adventures in Wonderland*, the King instructed the White Rabbit to read some verses. The rabbit asked the King, "Where do I begin?" The King replied: "Begin at the beginning and go on till you come to the end: then stop." Americans have not placed the election of Barack Obama as president in its proper context and, thus, in order to understand where we are today we must "begin at the beginning."

From Jim Crow to the New Racism Regime

The Obama phenomenon is the product of the fundamental racial transformation that transpired in America in the 1960s and 70s. The new racial order that emerged—the "new racism"—unlike Jim Crow, reproduces racial domination mostly through subtle and covert discriminatory practices which are often institutionalized, defended with coded language ("*Those* urban people" or "*Those* people on welfare"), and bonded by the racial ideology of color-blind racism (for a full discussion of "the new racism," see Chapter 4 in Bonilla-Silva 2001; cf. Smith 1995). Compared to Jim Crow, this new system seems genteel but it is extremely effective in preserving systemic advantages for whites and keeping people of color at bay. The new regime is, in the immortal lyrics of Roberta Flack's[31] song, of the "killing me softly" variety.

This new regime came about as the result of various social forces and events that converged in the post–World War II era: (1) the civil rights struggles of the 1950s and 1960s; (2) the contradiction between an America selling democracy abroad and giving hell to minorities at home which forced the government to engage more seriously in the business of racial fairness; (3) the black migration from the South that made Jim Crow less effective as a strategy of social control; and (4) the change of heart of so-called enlightened representatives of capital who realized they had to retool the racial aspects of the social order in order to maintain an adequate "business climate." The most visible positive consequences of this process are well-known: the slow and incomplete school desegregation that followed the 1954 *Brown v. Board of Education* Supreme Court decision; the enactment of the Civil Rights Act of 1964, the Voting Rights Act of 1965, and the Housing Rights Act of 1968; and the haphazard political process that brought affirmative action into life.

Unfortunately, alongside these meaningful changes, whites developed very negative interpretations of what was happening in the nation.[32] The concerns they expressed in the late 1960s and early 1970s about these changes (Caditz 1976) gelled into a two-headed beast in the 1980s. The first head of the monster was whites' belief the changes brought by the tumultuous 1960s represented the end of racism in America. Therefore, since they believed racism had ended, they began regarding complaints about discrimination by people of color as baseless and a product of their "hypersensitivity" on racial affairs. The second head of the beast was that a substantial segment of the white population understood the changes not just as evidence of the end of racism, but also as the beginning of a period of "reverse discrimination."[33] Hence, this was the ideological context that helped cement the "new racism."

Elsewhere I have described in detail how the new racial practices for maintaining white privilege operate ideologically, socially, economically, and politically (again, interested parties should see Chapter 4 in Bonilla-Silva 2001 and, for an update, see Bonilla-Silva and Dietrich forthcoming). Given the focus of this chapter, I just review briefly my analysis of developments at the political level. Nowadays three major factors limit the advancement of people of color in the political arena. First, there are multiple structural barriers to the election of black and minority politicians such as racial gerrymandering, multimember legislative district members, and the like. Second, despite some progress in the 1970s, people of color are still severely under-represented among elected (whites still show a preference to vote for white candidates) and appointed officials—the proportion of elected and appointed officials still lags well behind their proportion in the population. Third, because most minority politicians must either "compromise" to get elected or are dependent upon local white elites, their capacity to enact policies that benefit the minority masses is quite limited.

More significantly, in my early analysis on these matters I mentioned (but did not delve deeply into the matter) the emergence of a new type of minority politician. By the early 1990s it was clear that both major political parties (but the Democratic Party in particular) had learned from the perils of trying to incorporate veteran civil rights leaders such as Jesse Jackson. Regardless of the limitations of Jackson as a leader and of his "rainbow coalition" strategy of the 1980s, he and his coalition proved to be too much of a challenge to the "powers that be."[34] Hence, both parties and their corporate masters developed a new process for selecting and vetting minority politicians. After the Democratic Party co-opted civil right leaders such as John Lewis, Andrew Young, and the like, they began almost literally manufacturing a new kind of minority politician (the Republican Party followed suit later). Consequently today's electorally-oriented minority politician (1) is not the product of social movements, (2) usually joins the party of choice while in college, (3) moves up quickly through the party ranks, and, most importantly, (4) is not a race rebel.[35] The new breed of minority politicians, unlike their predecessors, are not radicals talking about "the revolution" and "uprooting systemic racism." If Republican, they are anti-minority conservatives such as Michael Steele (currently the chairman of the Republican National Committee), Bobby Jindal (governor of Louisiana since 2008), Alan Keyes (conservative commentator and perennial candidate for *any* office), J. C. Watts (former Congressman from Oklahoma and still a very influential leader in the GOP) and, if a Democrat, post-racial leaders with center to center-right politics such as Harold Ford (former congressman from Tennessee and currently head of the conservative Democratic Leadership Council (DLC) and an MSNBC commentator), Cory Booker (Newark's mayor since 2006), Deval Patrick (governor of Massachusetts since 2006), Adrian Fenty (D.C.'s mayor since 2006) and, of course, Barack Obama. Not surprisingly, plutocrats love these kinds of minority politicians because, whether Republican or Democrat, neither represents a threat to the "power structure of America."[36]

Obama's case is illustrative. Although during his carefully orchestrated presidential campaign he and his team touted his credentials as a "community organizer," Obama's real story at the moment of his political conception is quite different. During the campaign Obama said "community organizing is 'something I carry with me when I think about politics today—obviously at a different level and in a different place, but the same principle still applies.'" [37] His wife, Michelle Obama, added, "Barack is not a politician first and foremost" but "a community activist exploring the viability of politics to make change."[38] The historical record, however, is quite different. First, Obama accomplished quite little in his two years as a *paid*[39] community organizer (all reports, including Obama's own account in *The Audacity of Hope*, reveal he was very disappointed with the pace of change) and second, by 1987 he had all but abandoned Saul Alinsky's ideals of the community organizer and was dreaming of getting elected to office. Hence, in the same article, which is sympathetic to Obama, the author states the following:

> Based purely on his organizing background, one would have expected Obama to become a bread-and-butter politician, a spokesman for his constituents' immediate needs. Instead, Obama became a politician of vision, not issues—one who appealed to voters' values rather than their immediate self-interest . . . . Obama has also eschewed the retiring persona of the organizer. Initially awkward as a speaker, he became a charismatic politician whose run for president has produced something very much like a movement. And, while his campaign has used some techniques from community organizing to rally state-by-state support, it is the antithesis of the ground-up, locally dominated, naturally led network of community groups that Alinsky envi-

sioned. *Obama, in short, has become exactly the kind of politician his mentors might have warned against.*[40]

The record also shows that by the time Obama ran for office in 1996, he had already acquired many of the typical characteristics of post–Civil Rights minority politicians. After he won the Illinois state race in 1996, Adolph Reed, a black political science professor and contributor to various progressive magazines, said the following about Obama:

> In Chicago, for instance, we've gotten a foretaste of the new breed of founda-tion-hatched black communitarian voices; one of them, a smooth Harvard lawyer with impeccable do-good credentials and vacuous-to-repressive neo-liberal politics, has won a state senate seat on a base mainly in the liberal foundation and development worlds. His fundamentally bootstrap line was softened by a patina of the rhetoric of authentic community, talk about meet-ing in kitchens, small-scale solutions to social problems, and the predictable elevation of process over program—the point where identity politics con-verges with old-fashioned middle-class reform in favoring form over sub-stance. I suspect that his ilk is the wave of the future in U.S. black politics, as in Haiti and wherever else the *International Monetary Fund* has sway. So far the black activist response hasn't been up to the challenge. We have to do better.[41]

Obama negotiated Chicago Democratic politics quickly and success-fully and by 2002 had become the darling of the city's black elite, and soon after, of Chicago's elite. Christopher Drew and Mike McIntire in a 2007 article in *The New York Times* state that Obama raised "improbably" fifteen million dollars for his senate campaign.[42] But their characterization of this quick turnaround (from having problems settling his campaign debt from his loss to Congressman Bobby Rush in 2000 to the success of his campaign in 2004) as "improbable" is inaccurate because by 2003 Obama had already received the benediction from the Democratic Party elders and financiers. Paul Street describes this process as follows:

> A corporate, financial, national and legal vetting of Obama, with an empha-sis on the critical money-politics nexus of Washington, D.C., began in 2003. That's when "Vernon Jordan, the well-known power broker and corporate board member who chaired Bill Clinton's presidential transition team after the 1992 election, placed calls to roughly twenty of his friends and invited them to a fund-raiser at his home," according to Silverstein. The fund-raiser "marked his entry into a well-established Washington ritual—the gauntlet of fund-raising parties and meet-and-greets through which potential stars are vetted by fixers, donors, and lobbyists."[43]

Street states that "Obama passed this preliminary trial with *flying col-ors*" (My emphasis. 2009: xxiii). The people in the meeting liked his academic background, suave and cool style, and political outlook. Attendees such as Gregory Craig (big time attorney and former special counsel to Bill Clinton), Mike Williams (legislative director of the Bond Market Association), and other big wheelers appreciated that Obama was not a "racial polarizer" (that is, that he was not Jesse Jackson–like) and that he was not "anti-business." This explains the seemingly "improbable" victory of Obama in the 2004 Senate race and the 700 million dollars he was able to raise in the 2008 presidential campaign. According to an investigative report by Ken Silverstein (2006) and a book by David Mendell (2007), Obama rose quickly beyond the confines of Illinois because the American elite resolutely loved his "reasonable tone."

Therefore, post–Civil Rights minority politicians like Obama are not truly about deep change, but about compromise. If they were truly about fundamental change and frontal challenges to the American social order, they would not be the darlings of the two mainstream parties. Although some post–Civil Rights minority politicians may, from time to time, "talk the talk," their talk is rather abstract almost to the point of being meaningless and they seldom if ever "walk the walk." For instance, Obama talked during the campaign about corporate lobbyists, but said nothing about *corporate power*; complained about "big money" in politics yet raised more money than *any* politician in American history (see later about corporate donors versus the "little donors"); subscribed to the Republican lie about a crisis in Social Security and is likely to follow through with policies to "save" a program that is actually solvent;[44] and talked about alternative energy sources and clean energy yet was in bed with folks in the "clean coal" and "safe nuclear energy" camp (see chapter 1 in Street 2009. Also, readers should examine the commercials by the energy sector that ran on national TV in the late spring and early summer of 2009 and how they used Obama's speeches during the campaign to bolster their agenda).[45]

Based on all the information at hand there is no question that politicians like Obama are "accomodationist" (Marable 1991) *par excellence* and teach the "wretched of the earth" the wrong political lesson: that electoral, rather than social-movement politics,[46] is *the* vehicle for achieving social justice. In the next section I show that Obama's political road to the (still) White House fits to a T the practices and tone of post–Civil Rights minority politicians.

"'WHO ARE YOU?' SAID THE CATERPILLAR": ON THE MEANING OF OBAMA'S POLITICS

When questions arose during the campaign about Obama's progressiveness due to his support of FISA[47] and other seemingly reactionary positions he held, Obama said in an interview with *The New York Times* that "I am someone who is no doubt progressive."[48] However, true to the style of post–Civil Rights minority politicians, he insisted he did not like to be "labeled" as right or left and preferred to be regarded as a "non-ideological" and "pragmatic" politician. As the campaign advanced, Obama's non-ideological stand betrayed a conservative bent and some commentators questioned his commitment to "progressiveness." For instance, in harsh yet prophetic words, *Huffington Post* blogger Taylor Marsh labeled Obama's brand of progressiveness as "progressive canni-balism." He was referring to Obama's willingness "to do whatever he can to get elected, cannibalizing his own and our ideals as he goes; bringing as many people along as he can, including conservatives who will have no allegiance to what progressives have worked for over decades to achieve."[49]

In this section I restate doubts I raised about Obama during the campaign and argue his politics and tone were not, as so many liberals and progressives believed, *tactical* maneuvers to get elected but represented who Obama truly *was* and how he *will be* as president. Because the concerns I expressed about the Obama phenomenon in events during the campaign were on point, I reproduce them here almost verbatim. I maintain the present tense I used, but print the statements in a different font to distinguish them from the brief (and contemporary) discussion that appears after each one.

> The first concern I have is that Obama does not represent a *true* social movement, but an undercurrent of various actors and contradictory forces that did not necessarily agree on fundamental issues. Lacking a social movement with a common agenda, I believe his presidency will become problematic as we have no way of predicting his actions and will not have people "in the streets" to curb them if needed.

When I wrote this, many commentators thought Obama had a "grass-roots" approach to politics.[50] However, all his political praxis during the campaign was in line with mainstream party politics (in fact, all he did was *through* the Democratic Party) and did not emanate from or create a social movement.[51] The massive rallies and the 700 million-plus dollars he raised in the campaign[52] did not emanate from the organized (or unorga-nized, as many social movements follow a more spontaneous path [Piven and Cloward 1978]) efforts of activists with a common agenda. The man-tra of his campaign, "Change we can believe in," was so abstract that almost anything and anyone could have fit in. The most significant mat-ter, however, was that Obama supporters lacked a common agenda and belief system. What I surmised[53] during the campaign—that white sup-port was not indicative of post-racialism—has now been corroborated in post-election studies. Noted survey researchers Professor Tom Pettigrew from UC-Santa Cruz and Professor Vincent Hutchings from the University of Michigan found that Obama's white voters were just slightly less prejudiced than McCain's white voters. And because Obama's white voters were younger than McClain's, I suspect that as they age and face real life issues (e.g., getting a job, getting married, selecting a neighborhood and schools for their kids, etc.), they will regress to their racial mean—that is, will develop views similar to those of older whites today.[54] (Professor Pettigrew puts some weight on the fact that most young whites voted for Obama, while Professor Hutchings is less impressed with this fact.)[55]

> Second, none of the policies Obama has offered on the crucial issues of our time (health care, NAFTA, the economy, immigration, racism, the Wars, etc.) is truly radical and likely to accomplish the empty yet savvy slogan he adopted as the core of his campaign: *change*.

I will say a bit more about some of Obama's policy preferences later but want to point out here that few of his ardent supporters had a clue about his policy proposals and even about his positions on crucial issues. For instance, while on vacation in the summer of 2008, I had a discussion with several minority professors about Obama and they told me I was "too harsh" on Obama. As the discussion proceeded, I said, "I cannot not believe you are all for Obama so blindly given his support for the death penalty." One of them laughed and told me that Obama was not for the death penalty. I urged the colleague to check the matter on the Internet and, a minute later, the person said, "Well, but Obama has a *nuanced* position," to which I replied, "When one is *dead* there is no *nuance*."[56]

> Third, Obama has reached the level of success he has in large measure because he has made a *strategic* move towards racelessness and adopted a post-racial persona and political stance. He has distanced himself from most leaders of the Civil Rights movement, from his own reverend, from his church, and from anything or anyone who made him look "too black" or "too political." Heck, Obama and his campaign even retooled Michelle Obama[57] to make her seem less black, less strong, and more white-lady-like for the white electorate!

Obama's post-racial stand during the campaign was not a new thing. Those who have read his books *Dreams of My Father* and *The Audacity of Hope* are familiar with his long-standing attempt to be if not *beyond* race at least *above* the racial fray. Hence, I was not the least surprised when President Obama answered the only question he was asked about race in his first press conference by suggesting race was a factor in life but that he was dealing with America's "real" problems.[58] I was also not surprised when in his second press conference he answered a question by Andre Showell, a black journalist, about what specific policies he had enacted to benefit minority communities, with ideas reminiscent of how conservatives frame race matters!

> So my general approach is that if the economy is strong, that will lift all boats as long as it is also supported by, for example, strategies around college affordability and job training, tax cuts for working families as opposed to the wealthiest that level the playing field and ensure bottom-up economic growth. And I'm confident that that will help the African-American community live out the American dream at the same time that it's helping communities all across the country.[59]

As part of his post-racialism, Obama has avoided the term *racism* in his campaign until he was forced to talk about race. And in that "race speech" that so many commentators heralded and compared to speeches by MLK (a truly heretic view), he said Reverend Wright's statements "expressed a profoundly distorted view of this country—a view that sees white racism as endemic" and classified them as "divisive." This should be surprising to race scholars across the nation who regard racism as indeed "endemic" and know that race has been a "divisive" matter in America since the 17th century!

For readers of this book who are familiar with my work (particularly, Bonilla-Silva 1997 and 2001), it should not be surprising to learn that I agree with Reverend Wright about his claim that racism is endemic to America. Thus, I do not believe his statements were "divisive." As I suggested in my speeches, our nation has been deeply divided by race (and class and gender as well) since colonial times! Obama's speech was clearly a *political* speech intended to appease the concerns of his white supporters riled by the media-driven frenzy in March of 2008 based on a snippet of a sermon given by Reverend Wright.[60] The text of the speech[61] can be deconstructed as a play with five acts. In the first act Obama stated that America is a great country, but recognized that it is still a "work in progress." His campaign, Obama insisted, had worked to continue the long "march for a more just, more equal, more free, more caring and more prosperous America." In the second act he inserted his usual "I am the son of a black man from Kenya and a white woman from Kansas." In the third act Obama chastised Reverend Wright and expressed his profound disagreement with his views, but said he could not "disown him more than (he could) disown (his own) grandmother" who had also uttered racist statements in the past. In the all-important fourth act of the play, Obama justified the anger both whites and blacks have and stated that "racism" has affected both groups (he said white racial resentment was partly "grounded in legitimate concerns"). In the last act of the play Obama called for racial reconciliation and for all Americans to be our "brother's keeper" and continue working together "to build a more perfect union."

His speech had three serious problems. First, Obama assumed racism is a moral problem (he called it a "sin") that can be overcome through goodwill. In contrast, I have argued that racism forms a structure and, accordingly, the struggle against racism must be fundamentally geared toward the removal of the practices, mechanisms, and institutions that maintain systemic white privilege. Second, Obama conceived "racism" (in his view, prejudice) as a two-way street. In the speech he stated that *both* blacks and whites have legitimate claims against one another, that is, that blacks have a real beef against whites because of the continuing existence of discrimination and whites against blacks because of the "excesses" of programs such as affirmative action. Obama was wrong on this point because, as I explained in chapter 7, blacks do not have the institutional power to implement a pro-black agenda whereas whites have had this kind of power from the very moment this country was born.[62] He was also wrong because whites' claims of "reverse discrimination" do not hold much water empirically (see chapter 4 and Vincent Roscigno's 2007 book *The Face of Discrimination*). And when he hints at the "excesses" of the 1960s, which he did in this speech and has done in many other speeches, he is truly talking nonsense! The data shows that affirmative action has been at best a Band-Aid approach to deal with the hemorrhage of racial inequality. Third, Obama's post-racial call for everyone to "just get along"[63] so that we can deal with America's real problems shows the Achilles heel of his stand: he truly does not believe racism is a serious structural problem in America. Otherwise he would not insist—and he has continued this line of argument—that we must get on with America's *real* problems such as the economy, health care, the wars, and the like. Yet the speech accomplished its mission: it placated his white supporters who, from then on, hardly showed more concerns about Obama's racial views.[64] The speech, accordingly, can be classified as a "neoslave narrative" as sociologist Tamara K. Nopper has aptly suggested.[65]

Some readers may be surprised by the fact that many blacks liked Obama's "race speech."[66] This puzzle, however, can be solved. First, whites and blacks heard Obama's race speech and interpreted the controversy over Reverend Wright *differently*. A poll commissioned by Fox News indicated that whereas 40 percent of whites had doubts about Obama because of his relationship with Reverend Wright, only 2 percent of blacks did.[67] Thus, for blacks, his association with Reverend Wright was not a big deal. A CBS-New York Times poll taken in late March of 2008 showed that blacks regarded Obama's campaign and his "race speech" as having had a positive effect on "race relations."[68] Hence, blacks viewed the entire Obama campaign as a positive step on race relations. Second, progressive black dissenting voices on this speech and on all matters related to Obama did not get much play in the media. Hence, the black public did not see or hear on mainstream TV stations or on black stations or radio shows a critique of this speech. Third, the black masses experienced (and as I write these lines, still are experiencing) an understandable yet problematic *nationalist moment* that did not allow for meaningful dissent about Obama and his politics to be expressed in the black community (see endnote 127 on nationalism). Accordingly, all these factors help explain why blacks heard Obama's condemnations of racism and his comments about the continuing significance of discrimination, but paid little attention to his implicit definition of racism, his acquiescence to whites' claims of "reverse racism," or his rather desperate attempt to placate whites' concerns in the speech.

Fourth, as Glen Ford, executive editor of The Black Agenda Report, Adolph Reed, Angela Davis, Paul Street, and a few other analysts suggest, Obamania is a "craze."[69] His supporters refuse to even listen to facts or acknowledge some very problematic positions Obama has, such as his support for the death penalty.

Anyone who lived in the United States during the 2008 presidential campaign knows that the entire country was captivated by Obama who, despite my criticisms, is a truly outstanding orator, astute politician, and remarkably charismatic man. The problem, however, remains. If Obama's charisma and charming smile obfuscates us from asking the hard questions, probing his record, and acknowledging his actual positions on issues, we risk endorsing style over substance and flowery rhetoric over truly progressive positions.

Lastly, perhaps the most important factor behind Obama's success, and my biggest concern, is that he and his campaign mean and evoke different things and feelings for his white and nonwhite supporters. For his white supporters, he is the first "black" leader they feel comfortable supporting *because* he does not talk about racism; because he reminds them every time he has a chance he is half-white; because he is so "articulate" or, in Senator Biden's words, echoed later by Karl Rove, Obama was "the first mainstream African-American who is articulate and bright and clean and a nice-looking guy";[70] *because* Obama keeps talking about national unity; and *because* he, unlike black leaders hated by whites such as Jesse

Jackson and Al Sharpton, does not make them feel guilty about the state of racial affairs in the country.[71]

Since very early on in Obama's campaign, his white supporters were *not* on the same page as his minority supporters. I knew this based on how white colleagues, friends, students, and the general white population was framing and interpreting Obama. He quickly became for whites an Oprah- or Tiger Woods–like figure (and it was no small potatoes that Oprah encouraged him to run[72] and, after he entered the race, endorsed him wholeheartedly and campaigned for him), that is, a black person who has "transcended" his blackness and become a symbol.[73] For instance, Katie Lang, a white woman profiled in a *Washington Post* article entitled "How Big a Stretch? For Barack Obama, Winning the White House Would Mean Bridging the Biggest Gap of All," stated that: "Obama speaks to everyone. He doesn't just speak to one race, one group," and added, "He is what is good about this nation."[74] Mrs. Lang also said:

> Kind of like, if I could compare him to Tiger Woods. When I look at Tiger Woods, I see the best golfer in the world. So when I see Barack Obama, I see a strong political candidate. I do not see "Oh, that's a black man running for president, or African American or multiracial black." It's not what comes to mind first. What comes to mind first is: great platform, charismatic, good leader, attractive.[75]

And many whites, like Joyce Heran in the article I cite above, said without much hesitation that if Obama were like Jesse Jackson or Al Sharpton, they "probably wouldn't like him as much."[76]

In sharp contrast, for many nonwhites, but particularly for blacks, Obama became a symbol of their possibilities. He was indeed, as Obama said of himself, their Joshua[77]—the leader they hoped would take them to the Promised Land of milk and honey. They read between the lines and thought Obama had a strong stance on race matters. For the old generation desperate to see change before they die,[78] and for many post-Reagan generation blacks and minorities who have seen very little racial progress during their lifetimes, Obama became the new Messiah of the Civil Rights movement.

Since Obama's victory in the Iowa caucus, black America projected onto Obama its dreams, history, and pride. This, as I stated above, is understandable. In a country with a racial history such as ours and where successful black leaders end up killed (Martin Luther King Jr. and Malcolm X), vilified (Malcolm X, Minister Farrakhan, and Reverend Al Sharpton), or ridiculed (almost all black politicians), one understands why the possibility of a having a black president became a symbol of the aspirations of the entire black community. In interviews with dozens of blacks from across the nation after the Iowa victory, *The New York Times* reported they "voiced pride and amazement over his victory [in the caucus] and the message it sent."[79]

The love fest between blacks and Obama that began in January after an initial period of doubt[80] has not ended. As I finish writing this chapter, few public black figures or commentators have broken ranks with Obama.[81] Although blacks' nationalist moment has a *raison d'être*, people ultimately do not eat pride, cannot find a job by feeling good about themselves, or fight discrimination by telling white folks "We have a black president so you better behave" (would this have helped Harvard Professor Henry Louis Gates?).[82] Professor Ronald Walters, a black political scientist at Maryland, has wisely said about the honeymoon Obama is enjoying from black America that *"one should not let the honeymoon that President Obama is enjoying among blacks and their leaders extend too far into the future"* (my emphasis).[83]

"THERE IS NO USE TRYING; ONE CAN'T BELIEVE IMPOSSIBLE THINGS": DEBATING THE OBAMA PHENOMENON DURING THE 2008 CAMPAIGN

Given the Obama craze (and I am using the term sociologically), critical engagements on Obama during the 2008 campaign were mostly futile. There was almost no communication as facts meant very little.[84] Hence, when I mentioned in my engagements things such as,

- Obama received 46 percent of his money from corporate America and a lot through the magic of bundling;
- Obama said in a speech in Selma, Alabama, that we were "90 percent on the road to racial equality" (see endnote 77);
- Obama stated he wanted to expand the military by 90,000 and deepen the American intervention in Afghanistan;
- Obama's opposition to the war was suspect (his opposition was not anti-imperialist as documented by Paul Street in 2009 and by Matt Gonzales in his piece entitled "The Obama Craze" (see endnotes 43 and 2, respectively);
- Obama was an ardent believer in free market capitalism albeit with some regulation;
- Obama's civil rights program was nothing more than the liberal stance on race matters and not much different from Hillary's program;

- Obama's stand on foreign policy matters, whether Palestine, Iran, Venezuela, Cuba, Iraq, or Afghanistan, did not represent a break with American imperialist positions;
- Obama was the darling of the DLC ;[85]
- Obama's chief advisers from Chicago and Harvard were regarded as "non-ideological";
- or Obama's stand on FISA, religion, "personal responsibility," work-fare, and on, and on, and on,[86]

people either did not know these things ("Obama got more money from Wall Street than McCain?"—actually, Obama received more money from corporate America than McCain[87]) or, worse yet, knew them but argued these were *tactical* positions Obama needed to espouse in order to get elected. Of course, since Obama's stand on most of these matters *predates* his run for the presidency, they cannot be "tactical" positions. Obama's liberal and progressive supporters wanted to believe, in ahistorical fash-ion, that Obama was a stealth progressive who once elected would turn left.[88] But, paraphrasing Martin Luther King Jr., "leaders should not be judged by the color of their skin but by the *content of their politics*" and the content of Obama's politics was (and is) center to center-right on almost all fundamental matters. Black and progressive America, unfortunately, seems destined to learn this lesson after this "neo-mulatto"[89] rents the White House for a short while and does not do any meaningful renova-tion!

"'WELL! WHAT ARE YOU?' SAID THE PIGEON. 'I CAN SEE YOU'RE TRYING TO INVENT SOMETHING!'": MY PREDICTIONS DURING THE CAMPAIGN AND MY SCORECARD

Social scientists must always verify how their analyses hold up over time. In this section I restate predictions I made during the presidential cam-paign and assess my "batting average." I made two large predictions. First, I predicted the voices of those who contend that race fractures America profoundly would be silenced. Obama's blackness, I suggested, would become an obstacle for people of color as whites would throw it back at them—as well as his words and actions (and even Michelle's)[90] —as evidence that race was no longer a big deal in America.[91] Second, I argued Obama's election would bring the nation closer to my prediction about racial stratification in the United States becoming Latin America-*like* (see chapter 8). Obama's presidency, I claimed, would accelerate the pace toward *symbolic* unity without the nation enacting the social policies needed for all of us to be truly *"all* Americans." And like in Latin American countries, Obama's nationalist stance ("There's not a black America and white America and Latino America and Asian America; there's the United States of America")[92] might shut the door for the recognition of race as a central factor of life! *Obamerica* may bring us closer than ever to a "multiracial white supremacy"[93] regime similar to those in Latin America and the Caribbean where "racially mixed" folks are elected to positions of power without that altering the racial order of things or how goods and services are distributed in the polity.[94]

These are two broad predictions that cannot be easily assessed at this juncture. Although I believe both are happening—and the first one is clearly happening, I will let history and readers judge the accuracy of these two predictions. I now review more targeted predictions I made and offer a few new ones based on President Obama's first year in office. First, based on promises and remarks Obama made during the campaign, I predicted he would increase the size of the military, wait longer than planned for withdrawing from Iraq, increase the scope of the military intervention in Afghanistan and, more problematically, bomb Pakistan if he got "actionable intelligence." So how did I fare? Although the severe economic crisis has prevented President Obama from fulfilling his promise of increasing the size of the military by 100,000, Defense Secretary Gates announced in late July of 2009 that he was going "to increase the size of the U.S. Army by up to 22,000 troops."[95] Regarding Iraq, the president has already taken a much weaker and slower approach. Instead of the sixteen months he promised during the campaign, he is now talking about troop withdrawal in nineteen months and has stipulated that a "residual force" of between 35,000 and 50,000 will remain. He has justified the latter by arguing that most troops will not be "combat forces" but rather "advisory training" and "assistance" brigades. Euphemisms aside, we should be aware that 30,000 to 50,000 American troops in Iraq will be viewed as an occupying force no matter what we call them. It is also very unlikely that a peaceful and stable Iraq will be in place when American troops leave (presumably in 2010) given that the invasion created a "multi-faceted civil war" with "political, sectarian, and ethnic" tonalities.[96]

On Afghanistan, President Obama has already sent 21,000 troops increasing the size of the American forces to close to 60,000 even though he acknowledges that a successful campaign there must be fundamentally about winning "the hearts and minds" of the Afghan people. On Pakistan, reports indicate the United States has been bombing this nation for some time. President Obama himself authorized two drone attacks that reportedly killed at least fifteen and twenty-two people respectively just days into his administration. One report stated that, "Since September (2008), the US is estimated to have carried out about 30 such attacks, killing more than 220 people."[97] (The drone attacks continue and the BBC reports that since August 2008, nearly fifty strikes have killed 450 people in the region.)[98] And if Iraq was (and still is) a quagmire, increasing the scope of the intervention in Afghanistan and bombing Pakistan are even more problematic ventures. No foreign power has ever been able to conquer Afghanistan and the last one that tried (the Soviet Union) was forced out after eight years even though it maintained about 100,000 troops in the territory during its intervention. The Soviets lost more than 14,000 soldiers and rotated over 600,000 soldiers in this costly incursion.[99] To complicate matters further, whereas Iraq is a country of just 29 million people, Pakistan is the sixth-largest nation in the world with 179 million people and Afghanistan has close to 37 million people spread throughout a very harsh and difficult landscape. Hence, one needs not be a military expert to know that the size of the population, terrain, and history do not bode well for the success of an American military campaign in Afghanistan (Coll 2004) or for *any* kind of military intervention in Pakistan.

Second, I suggested Obama was going to put together a very conservative cabinet. As I predicted, the conservative people who advised him during the campaign are now the core of his cabinet. Worse yet, Obama's intention of mimicking Abraham Lincoln by having a "team of rivals" pushed his cabinet unnecessarily further to the right. I review the background of some[100] members of his Cabinet for the benefit of young readers:

- Hillary Clinton, after a long, contested, and divisive campaign where charges of racism were leveled against her and her husband,[101] was appointed Secretary of State.
- Bob Gates, Secretary of Defense for George W. Bush, was retained in the post. Bob Gates' pedigree is that he worked at the CIA and the National Security Council for twenty-six years and served at its director from 1991 to 1993 under President George H. W. Bush. He was also president at Texas A&M University and in that capacity decided not to accept the Supreme Court decision reversing the Hopwood decision, allowing race to be used as a factor in admissions. Secretary Gates has been instrumental in maintaining many of Bush's policies in Obama's administration.
- Larry Summers was a member of President Reagan's Council of Economic Advisers and was Secretary of the Treasury under President Clinton. He was appointed by President Obama as Director of the National Economic Council. This means he is Obama's chief economic advisor. Larry Summers' economic views are center-right.[102] He helped President Clinton pass a capital gains tax measure in 1999 and described the bill that deregulated the banking industry, which

is today regarded as the culprit for the current economic catastrophe in the world, in the following manner: "Today Congress voted to update the rules that have governed financial services since the Great Depression and replace them with a system for the 21st century."[103] But Summers is perhaps best known for his remarks at the National Bureau of Economic Research conference in 2005 where he speculated that women's underrepresentation in technical and scientific jobs may be based on genetics.[104] Summers' views on women were not surprising for many in the Harvard community because under his tenure as president of the institution the hiring and retention of women decreased significantly. He also had a contentious relation with minority faculty that became a matter of the public record after he reprimanded well-known African American professor Cornel West in 2002.[105] Professor West let people know his feelings and views on this matter and left the institution for Princeton.

- Paul Volker was Chairman of the Federal Reserve from 1979 to 1987 under Presidents Carter and Reagan and is now Chairman of the Economic Recovery Advisory Board under President Obama. As chairman of the Fed, Volker raised interest rates in the early 1980s so high that unemployment skyrocketed to levels not seen since the Great Depression (the official rate was about 11 percent in 1982 but if one includes the group labeled as "discouraged workers," the rate was probably closer to 15 percent). He also praised President Reagan for breaking the back of unions.[106]

- Timothy Geithner, former Chairman of the Federal Reserve Bank of New York is now Secretary of the Treasury. Although he has had, unlike other members of Obama's team, a relatively quiet history, Geithner overviewed matters in the most important Fed during the beginning of the current economic crisis and did relatively little to change things.[107] Michael Hirsch suggested in an article titled "Whose Plan Is This?" in *Newsweek* that Geithner's plan to deal with the so-called toxic assets (the bad loans that have lost much of their value in Wall Street) was the brainchild of Warren Buffet, an investor and head of Berkshire Hathaway Inc. who is reportedly the richest man in the world. Whereas critics such as Paul Krugman and Joseph Stiglitz and friends such as Robert Reich (former Secretary of Labor under Clinton) have urged for deeper market reforms, Geithner has followed much more modest reforms consistent with the wishes of Wall Street tycoons.[108]

Obama's Lincoln-like "team of rivals" has been described by independent journalist David Sirota as a "team of zombies!"[109] So far, President Obama does not have a *single* radical voice in his team except perhaps for

Hilda Solis (Secretary of Labor) and, arguably, Eric Holder[110] (Attorney General). Lacking progressive people in his cabinet, who will defend the interests of poor and working people in his administration? Who will push Obama to think hard about American interventions abroad? And let's not forget that Obama's cabinet is not as diverse as one would expect[111] and that the few people of color in his cabinet are in secondary positions (in most press conferences Obama is flanked by white folks).

Third, I suggested Obama was going to compromise on his promise of taxing the rich. He has already delayed doing so until 2010 when Bush's tax cuts expire and when he hopes the economy will have improved. But what will President Obama and his advisers do if the economy does not improve substantially by 2010?[112] Will they stick to the plan and raise taxes for those making $250,000 or more a year or continue on his "pragmatic" track and change course again? What will progressive Americans do if President Obama follows *McCainomics*? As most readers recall, presidential candidate John McCain was the one who said that taxing the rich was problematic because they created jobs and wealth in America. Delaying taxing the rich now and hesitating doing so in 2010 if the economy is not doing well indicate President Obama's economic views are in line with the "Chicago School."[113]

Fourth, I suggested Obama's health care plan was weak and that his "pragmatism" was going to make it even weaker. Specifically, I argued his proposed reform was far off from what the country needed: a universal, single-payer health care plan.[114] This was a bone of contention during the campaign as independent observers commented that Obama had the weakest health care plan of all the contenders for the Democratic Party's nomination. The big issue critics raised was that Obama's plan did not *require* everyone to have insurance. Instead, he hoped all in need would buy health care once it was made "affordable."[115] Unfortunately, by not requiring everyone to have insurance, Obama's plan would create the classic "free rider" dilemma. People in certain positions (e.g., students, independent workers, small business owners, etc.) can game the system by not buying insurance unless they get sick. And because Obama's plan requires HMOs to not exclude people for medical pre-conditions, free riders will not be penalized. If this version of the health care reform is enacted, the artificially high cost of health care will remain as HMOs will pass their increased costs on to the insured.[116]

Obama himself is not an advocate of a single-payer system and has tried to exclude members of his own party such as Congressman John Conyers from Michigan, a leading proponent of a single-payer system, from meetings on health care reform. Conyers, after he threatened to picket outside the White House, was invited to the summit and, later on, in a presentation at Thomas Jefferson University described the attendees of the meeting as follows: "It was very heavy with corporate health care interests—Big Pharma, insurance companies—the people who don't want single payer."[117]

Fifth, I predicted that because of Obama's weak stand on race and his post-racial persona and appeal, he was not going to enact any meaningful race-specific policies to ameliorate racial inequality. Obama's so-called middle ground position on race can be examined in chapter 7 of his book *The Audacity of Hope*. There he insists that although race still matters, "prejudice" is declining and as proof he heralds the growth of the black elite whose members do not "use race as a crutch or point to discrimination as an excuse for failure" (Obama 2006: 241). He acknowledges the existence of significant gaps between whites and minorities in income, wealth, and other areas and makes a tepid support for affirmative action, yet engages in a Bill Cosby–like critique of blacks and states they watch "too much television," engage in "too much consumption of poisons," lack an "emphasis on educational achievement," and do not have two-parent households (244–45). So what is his solution to deal with racial inequality? "An emphasis on universal, as opposed to race-specific, programs" which he believes "isn't just good policy; it's also good politics" (247).[118] He also discusses the problem of the black "underclass" and chastises those unwilling to accept the role of "values" in their predicament (254). Albeit he mentions that "culture is shaped by circumstances" (255), his emphasis is on behavior (see 255–57).

Is there evidence that President Obama's universalist stand has affected his decisions in office? I believe the $789 billion stimulus package his administration passed in early 2009, which gave control to localities on how to use the funds, is a case in point. Giving money directly to localities without any controls is quite problematic as localities have historically distributed funds in a way that preserves existing inequities.[119] Unless one adopts what john powell labels "targeted universalism"—a perspective that takes into consideration that people are differently situated in the social order and, thus, that some may need more resources than others— "universal" efforts such as this one will not reduce racial inequities.[120]

President Obama's "race lite" stand was vital during the campaign and remains so. He has avoided any serious discussion on race and, when forced to talk about it, has remained intriguingly vague. For instance, in an interview with ABC's George Stephanopoulos, he took seemingly all sides on affirmative action. He talked about the importance of *how* affirmative action is carried out, mentioned that race still matters, said his daughters probably will not need affirmative action, and hinted at a class-based program. In a comment on Obama's performance in the interview, Peter S. Canellos observed in *The Boston Globe* that Obama rarely deals with the substance of the policies, but focuses on the values, a tactic that seems to go well with his supporters.[121] In his first press conferences as president, for example, when asked about race matters, Obama has circumvented the questions and suggested he has bigger issues before him.

Further evidence of President Obama's weak stand on race matters was his decision not to attend the 2009 UN-sponsored World Conference on Racism at Geneva. The reasons he cited for not attending were quite similar to those of his predecessor—concerns about reparations and some attendees classifying Israel as a racist state. And in what should have been interpreted as a sign of disrespect by minority organizations, Samantha Power, Obama's national security aide, had a conference call with Jewish leaders to let them know how Obama was processing his decision on whether or not to attend this meeting (all interested parties should have been consulted).[122] Lastly, in his much-heralded trip to Ghana in July of 2009, unlike Presidents Clinton and Bush, who even apologized for slavery, Obama did not contextualize the sad state of much of Africa and excoriated African nations for their problems in "governance."[123]

Sixth, I criticized the progressive and liberal community in America for being in "silly season," to use Obama's terminology, regarding the amount of money he raised (close to 730 million dollars!), how he raised it (bundling), and for ignoring the implications this money would have in his administration (for a good discussion on these matters, see chapter 6 in Paul Street's *Barack Obama and the Future of American Politics*). Are we not concerned that Wall Street and HMOs *support* Obama?[124] Do we believe that 700 million dollars of donations will not affect his administration? (Assignment: Check which companies received bailout money and which did not and then assess if there is any relation to their contributions to Obama's campaign.)

These were my predictions and arguments about Obama and sadly[125] many have become a reality and others seem very likely. Obama is clearly not a stealth progressive, but a centrist, pro-market, traditional politician with a *quasi*-color-blind view about race matters in America. Obama himself has accepted part of this characterization as when, in a meeting with centrist members of his party in April of 2009, he described himself as a "new Democrat" and as a "pro-growth Democrat,"[126] both clear signifiers of his pro-business stance.

To be clear, my characterization of President Obama is political and policy-based rather than moral or personal. In fact, at some level I share a lot of the pride blacks, Latinos, and Asian Americans feel for Obama. In this sense, I am part of the nationalist moment I have mentioned in this chapter (but I have done my best *not* to let this nationalism[127] cloud my analysis). More significantly, I do not believe *all* of Obama's polices are wrongheaded. For example, the closing of the detention camp at Guantánamo Bay,[128] the cessation of so-called "enhanced interrogation techniques (torture),[129] his public statements about wanting to extend a hand to leaders of "rival nations,"[130] the possibility reforming our health care system (even if it ends up not delivering a single-payer system, a reformed bad system will be better than the current one), his support of the "Employee Free Choice Act" which would facilitate workers' efforts to get unionized (even though Obama has already hesitated and urged workers to find a "compromise" with the business community),[131] his new emission and mileage standards,[132] and his legislation to exert some control over the credit card industry[133] are good for the nation. Like so many Americans, I also believe President Obama is a more capable, dignified, and shining representative of this country in the world platform than his predecessor. There is little doubt that Obama projects to the world community a much better image of this nation and its possibilities. Even before he was elected, international polls showed that up to three-fourths of people in the world believed that "an Obama presidency would see improved U.S. relations with the rest of the world."[134] This early enthusiasm for Obama has remained high. A post-election poll, for instance, revealed that two-thirds of those surveyed in seventeen nations, compared to 47 percent in 2008, believed America's relations with the rest of the world will become better.[135]

Nevertheless, having clarity about who Obama is, what his policy stands, preferences, and proclivities are, and what his likely political trajectory will be are important matters as we can use this information to craft a better political strategy for the near future. The contour of such political strategy is what I address in the last section of this chapter.

"'TUT, TUT, CHILD!' SAID THE DUCHESS. 'EVERYTHING'S GOT A MORAL, IF ONLY YOU CAN FIND IT.'": LET SOCIAL JUSTICE NOT DIE AT THE ALTAR OF "PRAGMATISM" AND COLOR BLINDNESS

In this chapter I explained why I was not enchanted with Obama, his policies, and the meaning of his election for the nation. My overall claim was that the Obama phenomenon was not a "miracle" or an event that denotes how far we have come in the arena of "race relations,"[136] but the product of forty years of racial transition from Jim Crow to the regime I have labeled the "new racism." As such, instead of signifying the "end of racism," Obama's election as president may help bring to the fore a more powerful type of racial domination: a Latin America–like multiracial white supremacy order. In *Obamerica* the space for talking about race matters may dwindle as whites have gained the upper hand symbolically. Although little has changed in the fundamentals of the racial order, having a black man "in charge"[137] gives the impression of monumental change and allows whites to tell those who research, write, talk, and organize against racial inequality that they must be crazy. Whites can now say "How can racism be important in a country that just elected a black man as its president?" and add "By the way, I voted for Obama, so I cannot be a racist." (Racial ideologies are always work in progress; thus, the "*I voted for Obama, so* . . ." may join the list of semantic moves I listed in chapter 3.)

I also argued that Obama's politics and stand on racial matters epitomize the character of America's racial regime which, among other things, brought forth the post–Civil Rights minority politician. Although Obama is the most successful exemplar of this new kind of politician, the Democratic and Republican landscape is dotted with them and I forecast many will emerge as central political figures in the near future. Let us not forget, for example, that before Obama, former Secretary of State General Colin Powell could have run for president in 1996.[138] In that year an exit poll conducted the day of the election revealed that had Powell, rather than Bob Dole, been the candidate for the Republicans, he would have won the election.[139]

President Obama has emphasized his interest in "bipartisanship," on not being "ideological," and on his "pragmatic" approach to politics as policy.[140] But what does this mean and what does it imply? I argued his pragmatism and distaste for what he calls "ideology" betrays his center-right stand on most issues. My argument is not entirely original as *New York Times* writer David Leonhardt dissected Obama's policy views in a piece titled "Obamanomics" where he described Obama as a "University of Chicago Democrat" and suggested that "Obama simply is more comfortable with the apparent successes of laissez-faire economics."[141] More tellingly, Leonhardt wrote that "[i]nvoking pragmatism doesn't help the average voter much; ideology, though it often gets a bad name, matters, because it offers insight into how a candidate might actually behave as president."[142]

Interestingly, like all Democratic presidents and presidential candidates since Lyndon B. Johnson, Obama depends on a strong electoral support from minority communities. If at some point black and Latino supporters, who were crucial for Obama's victory,[143] realize he is not going to enact policies that will benefit them they may walk out of his electoral coalition. But since there are no other electoral options at this juncture, what political options are there for people of color and progressives to make sure the change they were promised is delivered?

"'ARE YOU CONTENT NOW?' SAID THE CATERPILLAR": TO-DO LIST FOR "CHANGE" TO BE DELIVERED

Since Obama emerged as a political possibility, I raised concerns about his lack of connection with social movements and about what he was calling a "grassroots movement"—in truth, Obama engaged solely in mainstream work in the party system with a predictably short shelf life. Accordingly, the first thing in the "to-do list" is to work hard in organizing social movements—the plural is important. If Americans truly want Obama's campaign slogan—"change we can believe in"—to become a reality, they must develop the vehicles and mobilize the people that will allow them to produce it. This is exactly the same suggestion I articulated before (see the second edition of this book and the Rowman & Littlefield website), but it is still valid since progressives have not advanced much in this political agenda and, in fact, wasted valuable time, emotions, money, and time in the cultish Obama phenomenon. The more Americans continue buying into mainstream politics, as they did in 2008, the less likely will they be able to effect the social change the nation needs. On this the words of Adolph Reed in 2007 ring as true today as when he wrote them:

> It's a mistake to focus so much on the election cycle; we didn't vote ourselves into this mess, and we're not going to vote ourselves out of it. Electoral politics is an arena for consolidating majorities that have been created on the plane of social movement organizing. It's not an alternative or a shortcut to building those movements, and building them, takes time and concerted effort.[144]

Second, in the process of building these social movements, we must develop *individual* and *collective* practices to resist class, race, and gender domination. These resistance experiences are the political school for those who truly aspire to live in an Amerika without the "k," in an America where real substantive democracy has emerged.[145] Far too many of the young (and the not-so-young) Americans who participated in Obama's campaign have not experienced the deep political experience of working *with* real people and *for* real causes in social movements. Thus, I urge liberals, progressives, leftists, and people of consciousness to move away from mainstream Democratic party politics and engage in social movement–type of work for health care reform, in anti-racist groups and campaigns, in pro-labor and feminist organizations, and in all sorts of anti-systemic political work. These experiences will immunize them against what passes as "politics" and "political participation" in this country and open their eyes and minds forever.[146]

Third, liberals and progressives must radicalize the spaces they inhabit no matter where and no matter what. They have become too passive and, for fear of creating controversy, avoid saying or doing much where they work or live. (This problem afflicted—or, perhaps, *facilitated*—the Obama campaign as those who participated were not encouraged to study the issues at hand deeply.) The not entirely self-imposed silence of the left has reduced the space for contestation in the public square. Although it is true that the "public square" in America is tilted to the center-right and that the media is not free as it is owned by corporations,[147] it is also true that progressives have retreated further reducing their already limited corner in the square.

Fourth, there is desperate need for critiques of President Obama from the left. On this, paraphrasing the lyrics of a song by Michael Jackson, "It don't matter if [our president is] black or white."[148] We must not stop debate, critique, and dissent because the president of the United States is black, white, Latino, or Asian. Only by organizing movements to oppose and challenge many of the policies President Obama is enacting, will we be able to change his political trajectory and the content of his policies. Unfortunately, far too many people in the American left have avoided any public engagement on Obama—whites, because they think that if they criticize him, they will be called "racist," and many people of color, because even though Obama is not "all that," they still think his victory has at least symbolic value.[149] Any true progressive, regardless of their race or gender, should never cease having a deep engagement in political matters. And if through this engagement one concludes a minority politician or a woman of any racial background does not represent the best interest of the people, one must say so loud and clear regardless of the consequences (do we remember the debate around the Clarence Thomas confirmation hearings?).[150] Not engaging in critique is not only a sign of cowardice and accommodation but is also self-defeating. By not criticizing President Obama's policies and actions now, we are digging our own graves as it will be even harder to do so in the future.

Finally, all I have suggested we should do to pressure the Obama administration to "do the right thing"[151] can be done in *creative* ways. The progressive community has become somewhat ossified and not moved up with the times. I have preached the need to *think* and *act* beyond the traditional repertoire of politics and tactics of the left and the Civil Rights movement before and repeat my claims again (again, see my comments in the "postscript" to the second edition and on the Rowman & Littlefield website). We need new ways of *doing* politics, organizing, and working with people to help folks see what is truly going on in the world they live in. Some of the strategies of the past (marches, sit-ins, political rallies, etc.) may still be part of our tool kit, but progressives need to listen to folks in the younger generation who can help them reinvent their political praxis. Accordingly, *Yes we can* use humor, as Michael Moore and others have showed, as an effective political weapon; *Yes we can* be postmodern in style and, on occasion, do truly "wacky" things (wouldn't it be great to do an all-white post-racial rally lampooning Obama's race views?); and *Yes we can* dare talk once again about the revolution and the significance of Malcolm X for racial and social change in *our* America (these are things and names that few dare mention these days). It is time the American left recovers from the political depression it has been in since Reagan was elected president in 1980.[152] It is time it takes a strong political dosage of Prozac and ends its vote-for-whomever-the-Democrats-nominate-for-president political option it has exercised since 1980—voting for the proverbial "lesser of two evils" always keeps evil in power.

If we do these things, we can recover from this maddening moment where things seem upside down. But if we wait until the next election and limit our political engagement to electoral politics—which has become the political praxis of far too many progressives—history is likely to, as Marx wrote, repeat itself: "the first time as tragedy, the second as farce."[153] The tragedy in this moment is that the first person of color elected to the highest office in the nation is a post-racial, accommodationist, so-called pragmatic and non-ideological man without connections to any social movement. The farce is that Obama may run in 2012 against Bobby Jindal—the ultra-conservative Asian Indian governor of Louisiana who has the backing of his party and even of Rush Limbaugh.[154] If this fateful match happens, whites and confused people of color will interpret it as the final proof of America's color blindness. If the farce materializes, getting out of the rabbit-hole I call *Obamerica* will be extremely difficult and the exchange between Alice and the Cheshire Cat may become "real":

> "But I don't want to go among mad people," Alice remarked.
> "Oh, you can't help that," said the Cat: "we're all mad here. I'm mad. You're mad."
> "How do you know I'm mad?" said Alice.
> "You must be," said the Cat, "or you wouldn't have come here."

Nevertheless, even if Jindal and Obama face off in 2012, it will not represent the "end of history."[155] If this match happens, the struggle for racial equality will become much harder, but people can *always* alter the course of history through their actions. People can indeed "make their own history."[156] We can make our president and his administration deliver the change he promised. "We the people" should do what Professor Cornel West suggested immediately after Obama was elected president:

> Barack Obama is a symbol, but we've got to move from symbol to substance. We've got to move from what he represents in a broad sense . . . . Can we

revitalize democratic possibilities on the ground with Barack in the White House? I think we can. We can put some serious pressure on him, and we can actually continue the democratic awakening among working people and poor people and push Barack in a progressive direction.[157]

Accordingly, it is time we "put some serious pressure" on President Obama to make sure "the happy summer days"[158] so many Americans dreamt about when he became president do not become a continuation of our long racial nightmare.

NOTES

1. Throughout this chapter I will use *Alice's Adventures in Wonderland* references. I do this because it fits the case quite well and because as a child this was one of my favorite books. All sections have titles partly derived from passages from the book.

2. This term entered our lexicon during this campaign and was in part produced by the reaction to Obama by the public, by the media, and by Obama's campaign team who wisely realized that the rock star–like adulation Obama was receiving was good for his electoral chances. An early voice critical of this nonsense was Matt Gonzalez, who ran for vice-president under Ralph Nader's ticket, in the article "The Obama Craze," *Counterpunch*, February 29, 2008, at www .counterpunch.org/gonzalez02292008.html.

3. The term "progressive" in the United States has various tonalities and people who call themselves such do not agree a hundred percent on tactics (electoral versus social movement politics) and even on the end game (democratic socialism, mixed-economy, radical democracy, etc.). However, they all repudiate corporate rule and patriarchy, and want to see an end to racial exploitation. They also support a more meaningful democracy where citizens are not spectators, but are at the core of the political process. Examples of progressives who were critical of Obama are Noam Chomsky, Angela Davis, Naomi Klein, and Cornel West.

4. During the campaign, there was a minimal and skewed debate, but at least there was a debate. Now that the Republicans, neoconservatives, and right-wing ideologues (almost the entire cast of the Fox News division, Rush Limbaugh, and others) have raised the intensity and frequency of their attacks and organized anti-Obama rallies such as the April 15, 2009 "Tea Parties," it is even harder for the views of progressives to receive any air time in the public square. In the spaces I debated the Obama phenomenon, the exchanges on all Obama-related matters has dwindled. Nowadays I just receive e-mails on what the right wing is saying about or doing to Obama.

5. Conservatives have created a mythology about academia: the idea that most intellectuals are left-wing oriented. In truth most people in academia are either Democrat or Republican and do not disagree with the *fundamental* components of this country, that is, they are all for the "free market," endorse the American version of "democracy," usually agree with American imperial ventures, and have

few qualms with the plutocracy that rules the nation. For propagators of this mythology, see David Horowitz, *The Professors: The 101 Most Dangerous Academics in America* (Washington, D.C.: Regnery Publishing, Inc., 2006). For a reality check, see Henry A. Giroux, *The University in Chains* (Boulder and London: Paradigm Publishers, 2007).

6. Regardless of my political leanings (and *all* scientists have them and they affect in multiple ways the work they do), it is possible for readers to judge the merits of my analysis as I do the best I can to back up every point I make and bring as much "data" as I can to bear whenever possible. In this sense, my commentary and analysis is indeed sociological.

7. From Bill Cosby to Bill Bennett; from John Lewis to Will Smith; from the Obamas (both) to far too many black and white pundits; the profoundly conservative, outdated, and empirically wrong claim of "now blacks have no more excuses" has reemerged. For a refutation, see Worni L. Reed and Berin Louis, Jr., " 'No More Excuses': Problematic Responses to Barack Obama's Election," *Journal of African American Studies* 13, no. 1 (2009): 97–109.

8. The exact quote of the second president of the United States is "Facts are stubborn things; and whatever may be our wishes, our inclinations, or the dictates of our passion, they cannot alter the state of facts and evidence." The quote can be found in the website of Law Professor Douglas Linder, Famous American Trials, "Boston Massacre Trials, 1770," at http://www.law.umkc.edu/faculty/projects/ftrials/bostonmassacre/bostonmassacre.html.

9. *Clear and Convincing Evidence: Measurement of Discrimination in America* (Washington, D.C.: Urban Institute, 1993).

10. Rivera, Amaad, Jeannette Huezo, Christina Kasica, and Dedrick Muhammad. "State of the Dream 2009." (Boston: United for a Fair Economy, 2009).

11. The report from the Bureau of Labor Statistics can be found at www.bls.gov/news.release/empsit.nr0.htm.

12. Earl Graves, Jr., "State of Black America: Wealth for Life," *Black Enterprise*, at www.blackenterprise.com/blogs/2009/04/08/state-of-black-america-wealth-for-life/.

13. Joe R. Feagin, "The Continuing Significance of Race: Antiblack Discrimination in Public Places," *American Sociological Review* 56, no. 1 (1991): 101–16.

14. 14. For a great review of the contemporary landscape of discrimination, see Devah Pager and Hannah Sheppard, "The Sociology of Discrimination: Racial Discrimination in Employment, Housing, Credit, and Consumer Markets," *Annual Review of Sociology* 34 (2008): 181–209.

15. In the 1960s, sociologist Paul M. Siegel wrote a very influential paper titled "On the Cost of Being a Negro," *Sociological Inquiry* 35, no. 1 (1965): 41–57, documenting the multiple and deleterious impact of racism on blacks. This idea was updated in the 1990s with the notion of "living while black," "driving by blacks," etc. In a recent paper, Shaun Gabbidon and Steven A. Peterson updated the evidence. See their paper, "LIVING WHILE BLACK: A State-Level Analysis of the Influence of Select Social Stressors on the Quality of Life Among Black Americans," *Journal of Black Studies* 37, no. 1 (2008): 83–102. I added in the quote in the text "brown" as many scholars have performed similar analyses for Latinos and Asians and documented that racism affects them adversely, too.

16. Professor William A. Smith has worked tirelessly to demonstrate that racism produces the syndrome he calls "racial battle fatigue." The constant thinking, preparing, expecting, and being concerned about the potential for racial discrimination creates an almost constant state of "fight or flight" in people of color with deleterious health consequences. See William A. Smith, Walter Allen, and Lynnette Danley, " 'Assume the Position . . . You Fit the Description': Psychosocial Experiences and Racial Battle Fatigue among African American Male College Students," *American Behavioral Scientist* 51, no. 4 (2007): 551–78.

17. Conservative race analysts, such as Hoover Institute Senior Fellow Paul Sniderman, have carried the academic torch for the white majority who insists that whites are mostly tolerant, that we still have a few bigots but few and far between, and that white views on crime, welfare, government intervention, and affirmative action are "principled" rather than race-based (see chapter 1). His latest book on race attitudes in the United States is *Black Pride and Black Prejudice* (Ewing, NJ: Princeton University Press, 2002).

18. I must state for the record that survey data suggest that the peak of the anti-immigration feeling in the nation happened in the middle part of the 1990s (65 percent of Americans opposed immigration in 1995 versus 39 percent in 2008). Jeffrey Jones, "Fewer Americans Favor Cutting Back Immigration," *Gallup.com*, June 10, 2008, at www.gallup.com/poll/108748/Fewer-Americans-Favor-Cut ting-Back-Imm igration.aspx. But one must be careful and not equate "survey results" with reality as on sensitive issues, as I have argued in this book, surveys may not measure in a precise manner people's feelings and be good predictors of their behavior.

19. Lou Dobbs has a show on CNN and for years had a segment entitled "Broken Borders." As the economy declined in 2008 and many immigrants from Mexico began returning to their country, Dobbs switched gears a bit and is now targeting the so-called war against drug dealers in Mexico and the "swine flu," both presented to his audience as the product of cultural dislocations.

20. Cities across America have enacted all sorts of legislation against undocumented workers ranging from fining landlords who do not check the citizenship status of their prospective tenants, involving local police in monitoring undocumented workers, and expanding local prisons to detain undocumented workers (cities are paid by the federal government for this service). A recent article by Leslie Savan, "Anti-Mexican Media Hysteria Makes Life More Dangerous for Latinos in the U.S.," *TheNation.com*, May 13, 2009, discussed the "media hysteria" since the outbreak of the swine flu and how it has deepened anti-Latino sentiment and stereotypes in the American population. You can find this article and many similar ones at www.alternet.org/tags/racism/.

21. For a discussion on the silliness of referring to the post-9/11 war as the "war on terror," see Dov S. Zakheim, "What's in a Name? Ending the 'War' on Terror," *The American Interest* at www.the-american-interest.com/article.cfm? piece=420.

22. The text on the debate regarding racial profiling can be found at www.pbs .org/newshour/bb/election/2000debates/2ndebate3.html.

23. Eric Lichtblau, "Bush Issues Racial Profiling Ban But Exempts Security

Inquiries," *The New York Times*, June 18, 2003, at www.nytimes.com/2003/06/18/us/threats-responses-law-enforcement-bush-issues-racial-profiling-ban-but-exempts.

24. The best book documenting the ineffectiveness of racial profiling is David A. Harris, *Profiles in Injustice: Why Racial Profiling Cannot Work* (New York: New York Press, 2003).

25. The video of Father Pfleger's comments can be seen in John McCormick and Manya A. Bracchaer, "Another Video from Obama's Church," *Chicago Tribune*, May 29, 2008, at www.swamppolitics.com/news/politics/blog/2008/05/another_video_from_obamas_chur.html.

26. Chris Matthews said on his show, *Hardball*, the following on February 12, 2008: "I have to tell you, you know, it's part of reporting this case, this election, the feeling most people get when they hear Barack Obama's speech. My, I felt this thrill going up my leg. I mean, I don't get that too often." You can see the video clip at www.huffingtonpost.com/2008/02/13/chris-matthews-i-felt-t_n_86449.html.

27. One student at a certain college in Nowhere, USA, sent me an e-mail letting me know she stopped reading my book after she saw I spelled America with a "k." I explained to her that as a college student, her attitude was reprehensible and silly: reprehensible, because the job of the scholar is to engage no matter what, and silly, because by not reading my book she guaranteed a low grade in her next exam. I also explained to her the meaning of the "k." America has gone a long way from the days of Ameri*kkk*a (the days of slavery), yet we still have a racial structure determining the life chances of all Americans and I signify that by including one "k" in the word "Amerika." Lastly, I told her that I will remove the "k" from Amerika, when Amerika removes racism from its midst!

28. Most liberal and progressive commentators bought Obama's arguments, ideas, and even style. Noteworthy examples were black public intellectuals such as bell hooks, Michael Eric Dyson, Manning Marable, and Cornel West (after some initial hesitation) who supported Obama almost uncritically. An example of the analysts who thought Obama unlikely, or very difficult, to be elected is Joe R. Feagin. See his comments, as well as those of five other analysts including me, in "The Social Significance of Race," at contexts.org/obama/.

29. Besides the articles and talks mentioned in the preface, I also made very specific predictions (including that Obama was likely to be elected by a decent margin) in an exchange sponsored by *Contexts*, a sociology journal. Please see Gianpaolo Baiocchi, Eduardo Bonilla-Silva, Joe Feagin, Enid Logan, Jeff Manza, and Josh Pacewicz,"The Social Significance of Barack Obama: An Online Exchange," *Contexts*, 2008, at contexts.org/obama/.

30. Given the arguments I raised in this book, whites' reaction to Obama is problematic yet understandable. His election is, in their eyes, confirmation they were *right* about the lack of significance of race in the social, political, and economic affairs of the country. Blacks' reactions are a bit more complex and somewhat unexpected, yet ultimately, also understandable. The nationalist euphoria in black America makes sense given that blacks have not seen much *collective* progress in thirty years. Hence, for the black masses, Obama's election seems like

their shining moment in American history. All believe Obama will do right by them and great expectations abound. And, for "successful" blacks (the segment Marable (1981) labels as the "black elite"), Obama's election seems like a confirmation of their own "rags to (not quite) riches" story. For them, Obama is the embodiment and expression of their *class* possibilities. For them, the immense "success" of one of them suggests that they can finally become middle and upper-middle class without the baggage of race affecting their lives. They may remain culturally black, but blackness may no longer be an impediment to their trajectory.

31. In 1973, R&B performer extraordinaire Roberta Flack made immortal the song *Killing Me Softly with His Song*. The refrain of the song goes,

> Strumming my pain with his fingers
> Singing my life with his words
> Killing me softly with his song
> Killing me softly with his song
> Telling my whole life with his words
> Killing me softly with his song

I have used the verse "Killing Me Softly" in talks as a metaphor of how contemporary racism "kills" people of color. Young readers who probably have never listened Mrs. Flack can hear her at www.youtube.com/watch?v=-B1wdau8uHU. For a very disturbingly *white* version of this song, see www.youtube.com/watch?v=OTynJ_p3DaE. (For readers not ready for prime time, this latter version represents "love" as only white as all the pictures in the video are of white people and Mrs. Flack, a beautiful black woman, does not appear at all!)

32. For books with interview data on this period that show this change see Judith Caditz, *White Liberals in Transition* (New York: Spectrum Publications Inc., 1976) and Bob Blauner, *Black Lives, White Lives* (Los Angeles and Berkeley: The University of California Press, 1989).

33. Two books on this broad subject are Jennifer L. Hochschild, *Facing Up to the American Dream* (Cambridge: Harvard University Press, 1995) and Martin Gilens, *Why Americans Hate Welfare* (Chicago: The University of Chicago Press, 1999).

34. See Manning Marable, "Jackson and the Rise of the Rainbow Coalition," *New Left Review* 1/149 (1989): 3–44.

35. Political scientists have been exploring this trend for a while and called it "deracialization." See, for example, Georgia Persons, ed., *Dilemmas of Black Politics: Issues of Leadership and Strategy* (New York: HarperCollins, 2009).

36. Still one of the best books on the "power structure" of America and how the system works is the classic yet magnificently updated book by William G. Domhoff, *Who Rules America Now?* William G. Domhoff, *Who Rules America? Power, Politics, & Social Change* (5th ed.) (New York: McGraw-Hill, 2006).

37. John B. Judis, "Creation Myth," *The New Republic*, September 10, 2008, at www.tnr.com/politics/story.html?id=2e0a7836-b897-4155-864c-25e791ff0f50.

38. Judis, "Creation Myth."

39. One must be careful not to equate the work and politics of paid "activists" with the work and politics of grassroots organizers. Although both may be moti-

vated by similar principles, unpaid work produces a totally different kind of political experience and generates a deeper political experience.

40. Judis, "Creation Myth," my emphasis.

41. "The Curse of Community," *Village Voice*, January 16, 1996—reprinted in *Class Notes: Posing as Politics and Other Thoughts on the American Scene* (New York: New Press, 2000), 13.

42. Christopher Drew and Mike McIntire, "After 2000 Loss, Obama Built Donor Network From Roots Up," *The New York Times*, April 3, 2007, at www .nytimes.com/2007/04/03/us/politics/03obama.html?_r = 1.

43. Paul Street, *Barack Obama and the Future of American Politics* (Boulder and London: Paradigm Publishers, 2009), pp. xxii–xiii. See also Ken Silverstein, "Barack Obama, Inc.: The Birth of a Washington Machine," *Harper's*, November 2006.

44. On this matter, see Dean Baker and Mark Weisbrot, *Social Security: The Phony Crisis* (Chicago: The University of Chicago Press, 2001) and Paul Krugman, "Played for a Sucker," *The New York Times*, November 16, 2007, at www.nytimes .com/2007/11/16/opinion/16krugman.html?ex = 1352955600&en = a87e0ffad19 b7b62&ei = 5090?ner = rssuserland&emc = rss.

45. The TV spot, created and paid for by the American Coalition for Clean Coal Electricity, also known as America's Power, uses a segment of a speech by Obama where he talked about clean coal energy and heralded it as a way to help us deal with our energy crisis as well as creating thousands of jobs. The spot can be seen at greenworldads.blogspot.com/2008/12/barack-obama-clean-coal-commercial-ad.html. And his support during the campaign has remained as he included in his stimulus package more than 3 billion dollars to continue the research on "clean coal technology." On clean coal Al Gore has accurately stated that "Clean coal is like healthy cigarettes, it does not exist." See by Brian Ross and Joseph Rhee, "RFK Jr. Blasts Obama as 'Indentured Servant' to Coal Industry," *ABCNEWS.com* at www.commondreams.org/headline/2009/04/21-8.

46. Arguably the weight of the historical evidence shows that *fundamental* social change is the product of social protest. See Frances Fox Piven, *Challenging Authority: How Ordinary People Change America* (Lanham, MD: Rowman and Littlefield, 2006).

47. FISA, the Foreign Intelligence Surveillance Act, was originally enacted in 1978. This act became extremely problematic as President Bush reportedly used it in an abusive way in violation of the 4th Amendment. In 2008, the act was going to be amended to make sure that those who provided information to the government (telecommunication giants) in violation of privacy rights could not be prosecuted, but Republicans derailed this by adding amendments to a bill sponsored by Senators Dodd and Feingold which were supported by then-Senator Obama. For a blow-by-blow account, see Jake Tapper, "Obama's FISA Shift," *ABC News*, July 9, 2008, at blogs.abcnews.com/politicalpunch/2008/07/obamas-fisa-shi .html.

48. Michael Powell, "Obama Addresses Critics on 'Centrist' Moves," *The New York Times*, July 8, 2008, at thecaucus.blogs.nytimes.com/2008/07/08/obama-addresses-critics-on-centrist-moves/.

49. Taylor Marsh, "Barack Obama's Progressive Cannibalism," *The Huffington Post*, December 8, 2007, at www.huffingtonpost.com/taylor-marsh/barack-obamas-progressiv_b_75933.html.

50. For examples of this view, see Risemay, "From apathy to action: Barack Obama's grassroots movement to mobilize and inspire the American public," *Matador Community*, March 19, 2007, at matadortravel.com/travel-writing/united-states/innovators/from-apathy-to-action-barack-obamas-grassroots-movement-to-m, and Amy Sullivan Sullivan, "A Leader of Obama's Grassroots Army," *Time.co.*, April 21, 2008, at www.time.com/time/magazine/article/0,9171, 1834670,00.html.

51. The literature on social movements is extensive and there are some definitional differences. Nevertheless, Stanley Aronowitz's definition in *False Promises* seems fitting:

> Social movements consist of more than their immediate demands for the redress of grievances. The precondition of sustained protest and contestation is a congealed community with broadly shared perceptions and values upon which agreement to act may be reached. Participants may retain their individual views, may be in conflict about many aspects of the movements' goals and program, but what marks their unity is not only shared enemies, but a strongly held sense that they share the same worldview (1991: xvii–xix).

52. Claire Cain Miller, "How Obama's Internet Campaign Changed Politics," *The New York Times*, August 21, 2008, at bits.blogs.nytimes.com/2008/11/07/how-obamas-internet-campaign-changed-politics/.

53. I stated my views on how blacks and whites regarded Obama to *The Wall Street Journal* writer Jonathan Kaufman who wrote a piece entitled "Race on Campus: Beyond Obama, The Unity Stops." I suggested that few of my white students, like few whites across the nation, had meaningful relationships with blacks, even those who claimed to be for Obama. I also pointed out that the racial views of white Obama supporters were not as progressive as those of his minority supporters and a few other things that were not mentioned in the article. See Jonathan Kaufman, "Race on Campus: Beyond Obama, the Unity Stops: After Campaign Rallies, Black, White Students Go Their Separate Ways," *The Wall Street Journal Online*, May 3, 2008, at online.wsj.com/public/article_print/SB12097767 0689464343.html.

54. For research that shows that younger cohorts are not as racially "tolerant" as people believe, see Scott Blinder, "Dissonance Persists: Reproduction of Racial Attitudes among Post-Civil Rights Cohorts of White Americans," *American Politics Research* 35, no. 3 (2007): 299–335, and Tyrone A. Forman and Amanda E. Lewis, "Racial Apathy and Hurricane Katrina: The Social Anatomy of Prejudice in the Post–Civil Rights Era," *Du Bois Review* 3, no. 1 (2006): 175–202. We still need, however, systematic longitudinal studies on cohorts to assess how their attitudes vary throughout important milestones in the lifecourse.

55. Professors Vincent Hutchings and Tom Pettigrew delivered papers at the conference "Still Two Nations?" at Duke in March of 2009 on their survey work on Obama and the 2008 election. The highlights of their findings were the following:

1) Obama's victory was the result of the "perfect storm" of factors—Obama's lucky situation in Chicago politics which allowed him to become a senator

in 2006, the extraordinarily high levels of black and Latino support for Obama, an economy in shambles, and an ineffective Republican candidate.

2) Despite the hoopla, white support for Obama (45%) in this election was in line with white support for Democratic candidates over the last 40 years.

3) Obama white supporters were not "beyond race." In answers to questions that have been used over the last thirty years to assess "racial attitudes," Obama white voters were just slightly less "prejudiced" than other whites.

4) A similar proportion of whites agreed with typical stereotypes of blacks, but Obama voters were more likely to *hide* this fact (the survey used by Professor Hutchings included an experiment where the mode of administration was varied randomly—face to face or self-administered—which allowed the examination of whether respondents report their beliefs consistently).

56. Paul Street, whose book I cited above, claims he noticed the same kind of blind support for Obama while he canvassed for John Edwards in Iowa. He reports the difficulties he experienced when he tried to discuss and debate with Obama supporters as they seldom had a clue of Obama's policy stands.

57. See AFP, "Michelle Obama Working Hard on New Image," *The Times*, June 24, 2008, at www.thetimes.co.za/Entertainment/CelebZone/Article.aspx?id = 789896.

58. Here is the exchange between President Obama and the journalist Ann Compton:

OBAMA: Ann Compton? Hey, Ann. You sound surprised.
QUESTION: I am surprised. Could I ask you about race?
OBAMA: You may.
QUESTION: Yours is a rather historic presidency. And I'm just wondering whether, in any of the policy debates that you've had within the White House, the issue of race has come up or whether it has in the way you feel you've been perceived by other leaders or by the American people? Or has the last 64 days before a relatively color-blind time?
OBAMA: I—I think that the last 64 days has been dominated by me trying to figure out how we're going to fix the economy, and that affects black, brown and white.

And, you know, obviously, at the inauguration, I think that there was justifiable pride on the part of the country that we had taken a step to move us beyond some of the searing legacies of racial discrimination in this country, but that lasted about a day.

And—and, you know, right now, the American people are judging me exactly the way I should be judged. And that is: Are we taking the steps to improve liquidity in the financial markets, create jobs, get businesses to re-open, keep America safe? And that's what I've been spending my time thinking about. OK. John Ward, Washington Times? Where's John?

The transcript of the press conference can be found at www.washingtonpost .com/wp-dyn/content/article/2009/03/24/AR2009032403036.html.

59. You can find the transcript of the press conference in www.huffingtonpos t.com/2009/04/29/obama-100-days-press-conf_n_193283.html.

60. History was made based on a snippet of a sermon (or perhaps, as I allude below, pasting snippets from several sermons) from a reverend, a church, a con-

gregation, and a religious tradition white America knew almost nothing about. Reverend Wright said about this in an interview with Bill Moyers the following:

> They know nothing about the church. They know nothing about our prison ministry. They know nothing about our food ministry. They know nothing about our senior citizens home. They know nothing about all we try to do as a church, and have tried to do, and still continue to do as a church that believes what Martin Marty said, that the two worlds have to be together. And that the gospel of Jesus Christ has to speak to those worlds, not only in terms of the preached message on a Sunday morning, but in terms of the lived-out ministry throughout the week.

The interview was excerpted by Mark Thomas, "Rev. Jeremiah Wright Appears on PBS' 'Bill Moyers Journal'," in *The Chicago Sun Times*, April 24, 2008, at www.suntimes.com/news/politics/obama/913847,wright042408.stng.

On March 21, CNN's Anderson Cooper in his blog exculpated Reverend Wright from most of the charges. Cooper listened to the entire sermon and found that the "chickens coming home to roost" comment was a quote from Edward Peck, the former U.S. Ambassador to Iraq and he did not find the "God damn America" statement in this sermon which suggests that someone did a job on this Reverend to hurt Obama's presidential chances. See Anderson Cooper's blog, "The full story behind Reverend Jeremiah Wright 9/11 sermon," *AC360*, March 21, 2008, at AC360.blogs.cnn.com/2008/03/21/the-full-story-behind-rev-jeremiah-wrights-911-sermon/.

61. The full text of his race speech in Philadelphia titled "A More Perfect Union" can be found at www.huffingtonpost.com/2008/03/18/obama-race-speech-read-th_n_92077.html.

62. A truly wonderful book outlining the role of race from the moment this country was born through today is Joe R. Feagin, *Racist America* (New York and London: Routledge, 2001).

63. Obama is cited in *Newsweek*, after the Wright controversy and the "race speech," saying the following:

> Race is a central test of our belief that we're our brother's keeper, our sister's keeper . . . . There's a sense that if we are to get beyond our racial divides, that it should be neat and pretty, whereas part of my argument was that it's going to be hard and messy—and that's where faith comes in.

Obama has milked this notion of our "brother's keeper" in many areas, but one cannot forget the religious, conceptual, and political implications of this statement as it pertains to how one addresses the racial problems of America. See Lisa Miller and Richard Wolfe, "Finding His Faith," *Newsweek*, July 12, 2008, at www.newsweek.com/id/145971/page/1.

64. A few weeks after this speech, Obama threw Reverend Wright "under the bus" (this expression became very popular in this campaign) and, later on, renounced his affiliation to the Trinity United Church of Christ. And a few weeks after these actions by Obama, a poll by The Pew Research Center for the People and the Press indicated that most Americans believed he had handled the contro-

versy well and 48 percent of whites agreed with this stand (although 45 percent disagreed). See people-press.org/report/?pageid = 1277.

65. You can read Nopper's speech on this matter in bandung1955.wordpress .com/2008/10/16/obama%e2%80%99s-%e2%80%98race-speech%e2%80%99-as-neoslave-narrative-2/.

66. Liz Halloran, "Obama's Race Speech Heralded as Historic: African-American Scholars and Leaders See This as the Presidential Candidate's Moment," *US News and World Report*, March 18, 2008, at www.usnews.com/articles/news/cam paign-2008/2008/03/18/obamas-race-speech-heralded-as-historic.html.

Even the usually critical people at The Black Agenda Report—and perhaps because of their one-dimensional class analysis—missed the point and focused mostly on the fact that Obama did not address class inequities as central to America's troubling racial history. See their comments at www.blackcommentator .com/269/269_cover_obama_race_speech_analysis_ed_bd.html.

67. Fox News, "Opinion Dynamics Poll," *FoxNews.com*, March 2008, at www .foxnews.com/projects/pdf/032008_release_web.pdf.

68. See CBS News and *The New York Times*, "Race Relations and Politics," *CBS-News.com* at www.cbsnews.com/htdocs/pdf/Mar08c-Race.pdf. A year later, after Obama's first hundred days in office, CBS did another poll with even more optimistic results. In their press release, they stated the following:

> For the first time in CBS News polling history, a majority of blacks are casting race relations in the United States in a positive light.
>
> Fifty-nine percent of African-Americans—along with 65 percent of whites—now characterize the relationship between blacks and whites in America as "good," according to a new CBS News/New York Times survey.
>
> Less than a year ago, just 29 percent of blacks said race relations were good. The percentage of blacks who say race relations are bad, meanwhile, has dropped from 59 percent last July to 30 percent today.
>
> Sixty-one percent of blacks say there has been real progress in getting rid of racial discrimination since the 1960s. That's up from 37 percent in December 1996. Eighty-seven percent of whites say there has been real progress since the 1960s.

69. Collective behavior analysts define crazes as all-involving phenomena where participants seem fanatical and devoted to the craze whether it is in the religious, economic, aesthetic, or political realm. For a classic statement on this matter, see Neil J. Smelser, *Theory of Collective Behavior* (New York: Free Press, 1962).

70. Xuan Thai and Ted Barrett, "Biden's Description of Obama Draws Scrutiny," *CNN.com*, February 9, 2007, at www.cnn.com/2007/POLITICS/01/31/ biden.obama/.

71. Many of the arguments I stated early in the campaign were articulated by other commentators. See David Greenberg's article in *The Washington Post*, "Why Obamania? Because He Runs as the Great White Hope," January 13, 2008, at www.washingtonpost.com/wp-dyn/content/article/2008/01/11/AR20080111 01414.html.

72. I watched *Larry King Live* and still remember the show in 2006 with Oprah and her friends where Mr. King asked her thoughts about a guy who was organizing an Internet campaign of "Oprah for President." She answered:

> WINFREY: You know what I would say to him, I would say, take your energy and put it in Barack Obama. That's what I would say.
> L. KING: Is that your favorite?
> WINFREY: That would be my favorite guy. I'm going to—I tried to call this guy, Mr. Mann, the other day.

See transcript of show in Lynn Sweet, "Oprah tells CNN's Larry King she wants Barack Obama to run for president," *Chicago Sun Times*, September 26, 2006, at blogs.suntimes.com/sweet/2006/09/oprah_tells_cnns_larry_king_sh.html.

73. Gary Kamiya, a writer for liberal journal *Salon*, wrote in February of 2008 a provocative piece entitled "It's OK to vote for Obama because he's black," at www.salon.com/opinion/kamiya/2009/04/29/race/. After he stipulated that his support for Obama was not exclusively based on his race, he bluntly stated:

> But if Obama were a white junior senator from Illinois with the same impressive personal and professional qualities—the same intelligence, empathy, speaking skills, legislative tenure and life story—there'd be no way he'd have the name recognition to mount a major campaign in the first place. And if he did manage to run, it's unlikely he would have inspired such a passionate and widespread following.

> Obama's charisma, which is his unique political strength, is real, but it cannot be separated from the fact that he's black. When Obama speaks of change and hope and healing divisions, his words carry an electric charge because of who he is: He *embodies his own message*, the very definition of charisma. As a black man offering reconciliation, he is making a deeply personal connection with whites, not merely a rhetorical one.

74. See Lynne Duke, "How Big a Stretch? For Barack Obama, Winning the White House Would Mean Bridging the Biggest Gap of All," *The Washington Post*, May 7, 2007, at www.washingtonpost.com/wp-dyn/content/article/2007/05/06/AR200705 0601255.html.

75. Duke, "How Big a Stretch?"

76. Duke, "How Big a Stretch?"

77. In speech in Selma, Alabama, he spoke of the Moses generation (the Civil Rights generation) and thanked them for bringing them 90 percent on the road to equality (this pleased some in the audience, even though it was factually wrong). There he laid claim to the mantel of the Joshua generation, who is charged with bringing his people to the Promised Land. Although he talked of generations, he clearly did not mind the implications of talking in singular about Joshua. The speech can be found at Lynn Sweet, "Obama's Selma speech. Text as delivered," *Chicago Sun Times*, March 5, 2007, at blogs.suntimes.com/sweet/2007/03/obamas_selma_speech_text_as_de.html.

78. See the profile of Evelyn Glore Ashford, a 93-year-old woman, by Thomas C. Fox in his piece for the *National Catholic Reporter* on April 28, 2009. There Mrs. Ashford said, like so many older African Americans, that " 'I'm just so glad I've lived to see this day. I've always had hope that blacks would be recognized for

their achievements and contributions. Now I see it's finally happening." The article can be read in ncronline.org/news/people/100-days-obama-leadership-black-pride-runs-high.

79. See Diane Cardwell, "Daring to Believe, Blacks Savor Obama Victory," *The New York Times*, January 5, 2008, at www.nytimes.com/2008/01/05/us/politics/05race.html.

80. The almost unanimous support Obama has now among the black masses was not so in 2007 and early 2008. See Kevin Merida, "Obama Wave Stuns Clinton's Black Supporters," *The Washington Post*, February 19, 2008, at http://www.washingtonpost.com/wp-dyn/content/article/2008/02/18/AR2008021802364.html.

81. An interesting exception is Michael Eric Dyson who was one of the first, if not the first, of black public intellectuals to endorse Obama and became his surrogate during the campaign (he appeared often in TV shows such as *Larry King Live* debating Hillary Clinton's supporters and, later on, McCain's supporters). But in June of 2009, he began criticizing President Obama and said, among many other things, that Obama "is willing to sacrifice the interests of African Americans in deference to a conception of universalism because it won't offend white people." He also suggested we need to hold him "accountable" and demand he addresses issues of race. His first critical engagement can be seen at www.allhiphop.com/stories/multimedia__video/archive/2009/05/29/21623176.as px.

82. In late July of 2009, Professor Gates, a world-renowned writer, scholar, and public figure was racially profiled in his own house. For details on this story, see Melissa Trujillo, "Henry Louis Gates Arrested, Police Accused of Racial Profiling," July 20, 2009, at www.huffingtonpost.com/2009/07/20/henry-louis-gates-jr-arre_n_241407.html.

83. In this article Professor Walters judged the first hundred days of Obama's presidency and gave him a B+ (and I think he was very generous). The article can be found at blackcommentator.com/322/322_aal_grading_obama_cover_pr inter_friendly.html.

84. In the afterword to her book *Dreaming Blackness: Black Nationalism and African American Public Opinion* (New York and London: NYU Press, 2009), Melanye T. Prince makes the same point and argues, as I do here, that the more we wait to engage Obama critically, the harder it will be to criticize him at all.

85. See Jason Horowitz, "Barack Obama, D.L.C. Clintonite?" *The New York Observer*, March 3, 2008, at www.observer.com/2008/barack-obama-d-l-c-clin tonite.

86. I discussed in endnote 47 the matter of FISA. The comment on religion refers to Obama's support for keeping President Bush's controversial faith-based initiative in place and the comment on "personal responsibility" and "workfare" refer to statements he made during the campaign (although he had made similar statements before and had included them in his *The Audacity of Hope*) chastising what he regarded as behavioral practices of poor blacks.

87. The Center for Responsive Politics, a non-partisan watchdog organization following campaign money based on reports to the National Election Commission, states in their website that Obama raised thirty-eight million compared to

McCain's twenty-eight from the "Finance, Insurance, and Real State" sector. In fact, McCain defeated Obama in the money primary meaningfully only in the "Energy and Natural Resources" and "Transportation" sectors while Obama defeated him handsomely in "Lawyers and Lobbyists," "Miscellaneous Business," and even in the "Health" sector. See the data at www.opensecrets.org/pres08/sectorallc.php?cycle=2008.

88. On this point, Adolph Reed mockingly commented in an article the following:

> A friend of mine characterizes this as the "we'll come back for you" politics, the claim that they can't champion anything you want because they have to conciliate your enemies right now to get elected, but that, once they win, they'll be able to attend to the progressive agenda they have to reject now in order to win. This worked out so well with the Clinton presidency, didn't it? Remember his argument that he had to sign the hideous 1996 welfare reform bill to be able to come back and "fix" it later? Or NAFTA? Or two repressive and racist crime bills that flooded the prisons? Or the privatizing of Sallie Mae, which set the stage for the student debt crisis? Or ending the federal government's commitment to direct provision of housing for the poor?

Adolph Reed, "Sitting This One Out," *The Progressive*, November 2007, at www .progressive.org/mag_reed1107.

89. See Hayward Derrick Horton and Lori Latrice Sykes, "Toward a Critical Demography of Neo-Mulattoes: Structural," in *Skin Deep: How Race and Complexion Matter in the "Color-Blind" Era*, edited by Cedric Herring, Verna Keith, and Hayward Derrick Horton, pp. 159–73 (Urbana: The University of Illinois Press, 2004).

90. Michelle Obama has made some statements as First Lady that I believe will be used against people of color.

91. During the campaign, MSNBC commentators Chris Matthews and Joe Scarborough, the first a Democrat and the second a Republican, pontificated in their shows about how irrelevant race had become in America. Matthews said many times that although he never attended school with blacks, his kids were color blind and had friends from all backgrounds. Scarborough, who is about twenty years younger than Matthews, mentioned often how people of his generation have no race issues and mingle with people from all racial backgrounds without hesitation. Interestingly, his TV and radio show are fundamentally "white shows."

92. Since his 2004 speech at the Democratic Convention, Obama has used this line often and it became ubiquitous in his campaign speeches.

93. Dylan Rodríguez, "Inaugurating Multiculturalist White Supremacy," *ILL-VOX: Blog of Anarchist People Of Color*, November 14, 2008, at illvox.org/2008/11/14/inaugurating-multiculturalist-white-suprema cy/.

94. More time needs to elapse before anyone can judge if my two big predictions held. But on the first one there is already increasing evidence that being critical of Obama is equated with sympathizing with or supporting the right wing. Juan Cole, for example, a distinguished liberal commentator and professor of political science at Michigan, was called all sorts of names by Taylor Marsh (a Democratic Party supporter and writer) because of a column he wrote in *Politico*

criticizing President Obama's decision of bombing Pakistan. In his popular blog he wrote the following about this state of affairs:

> The notion that we should not say something critical of the policy of a Democratic president because it might give aid and comfort to the rightwing enemy is completely unacceptable. It is a form of regimentation, and equivalent to making dissent a sort of treason. We had enough of that the last 8 years (it used to be from different quarters that I was accused of traitorously succoring the enemy).

His post was on January 27, 2009, and can be found at www.juancole.com/2009/01/cole-marsh-debate-on-obamas-bombing-of.html.

95. CNN, "Defense Secretary to Add Up to 22,000 troops to U.S. Army," July 20, 2009, at www.cnn.com/2009/POLITICS/07/20/us.military.increase/index.html.

96. For in-depth analysis and reporting on the Iraq invasion and its aftermath, see the Pulitzer Center on Crisis Reporting at pulitzercenter.typepad.com/death_of_a_nation/. For critiques of the strategy of arming certain tribes in Iraq to fight "the enemy," see Sumedha Senanayake, "Iraq: Plan to Arm Additional Sunni Groups Poses Risks," *Radio Free Europe Radio Liberty*, June 22, 2007 at www.rferl.org/content/article/1077279.html.

97. For reports on covert bombings in Pakistan and their impact, see "President Obama Orders Pakistan Drone Attacks," *TIMESONLINE*, January 23, 2009, at www.timesonline.co.uk/tol/news/world/us_and_americas/article5 575883.ece. See also, Sarah Baxter, "Obama Airstrikes Kill 22 in Pakistan," *TIMESONLINE*, January 25, 2009, at www.timesonline.co.uk/tol/news/world/us_and_americas/article5 581084.ece.

It is noteworthy that David Kilcullen, an army officer who served under General David Petraeus and a strong advocate of the "upsurge" in Iraq, in testimony before Congress objected to the missile attacks in Afghanistan. His objection was neither moral nor legal, but practical. In his words, "Since 2006, we've killed 14 senior Al Qaeda leaders using drone strikes; in the same time period, we've killed 700 Pakistani civilians in the same area. The drone strikes are highly unpopular. They are deeply aggravating to the population. And they've given rise to a feeling of anger that coalesces the population around the extremists and leads to spikes of extremism. . . . The current path that we are on is leading us to loss of Pakistani government control over its own population." See the article by Doyle McManus, "U.S. drone attacks in Pakistan 'backfiring,' Congress told," in *The Los Angeles Times*, May 3, 2009, at www.latimes.com/news/opinion/commentary/la-oe-mcmanus3-2009may03,0,7133284.column.

98. "Drones kill dozens in Pakistan," *BBC News*, July 8, 2009, at news.bbc.co.uk/2/hi/south_asia/8139739.stm.

99. See Arundhati Roy, *Soviet Intervention in Afghanistan: Causes, Consequences and India's Response* (New York: Stosious Book, 1987).

100. The list is larger and growing and includes other center-right oriented people such as Arne Duncan, Secretary of Education, and Susan E. Rice, Obama's appointee as U.S. Ambassador to the United Nations.

101. Dan Baiz, "Bill Clinton South Carolina's Ties," *The Washington Post*, January 22, 2008, at voices.washingtonpost.com/44/2008/01/22/bill_clintons_south_ carolina_t.html.

102. For an interesting exposé of Larry Summers' economic views and how they fit the current economic policies of the Obama administration, see Bill Moyers and Michael Winship, "The Intoxication of Larry Summers: Changing the Rules of the Blame Game," *CommongoundCommonsense.org*, April 9, 2008, at www.common groundcommonsense.org/forums/lofiversion/index.php/t107705.html.

103. Labaton, Stephen, "Congress Passes Wide Ranging Law Repealing Bank Laws," *The New York Times*, November 9, 1999, at www.nytimes.com/1999/11/ 05/business/congress-passes-wide-ranging-bill-easing-bank-laws.html.

104. Lawrence H. Summers, "Remarks at NBER Conference on Diversifying the Science and Engineering Work Force," can be found at www.president.harv ard.edu/speeches/summers_2005/nber.php. The American Sociological Association, among many other organizations, issued a statement stating that there are virtually no differences between men and women in "measures of verbal, mathematical, and spatial abilities" and that women, like men, "flourish in science, just as in other occupational pursuits, when they are given the opportunity and a supportive environment." Thus, the observed differences in employment patterns and compensations, which have been declining over time, are explained by social factors such as discrimination, socialization, social gender expectations, and the like. The statement titled "Statement of the American Sociological Association Council on the Causes of Gender Differences in Science and Math Career Achievement: *Harvard's Lawrence Summers and the Ensuing Public Debate*" can be found at www2.asanet.org/public/summers.html.

105. On the West controversy and Summers' lack of support for affirmative action, see Robin Wilson and Scott Smallwood, "Battle of the Wills," *The Chronicle of Higher Education*, January 18, 2002, at chronicle.com/free/v48/i19/19a00801 .htm. On the matter of how few women were hired or promoted during Larry Summers' tenure as president of Harvard, Marcela Bombardieri in her 2005 article in *The Boston Globe*, "Harvard Women's Group Rifts at Summers," wrote that: "Each academic year since Summers became president in 2001, the percentage of women offered tenured jobs has declined. In the last academic year, only four of 32 such offers were extended to women." The article is located at www.boston.- com/news/education/higher/articles/2005/01/19/ harvard_womens_group_rips_ summers/.

106. Patrick Martin, "Who is Paul Volcker? Obama Appoints a Longtime Enemy of the Working Class," November 29, 2008, at www.wsws.org/articles/2008/ nov2008/volc-n29.shtml.

107. See *The Wall Street Journal*'s piece "Who is Timothy Geithner?" November 28, 2008, at blogs.wsj.com/economics/2008/11/21/who-is-timothy-geithner/.

108. The article can be found at www.newsweek.com/id/192328. See also Tim Rich's piece, "Slumdogs Unite!" in *The New York Times*, February 7, 2009, criticizing Geithner and Obama's economic team at www.nytimes.com/2009/02/08/ opinion/08rich.html?_r=1&ref=opinion.

109. David Sirota's "Obama's Team of Zombies," February 6, 2009, can be found at www.creators.com/opinion/david-sirota/a-team-of-zombies.html.

110. It will be interesting to watch how long this Attorney General lasts and if he remains strong in his views. After a speech at the celebration of Black History Month at the Department of Justice in which he said that "Though this nation has proudly thought of itself as an ethnic melting pot, in things racial we have always been and continue to be, in too many ways, essentially a nation of cowards," President Obama rebuked him publicly. The test of his independence and progressiveness will be what he decides to do regarding the reports that the CIA lied to Congress about plans for various covert operations from 2001 to 2008 given that President Obama has all but said he does not want to prosecute anyone and prefers to "move forward." Obama's interview and Holder's speech can be accessed through Steven Rounds, "Obama Criticizes Holder's 'Nation of Cowards' Speech," March 7, 2009, at www.mainjustice.com/2009/03/07/nation-of-cowards-statement-receives-criticism-from-obama.

111. Jared Allen, "Black lawmakers irked by Obama's diverse cabinet," *The Hill*, December 22, 2008, at thehill.com/leading-the-news/black-lawmakers-irked-by-obamas-diverse-cabinet-2008-12-22.html.

112. Currently most economists believe the economy might see signs of recovery in late 2010. But given that they expect the unemployment rate to be hovering about 10.5 percent, classifying that as "recovery" is pie in the sky. In an article that appeared July 21, 2009, in *The Wall Street Journal* Ben Bernanke, Chair of the Federal Reserve, seems aware of this reality. He wrote that "accommodative policies [by the Fed] will likely be warranted for an extended period." This means that even though a few things are doing well, the economy is still unstable and fragile and thus the Fed has decided not to tighten monetary policy (raise interest rates) until the economy stabilizes. The article can be read at online.wsj.com/article/SB10001424052970203946904574300050657897992.html.

113. Obama taught law at Chicago and was influenced by the "Chicago School." Read Naomi Klein's incisive column in *The Nation*, entitled "Obama's Chicago Boys," June 12, 2008, where she documents the influence of the conservative, Milton Friedman-inspired Chicago School of economics on Obama. The article can be found at www.thenation.com/doc/20080630/klein. See also David Leonhardt, "Obamanomics," *The New York Times*, August 20, 2008, at www.nytimes.com/2008/08/24/magazine/24Obamanomics-t.html.

114. The group Physicians for a National Health Program define single-payer as follows: "Single-payer national health insurance is a system in which a single public or quasi-public agency organizes health financing, but delivery of care remains largely private." See their website at www.pnhp.org/facts/single_payer_resources.php.

115. See Paul Krugman's piece "Clinton, Obama, Insurance," *The New York Times*, February 4, 2008, at www.nytimes.com/2008/02/04/opinion/04krugman.html.

116. As I write this chapter, the debate is raging and it is not clear if Obama will move to the right to get some Republican support or listen to (or be pushed by) those in his party who have insisted for years on the necessity of a single-payer

system. One positive element is that Obama's team and Senate majority leader Harry Reid included a reconciliation process in the health care debate, which means that (1) the bill can pass with just fifty-one votes and (2) the measure has a deadline of October 15, 2009. See Jonathan Cohn's piece, "Reconciliation now has date: October 15," *The New Republic*, April 24, 2009, at blogs.tnr.com/tnr/blogs/the_treatment/archive/2009/04/24/reconciliation-now-has-a-date-october-15.aspx.

However, the big issue to look out for will be whether the *public* component of the measure—a Medicare-like system to guarantee access and affordability to every American regardless of income—remains in the final iteration of the bill. Obama will have to contend not only with Republicans, but with conservative Democratic senators such as Arlen Specter (PA), Max Baucus (MT), and Ben Nelson (NE). Baucus, as Chairman of the Finance Committee, is in a powerful position to mold the final version of the plan and has already said in public that he does not support a single-payer system. And Baucus, according to data from the Federal Election Commission, is the third-largest recipient of money from the health care and pharmaceutical industry. See Dan Eggen, "Health industry has donated millions to lawmakers," in *The Washington Post*, March 8, 2009, at www.washingtonpost.com/wp-dyn/content/article/2009/03/07/AR2009030701748.html. On May 7, 2009, Baucus held a meeting of the Finance Committee on health care reform and excluded all advocates of the single-payer system. This event was not reported widely, but Ed Schultz, in his *The Ed Show* on MSNBC aired a great segment on it on May 8, 2009. The segment can be seen at www.msnbc.msn.com/id/30031533/. Four days later, President Obama had a meeting with representatives of, among other groups, the American Medical Association, the Pharmaceutical Research and Manufacturers of America, the American Hospital Association, America's Health Insurance Plans, and the Service Employees International Union where all agreed to support health care reform and enact measures to cut costs. Yet, the emerging consensus of the reform in the making is that it will not be a single-payer system. See Michael A. Fletcher and Ceci Connolly, "Health Groups Vow Cost Controls," *The Washington Post*, May 11, 2009, at www.washingtonpost.com/wpdyn/content/article/2009/05/10/AR2009051002222.html?hpid=topnews.

As I finish this draft, several groups are organizing marches and are lobbying hard to make sure that the single-payer option is debated. However, based on the political landscape, Baucus' centrality to this process, and the president's pragmatic proclivities, I believe the health care reform that will be enacted will be very weak and may not even include a decent and large public option. For those interested in data and analysis on health care reform see the website of *American Health Care Reform.org* at http://americanhealthcarereform.org/.

117. Michael Vitez, "At Jefferson, Conyers Backs Obama Health Stand," *The Philadelphia Enquirer*, March 7, 2009, at www.philly.com/philly/news/breaking/40898352.html.

118. Like sociologist William Julius Wilson, who articulated this position in his books *The Declining Significance of Race* and *The Truly Disadvantaged*, Obama believes that a class-based or "universal" approach will help blacks and Latinos

as a good economy "will lift all boats." The problem with this policy is that it has not worked because even poor whites have racial advantages compared to poor blacks and Latinos and, accordingly, universal programs tend to benefit disproportionally not blacks but *whites*. It is noteworthy that Wilson changed his stand somewhat and now advocates for universal programs that are sensitive to race (see his shift in position in his 1996 book *When Work Disappears* and in his recent *More Than Just Race*). I cite below the work of john powell on this matter and I urge interested parties to read the work of Princeton sociologist Marta Tienda on the limits of universal social policies. For a short statement on her findings, see Marta Tienda, "Diversifying the College Campus," *Contexts*, 2008, at contexts .org/articles/fall-2008/diversifying-the-college-campus/.

119. For a great discussion about how race affected how funds were dispersed in the New Deal, see Ira Katznelson, *When Affirmative Action Was White* (New York and London: W.W. Norton, 2005).

120. Kirwan Institute for the Study of Race and Ethnicity, *Preliminary Report of the Impact of the Economic Stimulus Plan on Communities of Color*, February 25, 2009, at 4909e99d35cada63e7f757471b7243be73e53e14.gripelements.com/publications/ preliminary_report_on_stimulus_impacts_feb2009.pdf; john powell, "Post-Racialism or Targeted Universalism?" February 4, 2009, at 4909e99d35cada63e7f75747 1b7243be73e53e14.gripelements.com/publications/post-racialism_or_targeted_ universalism_powell_feb2009.pdf.

121. Peter Canellos, "On Affirmative Action, Obama Intriguing but Vague," *Boston.com*, April 29, 2008, at www.boston.com/news/nation/articles/2008/04/29/ on_affirmative_action_obama_intriguing_but_vague/.

122. See Sam Stein, "Obama Team Tells Jewish Leaders: UN Durban Text Crosses 'Red Line,'" *The Huffington Post*, April 15, 2009, at www.huffingtonpost .com/2009/4/14/obama-team-tells-jewish-l_n_186874.html

123. On Obama's problematic comments in Ghana and the real imperial interests behind his visit and statements, see Maulana Karenga, "Obama in Africa: Rethinking Reality and Responsibility," *Humanities and Social Sciences Online*, July 20, 2009, at h-net.msu.edu/cgi-bin/logbrowse.pl?trx=vx&list=H-Afro-Am& month=0907&week=c&msg=p52j8pOCTcv3J2XTvdJn0A&user=&pw=.

124. In a investigative report piece in *Harper's* magazine, titled "Sick in the Head: Why America Won't Get the Health-care System It Needs," Luke Mitchell documents that the HMOs, represented by an organization in Washington called America's Health Insurance Plans, *support* universal health care. What they do not support is, however, the enlargement of government-led programs such as Medicare and Medicaid or similar ones, that is, they want universal coverage but through market-based organizations. Such an approach is unlikely to do much to address the high costs of health care in America. The article appeared in vol. 318, no. 1905, in February 2009.

125. In many presentations on the Obama phenomenon, I was accused of being a "cynic" or a "pessimist." Nothing further from the truth; I tried to explain as best as I could and with the information I had at hand what I thought was happening in the country. And, as an analyst of color, my hopes and dreams are like those of Dr. King, to "one day live in a nation where [no one] will . . . be judged

by the color of their skin but by the content of their character." But the dream he had and that I share cannot happen unless, as he also said, we "make real the promises of democracy." Without letting true freedom ring, ineffective and timid reform will parade for real change and we may be as a nation not much better than before Obama was elected president. (Dr. King's "I have a dream" speech can be found at www.usconstitution.net/dream.html).

126. Jonathan Martin and Carol E. Lee, "Obama: 'I am a New Democrat,'" *Politico*, March 11, 2009, at www.politico.com/news/stories/0309/19862.html. New Democrats, a label used by people affiliated with the DLC, describe their views as follows on their website:

> New Democrats support policies to expand economic growth and ensure that all Americans have the opportunity to benefit from that growth; a fiscally responsible and efficient government; a secure homefront; and a robust foreign policy that includes trade, constructive U.S. leadership throughout the world, and a modern and strong military.

See www.house.gov/tauscher/ndc/about_ndc.shtml.

127. Nationalism is a peculiar social force. It can bond a "nation" (even when all nations are "imagined communities" [Anderson 1991]), it can help people in their struggles for liberation from the yolk of colonialism (but even here, what begins as progressive can—and often does—deteriorate into chauvinism), and it can be used to justify the most horrific atrocities, such as the cases of Nazi Germany, Rwanda, and Yugoslavia show. Thus, nationalism is like a sea urchin: it is delicious, but it is spiny and dangerous.

128. As I write this chapter some Democratic leaders of the Senate such as Virginia Senator Jim Webb are suggesting the need to keep the prison open until they process all the detainees. And in late May, with the support of most Democrats in the Senate, a bill passed *not* funding the closing of Guantánamo.

129. Unfortunately, Obama's "pragmatism" has affected even this positive development as he is already backtracking, for instance, on his promise of releasing pictures of prisoners who were tortured. See Jennifer Loven, "Obama seeks to block release of abuse photos," *AP White House Correspondent*, at news.yahoo.com/s/ap/20090513/ap_on_go_pr_wh/us_pentagon _abuse_photos. He also reversed himself on the "military tribunals" and has reinstated this Bush-era atrocity. See Lara Jakes, "Obama to revive military tribunals for GITMO detainees, with more rights," *The Huffington Post*, at www.huffingtonpost.com/2009/05/14/obama-to-revive-military-_n_203783.html.

130. It is commonplace to refer to Cuba, Venezuela, Iran, Nicaragua (with Daniel Ortega as its President), Bolivia, and other nations as our "rivals." But this assumes that the United States has a common "national interest" which these nations have presumably threatened. But if we see the United States as a nation divided along lines of class, gender, and race, then one must ponder whose interests are being defended when our leaders talk tough about these nations. For readers intrigued by this comment, I urge them to take a good introductory course to sociology where the idea of "national interest" is deconstructed.

131. Sam Stein, "Obama's Remarks On Employee Free Choice Act Make Labor

'Very Pleased,'" *The Huffington Post*, February 12, 2009, at www.huffingtonpost .com/2009/02/12/obamas-remarks-on-employe_n_166345.html.

132. Mike Allen and Eamon Javers, "Obama announces new fuel standards," *Politico*, May 19. 2009, at www.politico.com/news/stories/0509/22650.html.

133. Sudeep Reddy, "Obama pushes for legislation," *The Wall Street Journal*, May 11, 2009, at online.wsj.com/article/SB124186580127503661.html.

134. Ali Gharib, International Press Service, "Obama Clear Winner in World Opinion" at www.commondreams.org/headline/2008/09/12-2. But see also why a crucial segment of the world, the Muslim world, is not likely to be too impressed with Obama in Ala Al Aswany 's piece, "Why the Muslim World Can't Hear Obama," *The New York Times*, February 7, 2009, at www.nytimes.com/2009/02/08/opinion/08aswany.html.

135. Rudy Texeira, "World Publics Optimistic about Obama Presidency," *Center for American Progress* at www.americanprogress.org/issues/2009/02/opinion_020909.html.

136. Since early on, some black commentators who supported Obama expressed their concerns about how whites were framing this situation. Professor Roderrick J. Harrison, a demographer from Howard University, stated that, "Historic as this moment is, it does not signify a major victory in the ongoing, daily battle." See Rachel L. Swarns, "Blacks Debate Civil Rights Risk in Obama's Rise," *The New York Times*, August 24, 2008, at www.nytimes.com/2008/08/25/us/politics/25race.html.

137. I must state for the benefit of younger readers that the selection process that produces our candidates for the presidency guarantees that the interests of dominant groups in society (capitalists, men, and whites) will be safeguarded and represented (Domhoff 2006). However, I also want to stress that political power, as expressed in state politics, is not equivalent with having absolute political power. Why? Because although dominant groups exert economic and ideological power and through them shape the terrain and content of politics, the subaltern (working class, women, and racial minorities) always have the potential to raise hell and effect change. Otherwise change would be impossible.

138. Colin Powell fits many of the elements of the new type of post–Civil Rights minority politician. However, I must point out that on racial matters, Powell has maintained a decent record. Even during duress, he remained firm in his support for affirmative action and did not buy completely into the romantic view of America the post-racial nation. See Colin L. Powell with Joseph E. Persico, *My American Journey* (New York: Random House, 1995).

139. Martin Plissner, "Ready for Obama Already," *The New York Times*, February 7, 2007, at www.nytimes.com/2007/02/07/opinion/07plissner.html?_r=1.

140. In his books, speeches, and interviews, Obama has insisted on these three matters: the need for bipartisanship, the limits of ideologically driven politics, and the desire for a pragmatic view on policies concerned with outcomes. For an early assessment on Obama's pragmatism, see David Ignatius's article in *The Washington Post*, "The Pragmatic Obama: He's Shaping the Debate on Foreign Policy," at www.washingtonpost.com/wp-dyn/content/article/2007/08/22/AR 2007082202400.html.

141. Leonhardt wrote this piece, which can be found at www.nytimes.com/2008/ 08/22/business/worldbusiness/22iht-WBobama23.1.15544413.html, in August of 2008 and has since written two more long pieces based on interviews with now President Obama. His last piece, "After the Great Recession," can be found at www.nytimes.com/2009/05/03/magazine/03Obama-t.html?pagewanted=6 .

142. Leonhardt, "Obamanomics."

143. Ninety-four percent of black voters and sixty-seven percent of Latinos supported Obama. The latter vote was more crucial as almost all past Democratic candidates in the last elections received upwards of eighty-eight percent support (e.g., John Kerry received ninety percent of the black vote in 2004). Furthermore, the Latino vote was decisive in the all-important battleground states such as Pennsylvania, Virginia, and Nevada. For superb data on the elections, see the report by *conservative* analyst Joseph Gimpel, "Latino Voting in the 2008 Election: Part of a Broader Electoral Movement" for the anti-immigrant *Center For Immigration Studies* which can be located at www.cis.org/latinovoting (sometimes the data talks more loudly than the ideology of those who produce it).

144. Adolph Reed, "Sitting This One Out."

145. Political scientists have wasted a lot of time and paper in discussing the contours of democracy as they mostly focus on the *formal* (voting, replacing leaders, free speech, etc.) rather than the *substantive* components of democracy. For an exception, see Joshua Cohen, "Procedure and Substance in Deliberative Democracy," in *Deliberative Democracy: Essays on Reason and Politics*, edited by James Bohman and William Rehg (Cambridge, Mass.: MIT Press, 1997), 407–38.

146. Although I am a "successful" professor of sociology at a "major" university, my political roots go back to my work with pro-independence groups, with groups defending the rights of squatters, and with the student movement that led a major strike in the University of Puerto Rico in 1981. Later on, while a graduate student at the University of Wisconsin, I participated in campaigns against the American intervention in Central America and for divestment in South Africa and, later on, was active in the creation and development of a group called The Minority Coalition which demanded diversity at Wisconsin and produced some reforms in the late 1980s. And even though I am no longer a flaming radical activist, I remain committed to the cause of social justice and "fight the power" in my academic domain (let's not forget that twenty-five percent of Americans have college degrees, therefore, we must do organizational work in colleges and universities, too).

147. Since the publication in 1998 of Edward S. Herman and Noam Chomsky's *Manufacturing Consent* (New York: Pantheon), many books have appeared documenting corporate control of the media and its implications. Two exemplars are Ben Bagdikian, *The New Media Monopoly* (Boston: Beacon Press, 2004) and the book edited by Ellio D. Cohen, *News Incorporated: Corporate Media Ownership and Its Threat to Democracy* (New York: Prometheus Books, 2005).

148. Michael Jackson's song, "Black or White," appeared on his 1991 album *Dangerous.* I cited this point in speeches in 2008 before Jackson's tragic death in June 2009.

149. During the campaign I addressed this claim about the symbolic value of his election in two ways. First, I argued that the symbolic value of Obama for people

of color was different than that for whites. Whereas for people of color he is their Joshua, for whites he is a symbol of the post-racial America. Second, for those who kept saying how now "little kids" will be able to believe they can be anything they want to be, I pointed out that (1) minority children exhibit higher levels of self-esteem than white children and (2) having the symbol without the "opportunity structure" could create all sorts of dislocations in minority children as they can now be blamed if they do not achieve all they presumably can. On black children and their self-esteem, see the work of Professors Bernadette Gray-Little and Adam F. Hafdahl from UNC-Chapel Hill highlighted in a university press release at www.unc.edu/news/archives/jan00/graylit012400.htm.

150. The NAACP, the largest civil rights group in the nation, deliberated for too long on this case and when it issued its opposition to the nomination of Clarence Thomas to the Supreme Court, it was too late to make an impact. Although Thomas' record was clearly that of a conservative man who opposed almost *all* legislation and jurisprudence of interest to the Association, the group hesitated because of only one reason: Thomas was a black man and many members thought this fact alone would make him see the light once on the court. Almost twenty years later the folly of this thinking is crystal clear as Thomas has been one of the most conservative members of the court and has voted against all issues of interest to the NAACP.

151. This was the title of one of Spike Lee's best movies ever. I urge young readers of this book to check out this wonderful movie which challenges us all to examine the political question of what tactics we should use to challenge racial injustice in America.

152. In truth, this was part of the world-systemic economic and political restructuration brought by the rise of the neoliberal project. See David Harvey, *A Brief History of Neoliberalism* (Oxford: Oxford University Press, 2005).

153. Karl Marx, "The Eighteenth Brumaire of Lois Bonaparte," *Karl Marx, Selected Readings*, David McLellan, ed. (Oxford: Oxford University Press, 1982), 300.

154. After a disastrous response to President Obama's first address to a joint session of Congress, arch-conservative radio commentator Rush Limbaugh came to Jindal's rescue and likened him to Ronald Reagan. Associated Press, "Critics rip Governor Jindal's response," at www.boston.com/news/nation/articles/2009/02/26/critics_rip_governor_jind als_response/.

155. Francis Fukiyama made popular this term in the late 1980s and early 1990s through essays and his 1992 book, *The End of History and the Last Man* (New York: The Free Press). The thesis of Fukiyama is that the long struggles of humanity over ideology have ended and that liberal democracy was in fact the end of history. But this argument has a long hand as it is articulated by liberal theoreticians almost once every generation. Before Fukiyama, sociologist Daniel Bell wrote a similar tome entitled *The End of Ideology* in 1960. Interestingly, history continues forcing these authors to proclaim later on like religious leaders that "the end of time is coming soon."

156. Karl Marx, *Selected Readings*, 300.

157. This comes from the transcript of the interview Professor West did with Amy Goodman for her show, *Democracy Now*, which can be found at www.demo cracynow.org/2008/11/19/cornel_west_on_the_election_of. After an initial

period of reticence, particularly after Obama decided not to attend an event celebrating the 40th anniversary of MLK's assassination in Memphis, missed Tavis Smiley's "State of the Black Union" in New Orleans, and failed to mention MLK in his nomination acceptance speech, Professor West decided to support Obama critically. However, during the campaign and now that Obama is president, Professor West has continuously criticized Obama for his soft stand on race matters, for his continuation of America's imperial policies, and for his mild approach to class matters. For an early statement of his views, see the transcript of his June 28, 2007, interview in *Democracy Now* at www.democracynow.org/2007/6/28/ renowned_princeton_professor_cornel_west_assesses.

158. This is the last phrase of Lewis Carroll's *Alice in Wonderland*. The entire book is online at www.sabian.org/alice.htm.

10

‿

Conclusion: "The (Color-Blind) Emperor Has No Clothes"

Exposing the Whiteness of Color Blindness

If there is no struggle, there is no progress. Those who profess to favor freedom, and yet deprecate agitation, are men who want crops without plowing up the ground. They want rain without thunder and lightning. They want the ocean without the awful roar of its many waters. This struggle may be a moral one, or it may be a physical one, or it may be both moral and physical, but it must be a struggle. Power concedes nothing without a demand. It never did and it never will.

—Frederick Douglass, *My Bondage and My Freedom*

"I thought racism died in the sixties? But you guys keep talking, and talking, and talking about racism. Please stop using racism as a crutch!"

"Don't you think the best way of dealing with America's racial problems is by not talking about them? By constantly talking about racism you guys add wood to the racial fire, which is almost extinguished!"

"Race is a myth, an invention, a socially constructed category. Therefore, we should not make it 'real' by using it in our analyses. People are people, not black, white, or Indian. White males are just people."[1]

"A&M's tradition of focusing on race is a terrible mentality to teach a new generation. Dr. Eduardo Bonilla-Silva's book *White Supremacy & Racism in the Post–Civil Rights Era* is the latest evolution in this ritual that should have collapsed with the 1960s."[2]

Statements such as these have become standard examples of how most whites think and talk about racism in contemporary America. Those of us who are minority professors in the academic trenches hear statements like these from students, staff, and colleagues. I personally have been accused of being a "racist" because I use the category race in my analysis (as if by closing our eyes, racial fractures would disappear from society and we would all just be "Americans") and of spreading "racist propaganda"[3] (in the color-blind era, those of us who write about race and racism are the ones accused of fostering racial divisions). These statements are all emblematic of the racial ideology that in this book I labeled "color-blind racism." At the heart of these statements—and of color blindness—lies a myth: the idea that race has all but disappeared as a factor shaping the life chances of all Americans. This myth is the central column supporting the house of color blindness. Remove this column and the house will collapse.

Removing this column, however, is not an easy task, because whites' racial views are not mere erroneous ideas to be battled in the field of rational discourse. They constitute, as I argued in this book, a racial ideology, a loosely organized set of ideas, phrases, and stories that help whites justify contemporary white supremacy;[4] they are the *collective representations*[5] whites have developed to explain, and ultimately justify, contemporary racial inequality. Their views, then, are not just a "sense of group position"[6] but *symbolic expressions of whites' dominance*. As such, they cannot be simply eradicated with "facts," because racial facts are highly contested. In the eyes of most whites, for instance, evidence of racial disparity in income, wealth, education, and other relevant matters becomes evidence that there is something wrong with minorities themselves; evidence of minorities' overrepresentation in the criminal justice system or on death row is interpreted as evidence of their overrepresentation in criminal activity; evidence of black and Latino underperformance in standardized tests is a confirmation that there is something wrong (maybe even genetically wrong)[7] with them.

Given that this ideology—like all ideologies—cannot be simply impugned with facts,[8] my main goal in this book was to decode the components of color blindness and explain their functions. In chapters 2, 3, and 4, I demonstrated how color-blind racism's frames, style, and racial stories help whites justify contemporary racial inequality. Whites use these components like "building blocks"[9] to manufacture accounts on a variety of racial matters. In general, their accounts amount to, "Race does not matter that much today, so let's move on." For example, when whites are asked about affirmative action, they resort to the frame of abstract liberalism to oppose it: "Why should we use discrimination to combat discrimination? Two wrongs don't make a right. We should judge people by their merits and let the best person get the job or promotion, or be admitted into a good college." When whites are confronted with the reality of the tremendous levels of residential and school segregation in the United States, they argue race has nothing to do with these matters. Many resort to the naturalization frame and say, "This is a natural thing. People prefer to be with people who are like them." Alternatively, they use the abstract liberalism frame and proclaim, "People have the right of choosing to live wherever they want to live. This is America, for God's sake!" When whites are faced with evidence of discrimination, they acknowledge its occurrence but label the episodes as "isolated incidents" and proceed to blame minorities for playing the "race card." Finally, when whites are questioned about the whiteness of their social networks, they rebut, "This has nothing to do with race. It's just the way things are." And if this does not work, they can project the problem onto minorities and say, "It's blacks who do not want to be with us. I have seen how they self-segregate in their neighborhoods and even when they attend our colleges." Others may be embarrassed by the makeup of their social networks and feel compelled to insert semantic moves ("Well, that's true, but some of my best friends are black") or personal stories ("My best buddy in Vietnam was Samoan!") to save face.

These frames, as I argued, set whites onto paths of no return. By regarding race-related matters as nonracial, "natural," or rooted in "people's choices," whites deem almost all proposals to remedy racial inequality necessarily as illogical, undemocratic, and "racist" (in reverse).

Besides examining the components of color-blind racism, I discussed two other important features in the color-blind era. First, I explored in chapter 5 the contradiction between whites claiming to be color blind and their almost totally white pattern of social interaction. Second, I examined in chapter 7 the influence of color-blind racism on blacks. In chapter 5 I showed that whites, despite their professed color blindness, live in white neighborhoods, associate primarily with whites, befriend mostly whites, and choose whites as their mates. The contradiction between their professed life philosophy and their real practice in life is not perceived by whites as such because they do not interpret their hypersegregation and isolation from minorities (in particular blacks) as a *racial* outcome. For most whites, this is just "The way things are" or something that has nothing to do with race. In chapter 7 I concurred with most researchers[10] in showing that blacks exhibit a different attitudinal outlook on racial issues than whites. Blacks, unlike whites, believe discrimination is real and central in shaping their life chances and that the government must intervene in a number of areas to guarantee equality among the races (therefore, blacks are significantly more likely to support affirmative action, busing, and even reparations than whites). Blacks are also more likely than whites to engage in interracial friendship and intimacy. Nevertheless, I also documented how blacks are influenced by many of the frames of color blindness, directly and indirectly. Specifically, I underscored the large indirect effect of the frames of color blindness on blacks and how this blunts the oppositional character of their perspectives on racial matters. For example, many blacks endorse stereotypical views about themselves (e.g., blacks are lazy, less intelligent, or more athletic than whites), which leads them to adopt confusing standpoints (e.g., "Discrimination is very important, but we are a lazy people").

Finally, I examined "race traitors"—whites who do not dance to the tune of color blindness (see chapter 6). Unlike most social scientists, who posit that educated (mostly middle-class) white folks are racially tolerant and, hence, more likely to support the struggle for racial equality, my research suggested working-class women are significantly more likely than any other segment of the white population to be racially progressive. I also pointed out a number of other factors that racial progressives have in common that may explain their racial progressiveness, such as growing up in racially mixed neighborhoods, having extensive equal-status contacts with minorities, being center-to-left politically, and having dated across the color line. Although more research needs to be conducted to corroborate my findings, specify the set of circumstances (what sociologists call "variables") and the conditions that lead actors to become racially progressive, and determine why this segment of the white population is more progressive than others, I tentatively suggest that because working-class women experience at least two kinds of oppression (as workers and as women), they are more likely to empathize with racial minorities. In their narratives, many of these women used their own experiences as women to articulate their views on various hotly contested racial issues and, more specifically, to describe how discrimination occurs nowadays. Nevertheless, as in the case of blacks, I also showed that the "souls of [these] white folks"[11] are not pure, that is, that their racial progressiveness has some limits, as they too are influenced by color blindness.

The interview data in this book demonstrated that color-blind racism is central to old and young whites alike. Although older, working-class white respondents (mostly in the DAS sample) were less adept at using softer, more efficient versions of the frames and style of color-blind racism than were younger, middle-class, educated ones (mostly among the college students sample), both groups were attuned to this new ideology. Yet the fact that some whites are "compassionate conservatives" on race does not change in any way the reality that all are baptized in the waters of color-blind racism. Besides, even though younger, middle-class, educated whites seem better adept at using the arsenal of color blindness, many—particularly those who were already in the labor market or close to entering it—were as crude and unsophisticated as their poorer, less-educated brethren. To examine this matter more accurately, we need a panel study to follow college students over a ten-year period or so to assess whether or not, as they mature and deal with central life issues (e.g., getting a job, purchasing a house, getting married, having children), their color blindness becomes cruder.

The data also evinced color-blind racism forms an impregnable yet elastic ideological wall that barricades whites off from America's racial reality. An impregnable wall because it provides them a safe, color-blind way to state racial views without appearing to be irrational or rabidly racist. And an elastic wall—and hence a stronger one—because this ideology does not rely on absolutes (it prefers statements such as "Most blacks are" rather than "All blacks are"), admits a variety of ways of using its frames (from crude and direct to kinder and indirect), and allows whites to employ a variety of emotional tones for stating their views (from the angry "Darned lazy blacks" to the compassionate conservative "Poor blacks are trapped in their inferior schools in their cycle of poverty; what a pity").

Accordingly, my answer to the strange enigma of "racism without racists" is as follows. The United States does not depend on Archie Bunkers to defend white supremacy. (In truth, it never did, but that is *otros veinte pesos*.)[12] Modern racial ideology does not thrive on the ugliness of the past or on the language and tropes typical of slavery and Jim Crow. Today there is a sanitized, color-blind way of calling minorities niggers, Spics, or Chinks. Today most whites justify keeping minorities from having the good things of life with the language of liberalism ("I am all for equal opportunity; that's why I oppose affirmative action!"). And today, as yesterday, whites do not feel guilty about the plight of minorities (blacks in particular). Whites believe minorities have the opportunities to succeed and that, if they do not, it is because they do not try hard. And if minorities dare talk about discrimination, they are rebuked with statements such as "Discrimination ended in the sixties, man" or "You guys are hypersensitive."

The analysis of the interview data also sheds light on the methodological importance of using this kind of data for examining racial ideology. Had I relied on my survey results to analyze whites' racial views, it would have been difficult. Depending on which questions I had used to make my case, I seemingly could have argued three totally different positions.[13] Moreover, I could not have extracted from the survey data the stylistic and narrative elements of color blindness. Although this does not mean that surveys on racial attitudes are useless, it does mean that survey researchers must strive to develop research projects with a qualitative dimension. Otherwise they may either produce an artificial image of racial progress (see chapter 1) or miss central components of the contemporary racial ideological constellation.

One set of questions that I could not answer properly with the data at hand related to how color-blind racism affects other racial minorities and how whites see other racial minorities in our new, more complex multiracial America. *Preliminarily,* although conceding that we lack data sets that include all racial groups, involve questions on interethnic matters, and include in-depth interviews with all the racial and ethnic groups, I answer these questions as follows. First, the black-white continuum still provides the bulk of the themes and imagery for the development of the primary ideas associated with the dominant racial ideology.[14] Consequently, even when one asks generic questions about minorities, whites are likely to focus on the black-white debate. Second, the practices of the "new racism"—the post–Civil Rights set of arrangements that preserves white supremacy in a mostly "kinder and gentler" way—affect *all* minorities, but the "race effect" seems to vary by the degree of closeness to "whiteness" of the groups in question (phenotypically, culturally, and so forth). For instance, although Latinos experience housing discrimination, they are less likely to experience it if they are perceived as "white" than if they are perceived as "black."[15] Similarly, although whites tend to marry endogamously, when they cross the color line, they are more likely to do so with Latinos (particularly with those of a lighter hue) and Asians than with blacks. Lastly, the racial attitudes of racial minorities seem to fit their "ranking" in the new racial hierarchy in America: Asians have views that are closer to those of whites, Latinos' views are less like those of whites, and blacks' are furthest from whites' views.[16] Therefore, because of the aforementioned trends, I believe whites are already making important distinctions among the various racial minorities; that such distinctions have objective, subjective, and social interactional consequences for minorities themselves; and that the degree of "color blindness" among minorities correlates with their position in this new, more complex racial stratification order.[17] Yet, on all these crucial issues for the future of race relations in America, I claim, like most social scientists do, that more research needs to be done before we can adequately answer these questions.

Since I do not want to conclude this book on a pessimistic note, let me suggest a few of the political conditions necessary to fight color-blind racism. (Please see chapter 8 for a discussion of the politics and political strategies needed if the United States develops a Latin America–like racial stratification order.) First, blacks and their allies would be the core[18] of a new civil rights movement demanding equality of results.[19] I documented in chapter 7 that blacks, as a social collectivity, have a clear understanding of the basics of post–Civil Rights white supremacy and, therefore, their views and experiences ought to help guide this new movement. However, because color blindness has tainted their views, it is of cardinal importance that activists in the new movement educate the black masses on the nuances of color blindness. To launch a frontal attack on the "new racism" and its color-blind ideology, the black masses must be as racially conscious as the leaders of the new movement. In ideological terms, the movement must break with the hegemony color blindness has over all Americans.

Second, we need to nurture a large cohort of antiracist whites to begin challenging color-blind nonsense from within. Whites' collective denial about the true nature of race relations may help them feel good, but it is also one of the greatest obstacles to doing the right thing. In racial matters as in therapy, the admission of denial is the preamble for the beginning of recovery. Antiracist whites cannot just be "race traitors";[20] they must engage in struggles to end the practices and the ideology that maintain white supremacy. Individual racial treason without a political praxis to eliminate the system that produces racial inequality amounts to racial showboating.

These antiracist white activists,[21] as I suggested above, will most likely be working-class women. However, as in all social movements, the struggle needs to work to expand the coalition fighting the powers that be. This means that progressive activists need to work with all *vulnerable whites:* poor and working-class whites regardless of gender, whites in the lower middle class, and educated whites who in the past were so central to the struggle for civil rights in America. In order to persuade vulnerable whites to join the struggle, it is important to do ideological work with them (but see below). Hence, the third way of combating color blindness is for researchers and activists alike to provide counter–ideological arguments to *each* of the frames of color-blind racism. We need to counter whites' *abstract* liberalism with *concrete* liberal positions based on a realistic understanding of racial matters and a concern with achieving racial equality. For example, whites' thesis of "We are for equal opportunity for everyone and that's why we oppose affirmative action" must be countered with the concrete argument that because discrimination (past and present) affects minorities negatively, race-based programs and massive programs on behalf of the poor are the only ways of guaranteeing racial equality.[22] The racially illiberal effects of the do-nothing social policy advocated by whites must be exposed and challenged.

Fourth, we need to undress whites' claims of color blindness before a huge mirror. That mirror must reflect the myriad facts of contemporary whiteness, such as whites living in white neighborhoods, sending their kids to white schools, associating primarily with whites, and having almost all their primary relationships with whites. And whites' absurd claim that these facts of whiteness are just a "natural thing" must be deflated with research and exposed by journalists showing the social and personal processes that produce each of these aspects of contemporary white supremacy. Researchers also need to turn the analytical lenses on *white* segregation and isolation from minorities and begin documenting how this isolation affects whites' views, emotions, and cognitions about themselves and about minorities.

Fifth, whiteness must be challenged wherever it exists; regardless of the social organization in which whiteness manifests itself (universities, corporations, schools, neighborhoods, churches), those committed to racial equality must develop a personal practice to challenge it. If you are a college student in a historically white college, you must raise hell to change your college; you must organize to change the racial climate and demography of your college. If you work in corporate America, you must wage war against subtle and covert racism; you must challenge the practices that track minorities into certain jobs and preserve high-paying ones for white males. If you are a parent who spends most of your time housebound, you need to begin a campaign for racial change in your family interactions and attitudes; you must engage with racial minorities, opt for a multiracial rather than a white church, and move from your white neighborhood into an integrated one.

Finally, the most important strategy for fighting "new racism" practices and the ideology of color blindness is to become militant once again. Changes in systems of domination and their accompanying ideologies are never accomplished by racial dialogues—the notion of "Can we all just get along?" or "workshops on racism"—through education, or through "moral reform"[23] alone. What is needed to slay modern-day racism is a new, in-your-face, fight-the-power civil rights movement, a new movement to spark change, to challenge not just color-blind whites but also minority folks who have become content with the crumbs they receive from past struggles. This new civil rights movement, as I have mentioned elsewhere,[24] must have at the core of its agenda the struggle for equality of results. Progressives cannot continue fighting for "equality of opportunity" when true equality cannot be achieved that way. It is time to demand equality now!

I realize many of these proposals are very idealistic. I know quite well most whites are not up to the challenge of working to develop a country without white supremacy. For example, few whites would engage in a social movement or in personal practices that would rock the foundation of the status quo and their everyday lives. The idea of moving from a "safe" neighborhood into a "dangerous" one, for instance, is anathema to most white Americans ("Honey, do you want our kids to attend *bad* schools? Do you want us to *lose our investment in this house*?"). However, social movements do not depend on mobilizing the masses to get started (yet, as I suggested above, successful movements must make *broad appeals* and, at least, gain the sympathy of the majority to be victorious).[25] The history of social mobilization shows that organized, active, resourceful, and creative movements have been able to challenge all kinds of oppressive structures.[26]

If this new civil rights movement begins a concerted campaign to fight "new racism" practices and color-blind idiocy, this movement has a chance. If the leaders of this movement begin to say to America, "We will no longer accept poverty and urban decay, substandard schools and housing, inferior jobs, old- as well as new-fashioned discrimination, and racial profiling, in short, we will no longer accept second-class citizenship in this country," then this movement has a chance. If liberal, progressive, and radical organizations join in this new civil rights movement to eliminate racial disparity in the United States once and for all, this movement has a chance. If progressive religious leaders of various denominations begin to preach about the need to complete the civil rights revolution we started years ago and derail the forces that want to turn back the racial clock, this movement has a chance. If the millions of conscientious college students across the nation wake up and do the right thing, as they did during the Civil Rights era, this movement has a chance. If young people and workers in the United States realize that racial inequality ultimately helps preserve other forms of inequality,[27] this movement has a chance. Activists and researchers alike need to realize the basic truth in Frederick Douglass's words, "If there is no struggle, there is no progress. . . . Power concedes nothing without a demand. It never did and it never will." Change is made, not theorized, written about, or orchestrated by policy makers or researchers. Only by demanding what seems impossible today (equality of results, reparations, and the end of all forms of racial discrimination), will we be able to achieve genuine racial equality in the future.

*   *   *

IMPORTANT ADDENDUM TO
ORIGINAL CONCLUSION

The title of the original conclusion was "The (Color-Blind) Emperor Has No Clothes." Developments since the time I worked on that conclusion (1999–2000) suggest that a more fitting title for the chapter today would be "The (Color-Blind) Emperor Has *New* Clothes." The new "pants" of the emperor are from Latin America, by which I mean that racial stratification in the nation is becoming Latin America–like (the subject of chapter 8). The historical bi-racial order[28] (white-nonwhite) is morphing rather quickly into a more complex racial system. I suggest three new "racial spaces"[29] are developing (white, honorary white, and the collective black) and that this order will allow people to make different choices not just about their "identity" but also about their race.[30] Given these new spaces, the likelihood of collective action from the traditional or historical "minority race groups" (blacks, Latinos, Asian Americans, and Native Americans) is decreasing as the new order fosters individual practices of racial mobility. For example, people who would have been regarded as "black" twenty or thirty years ago can now successfully manufacture a different place for themselves in America. Actors and performers such as "The Rock," Vin Diesel, Keanu Reeves, Jennifer Rubin, and Jennifer Tilly, all "racially mixed" (again, only in this moment this claim is possible as during the Jim Crow period all of them would be assigned the "lower" race in the mix), work all sides of the racial spectrum as they can use their phenotypical capital (dare I say "honorary whiteness") to their advantage.[31]

This newly emerging racial landscape has received a boost from the new "shirt" the emperor began wearing since November 4, 2008: the Obama phenomenon. The election of *this* black man as president (and I will continue insisting on Obama's political and personal peculiarities) has accelerated the pace of the Latin-Americanization process and solidified further the house of color blindness. Why? Because Obama has worked the post-racial game and, as I argued in chapter 9, played perfectly the role whites have constructed for people of color (they "love" minority folks if they "behave," are nice to them, smile a lot, are "cool" and "respectable," and do not talk much about race). This game, which I argued is the true secret behind Obama's success, has placed a black person in power without that altering much the distribution of racial power or how social goods are distributed in the polity. Obama has helped establish what I called in the chapter a "multiracial white supremacy order"—a regime similar to those in the Americas or the Caribbean where people of color are in power without altering the "[racial] order of things" (Foucault 1973).

These two developments (the Latin-Americanization of the racial order and the Obama phenomenon) will make the struggle for racial justice much harder in years to come. In *Obamerica* (see endnote 2 in chapter 9) several factors will buffer racial conflict and limit the likelihood of race-based frontal challenges. First, the traditional racial groups are becoming less "stable" or unified as many members can now make legitimate claims to be something else. For example, immediately after Obama was elected president, many members of the "black elite" joined white America in their nonsensical preaching to poor blacks ("Folks, now you have a black president so you have no more excuses") (see endnote 7 in chapter 9). This segment which has always tried to distance itself from the "black majority" has now much more space to be something other than black. They can, as many formerly black and Indian people were able to do historically in the Americas and the Caribbean, struggle to create other classifications such as multiracial, bi-racial, or simply American. Thusly the strength of the "black" or "Latino" challenges will be diluted by this development.

Second, the segment or space I label "honorary white" will do a lot of the dirty work of policing racial boundaries and disciplining those in the "collective black." I expect to hear a lot of noise in the next decade about intra-racial or intra-ethnic struggle in the black, Latino, and Asian camps. That fight, however, will denote the efforts of segments within these communities to distance themselves from their groups of origin. And what may be read as intra-racial in the next years may soon become something else (for example, this "racial" discussion may become a "class" discussion among Americans about the behavior of the "poor"—likely to be the very dark segment of the population—and middle and upper-middle class honorary whites). The important thing to point out is that the dominant race in this society (whites) will no longer work alone in preserving the racial order as honorary whites and some individuals[32] in the collective black space will help them maintain the coordinates of the new order.

Lastly, as of November 4, 2008, white America has shouted to the world: "(Finally) We are ALL Americans." They have now attained the upper hand in symbolic racial politics as they can tell people of color "We have a black president, what else do *you people* want?" Although some commentators are pointing out the limits of the notion of America as a "post-racial" nation, it is also true that the space for talking and debating race matters in the public has decreased tremendously.

But all empires have fractures and all emperors are eventually replaced. In the case of the new racial order, I outlined in chapters 8 and 9 the weaknesses of the system and suggested things we may do in the struggle for racial justice. I highlighted the urgent need for new social movements to challenge the "matrix of domination"[33] in contemporary America. I also called for doing active political work among the new emerging racial majority in the nation (the collective black) as that work might produce a new historical bloc to fight the current racial order. However, I also expressed my pesoptimism about these possibilities. On the Latin Americanization front, I mentioned that once this type of regime took hold in the Americas and the Caribbean, they became entrenched and posed formidable challenges to those at the bottom of the racial well. In the case of my call for social movements, I pointed out that at least in terms of the Obama moment we are living, political participation has been limited to electoral politics which limits the likelihood of these movements ever developing. (I know there are many small movements dotting the political territory. My concern, however, is about how the massive participation of Americans—particularly the youth that threw itself into Obama—in mainstream politics has had the nefarious effect of *demobilizing* people and making them into political actors that do "politics" every four years.)

Notwithstanding my pesoptimism, history is what it is and no racial order can maintain itself forever. The oppressed (racially or otherwise) always resist domination and what seems like an insurmountable Mount Everest is always conquered (although some may die trying to reach its top). Accordingly, I end this third and hopefully *last* edition of this book mindful that slavery looked like a system that would never end and it did; that Jim Crow maintained people of color subjected for more than a hundred years[34] and it has all but died; and that the "new racism" with its Latin America–like extension looks like fast setting cement, but it will eventually collapse, too. I just hope I am alive when this happens and that my bones allow me to celebrate the real "end of racism" in the country that will then be properly called America with no "*k*'s."

NOTES

1. A colleague said something like this to me almost verbatim a few years ago in response to a presentation I gave about racism in sociology. Later on, the same colleague uttered a statement along the same lines to challenge a graduate student's presentation on whiteness. Denying the *social reality* of race because of its constructed nature (see chapter 1), unfortunately, has become respectable in academia. This position, which has been uttered by conservatives such as David Horowitz, has now been adopted by liberals such as Todd Gitlin and even radicals (or former radicals) such as Paul Gilroy. For the latter, see Paul Gilroy, *Against Race* (Cambridge, Mass.: Belknap, 2000).

2. Matthew Maddox, "Institutionalized Racism Continues at A&M: Sociology Professor's Book Will Continue Tradition of Racist Ideology on Campus," *Battalion*, October 2, 2002.

3. Maddox, "Institutionalized Racist Ideology."

4. Charles W. Mills, *The Racial Contract* (Ithaca, N.Y.: Cornell University Press, 1997).

5. This is Emile Durkheim's term. However, I use it here in Moscovici's sense. See Serge Moscovici, "The Coming Era of Social Representations," in *Cognitive Approaches to Social Behaviour*, edited by J. P. Codol and J. P. Leyens (The Hague: Nijhoff, 1982), 115–50.

6. Social psychologist Herbert Blumer conceived prejudice as a "sense of group position" and connected this "sense" to the hierarchical racial order. See Luigi Esposito and John W. Murphy, "Another Step in the Study of Race Relations," *Sociological Quarterly* 41, no. 2 (2000): 171–87.

7. Although color-blind racism need not use biological arguments to maintain

racial privilege, biological arguments creep back from time to time and have not yet been abandoned by at least a third of whites. For instance, in my own DAS, anywhere from 20 to 40 percent of whites believed biological stereotypes about blacks such as the idea that blacks are naturally more athletic than whites and blacks are sexually well-endowed. For an academic incarnation of this tendency, see Richard J. Herrnstein and Charles Murray, *The Bell Curve* (New York: Free Press, 1994).

8. If ideologies are about "meaning in the service of power," as Thompson argues, they must be countered with power. Counter–ideological battles alone cannot ultimately erode power crystallized in institutions and practices to maintain white privilege. John B. Thompson, *Studies in Theory and Ideology* (Cambridge, UK: Polity, 1984).

9. For data on New Zealand, see Margaret Wetherell and Jonathan Potter, *Mapping the Language of Racism* (New York: Columbia University Press, 1992).

10. See chapter 7 for references on blacks.

11. W. E. B. DuBois named one of his chapters "The Souls of White Folk," in *Darkwater* (Rahway, N.J.: Quinn and Boden, 1920).

12. "Otros veinte pesos" is a Puerto Rican expression that literally means "another twenty dollars" and is used to suggest that a side argument will take a long time to make and, therefore, that making it will distract from the main one.

13. See Eduardo Bonilla-Silva and Tyrone A. Forman, "'I Am Not a Racist, but . . .': Mapping White College Students' Racial Ideology in the USA," *Discourse and Society* 11, no. 1 (2000): 50–85.

14. On this point, see Joe R. Feagin, *Racist America: Roots, Realities, and Future Reparations* (New York: Routledge, 2000), 3.

15. On housing issues, see Douglas S. Massey and Nancy A. Denton, "Trends in the Residential Segregation of Blacks, Hispanics, and Asians: 1970–1980," *American Sociological Review* 52, no. 6 (1987): 802–25. On interracial relationships, see Zhenchao Qian and Daniel T. Lichter, "Measuring Marital Assimilation: Intermarriage among Natives and Immigrants," *Social Science Research* 30, no. 2 (2001): 289–312.

16. See Eduardo Bonilla-Silva and Karen Glover, "'We Are All Americans': The Latin Americanization of Race Relations in the USA," in *Changing Terrain of Race and Ethnicity*, edited by Maria Krysan and Amanda Lewis (New York: Russell Sage, 2004).

17. Bonilla-Silva and Glover, "We Are All Americans."

18. On black social movements in America, see Cedric J. Robinson, *Black Movements in America* (New York: Routledge, 1997).

19. For more on this, see the conclusion to my *White Supremacy*.

20. For this concept and an elaboration of the politics behind it, see the journal *Race Traitor*.

21. For a study of white antiracists in American history, see Herbert Aptheker, *Anti-Racism in U.S. History: The First Two Hundred Years* (New York: Greenwood, 1992).

22. For a book focusing on the former, see David Ingram, *Group Rights: Reconciling Equality and Difference* (Lawrence: University Press of Kansas, 2000). For a

policy suggestion that includes both, see William Julius Wilson, *When Work Disappears* (New York: Knopf, 1996).

23. Today, almost all religious groups in the United States abhor racism and have even denounced their past mistakes. For example, in 1995 the Southern Baptist Convention apologized to blacks for "condoning and/or perpetuating individual and systematic racism." Almost all religious groups advocate a moral crusade against racism, but few do anything beyond their occasional public statements. For a sensitive and intelligent analysis of religion and race in America, see Michael O. Emerson and Christian Smith, *Divided by Faith: Evangelical Religion and the Problem of Race in America* (New York: Oxford University Press, 2000).

24. Consult the conclusion of my *White Supremacy* for an argument on how this movement should be organized and a discussion of the need for a large movement agenda that includes class and gender concerns.

25. A good book for the basics of the social movement literature is Stanford M. Lyman, *Social Movements: Critiques, Concepts, Case-Studies* (New York: New York University Press, 1995). For a good book that argues that social movements need to make broad appeals and develop "connective structures" among different sectors, see Sidney Tarrow, *Power in Social Movements: Social Movements and Contentious Politics* (Cambridge: Cambridge University Press, 1998).

26. For an excellent collection of essays discussing the array of new and creative contemporary movements, see Enrique Larana, Hank Johnston, and Joseph R. Gusfield, eds., *New Social Movements: From Ideology to Identity* (Philadelphia: Temple University Press, 1994). For examples of how to build multiracial coalitions, see John Anner, ed., *Beyond Identity Politics: Emerging Social Justice Movements in Communities of Color* (Boston: Beacon, 1996).

27. This point has been made by, among others, Joe R. Feagin, in *Racist America* (New York: Routledge, 2000); his newer book, Joe R. Feagin, *Systemic Racism: A Theory of Oppression* (New York: Routledge, 2006); and Patricia Hill-Collins, in "Moving beyond Gender: Intersectionality and Scientific Knowledge," in *Revisioning Gender*, edited by Myra Marx Ferre, Judith Lorber, and Beth B. Hess (Thousand Oaks, Calif.: Sage, 1999), 261–84.

28. The American racial order was never truly "bi-racial" if by that one means white-black. Across the nation other groups were part of the racial order and, in some places, were more significant than blacks (e.g., Mexican Americans throughout much of the Southwest and Native Americans in states such as Oklahoma). The point, however, is that in most of the nation the color line was fundamentally structured around the white-non-white divide. However, see the work of Reginald Daniel, *More Than Black? Multiracial Identity and the New Racial Order* (Philadelphia: Temple University Press, 2002) for a discussion on "tri-racial isolates."

29. In the chapter here and in the previous edition I used terms such as "groups" and "strata" to refer to the three new collectivities I surmised were emerging. However, I also pointed out the inchoate and permeability of the boundaries of these groups. Lately (in truth, I used the term in 2004 in an article in the now defunct *Race and Society* journal as well as in talks on this matter), I have referred to these collectivities as "racial spaces" to denote more clearly their "in itself" rather than "for itself." This is also the case of racial formations in Latin

America and the Caribbean, that is, for many reasons, they seldom cohere as groups and act collectively. See Eduardo Bonilla-Silva, "Are the Americas 'Sick with Racism' or Is It a Problem at the Poles? A Reply to Christina A. Sue," *Ethnic and Racial Studies* 32, no. 6 (2009): 1071–82.

30. Sociologists of race and ethnicity make a distinction between "identity" as a mostly personal or subjective matter that may or may not correlate with your "race." Thus, a person that is regarded by most observers in a polity as "black" may call herself "white," "American," or "bi-racial." "Race" refers to the historico-political categories that are created in a racialized polity and have a strong externality, that is, actors are defined as such by others in the polity and have limited chances of challenging that characterization. In the above mentioned case, for instance, the person self-identifying herself as white or any other identity would be viewed and treated by most as black.

31. For an interesting discussion on this matter as well as on the way that "multiculturalism" is used in cinema, see Mary C. Beltrán, "The New Hollywood Racelessness: Only the Fast, Furious, (and Multiracial) Will Survive," *Cinema Journal* 44, no. 2 (2005) 50–67.

32. I have suggested in chapter 8 and in many of my writings and presentations on this subject that many individuals in the collective black space may help buffer conflict in their efforts to be "anything but (part of the collective) black." It is to their *individual* advantage to distance themselves from those in their space if they wish to attain racial mobility and, hence, will likely step all over their brethren on their way up.

33. All modern societies exhibit a complex hierarchical order that includes class, gender, and race and other social categories. Thus, although I have focused mostly on the racial aspects of the American social order, I have also alluded to and included in some parts of my analyses the need for movements that are cognizant of the fact of this complexity. For a good discussion on this matter, read *anything* written by philosopher Charles W. Mills.

34. An impressive recent book describing the resistance of blacks to Jim Crow and the centrality of militant struggle is Hasan Kwame Jeffries, *Bloody Lowndes: Civil Rights and Black Power in Alabama's Black Belt* (New York and London: NYU Press, 2009).

Bibliography

Aguirre, Adalberto, Jr. "Academic Storytelling: A Critical Race Theory Story of Affirmative Action." *Sociological Perspectives* 43, no. 2 (2000): 319–39.

Allport, Gordon W. *The Nature of Prejudice.* New York: Doubleday/Anchor, 1958.

America, Richard F. *Paying the Social Debt: What White America Owes Black America.* Westport, Conn.: Praeger, 1993.

Andersen, Margaret L. *Thinking about Women: Sociological Perspectives on Sex and Gender.* New York: Macmillan, 1988.

Anderson, Benedict. *Imagined Communities: Reflections on the Origin and Spread of Nationalism,* revised and extended. London and New York: Verso, 1991.

Anderson, Elijah. *Streetwise.* Chicago: University of Chicago Press, 1990.

Anner, John, ed. *Beyond Identity Politics: Emerging Social Justice Movements in Communities of Color.* Boston: Beacon, 1996.

Anti-Defamation League. *Highlights from an Anti-Defamation League Survey on Racial Attitudes in America.* New York: Anti-Defamation League, 1993.

Aptheker, Herbert. *Anti-Racism in U.S. History: The First Two Hundred Years.* New York: Greenwood, 1992.

Argyle, Michael, and Monika Henderson. *The Anatomy of Relationships.* London: Routledge, 1985.

Armour, Jody David. *Negrophobia and Reasonable Racism: The Hidden Costs of Being Black.* New York: New York University Press, 1997.

Armstrong, Clairette P., and A. James Gregor. "Integrated Schools and Negro Character." Pp. 101–49, in *White Racism and Black Americans,* edited by David G. Bromley et al. Cambridge, Mass.: Schenkman, 1972.

Aronowitz, Stanley. *False Promises: The Shaping of American Working Class Consciousness.* Durham, N.C.: Duke University Press, 1991.

Auletta, Ken. *The Underclass.* Woodstock, N.Y.: Overlook, 1999.

Ayres, Ian. *Pervasive Prejudice?* Chicago: University of Chicago Press, 2002.

Baker, Houston A. "Scene . . . Not Heard." Pp. 38–50 in *Reading Rodney King, Reading Urban Uprising,* edited by Robert Gooding-Williams. New York: Routledge, 1993.

Bartra, Roger. *Wild Men in the Looking Glass: The Mythic Origins of European Otherness.* Ann Arbor: University of Michigan Press, 1994.

Bauman, Zygmut. *Modernity and Ambivalence*. Ithaca, N.Y.: Cornell University Press, 1991.

Baumeister, Andrea T. *Liberalism and the "Politics of Difference."* Edinburgh: Edinburgh University Press, 2000.

Bay, Mia. *The White Image in the Black Mind: African-American Ideas about White People, 1830–1925*. New York: Oxford University Press, 2000.

Bell, Derrick. *Race, Racism, and American Law*. Boston: Little, Brown, 1992.

Bellamy, Richard. "Liberalism." Pp. 23–49 in *Contemporary Political Ideologies*, edited by Roger Eatwall and Anthony Wright. Boulder, Colo.: Westview, 1993.

Blanchard, Janice, and Nicole Lurie. "R-e-s-p-e-c-t: Patient Reports of Disrespect in the Health Care Setting and Its Impact on Care." *Journal of Family Practice* 53 (2004): 721–31.

Blauner, Robert. *Black Lives, White Lives: Three Decades of Race Relations in America*. Berkeley: University of California Press, 1989.

Bobo, Lawrence D., and Devon Johnson. "Racial Attitudes in a Prismatic Metropolis: Mapping Identity, Competition, and Views on Affirmative Action." Pp. 81–163 in *Prismatic Metropolis: Inequality in Los Angeles*, edited by Lawrence D. Bobo et al. New York: Russell Sage Foundation, 2000.

Bobo, Lawrence D., and James Kluegel. "Opposition to Race-Targeting: Self-Interest, Stratification Ideology, or Racial Attitudes?" *American Sociological Review* 58, no. 4 (1993): 443–64.

Bobo, Lawrence D., James A. Kluegel, and Ryan A. Smith. "Laissez-Faire Racism: The Crystallization of a Kinder, Gentler, Antiblack Ideology." Pp. 15–44 in *Racial Attitudes in the 1990s: Continuity and Change*, edited by Steven A. Tuch and Jack K. Martin. Westport, Conn.: Praeger, 1997.

Bobo, Lawrence D., and Fred Licari. "Education and Political Tolerance: Testing the Effects of Cognitive Sophistication and Target Group Affect." *Public Opinion Quarterly* 53, no. 5 (1989): 285–308.

Bobo, Lawrence D., and Susan Suh. "Surveying Racial Discrimination: Analyses from a Multiethnic Labor Market." Pp. 523–60 in *Prismatic Metropolis: Inequality in Los Angeles*, edited by Lawrence D. Bobo et al. New York: Russell Sage Foundation, 2000.

Bonilla-Silva, Eduardo. "Rethinking Racism." *American Sociological Review* 62, no. 3 (1997): 465–80.

———. " 'This Is a White Country': Racial Ideological Convergence among the Western Nations of the World-System." *Sociological Inquiry* 70, no. 2 (2000): 188–214.

———. " 'This Is a White Country': The Racial Ideology of the Western Nations of the World-System." *Research in Politics and Society* 6 no. 1 (1999): 85–102.

———. *White Supremacy and Racism in the Post–Civil Rights Era*. Boulder, Colo.: Rienner, 2001.

Bonilla-Silva, Eduardo, and Ashley Doane Jr., eds. "New Racism, Color-Blind Racism, and the Future of Whiteness in America." In *Whiteout: The Continuing Significance of Racism and Whiteness*. New York: Routledge, 2003.

Bonilla-Silva, Eduardo, and Tyrone A. Forman. " 'I Am Not a Racist but . . .': Mapping White College Students' Racial Ideology in the USA." *Discourse and Society* 11, no. 1 (2000): 50–85.

Bonilla-Silva, Eduardo, Tyrone A. Forman, Amanda E. Lewis, and David G. Embrick. " 'It Wasn't Me': Race and Racism in 21st Century America." *Research in Political Sociology*, forthcoming.

Bonilla-Silva, Eduardo, and Karen S. Glover. " 'We Are All Americans': The Latin Americanization of Race Relations in the USA." In *The Changing Terrain of Race and Ethnicity: Theory, Methods and Public Policy*, edited by Amanda E. Lewis and Maria Krysan. New York: Russell Sage Foundation, 2004.

Bonilla-Silva, Eduardo, and Amanda E. Lewis. "The 'New Racism': Toward an Analysis of the U.S. Racial Structure, 1960–1990s." Pp. 100–150 in *Race, Nation, and Citizenship*, edited by Paul Wong. Boulder, Colo.: Westview, 1999.

Bordieau, Pierre. "Social Space and Symbolic Power." *Sociological Theory* 7 (Spring 1980): 12–25.

———. *Distinction*. Cambridge, Mass.: Harvard University Press, 1984.

———. *Pascalian Meditations*. Stanford, Calif.: Stanford University Press, 1997.

Bourgeois, Philippe. *In Search of Respect: Selling Crack in El Barrio*. New York: Cambridge University Press, 1995.

Brodkin, Karen. *How Jews Became White Folks and What That Says about Race in America*. New Brunswick, N.J.: Rutgers University Press, 1998.

Brooks, Roy. *Integration or Separation? A Strategy for Racial Equality*. Cambridge, Mass.: Harvard University Press, 1996.

Bush, Roderick. *We Are Not What We Seem: Black Nationalism and Class Struggle in the American Century*. New York: New York University Press, 1999.

Caditz, Judith. *White Liberals in Transition: Current Dilemmas of Ethnic Integration*. New York: Spectrum Publications, 1976.

Campbell, Angus, and Howard Schuman. *Racial Attitudes in Fifteen American Cities*. Ann Arbor, Mich.: Survey Research Center, June 1968.

Clinton, Catherine. *The Plantation Mistress*. New York: Pantheon, 1982.

Coll, Stephen. *Ghost Wars: The Secret History of the CIA, Afghanistan, and bin Laden, from the Soviet Invasion to September 10, 2001*. New York: Penguin, 2004.

Collins, Sharon. *Black Corporate Executives: The Making and Breaking of a Black Middle Class*. Philadelphia: Temple University Press, 1997.

Crosby, Faye. *Affirmative Action Is Dead: Long Live Affirmative Action*. New Haven, Conn.: Yale University Press, 2004.

Cruse, Harold. *Plural but Equal: A Critical Study of Blacks and Minorities and America's Plural Society*. New York: Morrow, 1987.

D'Souza, Dinesh. *The End of Racism: Principles for a Multiracial Society*. New York: Free Press, 1995.

Darity, William A., Jr. "Stratification Economics: The Role of Intergroup Inequality." *Journal of Economics and Finance* 29 no. 2 (Summer 2005): 144–53.

Davis, Allison, Burleigh B. Gardner, and Mary R. Gardner. *Deep South: A Social Anthropological Study of Caste and Class*. Chicago: University of Chicago Press, 1941.

Dawson, Michael C. *Behind the Mule: Race and Class in African American Politics*. Princeton, N.J.: Princeton University Press, 1994.

———. *Black Visions: The Roots of Contemporary African-American Political Ideologies*. Chicago: University of Chicago Press, 2001.

DeMott, Benjamin. *The Trouble with Friendship: Why Americans Can't Think Straight about Race.* New York: Atlantic Monthly Press, 1995.

Denzin, Norman K. *The Research Act.* Englewood Cliffs, N.J.: Prentice Hall, 1989.

Denzin, Norman K., and Yvonna S. Lincoln. *Handbook of Qualitative Research.* Thousand Oaks, Calif.: Sage, 2000.

Desena, Judith N. "Local Gatekeeping Practices and Residential Segregation." *Sociological Inquiry* 64, no. 3 (1994): 307–21.

Doane, Ashley W. "White Identity and Race Relations in the 1990s." Pp. 151–59 in *Perspectives on Current Social Problems,* edited by Gregg Lee Carter. Boston: Allyn and Bacon, 1997.

Dollard, John. *Caste and Class in a Southern Town.* New York: Doubleday, 1957.

Domhoff, William. *Who Rules America?* New Jersey: Prentice Hall, 2006.

Dorn, Edward. *Rules and Racial Equality.* New Haven, Conn.: Yale University Press, 1979.

Dovidio, John F., and Samuel L. Gaertner. "Changes in the Expression and Assessment of Racial Prejudice." Pp. 119–50 in *Openmind Doors,* edited by Harry J. Knopke et al. Tuscaloosa: University of Alabama Press, 1991.

Dowding, Keith. *Power.* Minneapolis: University of Minnesota Press, 1996.

DuBois, W. E. B. *The Souls of Black Folk.* New York: Penguin, 1995.

Duke, David. At www.duke.org (accessed December 8, 2002).

Dunn, Thomas L. "The New Enclosures: Racism in the Normalized Community." Pp. 178–95 in *Reading Rodney King, Reading Urban Uprising,* edited by Robert Gooding-Williams. New York: Routledge, 1993.

Edin, Kathryn. *Making Ends Meet: How Single Mothers Survive Welfare and Long-Wage Work.* New York: Russell Sage Foundation, 1997.

Edsall, Thomas, and Mary D. Edsall. *Chain Reaction: The Impact of Race, Rights, and Taxes on American Politics.* New York: Norton, 1992.

Eliasoph, Nina. "'Everyday Racism' in a Culture of Political Avoidance: Civil Society, Speech, and Taboo." *Social Problems,* 46, no. 4 (1997): 479–502.

Emerson, Michael O., and Christian Smith. *Divided by Faith: Evangelical Religion and the Problem of Race in America.* New York: Oxford University Press, 2000.

Epstein, J. L. "After the Bus Arrives: Resegregation in Desegregated Schools." *Journal of Social Issues* 41, no. 3 (1985): 23–43.

Esposito, Luigi, and John W. Murphy. "Another Step in the Study of Race Relations." *Sociological Quarterly* 41, no. 2 (2000): 171–87.

Essed, Philomena. *Diversity: Gender, Color, and Culture.* Amherst: University of Massachusetts Press, 1996.

Esses, Victoria, John Dividio, and Gordon Hodson. "Public Attitudes toward Immigration in the United States and Canada in Response to the September 11, 2001 'Attack on America.'" *Analyses of Social Issues and Public Policy* 2 (2002): 69–85.

Fair, Bryan K. *Racial Caste Baby: Color Blindness and the End of Affirmative Action.* New York: New York University Press, 1997.

Fairclough, Norman. *Language and Power.* London: Longman, 1989.

———. *Critical Discourse Analysis: The Critical Study of Language.* London: Longman, 1995.

Farley, Reynolds. *The New American Reality*. New York: Russell Sage Foundation, 1996.

Fay, Brian. *Contemporary Philosophy of Social Science*. Oxford: Blackwell, 1996.

Feagin, Joe R. *Racist America: Roots, Realities, and Future Reparations*. New York: Routledge, 2000.

Feagin, Joe R., and Melvin Sikes. *Living with Racism: The Black Middle Class Experience*. Boston: Beacon, 1994.

Feagin, Joe R., and Hernán Vera. *White Racism: The Basics*. New York: Routledge, 1995.

Feagin, Joe R., Hernán Vera, and Nikitah Imani. *The Agony of Education: Black Students at White Colleges and Universities*. New York: Routledge, 1996.

Fehr, Beverly. *Friendship Process*. Newbury Park, Calif.: Sage, 1996.

Fine, Michelle, and Lois Weis. *The Unknown City: Lives of Poor and Working-Class Young Adults*. Boston: Beacon, 1998.

Firebaugh, Glenn, and Kenneth E. Davis. "Trends in Antiblack Prejudice, 1972–1984: Region and Cohort Effects." *American Journal of Sociology* 94 (1988): 251–72.

Fontana, Andrea, and James H. Frey. "The Interview: From Structured Questions to Negotiated Text." Pp. 645–72 in *Handbook of Qualitative Research*, edited by Norman K. Denzin and Yvonna S. Lincoln. Thousand Oaks, Calif.: Sage, 2000.

Foucault, Michel. *The Order of Things: An Archeology of the Human Sciences*. New York: Random House, 1973.

Frankenberg, Ruth. *White Women, Race Matters*. Minneapolis: University of Minnesota Press, 1993.

Fraser, James, and Edward Kick. "The Interpretive Repertoires of Whites on Race-Targeted Policies: Claims Making of Reverse Discrimination." *Sociological Perspectives* 43, no. 1 (2000): 13–28.

Gallagher, Charles A. "Interracial Dating and Marriage: Fact, Fantasy and the Problem of Survey Data." Pp. 240–254 in *Quality and Quantity of Contact: African Americans and Whites on College Campuses*, edited by Robert Moore. New York: University Press of America, 2002.

Gilroy, Paul. *Against Race*. Cambridge, Mass.: Belknap, 2000.

Goad, Jim. *The Redneck Manifesto*. New York: Touchstone, 1997.

Goldberg, David T. *Racist Culture: Philosophy and the Politics of Meaning*. Cambridge, UK: Blackwell, 1993.

Goldfield, David R. *Black, White, and Southern: Race Relations and Southern Culture, 1940 to the Present*. Baton Rouge: Louisiana State University Press, 1990.

Goldfield, Michael. *The Color of Politics: Race and the Mainsprings of American Politics*. New York: New York Press, 1997.

Gouldner, Helen, and Mary Strong. *Speaking of Friendship: Middle-Class Women and Their Friends*. New York: Greenwood, 1987.

Graham, Lawrence Otis. *Member of the Club*. New York: HarperCollins, 1995.

Gray, John. *Liberalism*. Minneapolis: University of Minnesota Press, 1986.

Grier, Peter, and James N. Thurman. "Youth's Shifting Attitudes on Race." *Christian Science Monitor*, August 18, 1999.

Hall, Stuart. "The Narrative Construction of Reality." *Southern Review* 17 (1984): 3–17.

Hallinan, Maureen, and Richard A. Williams. "The Stability of Student's Interracial Friendships." _American Sociological Review_ 52, no. 2 (1987): 653–64.

Hanchard, Michael G. _Orpheus and Power._ Princeton, N.J.: Princeton University Press, 1994.

Harrington, Michael. _The Other America: Poverty in the United States._ New York: Macmillan, 1962.

Harris, C. _Flying While Black: A Whistleblower's Story._ Los Angeles: Milligan, 2001.

Harris, David A. "Driving While Black: Racial Profiling on Our Nation's Highways." American Civil Liberties Union Special Report. _American Civil Liberties Union,_ June 1999. At archive.aclu.org/profiling/report/index.html (accessed December 8, 2002).

Hartigan, John, Jr. _Racial Situations: Class Predicaments of Whiteness in Detroit._ Princeton, N.J.: Princeton University Press, 1999.

Hartmann, Paul. _Racism and the Mass Media: A Study of the Role of the Mass Media in the Formation of White Beliefs and Attitudes in Britain._ Totowa, N.J.: Rowman & Littlefield, 1974.

Herrnstein, Richard J., and Charles Murray. _The Bell Curve: Intelligence and Class Structure in American Life._ New York: Free Press, 1994.

Hill-Collins, Patricia. _Black Feminist Thought._ New York: Routledge, 1990.

———. "Moving beyond Gender: Intersectionality and Scientific Knowledge." Pp. 261–84 in _Revisioning Gender,_ edited by Myra Marx Ferre, Judith Lorber, and Beth B. Hess. Thousand Oaks, Calif.: Sage, 1999.

Hoberman, John. _Darwin's Athletes._ Boston: Houghton Mifflin, 1997.

Hochschild, Jennifer. _Facing Up to the American Dream._ Princeton, N.J.: Princeton University Press, 1995.

Hughes, Michael. "Symbolic Racism, Old-Fashioned Racism, and Whites' Opposition to Affirmative Action." Pp. 45–75 in _Racial Attitudes in the 1990s: Continuity and Change,_ edited by Steven A. Tuch and Jack K. Martin. Westport, Conn.: Praeger, 1997.

Hunt, Darnell. _O. J. Simpson Facts and Fictions: News Rituals in the Construction of Reality._ Cambridge: Cambridge University Press, 1999.

———. _Screening the Los Angeles "Riots": Race, Seeing, and Resistance._ Cambridge: Cambridge University Press, 1996.

Hunt, Matthew O., Pamela Barboy Jackson, Brian Powell, and Lala Carr Steelman. "Color Blind: The Treatment of Race and Ethnicity in Social Psychology." _Social Psychology Quarterly_ 63, no. 4 (2000): 352–64.

Hwang, Sean-Shong, Rogelio Saenz, and Benigno E. Aguirre. "Structural and Individual Determinants of Outmarriage among Chinese-, Filipino-, and Japanese-Americans in California." _Sociological Inquiry_ 64, no. 4 (1994): 396–414.

Ignatiev, Noel. _How the Irish Became White._ New York: Routledge, 1995.

Ingram, David. _Group Rights: Reconciling Equality and Difference._ Lawrence: University Press of Kansas, 2000.

Jackman, Mary R. _The Velvet Glove: Paternalism and Conflict in Gender, Class, and Race Relations._ Berkeley: University of California Press, 1994.

Jackman, Mary R., and Marie Crane. " 'Some of My Best Friends Are Black . . .': Interracial Friendship and Whites' Racial Attitudes." _Public Opinion Quarterly_ 50 (Winter 1986): 459–86.

Johnson, Charles S. *Patterns of Negro Segregation*. New York: Harper & Brothers, 1943.

———. *Racial Attitudes: Interviews Revealing Attitudes of Northern and Southern White Persons, of a Wide Range of Occupational and Educational Levels, Toward Negroes*. Nashville, Tenn.: Social Science Institute, Fisk University, 1946.

Johnson, Monica Kirkpatrick, and Margaret Mooney Marini. "Bridging the Racial Divide in the United States: The Effect of Gender." *Social Psychology Quarterly* 61, no. 3 (1998): 247–58.

Kalmijn, Matthijs. "Intermarriage and Homogamy: Causes, Patterns, Trends." *Annual Review of Sociology* 24 (1998): 395–421.

Kane, Emily W. "Racial and Ethnic Variations in Gender-Related Attitudes." *Annual Review of Sociology* 26 (2000): 419–39.

Keen, Sam. *Faces of the Enemy: Reflections of the Hostile Imagination*. New York: Harper & Row, 1986.

Kelley, Robin D. G. *Yo' Mama's Disfunktional: Fighting the Culture Wars in Urban America*. Boston: Beacon, 1997.

Kincheloe, Joel L., and Peter McLaren. "Rethinking Critical Theory and Qualitative Research." Pp. 279–314 in *Handbook of Qualitative Research*, edited by Norman K. Denzin and Yvonna S. Lincoln. Thousand Oaks, Calif.: Sage, 2000.

Kinder, Donald R., and Lynn M. Sanders. *Divided by Color: Racial Politics and Democratic Ideals*. Chicago: University of Chicago Press, 1996.

Kinder, Donald R., and David O. Sears. "Prejudice and Politics: Symbolic Racism versus Racial Threats to the Good Life." *Journal of Personality and Social Psychology* 40, no. 1 (1981): 414–31.

King, Martin Luther, Jr. *A Call to Conscience: The Landmark Speeches of Dr. Martin Luther King, Jr.* Edited by Clayborne Carson and Kris Shephard. New York: Intellectual Properties Management, in association with Warner Books, 2001.

Kovaleski, S., and S. Chan. "D.C. Cabs Still Bypass Minorities, Study Finds: City Crackdown Called Sporadic." *The Washington Post*, October 7, 2003.

Kovel, Joel. *White Racism: A Psychohistory*. New York: Columbia University Press, 1984.

Kozol, Jonathan. *Savage Inequalities*. New York: Crown, 1992.

Lafer, Gordon. *The Job Training Charade*. Ithaca, N.Y.: Cornell University Press, 2002.

Larana, Enrique, Hank Johnston, and Joseph R. Gusfield, eds. *New Social Movements: From Ideology to Identity*. Philadelphia: Temple University Press, 1994.

Lerner, Gerda. *The Grimké Sisters from South Carolina. Rebels: Pioneers for Woman's Rights and Abolition*. New York: Schocken, 1967.

Levin, Jack, and Jack McDevitt. *Hate Crimes: The Rising Tide of Bigotry and Bloodshed*. New York: Plenum, 1993.

Lewis, Oscar. *The Children of Sanchez: Autobiography of a Mexican Family*. New York: Random House, 1961.

———. *La Vida: A Puerto Rican Family in the Culture of Poverty. San Juan and New York*. New York: Random House, 1966.

Lipset, Seymour. *American Exceptionalism*. New York: Norton, 1996.

Lyman, Stanford M. *Social Movements: Critiques, Concepts, Case-Studies*. New York: New York University Press, 1995.

Marable, Manning. *How Capitalism Underdeveloped Black America.* Boston: South End Press, 1981.

———. *Race, Reform, and Rebellion: The Second Reconstruction in Black America, 1945–1990.* Jackson: University Press of Mississippi, 1991.

Marx, Karl. *The German Ideology.* Edited by C. J. Arthur. New York: International, 1985.

Massey, Douglas S., R. Alarcon, J. Durand, and H. Gonzalez. *Return to Aztlan: The Social Process of International Migration from Western Mexico.* Berkeley: University of California Press, 1997.

Massey, Douglas S., and Nancy A. Denton. *American Apartheid: Segregation and the Making of the Underclass.* Cambridge, Mass.: Harvard University Press, 1993.

———. "Trends in the Residential Segregation of Blacks, Hispanics, and Asians: 1970–1980." *American Sociological Review* 52, no. 6 (1987): 802–25.

McConahay, John B. "Modern Racism, Ambivalence, and the Modern Racism Scale." Pp. 91–126 in *Prejudice, Discrimination, and Racism,* edited by John F. Dovidio and Samuel L. Gaertner. New York: Academic, 1986.

McConahay, John B., and J. C. Hough. "Symbolic Racism." *Journal of Social Issues* 32, no. 2 (1976): 23–46.

McCullough, Mary W. *Black and White as Friends: Building Cross-Race Friendships.* Cresskill, N.J.: Hampton, 1998.

McLellan, David, ed. *Karl Marx: Selected Writings.* London: Oxford University Press, 1982.

Mead, Lawrence M. *Beyond Entitlement: The Social Obligations of Citizenship.* New York: Free Press, 1986.

Media Action Network for Asian Americans. "A Memo from MANAA to Hollywood: Asian Stereotypes. Restrictive Portrayals of Asians in the Media and How to Balance Them." 2001. At www.manaa.org/a_stereotypes.html (accessed December 8, 2002).

Meehan, Albert, and Michael Ponder. "Race and Place: The Ecology of Racial Profiling African American Motorists." *Justice Quarterly* 19 (2002): 399–430.

Mendell, David. *Obama: From Promise to Power.* New York: HarperCollins, 2007.

Mills, Charles W. *Blackness Visible.* Ithaca, N.Y.: Cornell University Press, 1998.

———. *The Racial Contract.* Ithaca, N.Y.: Cornell University Press, 1997.

Moran, Rachel. *Interracial Intimacy: The Regulation of Race and Romance.* Chicago: University of Chicago Press, 2001.

Moscovici, Serge. "The Coming Era of Social Representations." Pp. 115–50 in *Cognitive Approaches to Social Behaviour,* edited by J. P. Codol and J. P. Leyens. The Hague: Nijhoff, 1982.

Moynihan, Daniel P., ed. *On Understanding Poverty: Perspectives from the Social Sciences.* New York: Basic, 1969.

Murray, Charles A. *Losing Ground: American Social Policy, 1950–1980.* New York: Basic, 1984.

Myrdal, Gunnar. *An American Dilemma: The Negro Problem and Modern Democracy.* New York: Harper & Brothers, 1944.

Neal, Patrick. *Liberalism and Its Discontents.* New York: New York University Press, 1997.

Nelson, Dana D. *National Manhood: Capitalist Citizenship and the Imagined Fraternity of White Men*. Durham, N.C.: Duke University Press, 1998.

Newman, Katherine S. *Declining Fortunes: The Withering of the American Dream*. New York: Basic, 1993.

Obama, Barack. *The Audacity of Hope*. New York: Crown Publishers, 2006.

Odum, Howard W. *American Social Problems*. New York: Holt, 1939.

Ogbu, John. *Minority Education and Caste: The American System in Cross-Cultural Perspective*. New York: Academic, 1978.

Oliver, Melvin, and Thomas Shapiro. *Black Wealth/White Wealth: A New Perspective on Racial Inequality*. New York: Routledge, 1995.

Omi, Michael, and Howard Winant. *Racial Formation in the United States*. New York: Routledge, 1994.

Orbuch, Terri L. "People's Account Count: The Sociology of Accounts." *Annual Review of Sociology* 23 (1997): 455–78.

Orfield, Gary, Susan Eaton, and the Harvard Project on School Desegregation. *Dismantling Desegregation: The Quiet Reversal of* Brown v. Board of Education. New York: New York Press, 1996.

Orwell, George. "In Front of Your Nose." In *The Collected Essays, Journalism, and Letters of George Orwell, Vol. 4*, edited by S. Orwell and I. Angus. New York: Harcourt, Brace, and World, 1946.

Park, Robert E. *Race and Culture*. Glencoe, Ill.: Free Press, 1950.

Peffley, Mark, and Jon Hurwitz. "Whites' Stereotypes of Blacks: Sources and Political Consequences." Pp. 58–99 in *Perception and Prejudice: Race and Politics in the United States*, edited by Jon Hurwitz and Mark Peffley. New Haven, Conn.: Yale University Press, 1998.

Penner, Louis A., John F. Dovidio, Donald Edmondson, Rhonda K. Dailey, Tsveti Markova, Terrance L. Albrecht, and Samuel L. Gaertner. "The Experience of Discrimination and Black-White Health Disparities in Medical Care." *Journal of Black Psychology* 35 (2009): 180–203.

Pincus, Fred. *Reverse Discrimination: Dismantling the Myth*. Boulder, Colo.: Lynne Reinner Publishers, 2003.

Piven, Frances Fox, and Richard Cloward. *Poor People's Movements*. New York:Vintage, 1978.

Poulantzas, Nicos. *Political Power and Social Classes*. Translation by Timothy O'Hagan. London: Verso, 1984.

Public Agenda. " 'Walking on Eggshells': Observations on How Americans Discuss Race." 1998. At www.publicagenda.org/specials/moveon/moveon8.htm (accessed December 8, 2002).

Qian, Zhenchao, and Daniel T. Lichter. "Measuring Marital Assimilation: Intermarriage among Natives and Immigrants." *Social Science Research* 30 (2001): 289–312.

Quillian, Lincoln. "Group Threat and Regional Change in Attitudes toward African-Americans." *American Journal of Sociology* 102, no. 3 (1996): 816–60.

Rawick, George P. *From Sundown to Sunup: The Making of the Black Community*. Westport, Conn.: Greenwood, 1972.

Reskin, Barbara, and Irene Padavic. *Women and Men at Work*. Thousand Oaks, Calif.: Pine Forge, 2002.

Ridgeway, Cecilia, and James Balkwell. "Group Processes and the Diffusion of Status Beliefs." *Social Psychology Quarterly* 60, no. 1 (1997): 14–31.

Ridgeway, Cecilia, Elizabeth Heger Boyle, Kathy J. Kuipers, and Dawn T. Robinson. "How Do Status Beliefs Develop? The Role of Resources and Interactional Experience." *American Sociological Review* 63 (1998): 331–50.

Rieder, Jonathan. *Canarsie: The Jews and Italians of Brooklyn against Liberalism.* Cambridge, Mass.: Harvard University Press, 1985.

Robinson, Cedric J. *Black Marxism: The Making of the Black Radical Tradition.* Chapel Hill: University of North Carolina Press, 2000.

———. *Black Movements in America.* New York: Routledge, 1997.

Roediger, David. *Colored White: Transcending the Racial Past.* Berkeley: University of California Press, 2000; London: Verso, 2002.

———. *The Wages of Whiteness.* London: Verso, 1994.

Rose, Sonya O. "Class Formation and the Quintessential Worker." Pp. 133–66 in *Reworking Class,* edited by John R. Hall. Ithaca, N.Y.: Cornell University Press, 1997.

Roscigno, Vincent J. *The Face of Discrimination: How Race and Gender Impact Work and Home Lives.* Lanham, Md.: Rowman & Littlefield, 2007.

Rubin, Lillian B. *Families on the Fault Line: America's Working Class Speaks about the Family, the Economy, Race, and Ethnicity.* New York: HarperCollins, 1994.

———. *Just Friends: The Role of Friendship in Our Lives.* New York: HarperCollins, 1985.

Rusche, SE and ZW Brewster. "'Because They Tip for Shit!': The Social Psychology of Everyday Racism in Restaurants." *Sociology Compass* 2, no. 6 (2008): 2008–29.

Russell, Katheryn K. *The Color of Crime: Racial Hoaxes, White Fear, Black Protectionism, Police Harassment, and Other Macroaggressions.* New York: New York University Press, 1998.

Ryan, William A. *Blaming the Victim.* New York: Random House, 1976.

St. Jean, Yanick. "Let People Speak for Themselves: Interracial Unions and the General Social Survey." *Journal of Black Studies* 28, no. 3 (1998): 398–414.

Sabini, John. *Social Psychology.* New York: Norton, 1992.

Schuman, Howard, Charlotte Steeh, Lawrence Bobo, and Maria Krysan. *Racial Attitudes in America: Trends and Interpretations.* Cambridge, Mass.: Harvard University Press, 1997.

Sears, David O., and Donald R. Kinder. "Racial Tensions and Voting in Los Angeles." Pp. 55–75 in *Los Angeles: Viability and Prospects for Metropolitan Leadership,* edited by Werner Z. Hirsch. New York: Praeger, 1971.

Sewell, William H., Jr. "The Concepts(s) of Culture." Pp. 35–61 in *Beyond the Cultural Turn,* edited by Victoria E. Bonnell and Lynn Hunt. Berkeley: University of California Press, 1999.

Sheatsley, Paul B. "White Attitudes toward the Negro." Pp. 303–24 in *The Negro American,* edited by Talcott Parsons and Kenneth B. Clark. Boston: Houghton Mifflin, 1966.

Sidanius, Jim, et al. "It's Not Affirmative Action, It's the Blacks." Pp. 191–235 in *Racialized Politics: The Debate about Racism in America,* edited by David O. Sears, Jim Sidanius, and Lawrence Bobo. Chicago: University of Chicago Press, 2000.

Siegelman, Peter. "Racial Discrimination in 'Everyday' Commercial Transactions: What Do We Know, What Do We Need to Know, and How Can We Find Out." Pp. 69–98 in *A National Report Card on Discrimination in America: The Role of Testing*, edited by Michael Fix and Margery Austin Turner. Washington, D.C.: Urban Institute, 1998. At www.urban.org/UploadedPDF/report_card.pdf (accessed December 8, 2002).

Sigelman, Lee, and Susan Welch. *Black Americans' View of Racial Inequality: The Dream Deferred*. Cambridge: Cambridge University Press, 1991.

Silverstein, Ken. "Barack Obama, Inc: The Birth of a Money Machine." *Harper's*, November 2006, p. 6.

Slack, Jennifer Daryl. "The Theory and Method of Articulation in Cultural Studies." Pp. 112–27 in *Stuart Hall: Critical Dialogues in Cultural Studies*, edited by David Morley and Kuan-Hsing Chen. London: Routledge, 1996.

Sloan, Irving J. *Our Violent Past: An American Chronicle*. New York: Random House, 1970.

Smith, Tom W. "Intergroup Relations in Contemporary America." Pp. 69–106 in *Intergroup Relations in the United States: Research Perspectives*, edited by Wayne Winborne and Renae Cohen. New York: National Conference for Community and Justice, 1998.

———. "Measuring Inter-Racial Friendships: Experimental Comparisons." Paper presented at the annual meeting of the American Sociological Association, August 6, 1999, in Chicago.

Sniderman, Paul M., and Edward G. Carmines. *Reaching beyond Race*. Cambridge, Mass.: Harvard University Press, 1997.

Sniderman, Paul M., and Thomas Piazza. *The Scar of Race*. Cambridge, Mass.: Harvard University Press, 1993.

Somers, Margaret. "The Narrative Constitution of Identity: A Relational and Network Approach." *Theory and Society* 23, no. 3 (1994): 605–49.

Steinberg, Stephen. *The Ethnic Myth*. Boston: Beacon, 1989.

Stouffer, S. A. *The American Soldier*, Vols. I and II. Princeton, N.J.: Princeton University Press, 1949.

Street, Paul. *Barack Obama and the Future of American Politics*. Boulder and London: Paradigm Publishers, 2009.

Taguieff, Pierre-André, ed. *Face au Racisme, Tome II: Analyse, Hypotheses, Perspectives*. Paris: La Découverte, 1991.

Taguieff, Pierre-André. *The Force of Prejudice: Racism and Its Doubles*. Minneapolis: University of Minnesota Press, 2001.

Tanur, Judith, ed. *Questions about Questions*. New York: Russell Sage Foundation, 1994.

Tarrow, Sidney. *Power in Social Movements: Social Movements and Contentious Politics*. Cambridge: Cambridge University Press, 1998.

Tatum, Beverly Daniel. *"Why Are All the Black Kids Sitting Together in the Cafeteria?": And Other Conversations about Race*. New York: Basic, 1997.

Terkel, Studs. *Race: How Blacks and Whites Feel and Think about the American Obsession*. New York: Doubleday, 1993.

Thomas, Alexander, and Samuel Sillen. *Racism and Psychiatry*. New York: Brunner/Mazel, 1972.

Thomas, Melvin. "Anything but Race: The Social Science Retreat from Racism." *African American Research Perspectives* (Winter 2000): 79–96.

Thompson, John B. *Studies in the Theory of Ideology.* Cambridge, UK: Polity, 1984.

Unzueta, Miguel M., Brian S. Lowery, and Eric D. Knowles. "How Believing in Affirmative Action Quotas Protects White Men's Self-Esteem." *Organizational Behavior and Human Decision Processes* 105, no. 1 (2007): 1–13.

Van Dijk, Teun A. *Communicating Racism: Ethnic Prejudice in Cognition and Conversation.* Amsterdam: Benjamins, 1987.

———. *Ideology: A Multidisciplinary Approach.* Thousand Oaks, Calif.: Sage, 1998.

———. *News as Discourse.* Hillsdale, N.J.: Erlbaum Associates, 1988.

———. *Prejudice in Discourse: An Analysis of Ethnic Prejudice in Cognition and Conversation.* Amsterdam: Benjamins, 1984.

———. *Racism and the Press.* London: Routledge, 1991.

Vigil, James Diego. *Barrio Gangs: Street Life and Identity in Southern California.* Austin: University of Texas Press, 1988.

Voloshinov, Vladimir N. *Freudianism: A Marxist Critique.* New York: Academic, 1976.

Walters, Ronald. *White Nationalism, Black Interests: Conservative Public Policy and the Black Community.* Detroit: Wayne State University Press, 2003.

Warner, W. Lloyd. "American Class and Caste." *American Journal of Sociology* 42, no. 2 (1936): 234–37.

Weber, Max. "Objectivity in Social Science and Social Policy." Pp. 50–112 in *Max Weber on the Methodology of the Social Sciences,* edited and translated by Edward A. Shils and H. A. Finch. New York: Free Press, 1949.

Webster, Yehudi O. *The Racialization of America.* New York: St. Martin's, 1992.

Wellman, David T. *Portraits of White Racism.* Cambridge: Cambridge University Press, 1993.

West, Cornel. *Race Matters.* Boston: Beacon, 1993.

Wetherell, Margaret, and Jonathan Potter. *Mapping the Language of Racism.* New York: Columbia University Press, 1992.

Wicker, Tom. *Tragic Failure.* New York: Morrow, 1996.

Wilson, William Julius. *The Declining Significance of Race.* Chicago: University of Chicago Press, 1978.

———. *The Truly Disadvantaged: The Inner City, the Underclass, and Public Policy.* Chicago: University of Chicago Press, 1987.

———. *When Work Disappears.* New York: Norton, 1996.

Yinger, John. *Closed Doors, Opportunities Lost: The Continuing Costs of Housing Discrimination.* New York: Russell Sage Foundation, 1995.

Zinn, Howard. *A People's History of the United States.* New York: HarperCollins, 1980.

Zuberi, Tukufu. "Deracializing Social Statistics: Problems in the Quantification of Race." *Annals of the American Academy of Political and Social Science* 568 (March 2000): 172–85.

Index

Note: Page numbers in *italic* type indicate figures or tables.

abstract liberalism frame: affirmative action in, 153–54; blacks and, 153–57; choices in, 35–36; definition of, 28; equal opportunity in, 28, 31–32; foundations of, 26–28; government intervention in, 34–35; individualism in, 28; meritocracy in, 32–34; segregation in, 34–35, 138; significance of, 26, 30–31
academics, politics of, 237n5, 239n17
Achilles Heel (magazine), 11
activists, paid vs. grassroots organizers, 241n39
Adams, John, 209, 238n8
Adorno, Theodor, 132
affirmative action: abstract liberalism frame and, 153–54, 208; attack on, 184–85; blacks on, 153–54, 164–66, 263; Bush, George H.W., opposition to, 17n2; effective, characteristics of, 148n7; equal opportunity and, 28; "I didn't own any slaves" response to, 80; "I was denied because of a minority" response to, 84–87; meritocratic approach to, 32–33; Obama, Barack, views on, 221, 230–231; "the past is the past" response to, 77–78; projection and, 64–66; public opinion on, 151, 262–263; racial progressives

on, 134, 137, 140–41; "yes and no, but . . ." response to, 60–62, 165
Afghanistan, Obama policy on, 226–27, 250n97
age, color-blind racism and, 70
Ali, José, 189
Alice's Adventures in Wonderland (Carroll), 207, 217, 236, 237n1, 240–41, 259n158
Alinsky, Saul, 215
All in the Family, 208
Allport, Gordon, 146
America in Black and White (Thernstrom and Thernstrom), 210
American Coalition for Clean Coal Electricity, 242n45
American Creed, 6, 30, 151
Americanism, xiv
American Revolution, 27
Amerika, 234, 240n27
anti-immigration movement, 211, 239n18
antiracism, 15–16
"anything but race," 62–63
Arab Americans, 194–95, 198
Archie Bunkers, 55, 95
Aronowitz, Stanley, 243n51
Ashford, Evelyn Glore, 247n78
Asian Americans: blacks and, 190–91; income of light- versus dark-

skinned, 185–86; interracial marriage among, 192; Latinos and, 189–91; political behavior of, 187–88; population of, 177–78, 199n4; racial attitudes of, 190–91, *191*; residential segregation among, 193; self-classification of, 195; social identity of, 187–88, 195–96, 205n63; white attitudes toward, 191
Asian Indians, 194–95
Asian women, white male attitudes toward, 118, 128n39
assimilation, 196. *See also* whitening
The Audicity of Hope (Obama), 219, 230
Auletta, Ken, 103

Barndt, Joseph, 103
Baucus, Max, 253n116
The Bell Curve (Murray and Hernstein), 210
Bernanke, Ben, 252n112
biological arguments, 29, 141
black elites, 270–71
The Black Agenda Report, 246n66
blacks: abstract liberalism and, 153–57; on affirmative action, 153–54, 164–66; Asian Americans and, 190–91, 233; collective group in tri-racial system, 179, 271, 275n32; color-blind racism in, 152–73; cultural racism and, 157–58; discrimination experienced by, 154, 160–63, 174n9; frames used by, 152–63, *154*, 264; future social identity of, 197; on government intervention, 156, 161; on interracial marriage, 166–69; Latinos and, 188–91; minimization of racism frame and, 160–63; naturalization frame and, 159–60; population of, 177; power of, 176n24; prejudice among, 172–73; racial stories of, 169–70; as racists, 172, 222; on reparations, 161, 170; research on, 151–52; on residential segregation, 155–57, 159–60; on reverse discrimination, 164–65; and rhetorical incoherence, 166–69; on school segregation, 155–57, 159; semantic moves by, 164–66; socioeconomic inequalities, 209–10; on social standing, 157–58, 161; styles of color-blind racism used by, 163–69; as supporters of Barack Obama, 222–24, 248nn80–81; 258n143; white attitudes toward, 124

blaming the victim, 25, 40, 83
blanqueamiento, 182. *See also* assimilation; whitening
Blumer, Herbert, 272n6
Bobo, Lawrence, 6, 7
Bolivians, 201n25
Bombardieri, Marcela, 251n105
Booker, Cory, 215
Bourdieu, Pierre, 125n7
bourgeoisie, 26–27
Brown, John, 132
Brown v. Board of Education (1954), 35
buffer groups, in stratified systems, 179, 182, 183, 190, 196–97, 200n18
Buffet, Warren, 228
Bush, George H. W., 17n2
Bush, George W., 195, 208, 211, 231, 242n45, 248n86
busing, 138, 151
Byrd, James, Jr., 29

Canellos, Peter S., 230
Carmines, Edward, 5
Carroll, Lewis, 207, 217, 236, 237n1, 240–41, 259n158
CBS-*New York Times* poll, 221–22, 246n68
Census Bureau, 178, 184
Chicago School, 252n113
Child, Lydia Maria, 132
China, 178, 199n5
choice: abstract liberalism frame and, 35–36; fallacy of arguments based on, 36. *See also* individualism
Christianity: Arab Christians, 204n57; whiteness and, 205n65

civil rights movement: new, 266–69,
271–272, 275n33; original, 131, 132
Clark, Kenneth, 4
class: color-blind racism influenced by,
70; white privilege and, 145; white
racial attitudes by, 132, 145
clean coal technology, 217, 242n45
Clinton, Bill (William Jefferson), 144,
231
Clinton, Hillary, 212, 227
code of the street, 104
Cole, Juan, 249n94
collective black group, 179, 271, 275n32
college, interracial interaction in,
109–11
color, skin. *See* colorism; pigmentocracy
color-blind politics, advocacy of, 5
color-blind racism: blacks influenced
by, 152–73; defined, 211; fighting,
266–68; ideology of, xv, 2–4, 48,
261–63, 273n8; Jim Crow racism
vs., 2–3, 213; liberalism and, 7; of
racial progressives, 134, 138,
141–45; research approaches to,
11–12, 264–65; in tri-racial system,
179, 195, 197; white supremacy
upheld by, 210–11, 239n17, 262.
See also frames; story lines; styles
of color-blind racism; testimonies
colorism, 182, 197, 205n64. *See also* pigmentocracy
compensation. *See* reparations
competitive racism, 30
Compton, Ann, 244n58
Connerly, Ward, 184
Conyers, John, 229–30
cool pose, 104
Cooper, Anderson, 244n60
Craig, Gregory, 217
crazes, defined, 246n69
cultural racism frame, 26; blacks and,
157–58; definition of, 28–29; motivation in, 40, 42; social standing in,
41–43
culture: minorities and, 116; as pigmentocracy criterion, 180–81
culture of poverty, 40, 51n35, 103, 172

Davis, Angela, 222
Davis, Kenneth, 5
The Declining Significance of Race (Wilson), 43, 253n118
defensive beliefs, 95
Denton, Nancy, 104
Detroit Area Study (1998), 12–13
diminutives, in color-blind rhetoric,
66–67
disclaimers. *See* semantic moves, in
color-blind rhetoric
discourse, whites' private racial, 72n2
discrimination: blacks' experience of,
154, 160–63, 174n9; effects of, 43,
79; as excuse, 46; existence of, attitudes about, 43, 45–46, 210; "I am
not black, so I don't know" attitude on, 59–60; life chances and,
41; minimization of racism and,
43–47; new racism and, 3, 183–84,
210–11; persistence of racial, 210–
211; "the past is the past" response
to, 79; racial progressives on, 134–
36, 139, 143; women's experience
of, 134, 143, 146. *See also* employment discrimination; reverse discrimination
Dobbs, Lou, 177, 195, 211, 239n19
Dollard, John, 25, 95
Dreams of My Father (Obama), 219
Drew, Christopher, 216
driving while black, 2
D'Souza, Dinesh, 212
DuBois, W.E.B., 66
Duncan, Arne, 250n100
Dyson, Michael Eric, 248n81

economic stimulus package, 230,
252n112
education: equal opportunity and, 31;
interracial interaction in, 109–11,
113; racial inequality addressed
through, 144, 147; tracking in, 109.
See also affirmative action; integrated schools; school segregation
emotions, racial issues and, 71–72, 98
employment, race and, 146, 239n20

employment discrimination: meritocratic approach to, 33–34; new racism and, 3
energy, Obama policy on, 242n45
Engels, Frederick, 11
Equal Employment Opportunity Commission, 83
equal opportunity, 28, 31–32
ethnic groups, success of, 82–83
Europe, racial politics in, 184
excuses, discrimination and, 46

False Promises (Aronowitz), 243n51
Fenty, Adrian, 215
Firebaugh, Glenn, 5
FISA. *See* Foreign Intelligence Surveillance Act (FISA)
Flack, Roberta, 241n31
Flores-Gonzales, Nilda, 189
Ford, Glen, 222
Ford, Harold, 215
Foreign Intelligence Surveillance Act (FISA), 242n47
Fox News (television show), 177, 221
frames, 25–49; abstract liberalism, 26–28, 30–36; blacks' use of, 152–63, *154*; cultural racism, 26, 28–29, 39–43; definition of, 10; flexibility of, 47–49; minimization of racism, 26, 29–30, 43–47; naturalization, 26, 28, 37–39; whites' use of, 30, 262–63, 265
Freud, Sigmund, 63
friendship: "anything but race" and, 62–63; blacks and interracial, 166, 174n8; college students and interracial, 110–11; incoherence in response to, 70; "some of my best friends are . . ." and, 57–58; "some of my best friends were . . ." and, 96–97; whites and interracial, 107–11, 126n18. *See also* interactions, black-white
Fukiyama, Francis, 258n155

Gabbidon, Shaun, 238n15
gang activity, 101n28

Gates, Bob, 226, 227
Gates, Henry Louis, 248n82
Geithner, Timothy, 228
Gibson, John, 177
Gilroy, Paul, 272n1
Gitlin, Todd, 272n1
globalization, and race, 184
Gore, Al, 242n45
government intervention: abstract liberalism frame and, 34–35, 144; blacks on, 156, 161; "I didn't own any slaves" response to, 79–80; "if others have made it" response to, 82–83; "the past is the past" response to, 77; projection and, 65. *See also* affirmative action; remedial policies; social welfare; welfare
Graves, Earl, Jr., 210
Gray, John, 26
Grimke sisters, 132
group formation, in tri-racial system, 186–87
Grutter vs. Bollinger, 184–85
Guantánamo, 255n128

habitus, 125n7. *See also* white habitus
Hall, Stuart, 54
Hannity, Sean, 177
Harrison, Roderick J., 256n136
hate crimes, 148n5
Heran, Joyce, 223
Herrnstein, Richard J., 210
Hirsch, Michael, 228
Holder, Eric, 229, 252n110
honorary whites: category of, 179, 194–96, 204n56; social identity of, 187–88, 270–71; status of, 197–98
Horowitz, David, 272n1
Hume, Brit, 177
Huntington, Samuel, 177
Hurricane Katrina, 29
Hutchings, Vincent, 219, 243n55
Hyman, Herbert, 4
hypersegregation, 109

"I am not black, so I don't know," 58–60

"I am not prejudiced, but . . . ," 57–58
identity, racial, 275n30
ideology: effectiveness of, 10, 152, 171; function of, 25–26; stories and, 75–76; style of, 53. *See also* racial ideology
"I didn't own any slaves," 79–82, 100nn12–13
"if others have made it," 82–83
immigrants: color-blind racism and, 211; illegal, 177, 211, 239n20; Latino, 188–89; Latino attitudes toward, 202n32; success of early, 82–83; survey data on opposition to, 239n18
immigration, opposition to, 211, 239nn18–20
incoherence: blacks and rhetorical, 166–69; in color-blind rhetoric, 53–54, 68–70; white versus black, 175n13
income, in light- versus dark-skinned groups, 185–86, *186*, 209–10
individualism: abstract liberalism frame and, 35–36; fallacy of arguments based on, 36; racism and, 6; segregation and, 28. *See also* choice
integrated schools, 109. *See also* busing; school segregation
intentionality, color-blind rhetoric and, 54
interactions, black-white: interest/empathy and, 124, 146–47; negative, 87–90; number of, 99, 107, 129n44; positive, 90–92; in school, 113–14. *See also* friendship
interpretation of research, 14–15
interracialism, white attitudes toward, 105
interracial marriage: acquaintance with, 96; "anything but race" and, 63; approval of, 118–20; blacks on, 166–69; children in, concern for, 64, 66, 73n17, 120–23, 135, 141; incoherence in response to, 68–70; increases in, 178; opposition to,

121–23; projection and, 64; racial progressives on, 133–35; reservations about, 120–21; survey results on, 105; in tri-racial system, 192; white attitudes on, 116–23, *117*
interracial relationships. *See* friendship; interracial marriage
Iraq, Obama policy on, 226
Israel, Obama administration and, 231
Italians, as minorities, 73n10
"I was denied because of a minority," 83–87

Jackman, Mary, 7, 10
Jackson, Jesse, 214, 222–23
Jackson, Michael, 235
Japanese Americans, 194–95
Jefferson, Thomas, 27
Jim Crow: color-blind racism versus, 2–3, 25, 213; reparations and, 79; stage Negroes and, 164
Jindal, Bobby, 215, 236, 258n154
job discrimination. *See* employment discrimination
jokes, racist, 56
Jordan, Vernon, 216
Joshua generation, Barack Obama's, 223, 247n77, 257n149

Kamiya, Gary, 247n73
Kant, Immanuel, 27
Keyes, Alan, 215
Kilcullen, David, 250n97
Kim, Claire Jean, 205n63
Kinder, Donald, 6
King, Larry, 247n72
King, Martin Luther, Jr., 1, 17n2, 220, 254n125, 259n157
King, Rodney, 29
Kluegel, James, 7
Krugman, Paul, 228

labor. *See* employment
laissez-faire racism, 7, 30, 33–34, 174n6
Lang, Katie, 223
language: avoidance of racial, in public, 54–56; whites' private racial, 72n2

Latin America, racial stratification in, 181–83
Latin America–like society, 173, 179, 183–85, 198, 205n65; and election of Obama, 225–26, 232–33, 270–71. *See also* tri-racial system
Latinos: Asian Americans and, 189–91; assimilated, 179; blacks and, 188–91; immigration attitudes of, 202n32; income of light- versus dark-skinned, 185; interracial marriage among, 192; population of, 177; race effect, 266; racial attitudes of, 188–89, *190*; residential segregation among, 193; self-classification of, *187*, 187, 195; social identity of, 187, 189, 195–96; white attitudes toward, 191
Lee, Spike, 258n151
Leonhardt, David, 233
Lewis, Oscar, 51n35
liberalism: characteristics of, 26–27; color-blind racism and, 7, 265; influence of, 27–28; racism and, 27–28; social reform and, 27–28. *See also* abstract liberalism frame
Limbaugh, Rush, 236, 258n154
Lincoln, Abraham, 227
Lipset, Seymour, 5
Losing Ground (Muray), 210

marriage. *See* interracial marriage
Marsh, Taylor, 218, 249n94
Marx, Karl, 9, 125, 236
Massey, Douglas, 104
Matthews, Chris, 212, 240n26, 249n91
McCain, John, xiv–xv, 208, 219, 224–225, 229, 249n87
McDermott, George, 29
McIntire, Mike, 216
Mead, Lawrence, 40, 103
media, racial stories reinforced by, 99
Memmi, Albert, 1
men, racial attitudes of, 145
Mendell, David, 217

meritocracy, 32–34
mestizaje, 181–82, 182
military, Obama policy on the, 226–27, 250n97
Mill, John Stuart, 27
Mills, Charles, 10
minimization of racism frame, 26; attitudes in, 43–44; blacks and, 160–63; definition of, 29–30; discrimination in, 43–47
minorities: color-blind racism and non-black, 266; culture of, 116; racial justice, possibility for, 270–72; racial spaces, 270; role constructed by whites for, 270; socioeconomic inequalities, 209–10; as supporters of Barack Obama, 222–24, 248nn80–81, 257n143; white supremacy order. *See also* Asian Americans; blacks; Latinos
minority politicians, post-civil rights': characteristics of, 214–15, 241n35; Obama as, 215–18
miscegenation, 181–82
Mitchell, Luke, 254n124
Moore, Michael, 235–36
morality: legislation of, 34; symbolic racism and, 6
Moscovici, Serge, 75
motivation, cultural racism frame and, 40, 42
multi-racialism, 178, 184, 199n6
Murray, Charles, 40, 103, 210

National Association for the Advancement of Colored People (NAACP), 258n150
nationalism: black, 222, 224; characteristics of, 255n127; in Latin America, 182–83; Obama election as challenge to traditional, xiv; as social force, 255n127
naturalization frame, 26; blacks and, 159–60; definition of, 28; fallacy of, 37; segregation in, 37–39, 111–16, 159
nativism, 211

The Negro American (Parsons and Clark), 4
negrophobia, 117, 148n10
New Democrats, defined, 255n126
Newman, Katherine, 29
new racism: emergence of, 183, 213; liberalism and, 26; Obama, Barack and, xiii–xv, 208, 212–17, 238n7, 240n30, 256n137, 256n140, 270–71; practices of, 3; race effect, 266. *See also* color-blind racism
news. *See* media
Nopper, Tamara K., 221

Obama, Barack: electoral politics vs. social movements and, 217, 234–36, 242n46, 257n146; Latin America like-society and, 225–26, 232–33, 270–71; Messiah-like practices, xiv; as minority politician, 215–18, 233; minority supporters of, 222–24, 248nn80–81, 257n143; new racism and, xiii–xv, 212–17, 238n7, 240n30, 256n137, 256n140, 270–71; progressivism of, 217–18; race and, 219–22, 244n58, 245nn63–64; race speech, analysis of, 220–22, 245nn63–64, 246nn66,68; symbolic value of election of, 235, 257n149; white supporters of, 218–19, 222–23, 243n53
Obama, Barack, campaign for the presidency: funding for, 216–217, 218, 224–25, 231, 249n87; post-racialism and, 219–22; predictions regarding analyzed, 225–32; success, reasons for, 216–17, 219, 222–23, 243n55, 270; supporters during, 218–19, 222–25, 233, 240n28, 243nn55–56, 248nn86–87, 257n149, 258n143; white vs. non-white experience of, 222–24; Wright, Jeremiah, association with and, 220–21, 245nn63–64
Obama, Barack, presidency analysis: Cabinet members of, 227–29; critiques, need for, 235; policy positions, 219–20, 225–32, 250n97, 252n112, 252n116, 255nn129–130; progressive debates on, 207–8, 237nn3–4, 249n94; racial inequality and, 230–31
Obama, Michelle, 215, 249n90
Obamania, 207–8, 237n2
Obama phenomenon, xiii–xv, 207–8, 212–13, 224–26, 232–34, 270
Oboler, Suzanne, 189
Oliver, Melvin L., 79
Omi, Michael, 172
oppositional identity, 104
O'Reilly, Bill, 177
Orwell, George, 198
otherization of blacks, 111

Pakistan, Obama policy on, 227, 250n97
Parsons, Talcott, 4
"the past is the past," 77–79, 170
Patrick, Deval, 215
people of color. *See* minorities
Peterson, Steven A., 238n15
Petraeus, David, 250n97
Pettigrew, Tom, 219, 243n55
phenotype, 180, 201n24
pigmentocracy: criteria of, 180–81, 182; epidermic boundaries in, 196; in Latin America, 182. *See also* colorism
playing the race card, 1, 29
policy. *See* public policy
politicians, new racism, 214–15. *See also entries for* Obama, Barack
poor whites, 132
Poulantzas, Nicos, 171
Powell, Colin, 233, 256n138
powell, john, 230, 254
power: of blacks, 176n24; of whites, 145
Power, Samantha, 231
prejudice: among blacks, 172–73, 270–71; Blumer's conception of, 272n6; in Latin America, 181; projection and, 65; racism versus, 172–73
Prince, Melanye T., 248n84

projection, as rhetorical tool, 63–66, 114–15
Protestant Ethic, 6
public policy, end of race-based, 184–85, 197

qualitative research, on blacks, 151–52

race: concept of, 8–9, 275n30; constructionist perspective on, 8–9; disappearance of, as official category, 178, 184–85, 197; globalization and, 184; invisibility of, to whites, 116; in Latin America, 181, 183; nationality as substitute for, 183; Obama, Barack and, 219–22, 244n58, 245nn63–64; Obama policies on, 230–31; social/economic effects of, 1–2; social reality of, 272n1. *See also* Obama, Barack
race card, playing the, 1, 29
race speech analysis, Barack Obama's, 220–22, 245n63–64, 246n66
race traitors, 16, 132, 264
racial attitudes: of Asian Americans, 190–91, *191*; of Latinos, 188–89, *190*; of whites, 191; of whites in post–civil rights era, 4–8, 210–11, 239n17
racial ideology, 9–10. *See also* frames
racial identity, 275n30
racial inequality, 209–10, 214, 230, 262–63, 266
racial justice, possibility of, 270–72
racial language: avoidance of, in public, 54–56; whites' private, 72n2
racial mobility, 270
racial optimists, 4–5
racial pesoptimists, 5–6
racial profiling, 211, 248n82
racial progress, public opinion on, 151
racial progressives, 131–47; characteristics of, 146–47, 264; class backgrounds of, 132–33; college students as, 133–38; definition of, 132; Detroit area residents as, 138–44; limitations of, 134, 138,
141–45; Obama campaign and, 237n3
racial spaces, 270
racial stories. *See* storytelling
racial stratification. *See* tri-racial system
racial structure, 9
racism: denial of, 2, 233, 267–68, 272n1; laissez-faire, 7; liberalism and, 27–28; Obama on, 220–21; prejudice versus, 172–73; religious groups, 274n23; reverse, 211; symbolic, 6–7; systemic versus psychological approaches to, 7–8, 9, 132, 172–73; whites justification of, 210–11, 262–63. *See also* color-blind racism; cultural racism frame
racism lite, 3
racists: acquaintance with, 92–95, 136, 141, 148n9; blacks as, 172
Reed, Adolph, 216, 222, 234, 249n88
relativism, 15
religion, and racism, 274n23. *See also* Christianity
remedial policies, 78. *See also* affirmative action; government intervention; reparations
reparations: abstract liberalism and, 31; blacks on, 161, 170; "I didn't own any slaves" response to, 80–81; "the past is the past" response to, 79, 170; racial progressives on, 134, 136
Republican Party, 178, 184
research: on blacks, 151–52; changing context for, 5, 11–12; on color-blind racism, 11–12, 211; conduct of, 30; data sources for, 12–13; interpretation of, 14–15; mixed methodology in, 5; political nature of, 13–14
residential segregation: abstract liberalism frame and, 35; among Asian Americans, 193; blacks on, 155–57, 159–60; among Latinos, 193; naturalization frame and, 37–39, 159–60; new racism and, 3; prob-

lems of, 112–13, 125, 146; public opinion on, 151; in tri-racial system, 192–93; whites and, 105, 112–13

reverse discrimination: affirmative action as, 61; blacks on, 164–65; cases filed alleging, 83; color-blind racism and, 211; "I was denied because of a minority" examples of, 83–87; racial progressives on, 136

rhetoric. *See* styles of color-blind racism

Rice, Susan E., 250n100

Rodríguez, Clara, 189

Rush, Bobby, 216

Saito, Leland, 188

Sanders, Lynn, 6

Savan, Leslie, 239n20

Scarborough, Joe, 249n91

school segregation: abstract liberalism frame and, 34–35, 138; blacks on, 155–57, 159; naturalization frame and, 37–39. *See also* integrated schools

Schuman, Howard, 5–6

Sears, David, 6

segregation: blacks and, 103–4; culture of poverty and, 103; hyper-, 109; incoherence in response to, 69; individualism and, 28; naturalization frame and, 37–39, 111–16, 159; projection and, 64; self-, 64, 69, 114–15; significance of, 103–25; whites and, 105–16. *See also* residential segregation; school segregation; white habitus

self-segregation, 64, 69, 114–15

semantic moves, in color-blind rhetoric, 57–63; "anything but race," 62–63; blacks and, 164–66; "I am not black, so I don't know," 58–60; "I am not prejudiced, but . . . ," 57–58; "some of my best friends are . . . ," 57–58; "yes and no, but . . . ," 60–62

sense of group position, 7–8

September 11, 2001 terrorist attacks, 205n65, 211

Shapiro, Thomas M., 79

Sharpton, Al, 223

Sheatsley, Paul B., 4

Showell, Andre, 220

Sidanius, Jim, 7

Siegel, Paul M., 238n15

Silverstein, Ken, 216, 217

single-payer health care plan, 229–30, 252n114, 252n116

Sirota, David, 228

skin color. *See* colorism; pigmentocracy

slavery: "I didn't own any slaves" story line, 79–82; participation in, 100n12; as social system, 100n13. *See also* reparations

Smith, Tom W., 108

Smith, William A., 239n16

Sniderman, Paul, 5, 239n17

Snow, Tony, 177

social change, effecting, 233–37, 271–72

social constructionism, 8–9

social distance, 105, *106–7*, 127n27

social identity theory, 123–24

social standing: blacks on, 157–58, 161; cultural racism frame and, 41–43; "if others have made it" response to, 83; minimization of racism and, 43; in tri-racial system, 186–87

social welfare, 32. *See also* welfare

Solis, Hilda, 229

"some of my best friends are . . . ," 57–58

"some of my best friends were . . . ," 96–97

Sotomayor, Sonia, 211

South Africa, 179

Soviet Union, 227

stage Negroes, 164

status construction theory, 123–24

Steele, Michael, 215

Steinberg, Stephen, 83, 184

stereotypes: Asian American acceptance of, 190, *191*; blacks' accep-

tance of, 157–58, 264; whites' acceptance of, 4, 272n7
Stevens, Thaddeus, 132
Stiglitz, Joseph, 228
story lines, 76–87, 97–98; definition of, 76; generic nature of, 76; "I didn't own any slaves," 79–82; "if others have made it," 82–83; "I was denied because of a minority," 83–87; "the past is the past," 77–79
storytelling, 75–99; blacks and, 169–70; function of, 75; ideology and, 75–76; story lines, 76–87, 97–98; testimonies, 76–77, 87–99
Street, Paul, 216–17, 222, 244n56
styles of color-blind racism, 53–72; avoidance of racial language, 54–56; blacks and, 163–69; diminutives, 66–67; explanation of, 53; incoherence in, 53–54, 68–70; intentionality and, 54; private discourse versus, 72n2; projection, 63–66; semantic moves, 57–63
Summers, Larry, 227–28, 251nn104–105
Sumner, Charles, 132
Survey of Social Attitudes of College Students (1997), 12–13
surveys, shortcomings of, 11–12, 239n18, 265–66
symbolic racism, 6–7
systemic racism, 7–8, 9, 132, 172–73

Taguieff, Pierre-André, 39
Tatum, Beverly, 112
"Tea Parties", 237n4
testimonies, 76–77, 87–99; acquaintance with racists, 92–95; interactions with blacks, 87–92; personal nature of, 76
Texaco case, 29, 50n21
Thernstrom, Abigail, 210
Thernstrom, Stephan, 210
Thomas, Clarence, 235, 258n150
Toossi, Mitra, 146
tracking, in education, 109
trinity formula, in stories about racist acquaintances, 92–95

tri-racial system, 179–98; buffer groups in, 179, 182, 183, 190, 196–97, 200n18; color-blind racism in, 179, 195, 197, 269–71, 274nn28–29; composition of, 179–80, *180*; conflict in, 179, 196–98; data on, 185–86, 193–94; emergence of, 183–85; group formation in, 186–87; interracial marriage in, 192; racial attitudes in, 188–91; residential segregation in, 192–93
Troutt, David Dante, xiv
Tyson Foods, 29

United States: cultural/political integrity of, 177; group formation in, 186–87; honorary whites in, 187–88, 194–96; incomes in, 185–86; interracial marriage in, 192; race-based policy in, 184–85; racial attitudes of strata in, 188–91; racial debate in, 271; racial politics in, 177–78, 183, 196–98; social change, effecting in, 233–37, 271–72; tri-racial system in, 179–81, 183–98
universal programs, 253n118
U.S. Constitution, 27

Vickerman, Milton, 197–98
Volker, Paul, 228
Voltaire, 27

Walters, Ronald, 224, 248n83
War on Terror, 195, 211
Watts, J.C., 215
Weber, Max, 13
welfare, 57. *See also* social welfare
Wellman, David, 8
West, Cornel, 40, 103, 228, 236–37, 258n157
white habitus: characteristics of, 124; consequences of, 104; definition of, 104; implications of, 125; and interracial marriage, 123; segregation and isolation of, 105–16. *See also* whiteness

whiteness: challenging, 267–68; as
Christian-only identity, 205n65;
failure to acknowledge, 114–15; as
norm, 112, 115–16; power of, 145.
See also white habitus
whitening, 192. *See also* assimilation;
blanqueamiento
white privilege: class and, 145; failure
to acknowledge, 81–82; maintenance of, 183; sense of group position and, 7; systemic character of,
8, 9, 132
whites: against color-blind racism,
266–69; honorary, 179, 187–88,
194–98; interactions of, 87–92, 99;
interests of, 10; poor, 132; private
racial discourse of, 72n2; racial
attitudes of, 1, 4–8, 191, 210–11,
261–62, 272n7; as supporters of
Barack Obama, 218–19, 222–23,
243n53; symbolic value of Obama
to, 235, 257n149
white superiority, 129n44
white supremacy: color-blind racism
and, 266–67; concept of, 9; in Latin
America, 181–82; multiracial, 270;
Obama election, effect on 232–33;
in tri-racial system, 179, 197–98
Williams, Mike, 217
Wilson, William Julius, 40, 43, 103,
253n118
Winant, Howard, 172
Winfrey, Oprah, 223, 247n72
women: discrimination experienced
by, 134, 143, 146, 228, 251n104; ideology challenged by, 171; as racial
progressives, 132, 144–46, 264
women, Asian, 118, 128n39
Woods, Tiger, 178, 223
working class: ideology challenged by,
171; male resistance to progressivism in, 145; racial progressives in,
132, 144, 147; white privilege and,
145
Wright, Jeremiah, 220–21, 244n60,
244n64

Yancey, George, 195
"yes and no, but . . . ," 60–62, 165

Zubrinsky Charles, Camille, 193

About the Author

Eduardo Bonilla-Silva is currently a professor of sociology at Duke University. Bonilla-Silva is most known for his 1997 article, "Rethinking Racism: Toward a Structural Interpretation," in the *American Sociological Review*, in which he challenged sociologists to abandon the sterile soil of the prejudice problematic. He is the author of four books, namely, *White Supremacy and Racism in the Post–Civil Rights Era* (2001), co-winner of the 2002 Oliver C. Cox Award; *White Out* (with Woody Doane); *Racism without Racists* (currently out in a third edition); and *White Logic, White Methods: Racism and Methodology* (2008), with Tukufu Zuberi, co-winner of the 2009 Liver C. Cox Award. He received the 2007 Lewis A. Coser Award for theoretical agenda setting given by the theory section of the *American Sociological Association* and is currently working on book titled T*he Invisible Weight of Whiteness: The Racial Grammar of Evryday Life in the USA.*